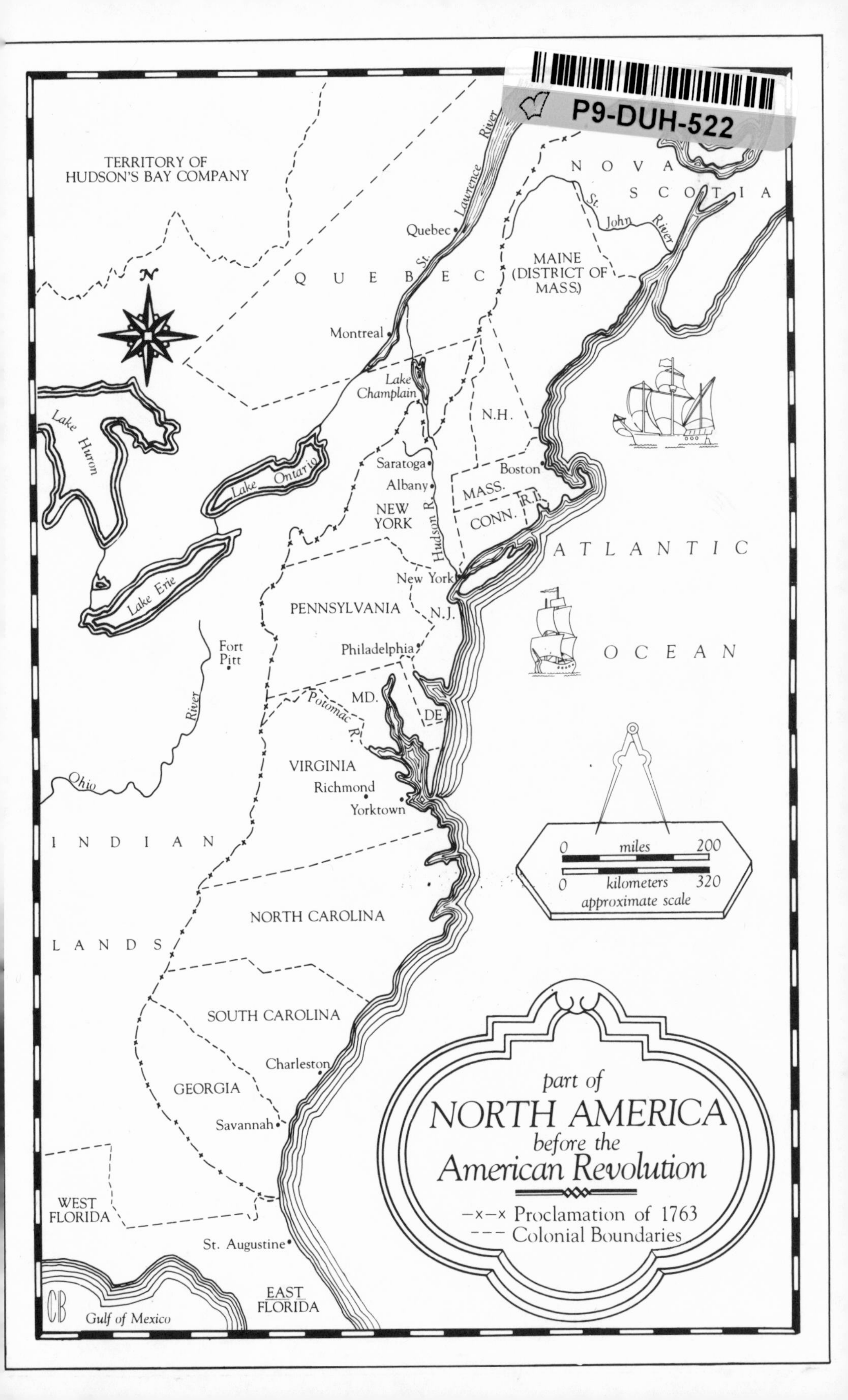

TERRITORY OF HUDSON'S BAY COMPANY
N
QUEBEC
Quebec
St. Lawrence River
Montreal
NOVA SCOTIA
St. John River
MAINE (DISTRICT OF MASS.)
Lake Champlain
Lake Huron
Lake Ontario
Lake Erie
N.H.
Saratoga
Albany
Boston
MASS.
R.I.
CONN.
NEW YORK
Hudson R.
New York
ATLANTIC
OCEAN
PENNSYLVANIA
N.J.
Philadelphia
Fort Pitt
River
Ohio
MD.
DE.
Potomac R.
VIRGINIA
Richmond
Yorktown
INDIAN
LANDS
NORTH CAROLINA
SOUTH CAROLINA
Charleston
GEORGIA
Savannah
WEST FLORIDA
St. Augustine
EAST FLORIDA
Gulf of Mexico
CB
0 miles 200
0 kilometers 320
approximate scale
part of
NORTH AMERICA
before the
American Revolution
—x—x Proclamation of 1763
--- Colonial Boundaries

BURGOYNE
OF SARATOGA

BY THE SAME AUTHOR

THE FLAMENCOS OF CÁDIZ BAY

THIEF-TAKER GENERAL:
The Rise & Fall of Jonathan Wild

THE MACARONI PARSON—
A Life of the Unfortunate Doctor Dodd

BURGOYNE OF SARATOGA

A BIOGRAPHY

Gerald Howson

Published by TIMES BOOKS, a division
of Quadrangle/The New York Times Book Co., Inc.
Three Park Avenue, New York, N. Y. 10016

Published simultaneously in Canada by
Fitzhenry & Whiteside, Ltd., Toronto

Library of Congress Cataloging in Publication Data

Howson, Gerald.
Burgoyne of Saratoga.

Bibliography: p. 333
Includes index.
1. Burgoyne, John, 1722–1792. 2. United States—
History—Revolution 1775–1783—British forces.
3. United States—History—Revolution—Campaigns and
battles. 4. Generals—Great Britain—Biography.
5. Great Britain. Army—Biography. I. Title.
DA67.1.B8H68 973.3'41'0924 [B] 78–53303
ISBN 0–8129–0770–1

Manufactured in the United States of America

Maps by Clarice Borio

TO REBECCA AND ROBERT

ACKNOWLEDGMENTS

GREAT BRITAIN

To the Right Hon. the Marquess of Bath for permission to use and quote from the *Thynne Papers* at Longleat and to Miss B. M. Austin, Librarian to the Marquess of Bath, for sending me a typescript copy of General Burgoyne's letter to Lord Rochford from Boston.

To Mr. John Brooke, National Register of Archives, for his helpful advice and assistance.

To Mr. M. S. Bond, Clerk of the Records, House of Lords, for his assistance.

To Mr. R. Sharpe France, County Archivist, Lancashire Record Office, Preston, for sending me copies of MSS.

To Miss P. L. Bell, County Archivist, and Miss Y. Rhymes, Assistant Archivist, County Record Office, Bedford, for sending me copies of MSS.

To Mr. C. C. Johnston, the Scottish Record Office, Edinburgh, for sending me copies of MSS.

To Professor Alastair Smart, Department of Fine Art, University of Nottingham, for assistance in tracing Ramsay's portrait of Burgoyne.

To Maj. General E. B. de Fonblanque, CB, CBE, DSO, for his kind help in trying to trace his grandfather's papers relating to Burgoyne.

To the Staff of the Public Record Office, London, for their assistance.

To the Staff of the British Library, the Manuscript Room, the Map Room, and the Print Room, British Museum, for their assistance.

To the Staff of the Westminster Public Library, Buckingham Palace Road, Archive Department, for their assistance.

To the London Library, without whose facilities and without the assistance of whose Staff this book could not have been attempted.

To Mr. Derek Barlowe, for his assistance.

To Mr. Michael Dempsey, for reading this manuscript and for his valuable advice and help.

Finally, to my wife, for her patience and encouragement during the years in which this book was researched and written.

PORTUGAL

To Coronel Henrique Garcia Pereira, Oficial Bibliotecário da Academia Militar, Lisbon, for sending me the delightful drawing of "Brigadeiro Burgoyne" charging at the walls of Valencia d'Alcántara.

UNITED STATES OF AMERICA

To the Director and Staff of the William L. Clements Library, University of Michigan, Ann Arbor, for their assistance and for sending me microfilms of manuscripts in the Germain and Clinton Papers and for their permission to quote therefrom.

To the Staff of the New York State Library, Albany, for sending me typescripts and photostats of manuscripts.

To the Staffs of the Harvard University Library, Boston Public Library, and New York City Public Library, for their assistance.

To Michael Phillips, Park Historian, Saratoga National Historical Park, for his valuable help and advice.

To Richard Saunders Allen, Programme Manager of the New York State Bicentennial Commission, for his hospitality, help, and kindness during my visit to Albany and Saratoga.

To Todd Pulliam and Faith Fogerty, of Altamount, New York, for their hospitality and invaluable help during my stay in Albany.

To Paul Wohl, for his kindness, help, and hospitality during my stay in New York.

To Raymond LeDuc, Jr., for driving me over the whole territory of Burgoyne's campaigns, from Montreal to Albany and Boston.

Finally, to Raymond and Constance LeDuc, for their kindness and hospitality during the months spent at Cambridge, Massachusetts, researching for this book.

CONTENTS

ILLUSTRATIONS

MAPS

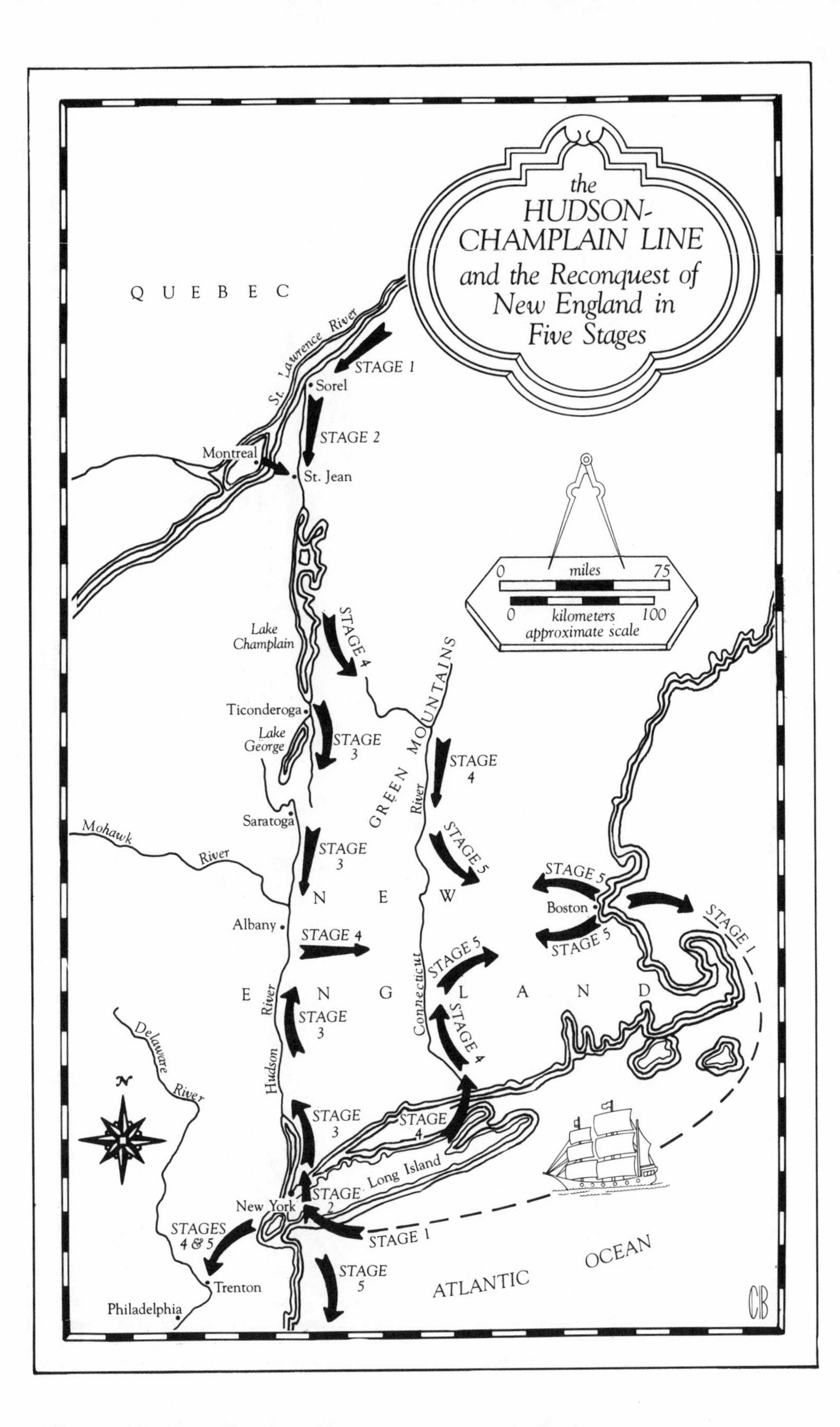
the HUDSON-CHAMPLAIN LINE and the Reconquest of New England in Five Stages
QUEBEC
St. Lawrence River
STAGE 1
Sorel
STAGE 2
Montreal
St. Jean
miles
0
75
kilometers
0
100
approximate scale
Lake Champlain
STAGE 4
GREEN MOUNTAINS
Ticonderoga
Lake George
STAGE 3
STAGE 4
Saratoga
River
Mohawk
River
STAGE 3
STAGE 5
STAGE 5
Boston
STAGE 1
N E W
Albany
STAGE 4
STAGE 5
STAGE 5
E N G L A N D
Connecticut
STAGE 4
Hudson River
STAGE 3
Delaware River
N
STAGE 3
STAGE 4
Long Island
STAGE 2
New York
STAGES 4 & 5
STAGE 1
STAGE 5
Trenton
Philadelphia
ATLANTIC OCEAN
CB

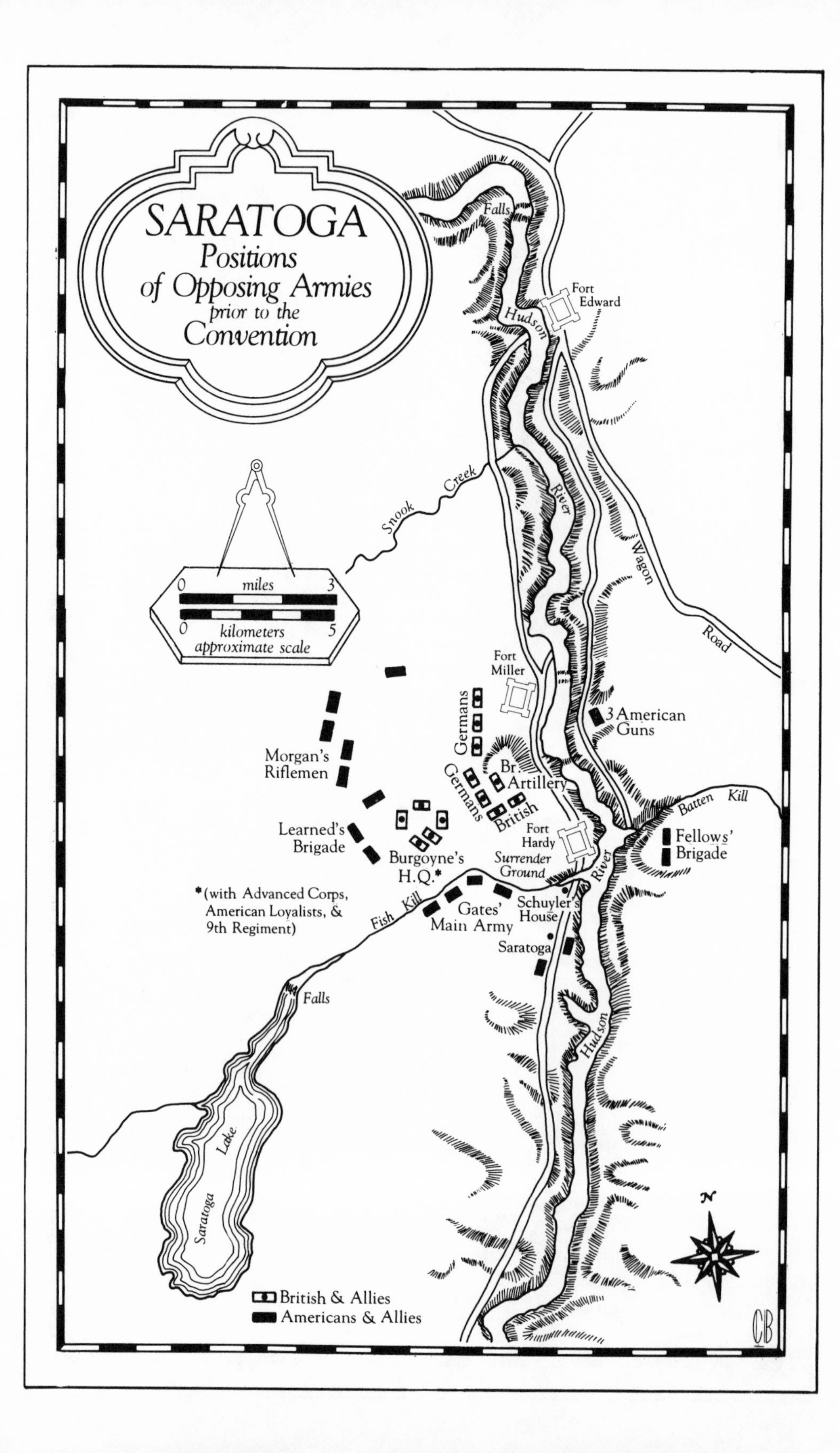
SARATOGA
Positions of Opposing Armies prior to the Convention
0 miles 3
0 kilometers 5
approximate scale
Falls
Fort Edward
Hudson
River
Snook Creek
Wagon Road
Fort Miller
Germans
3 American Guns
Morgan's Riflemen
Br. Artillery
Germans
British
Batten Kill
Learned's Brigade
Fort Hardy
Fellows' Brigade
Burgoyne's H.Q.*
Surrender Ground
River
*(with Advanced Corps, American Loyalists, & 9th Regiment)
Fish Kill
Gates' Main Army
Schuyler's House
Saratoga
Falls
Hudson
Saratoga Lake
N
British & Allies
Americans & Allies
CB

FOREWORD

IT is usual to describe Saratoga as one of the decisive battles of the world for the simple reason that it ensured the success of the American Revolution and so led to the creation of the United States of America. Of course, there are always people who prefer to argue that, whichever way the battle had gone at Saratoga, the Americans would still have won their Revolution because they were carried forward, so to speak, by a tide of history; but this is rather like saying that it would have made no difference if the Persians had won at Marathon and conquered Greece, if the Arabs had won at Tours and conquered western Europe, or if the Germans had won the Battle of Britain. Had any of these things happened—and they very nearly did—the world now would be an unimaginably different place. Just as we in Britain knew by October 1940 that ultimate victory was possible despite everything, and began to tell one another it was certain, so in October 1777 the Americans knew that ultimate victory was possible despite everything, and began to tell one another it was certain. It was the turning point of the war and the Americans are right to regard the event with pride.

To Americans, moreover, there was something dramatically, even symbolically, proper in the fact that the British commander at Saratoga was General John Burgoyne. He typified to perfection the Old World of privilege, artificial manners, fastidious taste, and cynical libertarianism that the plain, no-nonsense American farmers and backwoodsmen, who were fighting for their liberty and a free republic, feared and detested. Perhaps this is why even scholarly historians nowadays invariably call him "Gentleman Johnny." Yet, so far as I can discover, he was never called that in his lifetime or, for that matter, for over a century after his death. Indeed, the inventor of this inspired nickname seems to have been none other than Bernard Shaw, who introduced General Burgoyne as a character into his play *The Devil's Disciple*.[1] Another touch of mystery and raffishness is added to our mental picture of the handsome general by the fact that his biographers tell us practically nothing about his birth except that it occurred in 1722, which it did not, and that there was a scandalous rumor connected with it, which might or might not have been true. Perhaps it would be as well, therefore, to begin by establishing both the place and the date of his birth.

BURGOYNE
OF SARATOGA

"Brigadeiro Burgoyne." This attractive, but little-known, drawing from a manuscript in the Academia Militar, Lisbon, shows Burgoyne at his brilliant capture of Valencia D'Alcántara in 1762. (*Courtesy of the Academia Militar, Lisbon.*)

CHAPTER I

HINT OF SCANDAL

PARK PROSPECT was a row of five houses, overlooking St. James's Park in London, which stood at the east end of Birdcage Walk near the present Parliament Square. They were demolished over two hundred years ago, but some idea of their appearance can be gained from the nearby houses in Queen Anne's Gate, with their beautifully carved doorways and air of dignified repose. In the 1720s it was a part of Westminster where the nobility and the underworld lived side by side. Queen Square, Park Street, and Dartmouth Street contained nearly two score earls, viscounts, barons, dowager duchesses, and army officers. Fifty yards away the dense rabbit warren of medieval timber houses around Thieving Lane and Little Sanctuary contained several thousand cutthroats, pickpockets, and whores. Thus the sleep of the Quality was disturbed once a week by the uproar from the Cockpit, where cockfights and rat-killing competitions were held, and several times a week by the explosion of pistols and the clash of swords, as parties of thief-takers and constables tried, often in vain, to wrest highwaymen and footpads from their strongholds.

It was in the second house from the east end of Park Prospect that General John Burgoyne was born on 4 February 1723. He was christened next day at St. Margaret's, Westminster, which even then was one of the most fashionable London churches, and his parents were registered as John and Anna Maria Burgoyne.[1]

The Burgoynes were an ancient family of solid, prosperous farmers who had come over, as the name implies, from Burgundy and been settled in Bedfordshire and Cambridgeshire for nearly five hundred years. They attributed the establishment of their fortunes to John of Gaunt, Duke of Lancaster, who had granted them some manors in a quaint rhyming deed which ran:

I, John of Gaunt,
Do give and do graunt
To Johnny Burgoyne
And the heirs of his loyne
All Sutton and Potton
Until the world's rotten.

Genealogists have pointed out regretfully that while the rhyme is old, it is probably not authentic, for there is some doubt whether John of Gaunt had the right to grant Sutton or Potton to anybody. Besides, in one version of the rhyme it is Roger, not Johnny, who is given the manors. The Burgoynes did, however, acquire land in Warwickshire as payment for assisting Henry VIII in the destruction of the monasteries, and in 1641 John Burgoyne was knighted by Charles I and became the first baronet. Nevertheless, he and all the Burgoynes sided with Parliament against the king in the Civil War that broke out shortly afterwards.

The third baronet, Sir John Burgoyne, was Burgoyne's grandfather. He married Constance Lucy of Warwickshire, a descendant of that Sir Thomas Lucy who, according to tradition, tried to arrest Shakespeare for poaching and was satirized in revenge as "Justice Shallow," the bumbling magistrate with a dozen white "louses"* in his old coat. By Constance, Sir John had seven children. The first, Sir Roger, succeeded to the title and continued the main branch of the family at Sutton, though his wife left him before he died, and, as soon as he died, married the son of Sir Christopher Wren. The third son, Thomas, became a linendraper, and one of his sisters married into the same business. Of the other children we know practically nothing, except that one girl married a doctor and one son was called "Lucy," which, although in honor of his mother's family, must have been embarrassing for him.

The second son, John, was Burgoyne's father, and, according to our only informant, Miss Warburton (Burgoyne's niece), he joined the army and became a captain. However, his obituary notices called him major, and the Army Lists, which began in 1740, made no mention of him. The title may have been self-awarded, for any young man who could afford a smart pair of gloves, a brocaded hat, some lace, and a sword could call himself "Captain" without being challenged and use his rank as a license for riotous behavior. Furthermore, second sons

*"Louses," not lice, making a triple pun. Shallow had a dozen white *Luces* (pike) embroidered on his coat—his family emblem, and an allusion to Sir Thomas Lucy. Parson Evans misconstrued this as "louses," adding that "it agrees well passant. It is a familiar beast to man, and signifies love." He was thinking of crab lice, thus implying that Sir Thomas Lucy was not only dirty but lecherous. (*Merry Wives of Windsor*, I.1.).

were something of a universal problem, like maiden aunts. Inheriting neither title nor fortune, they considered themselves too grand to go into trade, as the youngest sons could do without losing face. Their best hope was to marry an heiress, and in this Captain John Burgoyne was successful. Indeed, it appears to have been the only real success of his life. She was Anna Maria Burnstone, of Hackney, which was not then the dreary East End slum it has been for two centuries, but a prosperous village full of bankers and merchants from London. Besides being rich, she was remarkably beautiful, remaining so until old age.

John Burgoyne moved into the house in Park Prospect, which belonged to Lord Bingley, between June and November 1713. This suggests that he married Anna Maria that year. Nine years were to pass before the birth of their first and only registered child, and one of the sponsors at the christening was Lord Bingley. Lady Bingley thereupon started a story that her husband was not only the godfather but the real father as well. The story gained ground, and by the time Burgoyne became famous fifty years later it was common gossip. In November 1775, Dr. William Cole, a Cambridge don who wrote down everything he heard and saw, was told that Burgoyne, whose description of Bunker Hill had just been read out, was "the natural son of a man of Quality & no ways related to the Sutton or Potton Family"; and two years later (5 October 1777), Horace Walpole told his friend Mason that "Burgoyne the Pompous is a natural son of Lord Bingley."[2]

By the nineteenth century the rumor was accepted as fact, and the distinguished American historian George Bancroft sneered at Burgoyne as a man who was ready to sacrifice anybody, including his friends, and anything, including his political principles, to achieve his "darling object": to efface the shame of his illegitimate birth by winning military glory. The Burgoyne family grew angry, and when they commissioned Edward de Fonblanque to write the general's biography they hoped he would scotch the story once and for all.[3] De Fonblanque began by pointing out that if Bancroft or anyone else had bothered to consult a standard work such as *Burke's Peerage* he would have discovered that Burgoyne was *not* illegitimate, for his parents were married. He next quoted a letter written in 1823 from Burgoyne's niece, Miss Warburton, to Burgoyne's daughter, Caroline (who in fact was herself illegitimate, but that was passed over). Miss Warburton admitted that the captain, Burgoyne's father, was "one of those fine gentlemen about town who contrive to run through their means and finish their days in the King's Bench" (i.e., the debtors' prison in Southwark) and that he "dissipated" his wife's money. Nevertheless, Miss Warburton had always understood that they remained on the most affectionate terms all their lives. Furthermore, if any of Anna Maria's straight-laced friends had suspected the *slightest* impropriety in her behavior they would have dropped her at once. They never did drop her, so she must have been innocent; and that, concluded de Fonblanque hopefully, was that.

Unfortunately, in the same year that de Fonblanque published his life of Burgoyne (1876), Lord Bingley's will, which had been unknown to the world at large until then, was discovered and published. Some of its clauses were so odd and suggestive that they put a different complexion on the whole affair. Lord Bingley, it should be explained, was not an aristocrat by birth, but was born Robert Benson, son of a rascally Yorkshire attorney "of no extraction." By good looks and sheer ability, he married an heiress, became Chancellor of the Exchequer under Queen Anne, and made a fortune out of that vast swindle, the South Sea Bubble. He was a strange, hard, secretive man and a notorious womanizer. His great house in Cavendish Square, London, was more like a prison than a home, with tiny windows and a high wall all round to keep out prying eyes. In later years it attracted some strange tenants. The Duke of Portland won it at cards and gave it to his son, who heightened the wall behind with an iron and glass screen eighty feet high, so that neighbors could not see even into the garden. There he lived in solitary darkness until he died. After that, it remained empty for many years, being supposed the scene of nameless crimes and haunted by ghosts. In 1906 it was pulled down for lack of a purchaser.

Lord Bingley died in 1731, and his will was made known to his family and beneficiaries. His small house in Old Queen Street (which backed onto Park Prospect) he left to his wife. His great house and largest estates he left to his daughter Harriet. He left £7,000 to his only acknowledged illegitimate daughter, Mary Johnson, provided she changed her name to Mary Benson. Next he left £400 a year to Anna Maria Burgoyne, plus the house in Park Prospect where she lived, and the use of a house in Cheshunt, Hertfordshire, called "The Nunnery," together with all its furniture, plate, jewels, etc., for the rest of her life. He added that he forgave John Burgoyne, her husband, the debt he owed him. Next came sums of money to "two or three widows," and to his godson John Burgoyne, *provided he changed his name to Robert Benson*, and that Harriet did not have any children. Next came another godson, Robert Benson, son of Lord Bingley's cousin Samuel Benson (who retained ownership of "The Nunnery," where Mrs. Burgoyne was to live, if she wished). At the bottom of the list came Lord Bingley's remaining right heirs, who were left very little indeed.

Colonel Horatio Rogers, an American scholar who was then editing the diary of Lieutenant Hadden, one of Burgoyne's officers at Saratoga, pointed out that this will was very strange, whichever way one looked at it. Why was young Burgoyne preferred to other godsons related to Lord Bingley by blood? Why was Anna Maria so favored, in a way that gave her security for life? Why the mention of the debt owed by Burgoyne's father? What could it mean, after all, but that Lord Bingley was Burgoyne's real father? There were other implications too which Rogers hinted at but, because of the conventions of the time, was unable to state bluntly. De Fonblanque had been even more roundabout; but what de Fonblanque had been trying to deny, and Rogers to assert, was that Anna Maria Burgoyne had slept with Lord Bingley to pay off her her husband's debts, and that young John Burgoyne was the result.[4]

There the question has rested until now. There may have been another explanation for the will. Lord Bingley may have disliked his Yorkshire relatives. Burgoyne's father may have been unable to produce children and may have acquiesced in an arrangement by which Lord Bingley gave them what they both wanted: a child. Without a divorce case, which would have brought the details into the open, we can never know. The truth would not matter very much if we could be sure that it had no effect on Burgoyne's character and, in consequence, his behavior.

Mere illegitimacy would hardly have worried Burgoyne. It was quite common in the 1720s, and he himself had four illegitimate children of whom he was not in the least ashamed. One became a distinguished field-marshal. But to be the product of a financial transaction to make up for his father's incompetence, or of an arranged coupling to make good his father's sterility, as though he were a farm animal, would not have been so easy to shrug off. Moreover, there is evidence to suggest that Burgoyne regarded his father with contempt, even hatred.

Miss Warburton mentioned that his father had died in the King's Bench prison. By placing this statement at the beginning of his book and never referring to it again, de Fonblanque creates the impression that this happened when Burgoyne was still a child. While searching the King's Bench records for information about this, I discovered to my surprise that in fact it happened when Burgoyne was middle-aged, and rich and influential enough to have rescued his father without difficulty. Yet for some reason he failed to do so. This episode, however, belongs to a period which will be dealt with later.

At the age of ten (1733) Burgoyne was sent to Westminster, which in those days was considered by many to be more civilized and cultured than Eton. It was a school that prided itself on the thoroughness of its training in Latin and on the importance it attached to teaching a good style of English. That it was successful can be seen from a list of some of the pupils: Lord Chesterfield, Edward Gibbon, William Cowper, Charles Churchill, Lord Shelburn, Lord Mansfield, Lord George Germain (who, whatever hs failings, wrote a marvellously elegant and concise prose), and Richard Cumberland, the dramatist who became Germain's secretary. It was probably neither more nor less brutal than any other of the great public schools of the time, despite the broadsheet that described it as "fatal, flogging Westminster." Nevertheless, the shock to a new boy ten years old can be judged from the desperate letter written by a child who was one of Burgoyne's contemporaries:

> MY DEAR, DEAR MOTHER,
> If you don't let me come home, I die—I am all over Ink and my fine clothes have been spoilt—I have been tost in a blanket and seen a ghost,
> I remain, my dear dear Mother,
> Your dutiful and most unhappy Son.

Burgoyne, living so near, probably did not have to board in the spartan lodgings provided by local landladies (only scholars lived in the dormitory), but was allowed to sleep at home, and so was spared the worst of the horrors.

By a stroke of fortune, however, in that same year a new headmaster, Dr. John Nicoll, came to Westminster and much of this was to change; in fact, it is in Dr. Nicoll that we can recognize the first signs of a strong influence on Burgoyne's character.

Dr. Nicoll was a man with ideas ahead of his time. A devout Christian of deep learning, he had unshakable faith in moral example and a lofty contempt for the cane as a means of instruction; had an ex-pupil been inspired to write an eighteenth-century *Tom Brown's Schooldays*, the name of Dr. Nicoll would be as well-known as that of Dr. Arnold of Rugby. Nevertheless, he was the kind of man about whom stories were remembered years afterwards. Richard Cumberland, for instance, tells how he escaped from prayers with some other boys to go and break up a Quakers' meeting and was later called to account by the doctor. "I presume he saw my contrition in my face, when turning a mild look on me he said aloud 'Erubuit, salva res est'—*He has blushed; all is well*—and sent me back to my seat." Under Nicoll, public contempt was a punishment compared to which a beating would have been considered an acquittal. Thus, a story tells of a boy who was convicted of a crime considered too dishonorable to name. Dr. Nicoll asked what punishment the seniors thought it deserved. "The severest that can be inflicted," they replied. "I can inflict none more severe than you have given him," said the headmaster and dismissed him, adding that he was convinced it could not happen again.[5]

In later years Burgoyne was to adopt the same method and use almost the same language in dealing with his officers who had disgraced themselves. Once, confronted by an officer who had committed the capital offense of leaving his post for some private business, Burgoyne let him off with a reprimand and published in General Orders afterwards, "The Officers of this Army do not want an example of Punishment to impress upon their minds the great principles of their Profession," adding that he forgave and would forget the fault in question, "convinced that it is impossible it should happen twice."[6]

Burgoyne, however, did not stay long at Westminster. At the age of fourteen he joined the army as a sub-brigadier in the 3rd Troop of Horse Guards. He received his commission on 8 August 1737, and the fact that his name remained on the school list until 1738 suggests that he left suddenly and without informing them. Perhaps a vacancy in this most exclusive of regiments presented itself and his father did not want to miss the opportunity, for in the army Burgoyne would at least be paid a tiny salary. The initial cost may well have been formidable, however, for although commissions were not invariably bought if candidates were suitable and their parents could exercise influence, only orphans and high nobles could enter the army gratis under the age of sixteen. A commission of sub-brigadier (the lowest commissioned rank in the Horse Guards and the equivalent of cornet in the cavalry and ensign in the infantry) cost £1,200. There was, besides, a mountain of items to be bought, including a tent, bedding, a full suit of clothes, frock suits, hats, cockades, garters, gloves, an abundance of lace, a sword, pistols, eighteen pairs of stockings, twenty-four shirts, a Portugal cloak, shoes, boots, spatterdashes, "and all the other necessaries, to appear as an Officer and a Gentleman."[7]

CHAPTER II

OFFICER, GENTLEMAN, DEBTOR

AT that time there was no organized army, in the modern sense, no real War Office, no general staff, no commander-in-chief, no recruiting centers, no officer training, scarcely even any barracks. The king was the captain-general. In wartime a senior general officer was temporarily appointed as commander-in-chief, which meant that he was a confidential adviser to the king and a liaison officer among the various ministers, the war departments, and the generals in the field. Strategy and the running of the war were determined and carried out by one of the two Secretaries of State. The Secretary of State for the Northern Department dealt with campaigns and politics in northern Europe, while the Secretary for the Southern Department dealt with southern Europe, America, Canada and the other colonies. The Secretary-at-War dealt only with routine matters such as commissions, movement, and supply (but not the raising of supplies) and carried out in detail the instructions of the Secretaries of State. The Master General of Ordnance was chief of the Board of Ordnance and dealt with everything to do with not only the Royal Artillery, but also with arms, ammunition, bedding, tents, wagons, fortifications, hospitals, military prisons, the building of such barracks as there were, and even the repair of the Royal Observatory at Greenwich. He also had complete control over sappers and engineers (the corps of engineers containing about sixty officers, with their men). The Board of Ordnance, a law unto itself, managed its own pay and transport, and it was notorious for the jealousy with which it guarded its ancient protocol and the slowness with which it carried out requests. The War Office, as the Secretary-at-War's department was sometimes called, and the Board of Ordnance were always encroaching on each other's prerogatives, always bickering, and always resentful of interference from outside; and the only times they ever seemed to be in concordance were when they accidentally combined to frustrate the grand strategic plans of a Secretary of State who was trying to win a war. They were all housed in small and pretty buildings near St. James's Palace and at Woolwich, though often the Master General of Ordnance would conduct business from his own home. Nothing more different from the Pentagon, or that great grey building that now lurks by the Thames, like a sullen threat, can be imagined. Yet they were almost certainly far more pleasant to work in and could on occasions be remarkably efficient. During the Seven Years' War, which, although spread out over half the globe from India to America, was the most successful war in British history, the two war departments that ran it employed between them scarcely more than thirty people, including porters and cleaning women.

The army itself was an amazing patchwork of free enterprise and state control, and this was nowhere more apparent than in the methods by which new regiments were created. They could be raised either by the king or by private persons. When the king raised a new regiment, he issued the commissions gratis to the officers and paid for the recruiting, uniforms, weapons, and stores entirely out of Treasury funds. Officers, of course, were expected to provide their own clothes, weapons, and equipment, and, if they were promoted on joining the new regiment, they had to pay for their promotions. This relieved the burden on the public to a certain extent.

When a private individual wanted to raise a regiment, he first had to convince the Secretary-at-War that he could do so more cheaply than the king could. This meant that before making his proposal he had already to have found enough officers willing to join immediately and to have his stores and clothing. He had also to find a powerful patron who could speak to the Secretary, or better still the king, on his behalf. If he could overcome all these obstacles, it proved at least that he was a serious person, and the rest was comparatively easy.

Having received his commission to raise the regiment with himself as colonel and a sum of money from the Paymaster-General to meet the expenses he had stipulated, he employed officers to do the work of recruiting, contracted the tailors to make the uniforms, and negotiated with the officers who had applied, or agreed, to staff the regiment. He could design the uniform himself if he wished, within certain limitations, and needed only the king's approval to use it. He could station the regiment wherever he could find land—in his own garden, if it were big enough. The important point was that all the officers who joined his regiment had to buy their commissions from him. Once the regiment was established, he received an annual sum of money from the War Office to keep it running, and from this he could draw off a percentage into his own pocket. Clearly, the colonel commandant of a regiment which he had raised himself was in a better position, financially at least, than the colonel of a regiment raised by the king, for he was not the commandant so much as the proprietor. As such, he delegated the actual duties of day-to-day organization to his commanding officer, who was sometimes a lieutenant-colonel but usually a major. This meant that the highest posts in the army were held by rich men, or men with aristocratic connections, who drew between £1,000 and £2,000 a year from their regiments besides their pay as full colonels, and who visited their regiments perhaps twice a year while the real work was done by experienced officers who came from families with modest incomes, and whose strong devotion to their profession compensated for their hard lives and the near impossibility of ever rising any higher.

No one seemed to know whether the buying and selling of commissions was strictly legal or not, but over the centuries it had become such an important part of the system that the army would have collapsed without it. One reason for this was that no one had a right to a pension. Pensions were given personally by the king to a small number of officers and men who had some special claim to distinction—a mere wound received in battle was not enough. Therefore, a lieutenant-colonel of the infantry, wishing to retire but with no pension to look forward to, was more or less obliged to sell his commission at the market price, £3,500, which he had paid over the years in stages with each promotion. If he was in the Guards, he could expect £6,700.

Also largely within the realm of private enterprise was everything to do with what we now call "logistics"—transport, supply, hospitals, etc. Even the drivers of the horses that pulled the guns and ammunition wagons were hired locally and temporarily, although they were issued with broad hats, white smocks, and whips.

At the same time, there were many rules and regulations enforced strictly on the whole army. Drill, of course, drum beats (the bugle was not yet used for reveille and other calls), and weapons were standardized, as were the order of march, court-martial procedures, garrison rules, the keeping of Orderly Books (diaries of daily General and Company Orders), and the basic color of the uniforms: infantry, for instance, had to wear red coats. Even the exact distances in yards between tents, and the exact placing and order of tents, were specified and kept to when regiments set up camp at the end of the day's march. It might be expected that in such an army the regiments would have grandiloquent, or certainly romantic, names, but in fact they were simply numbered (e.g., 9th Regiment of Foot). However, because the colonel was by far the most important person in the regiment, it was often referred to by his name (e.g., 9th, Ligonier's, Regiment of Foot).

The practice of giving regiments local names did not become popular, let alone official, until the end of the century. Present-day talk of preserving the "old county regiments" is really nonsense, therefore; since, like so many "ancient traditions," the whole thing was a Victorian invention, if a worthy one.

Punishments were ferocious. Sentences of five hundred, eight hundred, and a thousand lashes were commonplace. Each camp had a "black hole," totally dark but by regulation not damp eough to endanger health, into which certain offenders were put for a day or two; each garrison had a "wooden mare"—a kind of gymnasium horse with a sharp ridge along its back, on which a soldier would be seated with 50-pound weights attached to his feet. Lesser punishments included "tying neck and heels," running the gauntlet, clubbing (beating with heavy sticks), booting (beating with a jackboot or, later, a belt), cobbing (more or less the same as clubbing), and bottling (shutting up in a small box).

The matter of soldiers' pay was so complicated and chaotic that it was regarded as a bad joke by the entire nation, although many decades were to pass before even minor reform was attempted. Let it be said that by the time the "gross off-reckonings," "poundage," "hospital," etc., had been deducted from a soldier's pay of eightpence a day, he was lucky if he was left with a halfpenny.

As a sub-brigadier in the Horse Guards, Burgoyne was better off, though barely. His pay was eight shillings a day, from which seven shillings and sixpence had to be deducted for "constant expense." This left sixpence a day on which to maintain his status as an officer and a gentleman (in the Horse Guards at that), from which a further ten shillings or so would have to be subtracted at the end of the year to replace worn-out clothing. It is as well to bear these facts in mind when reading of the jealousies that existed between officers over promotion and of the tricks they employed to raise money to buy it. There is no sensible method, by the way, of translating these sums into modern terms. Sixpence in 1738 could possibly be said to represent £1 ($2) in 1978, but the purchasing power of money was quite different in the preindustrial age.

Burgoyne remained in the Horse Guards for six-and-a-half years, during which he received a thorough grounding in everything to do with cavalry—indeed, he was to remain by temperament a cavalry officer all his life. However, he obtained no promotion, and exchanged into the 1st Royal Dragoons as a cornet on 23 April 1744. The War of the Austrian Succession was now in full swing, and the "Royals" formed part of the British contingent of the Anglo-Allied army under the Duke of Cumberland. All the dragoon regiments serving abroad had their establishments increased by one cornet per troop (thirty-six cornetcies in all), and since such commissions were gratis, it is possible Burgoyne made £1,200 by the sale of his sub-brigadiership in the Horse Guards. Even if he had to buy his commission in the Royals, he would still have made a profit of £200. According to one report, Burgoyne joined the Royals at Lassines in Flanders at the end of the month. This would suggest he was at the Battle of Fontenoy a year later, when the Duke of Cumberland's army was defeated by the Mareshal Saxe (whose writings Burgoyne was to study carefully—indeed, he was one of the first subscribers to an English translation of Saxe's extraordinary work on the art of war, *Mes Rêvèries*, which appeared in 1757). During the battle the Royals lost forty-eight men and over a hundred horses. In the autumn, most of the British regiments were brought back to England to meet the threat of Bonnie Prince Charlie's invasion from Scotland. The 1st Royal Dragoons were deployed north of London as part of the forces protecting the capital.

Meanwhile, on 22 February Burgoyne had been promoted to lieutenant, filling the vacancy left by a Lieutenant John Surtees, which suggests again that the promotion may have cost him nothing. On 1 July 1747, he was promoted to captain. This was possibly financed by what was left from the £1,200 out of his sub-brigadiership (if any money still remained), by his family, or perhaps by card playing.[1]

De Fonblanque tells us that while at Westminster Burgoyne made friends with James Smith-Stanley, eldest son of the 11th Earl of Derby. Smith-Stanley insisted on calling himself "Lord Strange," which was a title the Derby family had somehow picked up a hundred and fifty years before, when the first Lord Strange had been proprietor and manager of the theatrical company in which Shakespeare wrote and acted. The story that they were friends at Westminster is doubtful, however. Lord Strange was six years older than Burgoyne and four years senior to him (in a public school even one year's difference creates a social barrier which nothing, not even a homosexual "crush," can break) and had left by 1735, when Burgoyne was still a junior. More probably they became friends afterwards. What is certain is that the friendship was to have the greatest influence on Burgoyne's life and career.

In 1748 the regiment was sent to Preston to control an outbreak of riots among the unemployed weavers whose trade had been depressed by the war. During his off-duty social rounds, Burgoyne met and became infatuated with Miss Frances Poole, daughter of a Cheshire baronet. The Earl of Derby, however, had a smart town house in Preston, and his great country house at Knowsley not far away, where Burgoyne and his fellow officers were always welcome. There he met Lady Charlotte Stanley, Lord Strange's sister and the youngest of the Earl's six daughters. His attitude to Frances changed:

After hard Conflict, Passion cool'd;
Discretion, Reason, Honour rul'd,
O'er the subsiding Flame;
Till Charlotte to my vacant Breast
With kindred Charms and Virtue blest
A sweet Successor came.

That was how he remembered the affair in later years, in a verse which he wrote to Frances when she married Lord Palmerston.[2]

John Burgoyne and Lady Charlotte fell in love. She was a slim, quiet girl, not perhaps a raving beauty but attractive (as her portrait and some surviving letters show) because of her gentleness and shrewd sense of humor.* For all her reserve and delicate physique, she had strength of will; for she ran away with Burgoyne and married him, in the face of her father's fury and promise to cut her off without a penny.

The wedding, which took place on 14 April 1751 at St. George's Chapel, Curzon Street, Mayfair, was conducted by the notorious Doctor Keith, who, although over eighty, was often so drunk that he would muddle the words of the ceremony. Under the law, running off with an heiress was a serious offense (and could under certain circumstances even be a capital felony), with the result that Dr. Keith's quasi-legal service in secret marriages was unassailably popular, no matter how exorbitant his fees or outrageous his behavior. A recent attempt to stop his activities by sending him to prison had failed, for he had kept open his "shop," as he called it, by employing impoverished curates in his stead, and, from the safety of the jail, built up a stronger practice than before.[3]

Although Lord Strange approved of the marriage and tried to mollify his father, the 11th Earl was unmoved. Burgoyne, therefore, soon found that to maintain his position as a captain of the dragoons and a hard-drinking, hard-gambling man-about-town, and to support a wife without a penny of her own, were quite beyond his means. On 31 October he sold his commission for £2,600 and sailed for France with Lady Charlotte to avoid his creditors.

Miss Warburton tells us that they settled at Chanteloup, in Touraine, where they made friends with the Duc and Duchesse de Choiseul,† who

* A humor which could be sharp: In writing to the above Lord Palmerston about the decease of the minister Lord Egrement, she observed, "His sudden death, I suppose, would not at all surprise you, for he was the sort of man to expect it from." (Brian Connell, *Portrait of a Golden Age* [Boston: Houghton Mifflin Co., 1958], p. 38; in England as *Portrait of a Whig Peer* [London: André Deutsch, 1957].

† At this time Choiseul was still the Comte de Stainville (he was created Duque de Choiseul in 1758). I have preferred to keep the anachronistic "Choiseul" here, however, for that is the name by which history remembers him.

Piazza di Spagna, Rome, in 1750. This was the center of the British colony, and the Burgoynes stayed in one of the houses overlooking the square. From *Veduta di Roma* by G. B. Piranesi, Vol. 1, No. 23. (*Courtesy of the Trustees of the British Museum.*)

lived in splendor nearby. This is hardly likely, for Chanteloup was not a village but a château near Amboise about the size of Buckingham Palace. The Burgoynes could not have afforded it and Choiseul did not live there until ten years later, in 1761.[4] Nevertheless, there is no doubt that Burgoyne and Choiseul, the future chief minister of France and Pitt's great adversary in the Seven Years' War, did meet somewhere, for they established a firm friendship that survived two bitter wars between their countries and ended only with Choiseul's death in 1785. When Choiseul was sent as ambassador to the Vatican in October 1754, he invited Burgoyne to join him as soon as Lady Charlotte had recovered from the birth of her daughter, Charlotte Elizabeth. We have brief glimpses of the Burgoynes on this holiday as seen by the young Scottish architect, Robert Adam, who was introduced to them at Aix-en-Provence on 21 December. Burgoyne took Adam along to dinner with the governor of Provence and then spent the whole night gambling, while Adam looked on, exhausted and uncomfortable in the company of what he regarded as clever and glittering, but heartless and amoral, people. Adam met them again in Florence during the carnival of February 1755, where Lady Charlotte danced with him frequently because "she didn't like the foreigners."

In March or April the Burgoynes settled in Rome, apparently staying with Choiseul. At this time Choiseul had living with him the painter Hubert Robert, whose specialty was highly romantic views of ruins in mountain landscapes: an obelisk, perhaps, or a moss-covered "trophy," with waterfalls or arching trees in the background, and a few peasants or soldiers in heroic postures adding human scale to a scene bathed in the light of an eternal late afternoon in summer. Frequent and welcome guests to the house were the painters Fragonard, Greuze, and Vernet, who were studying at the French Academy. The "modern artist" in Rome was the temperamental Piranesi, who involved everybody he met—English, French, and Italians—in his violent quarrels. However, each new set of engravings he showed to his friends, with their sensational effects of perspective and buildings of gigantic, almost muscular, strength, caused astonishment and surprise.

Rome was a small city consisting largely of ruins, monuments, and wide open spaces. It was full of Englishmen on the Grand Tour, most of whom lived in the neighborhood of the Piazza di Spagna. Here Lady Charlotte called on Robert Adam at his apartment and made him show her all the new clothes he had bought in Italy, having "no objection to anything but my red suit, which colour she could not put up with, but upon my assuring her ladyship I would soon be master of the prettiest suit of silk cloth Rome could afford she was quite satisfied."

She introduced Adam to her friends the Elliotts, because they too were Scottish; but Mr. Elliott turned out to be "a most insignificant trifling mortal" obsessed with "Genteelity," whose talk consisted of nothing but titles, orders of knighthood, stars, garters, ribbons, and pedigrees. In the same circle was a curious creature called "the abbé Grant," who was supposed to represent some Scottish religious body but in fact served as a go-between and fixer-of-introductions for the English in Roman high society. There were also a number of dukes and earls in search of edification at the fount of antiquity, accompanied by their cultural tutors, who were sarcastically called "bear-leaders." Among such tutors was the extraordinary Robert Wood, who had just returned from a dangerous exploration of Egypt and Syria to discover the truths behind Homeric myths. Wincklemann, who has the dubious distinction of being the father of modern art history, was then engaging in an angry controversy with Piranesi over the relative merits of Roman versus Greek architecture, and taking his part on behalf of Greece was Allan Ramsay, the portrait painter and classical scholar.

All these friends would go on excursions to historic sites or search for lost ones, such as Horace's Sabine villa, and in the evenings attend a *conversazione* at one of the great houses, or the unbearably dull amateur dramatics which the Princess Borghese would hold at her villa, or, better, a dinner at the Elliott's or the Burgoyne's. Afterwards they would go for a moonlight walk through the ruins and along the banks of the Tiber, watching the young Romans and their girl friends strolling arm in arm among the tombs and columns. Their walk would take them back to the Piazza di Spagna, where they would refresh themselves with ice cream and fruit before climbing the Spanish Steps and going, via the Villa de Medici, to the Pincio gardens. Here they could watch the grandest gentlemen in Rome, cardinals, monsignori, princes, sauntering in disguise beneath the trees with their ladies, masked and veiled, and looking at the burlettas and harlequinades being performed in brightly colored booths. It became a kind of game to guess who was with his wife, or cousin, or mistress.

Toward the end of the year Allan Ramsay painted Burgoyne's portrait. Until recently, this picture was known only by two copies made by unskillful artists (one, indeed, made poor Burgoyne look like a papier-mâché doll), but happily the original was discovered some years ago in a private collection. It turns out to be an excellent life-size study, immediately recognizable as the same Burgoyne who was painted ten years afterwards by Sir Joshua Reynolds. He is standing in the Colosseum, leaning on a wall with brocaded hat in hand, in a typical eighteenth-century pose. He wears the red jacket and buff waistcoat of the dragoons, and gazes at the spectator as if to say "*Sic transit gloria mundi.*" However, while he is lit from the *left*, the Colosseum is lit from the *right;* for Ramsay had simply filled in the background from a sketch he had made the year before without correcting the inconsistency.[5]

John Burgoyne in Rome, 1756, by Allan Ramsay. This is the recently discovered original of a much-copied portrait. (*From a Private Collection.*)

By this time, war had broken out between Britain and France; Choiseul had gone to Vienna, and the French no longer invited the English to soirees. The Burgoynes left for England.

Whatever the reasons that forced him to go to Europe in the first place, Burgoyne undoubtedly profited enormously from his long European stay. He could now read and speak French (though he always wrote it awkwardly) and had a smattering of Italian. He had not only been exposed to large doses of what we today call "culture," but through Choiseul, the protector of the Encyclopedists, had actually met many of the leading writers and artists of the age and been in contact with the most advanced ideas in Europe. It was an experience that rarely fell to a British military man. Fragonard and Hubert Robert influenced him in a more subtle and permanent way, for the imagery and atmosphere of their paintings pervades the plays, songs, and musical dramas that he wrote in later life. Perhaps of most use to his career as an officer was the skill he had attained in all the varieties of gambling, at which he was now so adept as to qualify as a professional.

Back in England, Lady Charlotte effected a reconciliation with her father, who settled on her an income of £400 a year and began to use his influence on behalf of his son-in-law. Burgoyne bought a house in Woodmansterne in Surrey. It was called "The Oaks," after a grove of ancient oaks on Banstead Downs, and was leased by the owners to a group known as "The Hunting Club." Perhaps Burgoyne heard of it through them or perhaps he liked it because its proximity to Sutton, Surrey, reminded him of his family's home in Sutton, Bedfordshire. It was little more than a derelict alehouse used for weekend festivities, and as soon as Burgoyne had bought the lease, he began to redesign it completely. He added a handsome dining-room (42 feet × 21 feet 6 inches) with a decorated curved roof and coved elliptical ends. There was a sculptured chimney piece flanked by medallions, and round each of the curved ends ran a cornice supported by eighteen corinthian columns. "A better proportioned apartment," wrote Brayley, the Surrey antiquarian, in 1850, "or one more pleasing in its general effect, can rarely be seen." The facade of the house was decorated with battlements to give it an appropriately military appearance. Since Burgoyne is believed to have designed his own house near Preston, it is probable that he had a hand in the redesigning of "The Oaks" as well.[6]

By the end of the year (1756) Burgoyne had bought his way back into the army as a junior captain of the 11th Dragoons, persuaded by his friends and relations that promotion would be swift and sure. Even so, he was not entirely satisfied, for during his five years' absence many of his junior officers had naturally overtaken him, and after a year in the army the promised favors were still not forthcoming.

"I must say," he hinted to Major Warde, his commanding officer, on

Lady Charlotte Burgoyne, 1770, by Allan Ramsay. (*From a Private Collection.*)

23 November 1757, "that the circumstance of serving *under* so many men whom I had commanded appeared so disagreeable to me, when my friends proposed my entering a second time into the army, that I should not have suffered any application to be made for me had I not had good assurances that I should not long continue a Captain. . . ." He went on to say that in view of his age (thirty-four) and previous service he had expected more "indulgencies" than might usually be granted to a junior captain. He ended, "I have great reason to believe that I shall not be disappointed in the first of these expectations" (i.e., promotion) "and I return you a thousand thanks for the manner in which you deal with me in regard to the last" (i.e., indulgences—which doubtless meant ample leave).

Eight months after this, Burgoyne was to have his first experience of responsibility in action. The Seven Years' War, which Americans know as the French-and-Indian War and which some describe as the first world war, was now in its third year. Britain and Prussia were fighting against France, Austria, Russia, and Sweden. Frederick the Great of Prussia had won two brilliant victories, but for Britain the war had been going badly. In America, where fighting had been waged sporadically but cruelly all along the frontiers from Canada to Louisiana, General Braddock's army had been annihilated near Fort Duquesne (Pittsburgh) and Abercrombie's Highlanders had suffered a terrible defeat at Ticonderoga. In Europe, Britain had done little beyond lose Minorca (for which the unfortunate Admiral Byng had been shot—"to encourage the others," said Voltaire) and sail the fleet up and down the Channel.

Nevertheless, although most people were unaware of the fact, things were changing for the better. News of Clive's astonishing successes in India was on its way to England. In June, Pitt and the Duke of Newcastle formed their coalition. Newcastle was to manage Parliament, and so provide the funds, and Pitt, as Secretary of State for the Southern Department, was to manage the war. Among the new measures he proposed were more positive attacks on the French coast, the idea being to draw French forces to the Channel and relieve pressure on Frederick.

Two futile raids were first mounted against Rochefort and St. Malo, where the British found the defenses too strong for them and retired. Lord George Sackville, second-in-command of the army, quarreled with the commander of the fleet, Admiral Howe, at the end of which Howe swore never to speak to him again. This incident was to be remembered during the American Revolution. Burgoyne took part in these raids but has left no account of them.

A third raid was planned and put under the command of General Bligh, whom Walpole described as "an old general routed out of some horse armoury in Ireland." His instructions were no more precise than "to carry a warm alarm along the coast of France." "Who could the descent alarm," asked a newspaper writer afterwards, "but a few peasants, and a few old women for fear they should not be ravished?" Burgoyne went with his 11th Dragoons, who, as was their proper function, were to fight on foot.

The place selected was Cherbourg. When the troops landed they found that the garrison had abandoned the town and its fortifications. They spent the next few days waiting while the engineers tried to destroy the defense works and basin, which, according to a stone monument, had been built by Cardinal Fleury thirty years before to stand "for all eternity." During this time the soldiers broke free of discipline and rioted in the town, raping several women, murdering some citizens, and setting fire to some houses. After Bligh had summarily hanged one or two, order was restored and the fleet set sail for England. Before landing, however, Bligh decided that more could be done and changed course back to France. Knowing that St. Malo was too well fortified to be attacked from the sea, Bligh chose St. Cast a few miles to the west, perhaps with the intention of approaching St. Malo from the rear.

Prior to disembarkation there was an argument between Admiral Howe and Bligh over where best to land the force, Bligh finally insisting on the place Howe objected to as being the most dangerous. Ten thousand men were set ashore and marched inland to Matignon, with no reconnaissance being made to ascertain the position, the strength, or even the existence of any French force in the area. Burgoyne tells us that the transport consisted of three wagons for all purposes, while "the sick and wounded alone could not have been properly contained in a dozen."

"Two days after the landing," wrote Burgoyne, "a deserter came in from the enemy who informed the Generals that the Duc d'Aiguillon, with an army double our number, was within six miles, and that he was pushing to get between Matignon, where the gross of our army lay, and the sea." The situation was now (to use Burgoyne's word) "critical." The army retreated pell-mell to the St. Cast bay and started to embark. It was noticed that during the confusion of trying to organize boats and countermand the orders to other boats *still landing provisions from the fleet*, the quartermaster-general, Colonel Clerk, who was supposed to be directing these operations, was sitting on a stone quietly reading a copy of the *London Gazette* (in order to discover, it was said, if any of his friends was in the list of new promotions). The bay was almost circular, bounded on the left (east) by high rocks stretching out into the sea, and on the right (west) by a steep hill with a village on its summit. The British had taken the one precaution of digging a breastwork along the head of the curving beach. As the last troops poured over this breastwork the enemy appeared on the surrounding hills. Howe brought the frigates and bomb-ketches in as close as their shallow draught would allow and opened a bombardment against the hillsides. The grenadier companies were detached from the regiments and, with the Guards, drawn up behind the breastwork from one end of the bay to the other, to protect the retreat. Burgoyne's regiment, dismounted, was posted on the right, at the foot of the hill below the village. At nine the French began their attack, but they were held back by the bombardment from the ships. At ten they mounted a battery of their own which, said Burgoyne, "did not hurt us much. Soon afterwards, C. and myself . . . perceived a very large body pushing with great expedition upon the hill on the right, in the intention to flank us. Of this we immediately informed the Generals, but received no order how to act, and were obliged to determine upon our own authority to wheel the divisions we commanded so as to front the enemy. A short time afterwards I received orders to lead three hundred men up the hill, but this was countermanded before I had got forty yards, and the whole battalion was ordered to occupy the rocks on the left, towards which another column of the enemy was advancing." (In other words, the battalion was to be taken right over to the far side of the bay, across the enemy's fire.) Having carried out this idiotic order, Burgoyne was told to embark his men.

Eventually the French gained the breastwork and thereafter had little to do but pick off the Guards and grenadiers who were standing defenseless in the water or trying to hide themselves among the rocks. All the grenadiers and part of the 1st Regiment of Foot Guards were left behind. Officially, casualties were said to have been under a thousand, but Burgoyne wrote that the true figure was between seventeen and eighteen hundred killed, taken prisoner, and wounded.

General Bligh was disgraced when he returned to England. Similarly, the Duc d'Aiguillon was disgraced when he returned to Versailles. Knowing that the British would soon have to sail away again, he had refrained from wasting lives in reckless attacks on them. As a result, it was charged against him that he could have captured the whole British force if only he had seized his heaven-sent opportunity and pushed straight to the coast.

In Parliament, Pitt's opponent Henry Fox likened these raids to "breaking windows with guineas."[7]

CHAPTER III

RAISING A REGIMENT OF HORSE

A new kind of cavalry had been making itself increasingly formidable on the battlefields of eighteenth-century Europe: the "hussars" of Austria-Hungary. They were mounted on horses smaller than were used for ordinary cavalry, and their name derived, perhaps, from the Italian word *corsario* (marauder). Descendants of the pony-mounted horsemen of Asia, they retained traces of their Asiatic origins in their costume. Nowadays, the small fur busby with a plume sticking up from it, the short fur cloak, and the jacket with its parallel bars of braid across the front irresistibly call to mind the words "comic opera," but there was nothing "comic opera" about their effectiveness. They could move at speed for nine days at a stretch without resaddling, collect intelligence over a wide area, and deliver surprise blows deep in enemy territory. Frederick the Great, quick to adopt them in Prussia, told his generals, "They are the eyes and ears of your army." Accordingly, King George II determined to raise a corps of hussars in Britain. However, like the dragoons, they were to be trained to fight on foot as well as on horseback and so were to be called "Light Dragoons."

The first two regiments of Light Dragoons were numbered the 15th and 16th. The 15th was raised by the king and given to Lieutenant-Colonel George Elliott, a cavalry officer of ability and experience. He became famous during the American Revolution as the "Cock o' the Rock" who defended Gibraltar during its long siege, for which he was created Baron Heathfield. De Fonblanque tells us that Burgoyne was appointed to raise the 16th because of his merit. This is not strictly true, for, although he proved an excellent colonel, he raised the 16th as a private venture, and the means by which he obtained the colonelcy provide a good illustration of how such things were done.

On his return from St. Cast, Burgoyne found that his "expectations" of promotion were more than fulfilled and that the influence of his father-in-law, now that they were reconciled, was really beginning to show results. He was promoted straight from captain to lieutenant-colonel (at a cost of £2,300), and at the same time given, or allowed to buy, a commission as a captain-lieutenant in the Coldstream Guards (at a further cost of between £1,500 and £2,600). Thus, from being a rather elderly captain he became, almost overnight, the youngest serving lieutenant-colonel in the army, besides being an officer in the Guards. This brought a combined income of well over £3,000 a year, which was a great improvement on the £1,343 10s he had earned as a captain and greater still on the £103 17s 6d he had earned as an ensign. Nevertheless, that the cost was heavy at first is indicated by the fact that early in 1759 he leased "The Oaks" to his father-in-law, though apparently he continued to live there for a few years more.[1]

When proposals to raise the Light Dragoons first began to be heard, Burgoyne, through the influential channel of his family, was able to persuade the Secretary-at-War, Lord Barrington, that he could save public money by supplying horses at £2 a head cheaper than the king would be able to do, i.e., at £13 each instead of £15. Presumably he was able to manage this through his racing friends. Accordingly on 4 August 1759 a royal warrant was issued to "our Trusty and Well loved John Burgoyne Esqre. to raise by beat of drum or otherwise" the 16th Regiment of Light Dragoons. It was to consist of four troops, each with seventy-one privates, two drummers, three corporals, and three sergeants. Headquarters were to be established at Northampton. The mounts were to be smaller than ordinary cavalry horses, none to be more than fifteen hands high.

There was never much difficulty in finding officers. The real problem was finding the men. The army was not popular with ordinary people. Unlike the navy, whose men were at sea, the army in peacetime was looked upon as a danger to civil liberties. Hence no king or Parliament dared press men into the army as they did into the fleet, for people would not have stood for it. Recruiting officers therefore had to use every device they could think of to persuade, cajole, or inveigle men into serving their "king and country."

Burgoyne wrote an advertisement which he had printed and posted up all over Northamptonshire. The body of it ran:

> You will be mounted on the finest horses in the world, with the finest clothing and the finest accoutrements; your pay and privileges are equal to two guineas a week; you are admired by the fair, which together with the chance of getting switched to a buxom widow or of brushing with a rich heiress renders the situation truly enviable and desirable. Young

men out of employment or uncomfortable—"There is a tide in the affairs of men which taken at the flood leads on to fortune". Nick in instantly and enlist.

Burgoyne was right to be careful in stating that the pay and privileges (undefined) were *equal* to £2 2s a week, for after deductions what the Light Dragoon private actually received can be worked out as £3 5s *a year*.[2]

Perhaps the least untruthful claim in Burgoyne's advertisement was that his troopers' clothes would be "the finest." Indeed, they could hardly be less if he was to keep ahead in fashionable society. Although uniforms were becoming more standardized by this time and the king had ordered that the uniforms of the two regiments were to be alike (the jackets had to be shorter than those of ordinary cavalry), Burgoyne provided uniforms that were strikingly smart.*

Recruiting went moderately well (about forty a week), and in October it was decided to increase the regiment by two troops, although some of the existing troops were not complete. The reason for this was that Lord Harcourt was looking for a place for his son and had decided that the position of captain in the 16th Light Dragoons would do very nicely. He offered, therefore, to supply two complete troops, with their horses, provided his son could be the captain of one of them. Despite this windfall, Burgoyne was having difficulties with Lord Barrington. His horses, he said, had cost £15 after all, the difference had put him £800 out of pocket. He requested that this be made up. Barrington agreed to £1 out of the £2 difference, explaining that the public could not be expected to supply out of its own funds what had been promised free by private individuals. When the two additional troops were announced, Burgoyne wrote on 25 October asking for a chaplain (another commission to sell) and some "hautboys" (oboe players) such as Elliott had in his 15th Light Dragoons. He now demanded the remaining £1 per horse, protesting that he was still £400 out of pocket. Why should public economy suddenly begin with him? He ended with a threat that if Barrington continued to refuse, he would take the matter up in Parliament. This meant that his brother-in-law, Lord Strange, would accuse Barrington in the House of Commons of victimization—

*Jackets were red, with black facings (cuffs, collars, and lapels), turned up in black with white linings. Waistcoats, breeches, buttons, and shoulder straps were white. Officers wore silver lace. Leather was tanned, but the saddlecloths were black laced richly with white (silver for officers). Worked into the pattern was the motto *Aut cursu cominus armis* (freely translatable as "Victory or Death") and *16 LD* in a wreath of roses and thistles. The dragoon wore a red cloak over his shoulders, with a black cape lined with white. The helmet, which rather resembled a coal scuttle in shape, was copper japanned in black. Above was a short brass crest plumed with red horsehair. In 1766 the regimental black was changed to blue, and the white waistcoat and breeches to buff. The drummers wore black with white facings.

an unwelcome prospect since Lord Strange was one of the most eloquent speakers in the House.

On the 27th Barrington wrote Burgoyne two letters. One was genial and dealt with technicalities. The business of Captain Harcourt, he said, was excellent. It was a pity that Major Vaughan, a candidate for admission to the regiment, could not raise a troop for himself in the "same frugal way." Vaughan would have to be dropped and his position offered to Mr. Jennings (he hoped on Burgoyne's warm recommendation) or "any other young man of fashion and fortune who will accept it with thanks." The second letter was in that tone of injured righteousness tempered by firm common sense that is always adopted by a man in a strong bargaining position. "There is so little regard for the public to be found in mankind," he began, "that I must neither be surprised or offended, that you do not give me the least credit for anything of that sort. . . ."

Major-General Elliott (who had been promoted), he pointed out, was an officer with a long and distinguished record. He had been appointed to command because he deserved it, and his regiment, with its *douceur* of oboe players, etc., had been raised by public money. Mr. Burgoyne had been a captain only a year and a half ago. After "a series of favours of which the army does not furnish a precedent, and to which with all his amiable and valuable qualities as a man he had not the least claim to as a soldier," Burgoyne had obtained, at his own request, permission to raise a regiment under certain conditions. These conditions he was now trying to wriggle out of. However, more money for the horses was out of the question, for the Treasury had already passed its allocations. Next, was Burgoyne not aware that no regiment in England had a chaplain and that oboe players were considered not as a perquisite but as so much extra pay to be deducted from the colonel's salary? As for Burgoyne's wondering why public economy should begin with him, "where can it begin more properly, as in a regiment commanded by a man, who was a captain a year and a half ago?" In words that expressed the eighteenth-century British philosophy regarding every limb of the body of the state, be it government, church, army, navy, civil service, police, or prisons, Barrington summed up:

> If an officer, by the length or merit of his services, has a claim to preferment, he should have it *gratis;* but when a young *gentleman*, who has no such pretension, is put over the heads of older and better soldiers, he should buy it. In short, the public should be paid in services or in savings.

After warning Burgoyne that the threat of the House of Commons was no way to frighten him, Barrington ended on a more friendly note. His anger, he said, had been caused by Burgoyne's having written "the least courtly letter that was ever written by an officer to a Secretary at War." Nevertheless, the regiment had been raised with surprising speed. It would be a good one, he was sure. Burgoyne could have his chaplain (and the commission money) if the regiment went abroad. "You are a man of sense, honour, and merit," and he promised that he would always assist Burgoyne when the right time came, "however you may speak or write about me."[3]

By January 1760 the regiment was nearly complete, and Burgoyne stipulated that the only cornets who would henceforth be admitted were those who could bring in fifteen horses with them or as many as £315 could buy. In February it was marched to Scotland and back, and in the autumn it was told to be ready for service abroad. It was transferred down to Surrey, and training was done on Wimbledon Common and Putney Heath, conveniently near Burgoyne's home, "The Oaks." There exists a letter dated 24 October to Barrington in which Burgoyne explains that Kingston-on-Thames is not large enough for his detachment and asks that his quarters be enlarged to include Hampton and other neighboring villages.[4] The next day, however, King George II died, and all military operations were postponed until the political situation became clearer.

George III was twenty-two when he ascended the throne. He was a well-meaning, intelligent, and strong-minded young man, but he was inexperienced, shy, and very much influenced by his confidant and adviser, Lord Bute, who was an intellectual. He had taken immense pains to educate the prince in the duties of a constitutional monarch, according to his Whig principles, but he was not a practical politician and, most serious of all, he did not have a seat in the House of Commons. However, he was a man who did not seem to know whether he wanted power or not, and his position of intimacy with the new king excited great jealousy and suspicion among the professional politicians in Parliament. To make matters worse, Prince George had, in the tradition of crown princes (and especially Hanoverian crown princes) been at odds with his grandfather George II, just as George II had been at odds with George I. Thus, a fundamental fact of the confused British politics of this period is that every politician and minister had to make up his mind whether to place his stakes on the present court, which meant certain office and power now, or on the opposition centered around the future king (the phrase was "Leicester House," where the Prince of Wales's family lived and where, consequently, members of the opposition were welcome guests), which meant possible, but not certain, office and power in the future. After Pitt's great triumphs, King George II had come to support the war. The prince, therefore, had opposed it, and now that he was on the throne, he was anxious to bring it to an end. What he really wanted to do—with the help of Lord Bute—was to clean the Augean Stable of political corruption in England. Peace negotiations were opened with France, against the Cassandralike warnings of Pitt, who declared that Choiseul was not to be trusted.

Meanwhile, Burgoyne had reached a critical stage in his military career. A colonelcy of a regiment was no more than a necessary step toward realizing the proper ambition of every active officer, which was to become a general. This was more likely to be achieved if he became a member of Parliament. In Parliament an officer could form political connections and draw attention to himself by his speeches. His name would come to the ear of the Secretaries of State and through them to the ear of the king. Provided he did not do anything outrageous, such as become a maverick or vote consistently with the opposition (though he could do so on occasion to show he had a mind of his own), he would eventually be on the short list of officers considered for high command. There was really no other way. As a mere colonel and regular officer it would have been quite possible for Burgoyne to stay in Northamptonshire (or Surrey) and do little more than inspect his regiment and make visits to London for the rest of his life. Even if a war called his regiment to active service, the important appointments would be made over his head and given to officers who were close to ministers. Wolfe had been a lonely exception, but even he had owed his command to the influence of his colonel, Lord George Sackville (Germain), who had understood his great gifts and forced his promotion through against jealousy and opposition. Moreover, had he survived Quebec, there is no doubt that as soon as he returned to England Newcastle would have found a seat in the Commons for him somehow. "If you wish to make a figure in your country, you must first make a figure in Parliament"—this was the great rule, and it applied regardless of profession.

Burgoyne's opportunity came at the general election of 1761. Sir William Peere Williams (an officer in Burgoyne's regiment) had bought some burgages (freeholds, etc., carrying votes) at Midhurst in Sussex and proposed Burgoyne as a candidate.

To anyone unfamiliar with them, British politics in the middle of the eighteenth century must appear hopelessly complicated. Although there were two parties, Whig and Tory, the differences between them were very unclear indeed. There were no party organizations, still less party policies. The troubles of the time arose not so much from opposition between Whig and Tory as from opposition between "factions"—the groups gathered around the important holders of office or around the leaders among their opponents. What really counted were personalities, family ties, and local traditions. Burgoyne, for instance, was a Whig because his brother-in-law, Lord Strange, belonged to a great Whig family; but he voted usually where his interest lay, and sometimes according to his conscience, even if this meant voting against the government (which was sometimes called "the court" and sometimes "the Administration").

The electoral system was antiquated, picturesque, and corrupt. Representation bore no relation to population. Some decayed counties, like Cornwall, still had over forty seats; new and growing places like Birmingham had none. Every county sent two members, as did every borough—a tradition dating back to the Middle Ages. Franchise varied from borough to borough, some seats having six or less voters and some six thousand. Local nobles would insist on the election of their protégés, and the administration would compete with other groups to buy seats by bribing the electors. Indeed, no one would go to the polls at all unless liberally treated with beer, beef, and, very often, money and free suits of clothes. Elections, therefore, were noisy, violent, drunken occasions enjoyed by everybody except those who had to pay for the festivities and those who had their arms, legs, or heads broken.[5]

Burgoyne's election at Midhurst was not very exciting, however. Sir William Williams did a deal with the opponents by which Burgoyne and the opposing candidate, William Hamilton (who was later to marry the famous Emma, Nelson's Lady Hamilton), had one of the two seats each. Williams was to receive £1,000 for this accommodation, but Hamilton never paid it.

A few weeks after the election, the political situation changed yet again. Pitt warned that France and Spain were on the point of forming a secret alliance and that the peace negotiations should be dropped at once. He was ignored and so resigned, his place being taken by Lord Egremont. It turned out, however, he was right, and military operations were resumed.

A corps of six thousand troops, among them a detachment of the 16th Light Dragoons under Sir William Williams, was sent to Belle Isle, south of Brittany, to capture the old fort built by Vauban. As his rank prohibited him from commanding a mere detachment, Burgoyne went along as a volunteer. He left his wife, who had tried to dissuade him from going, some lines of verse as a reassurance. Have faith, he wrote, in Heaven!

> The Power that formed my Charlotte's heart
> Thus tender, thus sincere
> Shall bless each wish that love can start,
> Or foster absence there.

Safe in the shadow of that Power,
I'll tread the hostile ground;
Though fiery deaths in tempest shower,
And thousands fall around.[6]

Almost immediately on landing, Sir William Peere Williams walked straight into the line of fire and was killed. Everyone believed it was suicide. His debts had become hopeless, and he was determined to avoid a debtors' prison. The attack was repulsed with the loss of five hundred men. While the British fleet lay offshore preparing another attack, the women of the town put on red jackets and rode along the cliff tops (those who could not find horses or donkeys being mounted on cows) to give the impression that the garrison was fully manned. A second landing was made eventually, and after a two-month siege the fort surrendered.

Burgoyne, not the man to put up with garrison duty in an isolated fort if he could help it, contracted a convenient fever and returned to London in November. He stayed at 2 Chesterfield Street, a smart Mayfair house he had recently rented for his mother to live in. We have a polite letter from this address to a general's widow, Mrs. Prideaux, who had been begging Burgoyne to find a place for her young son in his regiment. He explained that he already had too many cornets in the regiment who ought still to have been at school.

> I have hitherto made it a point to get part of my regiment upon every active service where Dragoons could be employed & am now labouring, & shall continue to do so through the winter, to have the whole sent to Germany early in the spring; I submit to you, Madam, with what propriety I could press an application for service & at the same time admit an officer incapable of doing duty.[7]

Burgoyne's wire-pulling to get his regiment into action again soon produced results. Britain, alarmed at the new alliance between France and Spain, declared war on Spain on 2 January 1762. France made threatening noises at Portugal in an attempt to frighten the young king, José I, into declaring war on Britain. José, refusing to turn against an old and loyal ally (and the world's greatest consumer of port wine), sent to England for help, offering to finance a British expeditionary force of seven or eight thousand men. Pitt, now in opposition, urged Parliament to accept. "I do not mean that we should carry the King of Portugal on our shoulders," he declaimed, "but only that we should set him on his legs, and put a sword into his hand!" The British hurriedly scraped together 3,028 men and sent them to Portugal under Lord Loudoun, promising another four thousand to follow.[8] Among the regiments ordered to go was the 16th Light Dragoons.

Burgoyne was to command the entire contingent of British cavalry and while in Portugal to hold the local rank of brigadier-general. Sending orders for the detachment at Belle Isle to go to Lisbon immediately, Burgoyne sailed in early June, taking Lady Charlotte, and perhaps their daughter Charlotte Elizabeth as well, with him.

In the Academia Militar in Lisbon there is a drawing which shows how well Burgoyne could dress a part. "Brigadeiro Burgoyne" wears a black cavalier moustache and beard, giving him very much the air of a swashbuckling *beau sabreur* on his prancing horse, as he leads his men to storm the gates of Valencia d'Alcántara. This was perfectly appropriate to the role he played in this campaign, which was so full of untoward and slapstick incidents that it is still remembered as "*La Guerra Fantástica*" ("The Fantastic War").[9]

CHAPTER IV

LA GUERRA FANTÁSTICA

THE Burgoynes arrived in Lisbon with the British expeditionary force on 16 June.[1] For the next few days the harbor was crowded with ships trying to disembark their troops in an orderly manner, no preparations having been made for their reception, or even ground set aside for their camps.

Seven years previously (1755), Lisbon had been destroyed by one of the most famous earthquakes in history. First Minister Don Sebastião José de Carvalho, Condé D'Oeyras, better known by his later (1770) title of Marquès de Pombal, had energetically rebuilt the city in the splendid baroque style called "Pombalesque." The enormous cost of this had emptied the Treasury. There had been no money for defense and the army had, almost literally, melted into the ground. At the first hint of war, Pombal had tried to create a new army, and by January 1762 he had contrived to collect a force of sixty thousand unarmed, untrained, ragged, and barefoot men. To organize this he had employed some English officers under Lord Tyrawley, the ambassador who was for a time commander-in-chief. Tyrawley had little interest in this work, convinced that both the Portuguese and Spanish armies were mere rabble. "Ten thousand disciplined soldiers," he wrote to Pitt, "might take their choice whether they would advance on Lisbon or Madrid."

Pombal, therefore, engaged the services of Wilhelm Schaumbourg-Lippe Bückebourg, the reigning count of Schaumbourg-Lippe, a small principality in northwestern Germany. He was a natural son of King George I of England, by the king's German mistress the Duchess of Kendal, and commander, since 1757, of George II's Hanoverian artillery. Although only thirty-eight years old, he was a veteran of two wars and was generally regarded as the best artillery officer in the world. He devoted his later years to a military academy, where he propounded theories of military science that forecast the great nationalistic wars of the next two centuries.

Count Lippe's appearance was unforgettable. His face was so long that it seemed to be all profile. He was tall and thin, and when he wore his great hat over his long flowing hair and carried his tiny sword at his side, the effect was overwhelmingly comic. Spanish generals reconnoitering the frontier saw this extraordinary figure through their telescopes and cried out, "It's Don Quixote!" Appointed *marechal general* of the Anglo-Portuguese army, Count Lippe established his headquarters at Pedrouces, outside Lisbon on the banks of the Tagus and conveniently near the arsenal.

Shortly after their arrival, the British officers were invited to a banquet by King José. When they arrived at the palace gates they were surprised to see the sentries, on their knees and with hands outstretched, begging for alms from passersby. Burgoyne and his fellow officers were even more surprised, indeed shocked, to discover that the waiters-at-table were none other than the officers—the captains, majors, and colonels—of the Portuguese regiments that were to accompany them to the frontier. It transpired that these officers had been the household servants of the generals, who, being unable or unwilling to pay them wages, had given them commissions in the army instead. They were little better off as officers, however, than they had been as butlers, footmen, and cooks; for they still received no wages and were obliged to follow humble trades in their spare time, such as pawnbroking and barrelmaking, to avoid starvation, while their wives took in washing.

Count Lippe was determined to instill a martial spirit into his new army. He decreed that any officer who suffered insult without demanding satisfaction would be cashiered. In Germany he had sometimes resorted to practical jokes as a part of training. Once he had placed a mine, time-fused, beneath his headquarters tent and casually informed his staff of the fact thirty seconds before it was due to explode. It had been his pleasure to sit with his officers at dinner while his gunners, from a suitable distance, tried to hit the flag flying above his tent. It is said that he adapted this trick in Portugal to point a different moral: That is, he expressed his contempt of the Portuguese artillery by offering a prize to any gunner who could hit the flag above the marquee during a return banquet which the British officers gave in honor of the Portuguese generals. When his distinguished guests showed their anxiety at the cannonshot hurtling past them, he observed that he was merely following the example of Diogenes the philosopher, who had once, during a practice by inexpert archers, sat down in front of their target in order to ensure his own safety.[2]

The Spaniards had mobilized an army of forty-two thousand men on the frontier and, accompanied by five thousand French "advisers," had crossed into Portugal at the beginning of May. Their strategy was simple. Portugal is protected along its border by a deep barrier of mountains. The Spaniards, therefore, divided their army into three wings: one in the north, one in the center, and one in the south. The three wings were to thread their way through the mountains and converge on the central plain of Alentejo. There they would unite and advance on Lisbon in overwhelming strength. The northern wing had already invaded the province of Tras o Montes and was advancing toward Oporto. The center wing had captured the fortress of Almeida, which had been compelled to surrender when the governor had inadvertently blown up his own magazines and himself with them. The southern wing was massing by the Tagus on the approaches to Lisbon itself. Nevertheless, they were advancing with extraordinary slowness and were still in the mountains by the end of July, by which time Lippe's mixed army was ready to move.

Burgoyne was given a brigade of five hundred British cavalry, five hundred British infantry, one thousand Portuguese cavalry, and one thousand Portuguese infantry and was ordered to proceed along the Tagus to Sardoal by way of Santorem. On 3 August he wrote to Lieutenant-General Townshend from Sardoal, which he had just reached after an appalling march. It had been impossible to find wagons for all the baggage on any one day, only some small carts drawn by oxen at oxen pace. To make up time he had marched his men fourteen hours a day. The baggage not on carts or wagons had had to be carried by the baggage guards, who were now down with sunstroke and fever. Three boatloads of baggage still lay at Abrantes, seven miles away, where they had been for six days. There were absolutely no horses, mules, or carts to be found anywhere; it was almost as if the local peasants were driving away their animals before the army arrived. The heat was extreme; yet his men had not eaten for twenty-four hours, and his horses had had no straw for two days. Nor was there any sign of there being any food in the foreseeable future. His men had to sleep on the ground or on bullrushes because the locals refused to let them have any straw.[3]

Lord Loudon approched Pombal and tactfully tried to shift the blame for this total lack of cooperation onto the minister's underlings. Pombal, however, continued "very shy upon all articles to do with mules, horses (especially for artillery), bread, corn, etc." He explained that only oxen were used in Portugal and that all horses were imported from Spain, blaming Loudoun and Tyrawley for not having found this out before mounting the expedition. With some reluctance, he produced six hundred mules, but Loudoun had to reject all but thirty of them as useless. On top of this there was a contretemps over honor. In eighteenth-century armies there was always a question as to which brigades should march and fight on the right (the senior side) and which on the left. Pombal had agreed that the British should take the left when in Portugal and the right when in Spain—if they ever got there. Now he insisted that the British should take the left both in Portugal and in Spain. The British were not only offended but anxious. Light infantry and advanced corps companies were usually placed on the right, from which attacks were often mounted. It was not reassuring to leave this vital offensive action to demoralized and disorganized Portuguese.

The truth was that Pombal, whom Walpole described as "the profoundest and most desperate politician of the age," was intensely unpopular. He had expelled the Jesuits two years previously after the discovery of a conspiracy for which he held them responsible.[4] The nobles and priests had been dumbfounded at his impudence, and he had exploited their confusion by forcing through reforms of every kind. Now they were recovering from the shock and doing everything in their power to inflame the superstitious peasantry against him. Thus while British officers accused Pombal of deliberately thwarting them from motives of national pride and jealousy, he was finding it difficult to ensure that a single order of his would be obeyed.

Colonel Anderson, attached to a Portuguese force under the Condé de San Jago, wrote to Burgoyne of the difficulty of gathering intelligence. "The peasants do not look on the Spaniards as their enemy; they think their cause the cause of the Jesuits and the cause of God. The people of condition, the excellencies and Hidalgos, have so insuperable a hatred to the Minister, as to sacrifice their king, their country, and even their honour, to feed it. I have, however, the happiness to be under as honest a man as ever lived, with as good a heart as it is possible to imagine."[5]

Unhappily, the Spanish commanders failed to understand the situation and instead of taking advantage of a welcome that would have guaranteed them an easy and pleasant march to Lisbon, treated the Portuguese peasants as near-heretics and persecutors of the Jesuits. The invaders indeed behaved in apparent ignorance of that code of honor which is supposed to have existed in armies in the eighteenth century, destroying villages, slaughtering the inhabitants, and burning and looting in the towns. Goaded into resistance, the Portuguese peasants broke down bridges, drove away their livestock, and tortured and mutilated such Spanish soldiers as they could catch. An angry correspondence began between the enemy commanders over these atrocities, "hitherto unusual in Wars between Christian princes." It is curious to note that while all this was going on, the Queen of Portugal continued to write to her mother, the Queen Mother of Spain, as though there were no war on at all, and her letters were actually delivered.[6]

With the threat to Oporto and the wine trade becoming serious, the alarmed British sent a naval squadron to protect the wine factories. A small British force, working with now enthusiastic Portuguese guerrillas, effectively blocked the mountain passes and forced the Spanish divisions to retreat. This saved the wine trade but had the unfortunate result of allowing these divisions to join the Spanish army advancing into Portugal in the center. Burgoyne's position was now precarious. With his three thousand men he was covering the territory between Vila Velha de Rondão, on the Tagus, and Portalegre twenty-five miles to the south. Facing him was a Spanish corps of fourteen thousand men under General D'Aranda, with other divisions threatening to encircle him on the north and south. If the Spanish armies succeeded in joining on the central plain, this would force the British and Portuguese to a pitched battle on disadvantageous ground and against superior numbers. If the Portuguese collapsed, the British force could find itself swamped by an army twelve times its size. Lippe could do little else but strike at sensitive points before the movement got any further forward. He asked Burgoyne to try the desperate remedy of attacking the headquarters and magazines inside Spanish territory at the ancient walled town of Valencia d'Alcántara.

By a forced march Burgoyne took his little force across the mountains so quickly that the Spaniards did not even know he had moved. He had no maps and depended entirely on guides who gave him contradictory information. All he knew was that if he kept on the Pitteranha road, which he had found, he would come to the town lying in the plain below. The town had only three important gates—one facing him, one to the east on the Alcántara road, and one to the south facing high mountains. "I was informed that patrols were not regular, nor at a distance; that there were no advanced piquets, no barricadoes, and that the only guard was in the great square."

Arriving on the heights above the town and keeping well out of sight, he divided his forces. Major Luttrell was sent with the Portuguese grenadiers to work his way around the town to the eastern road, thus cuting off communication with Alcántara. With his grenadiers went some Portuguese cavalry and twenty-four of the 16th Light Dragoons under a captain. Their flanks were protected by a crowd of armed peasants and "irregular infantry." Lord Pulteney, with the British grenadiers, was ordered to storm the gate in front, on the Pitteranha road. Portuguese irregulars were ordered to enter by the south gate and occupy houses on either side of the entrance. Major Somerville was to take the rest of the Light Dragoons around to the north, block off the town on that side, and give support to whichever party required it.

The town was therefore to be attacked on three sides at once, at sunrise. The Portuguese were given the longest route "to reserve the English for a rush into the town, in case I should find we were discovered, while the different divisions were taking their posts. About four miles from the town I found a convent which was on a very strong post, and I left in it a hundred men."

Unfortunately, his guides had misinformed Burgoyne as to the distances, and while he was waiting for the different parties to reach their stations, he saw that dawn was coming on fast. There was nothing to do but drop the whole plan and charge straight in with the Light Dragoons while there was still a chance of surprise. Burgoyne led his corps "at three-quarters speed" to the gates, and forty men led by Lieutenant Lewis pushed into the town swords in hand. The entrance clear, Burgoyne followed with the rest.

> The guards in the square were all killed or taken prisoner, before they could use their arms, and the ends of the streets were possessed with very little resistance. By the time the body of the regiment was in the square, a few desperate parties attempted an attack, but all perished or were taken. The only firing that remained was in single shots from windows, which did not continue long after the grenadiers came up. I was obliged to treat the people who persisted in it without quarter, and at last got some priests whom I forced through the town, to declare that the town should be set fire to at the four corners, unless all doors and windows were instantly thrown up. Before they had proceeded down one street, the people had seen their error, and all was quiet.

Light Dragoons were sent into the countryside to round up all who had escaped. A sergeant and six men ran into twenty-six Spanish dragoons under a subaltern. They killed six and made the rest prisoners, taking all the horses. Before retiring, Burgoyne's force blew up the magazines and spiked all the cannon. They took away with them the Spanish general, Don Miguel de Irumbeni y Kalanca, his aide-de-camp, a colonel, two captains, seventeen subalterns, fifty-nine privates, three colors, and a number of hostages to ensure the good treatment of his wounded, who would be exchanged for the hostages later, "and for the payment of a year's king's revenue for sparing the convents and the town."[7]

In fact, Burgoyne had destroyed the Regimiento de Sevilla (twelve hundred men) and cut the communications center of the Spanish invasion. The effect of his success was out of all proportion to the numbers involved. The Portuguese, at first bewildered and then sunk in gloom, were now wildly elated. The British, hitherto distrusted and denied every kind of help, were now the heroes of the hour and feted everywhere with fiestas and fireworks. Here were allies indeed! Count Lippe praised the courage and "generosity" of the British troops, "& it deserves Admiration that in an Affair of this kind the Town & the inhabitants Suffer'd very little, which is owing to the good order Brigadier Burgoyne kept up even in the heat of the Action." He wrote to Lord Bute, setting out in detail the success due entirely to the "remarkable valour, conduct, and presence of mind of Brigadier Burgoyne . . . and it is my duty to mention this officer to your Lordship as a most excellent one, and extremely worthy of his Majesty's remembrance."[8] A few days later Burgoyne received a personal letter from Pombal enclosing a diamond ring as a present from King José. In his own dispatch Burgoyne attributed the success entirely to "the admirable, though not uncommon, valour of the troops I had the honour to command." He went on to praise Major Somerville for his judgment, spirit, and humanity, "and I do not know for which of these qualities he deserves most commendation."

Among Burgoyne's correspondence of this time are letters which show the administrative problems he had to deal with in the midst of all this campaigning. There is a note to Lord Loudoun, dated 22 September, asking him to expedite the courts-martial of three deserters, as there had been several desertions lately. These were probably the unfortunates who, de Fonblanque tells us, were sentenced to a thousand lashes each. Captain Edward Walpole, Horace Walpole's nephew, had started badly in the regiment. However,

> his behaviour since his arrival in Portugal where he has been trusted with a separate command allows me the satisfaction of mentioning his name to you in a very different manner from what his habit of dissipation authorized me to do when I had the honour to talk to you upon his preferment in England. I never doubted his talents for the service; I am now convinced he is capable of steadiness to employ them. . . .

And Burgoyne went on to recommend Walpole's promotion to major. Unfortunately, Burgoyne was mistaken, for he was to have more trouble from Walpole later on. In the same letter, Burgoyne recommends that young Cornet Duperron should be transferred to the infantry, for, though a "very diligent, good officer, he is very unfit for the Dragoons as an incorrigible bad Horseman and unacquainted with every part of horse Service." Nevertheless, Duperron's private circumstances make him "a subject of compassion," and a posting to a regiment of foot would "make him and his family happy."[9]

Burgoyne had his own career to think of. Before leaving for Portugal he had applied to Lord Bute for promotion to the rank of full colonel. This had been refused, as there were several officers of longer service who had higher priority. In August Burgoyne had protested to

Townshend (the new Secretary-at-War), for his equals, Clinton, Fitzroy, and Brudenell, had all recently been promoted purely on account of their family influence. He too had applied on grounds of his family interest. "Upon any other ground, I should blush to ask it," he claimed and added that if any of his three friends had made their claim on grounds of merit of service, no doubt they would have had to wait a long time. "But when the Government thinks proper to allow family weight and protection to take place, I will be bold to offer my claim, from the honour of Lord Strange's application, upon the same list as Mr. Clinton and Mr. Fitzroy, and my want of success will give me more pain as a slight to my patron than as a disappointment to myself." Burgoyne's contemporaries, who were no more modest than we are, felt it was rude and immodest to boast over one's personal achievements, but not so to proclaim one's good family.

Yet King George III was, rightly or wrongly, trying to diminish corruption, and one of the means he was using was making sure that his approval of the six-monthly promotion lists that were presented to him was no mere formality. Townshend was therefore able to send Burgoyne a pained reply, rather in the same tone that Barrington had used before. He was shocked and hurt that Burgoyne should suspect hidden motives where none existed. Had he had the slightest evidence that the king had meant otherwise than what he had said and had his respected friend Lord Strange suspected anything either, he would have acted at once. Burgoyne certainly seems to have had the knack of rubbing Secretaries-at-War the wrong way.

Meanwhile, Burgoyne's brigade was ordered north to oppose the combined Spanish armies crossing the Duoro River. The numbers against them were overwhelming, and it was not long before the Anglo-Portuguese army lost both Castello Branco and Vila Velha de Rondão on the Tagus. The way was open to Lisbon, and the Spanish division at Valencia d'Alcántara was now sufficiently protected to repair the dislocation inflicted on it by Burgoyne's attack.

Burgoyne hovered about Vila Velha, and when he saw that the Spaniards had detached a large force in pursuit of the British under Lord Loudoun, he decided that this was an opportunity to strike a blow as effective as the one at Valencia d'Alcántara. "At Sun Set," he writes in his dispatch, "I had the Opportunity of reconnoitring all the Avenues to his Camp." He saw that the Spaniards had left six pieces of artillery, with cavalry and picquets, on the plain in front of the town and that in their elation they had left the camp poorly guarded.

> Upon these observations I determined to attempt a Surprise, by marching a Detachment round the Enemy's Camp by a Path I had discovered over the mountains to a difficult but practicable Ford about a League up

> the River. Accordingly I put a Detachment in March as soon as I returned to Camp, but so much time had been employ'd in examining the Ford and in passing the Defiles of the mountains, that Colonel Lee, who commanded it, found he could not reach his Destination before Day light, and very prudently retired to Camp.

Colonel Charles Lee was a clever, blustering military adventurer—red face, large nose, receding chin, bushy moustache, bibulous eyes, and of a wirelike thinness—who was in later life to join the American rebels and became for a time, until he quarreled with him, Washington's second-in-command.

The Spaniards, having neglected to picquet their own camp properly, had nevertheless set up posts overlooking Burgoyne's to watch his movements. The next day (4 October), therefore, Burgoyne sent off his detachments in groups of ten to avoid arousing suspicion. By evening a hundred grenadiers had surreptitiously marched away into the hills and were assembled at the head of a ravine. After dark Burgoyne led the main force of five hundred Light Dragoons, two hundred Royal Volunteers, and fifty Portuguese "St. Pazo Horse" to the ford and then returned to camp to supervise his artillery. This was intended to divert the enemy's attention by directing their fire onto the two hills that overlooked the Spanish camp—one above the village and the other with a castle at its top—and the guns had to be drawn into position with the utmost quietness.

All these maneuvers went according to plan. Burgoyne narrated briefly:

> About two in the morning I had the Satisfaction to find by the confused Cries of the Enemy, that Colonel Lee was in their Camp, and a few minutes after I perceived by their irregular and retiring Fire, that he was pushing them towards their Magazines, and that they were flying in Confusion. I immediately began a firing from all my Cannon [against the two hillsides], & continued until an Officer called out all parts carried.[10]

The six cannon were spiked, the magazines blown up, and a large number of Spaniards killed (though no figures are given). Burgoyne's own casualties were trifling, and he succeeded also in taking away all the food stores and pack animals. By temporarily cutting the Spaniards' supply line and throwing their rear into confusion, Burgoyne weakened the impetus of their advance. There was delay while D'Aranda brought up reinforcements, and it was a fortnight before the offensive got under way again. Two weeks later the autumn rains started in earnest, and the whole invading army turned about and withdrew over the frontier. The British and Portuguese armies went into winter quarters.

The news of his exploits soon reached London, and in November Burgoyne received a letter from Lord Bute to say that his desired promotion to full colonel, out of consideration to Lord Strange "and your own merit," had been granted to him, retroactive to 8 October. On 18 March the following year he was officially appointed colonel commandant of his regiment.[11]

There was no doubt in anyone's mind that Brigadeiro Burgoyne's exploits in the campaign had indeed been brilliant. His planning had been careful and thorough, his dispositions excellent, and his leadership dashing. His two counterattacks had tipped the balance against the Spaniards, saved Lisbon, and shown the true effectiveness of light cavalry when properly employed. Not even his friend Elliott's success at Emsdorf in Germany, where his 15th Light Dragoons had defeated five French battalions, had been more resplendent.

In January 1763 peace negotiations brought hostilities to an end. The 16th Light Dragoons were ordered to sell all their horses in Portugal and return home.[12] Colonel Burgoyne and his wife set sail for England. King José allowed him to take away the colors he had captured at Valencia d'Alcántara.

CHAPTER V

UPROAR, VIOLENCE, AND A *FÊTE CHAMPÊTRE*

AS soon as the Peace of Paris was signed, Britain began to reduce her armed forces to a bare minimum. Colonel Burgoyne's chief concern was that his regiment should not be among those disbanded, and accordingly he set about bringing it to the highest pitch of smartness and efficiency. To some degree his exploits in Portugal helped his purpose, for many of the tougher and more adventurous young men of quality who intended to become soldiers were determined, if it were at all possible, to join the Light Dragoons.

Burgoyne drew up a "Code of Instructions" for the guidance of the new officers who were "as much particularized by their youth and inexperience as by their rank and fortune."[1] Although the purpose of this was to remedy the complete lack of officer training, his method was informal. He did not intend, he wrote, "to offer anything . . . as the orders of a commanding officer, but as the sentiments of a friend, partly borrowed and partly formed upon observation and practice. . . ."

Burgoyne did not believe that officers should, or could, be promoted from the ranks. On the contrary, "the ranks of corporal and sergeant should be considered as the most signal honour that a man from the ranks could attain." From the extract that has survived, it is uncertain whether Burgoyne believed this as a universal principle or merely accepted it as a fact of life in his time. His mentioning it at all suggests that he was arguing a principle, perhaps on the grounds that an officer from the ranks would never be able to maintain the social distance between himself and the men necessary for proper discipline. Outdated and reactionary though this now sounds, it should be remembered that whereas in a modern army soldiers respect and trust a "ranker" (assuming he is a competent officer) as one of themselves who has made good, in the eighteenth century they might well have despised him as one no better than themselves, aping the airs and graces of a gentleman.

Regarding the maintenance of discipline, there were two schools of thought. The Prussians trained men "like spaniels, by the stick," and reduced human nature "to as low as it would bear." The French went to the other extreme of appealing to the soldiers' sense of honor. However, people who argue from theory instead of practice and put all their faith in human rationality are "commonly deceived in their expectations"; for the French were, indeed, the worst disciplined troops in Europe. The English required "a just medium between the two extremes."

This, of course, was not easy to achieve, for to succeed "where minds are to be wrought on requires both discernment and labour. . . . Admitting then that *English soldiers are to be treated as thinking beings*, the reason will immediately appear of getting insight into the character of each particular man, and proportioning accordingly the degrees of punishment and encouragement." This sounds the plainest common sense, yet how many officers even today are really prepared to take the trouble Burgoyne was enjoining his officers to take more than two hundred years ago?

Burgoyne had a strong objection to his officers' swearing at soldiers, for it broke the strict demarcation that should exist between them. However, "there are occasions, such as during stable or fatigue duty, when officers may slacken the reins so far as to talk to soldiers; nay, even a joke may be used, not only without harm but to good purpose, for condescensions well applied are an encouragement to the well disposed, and at the same time a tacit reproof to others." On the other hand, he believed, contrary to the conventions of the time, that among officers a complete social equality should exist when off duty, "for any restraint upon conversation (off parade), unless when an offence against religion, morals or good breeding is in question, is grating . . . and it ought to be a characteristic of every gentleman neither to impose nor to submit to any distinction, but such as propriety of conduct or superiority of talent naturally create."

Burgoyne believed that only an educated man could make a good officer, and he laid out a program of self-improvement for his officers which was considerably ahead of its time. They should learn French, not only because "in foreign service gentlemen will find themselves at the greatest loss" without it, but because all the best books on military science were written in that language. Mathematics and drawing too were essential to service in the Light Dragoons.

His basic rule, however, was that an officer should never enforce a duty on others which he could not perform himself. Burgoyne was pained to see young officers who had learned to ride but had never learned why the horses obeyed them. Even in old and celebrated regiments, one could see "bits ill fitted, accoutrements slovenly put on, twisted stirrups, saddles out of their places, etc.," and the officers blithely unaware that anything was wrong. *His* officers, therefore, must be prepared, from time to time, to forget their rank and be willing to accoutre and bridle horses themselves, until they became thoroughly acquainted with the use of every buckle and strap. Similarly, they should learn the elements of veterinary medicine and know how to shoe a horse as well as the best NCOs. In this way, the men "will acquire a nicety and pride about their equipment which they will never lose. . . ."

Whatever may have been the means by which Burgoyne obtained his regiment (and they were hardly exceptionable at that period), once he had obtained it he proved to be a model officer who had no intention of treating his post as a mere sinecure from which to draw £1,500 a year. He knew that the best guarantee of survival was not glamour but catching the eye of the king. His opportunity came on 18 June 1764, when the brigade of Light Dragoons was reviewed on Wimbledon Common. The king was so pleased with the appearance of "Burgoyne's Light Horse," as he called them, and so impressed by the faultless skill with which they executed their intricate maneuvers, that all talk of disbanding the regiment was dropped. Two years later King George and Queen Charlotte again reviewed the brigade, which consisted now of only two regiments, and ordered that Elliott's 15th be called "The King's" and Burgoyne's 16th "The Queen's" Light Dragoons as a mark of approbation. Thereafter, the review of the two regiments became an almost annual event, sometimes on Wimbledon Common and sometimes on Blackheath. Burgoyne's methods had been justified, and the regiment was to have a long and distinguished history. Today, it is known as the 16th/5th Lancers.[2]

While attending to his regiment, Burgoyne was also attending to his future as a politician. On returning to England he took his seat in Parliament, as member for Midhurst. These were years of political confusion, for in the twelve years between the end of the Seven Years' War and the beginning of the American Revolution, there were no less than six successive administrations. Bute resigned in April 1763, to the relief of almost everyone except the king. He was hounded by jealousy and suspicion, but the last straw had been the complicated and inexplicably lenient terms of the Peace of Paris, which, said John Wilkes, resembled the Peace of God, in that it passed all understanding.

Bute was succeeded by his Secretary of State for the Northern

Department, George Grenville. He was conscientious, hardworking, and businesslike, but pedantic and on occasion stubbornly obtuse. Being the first minister to bother with reading the dispatches from America, he became concerned over how to raise money to pay for the defense of the colonies. The result of his cogitations was the Stamp Act, which Parliament passed with scarcely a demur, quite unaware of the tremendous consequences this would have. There were other matters far more pressing to claim their attention.

There was the heated question, for instance, of who should be regent in the event of the king's death. King George wished to exclude his brother Prince Edward, but he kept his feelings secret to avoid offending his family. Therefore, he named nobody. But as Queen Charlotte was the natural choice, but had not been named, Grenville and others assumed a conspiracy was afoot to nominate the king's mother, Augusta, the princess dowager. It was widely, and erroneously, believed that she was Bute's mistress, and a storm arose because it was believed, again quite wrongly, that Bute was making a cunning bid to return to power. Another crisis was caused by the Wilkes affair.

John Wilkes had been Bute's harshest critic. When Grenville had announced, through the King's Speech at the opening of the new session of Parliament, his administration's program, Wilkes had caustically written, in his paper *The North Briton*, that the new ministry had merely brought changes of men, not of measures. However, an attack on the King's Speech, although the speech was written by Grenville, was held to be an attack on the king, and Wilkes, although an MP, was arrested on a general warrant for "the authors, publishers and printers" of *The North Briton*. The populace, crying "Wilkes and Liberty!," rallied to his support, and there was a whirl of riots in Middlesex and London. Meanwhile, the question of the legality of general warrants, which empowered constables to arrest people without names being specified, became the subject of a major debate in Parliament (eventually, they were declared illegal).

Burgoyne was a supporter of Grenville's administration in a lukewarm way, but on the question of general warrants he suddenly became "very earnest to avoid a decision of it at this juncture. I am also very desirous . . . to speak my sentiments in the House, and . . . I humbly offer myself to second any motion for postponing the question." Grenville refused his offer, and although Burgoyne spoke in the debate his speech was not recorded. He was a man of mild political convictions and suffered the fate of all such people—that is, he frequently found himself on both sides at once. On this occasion he probably disapproved of general warrants in principle but did not wish to embarrass his friends (such as Lord Sandwich and Henry Luttrell) who were trying to crush Wilkes.[3]

Burgoyne did not speak much in Parliament in these years, and perhaps it is a pity he ever spoke much at all. It is extraordinary that the commander who insisted that his officers should learn to write accurately and swiftly always forgot his own precept when he rose to address the House or sat down to write a letter to a minister. The source of the trouble may have been that at this time Burgoyne seems to have been trying to curry favor with William Pitt, whom many supposed would be the next head of government, and in doing so to have emulated the great man's literary style. He could not have chosen a worse master. Except in his instructions to generals (and not always then) Pitt was incapable of writing clearly about anything. Later in the year (1766) Burgoyne set off for a tour of the battlefields of the Seven Years' War in Europe and asked Pitt for letters of introduction. Pitt's reply contained the following appalling sentence:

> I will not attempt at present to give expression in any degree to the extent of what I feel from the friendly assurances of the sentiments with which you honour me; little as I have merited such a favourable suffrage where you, Sir, so kindly attribute deserving, I can only beg you to be persuaded that if it be proud and happy in the honour of a justly valued friendship can give a pretension to it, I shall hope you will not find me without some title to the place you are so good to give me in yours.

To this Burgoyne replied:

> But howsoever flattering or advantageous have been the effects of your friendship, it is in the possession of it that I exult; and not to wrong my feelings, I must still trust to the conceptions of a great and benevolent mind, and not to my own feeble expression, to represent that respect, that gratitude, and that zeal with which I solicited, with which I embrace, and with which I study to cultivate, the sentiments your Lordship professes towards me.[4]

This is not English so much as imperial Chinese, and it was a style that Burgoyne cultivated more and more, with progressively worse effect, as he grew older.

During the weeks of preparation for his departure, Burgoyne commissioned Sir Joshua Reynolds to paint his portrait. The result is the fine picture now in the Frick Collection in New York. According to Reynolds' biographer Tom Taylor, the two were already friends by this time and met frequently at such places as the Green Room of Drury Lane Theatre, and at the dinners of the Thursday Club, a group of whist-playing friends of George Selwyn's, which were held at the famous Star and Garter tavern in Pall Mall. This place, which appears so frequently in memoirs of the period, was notorious for its high prices, but the wine was perhaps the best available in London. The

Colonel John Burgoyne in 1766, by Sir Joshua Reynolds. (*Courtesy of the Frick Collection.*)

Dilletanti Society (a group devoted to the study of classical art) met here also, as well as the first cricket club in England, founded in 1774 by Sir Horace Mann and the vicious young Duke of Dorset, who was later to run off with the wife of Burgoyne's nephew.

Burgoyne left England in July 1766 and went to Berlin. Apparently he was not granted an audience by Frederick the Great (for if he had been, he would have said so), but he was able to see something of the Prussian army and to copy a paper on military strategy which Frederick had written for General Fouquet in 1758. Its subject was the methods of fighting developed by the Austrians in the recent campaigns, which Frederick called "the new war for positions," and how to combat them. Burgoyne wrote on the back of his copy (the essay was several thousand words long) "of great curiosity and value"; and indeed it would appear he tried to apply some of the suggestions in this paper both at Ticonderoga and at the two Battles of Freeman's Farm eleven years later. From Berlin he went to Brunswick, Dresden, and Prague, examining battlefields on the way. Determined to see the new Austrian emperor, Joseph II, if only from a distance, he went to the headquarters at Teuchtbrod, where Joseph was supervising the army exercises. All foreign officers were prohibited. "To ask leave that had been refused to men of the first rank," he wrote to his friend Major-General Elliott, "was in vain, but by a little intrigue, a good deal of perseverance, and perhaps more assurance than I ought to boast of, I have succeeded to be present incognito at the practice of the principal manoeuvres." From there he went to Vienna and, by way of the Rhineland, to France, where he stayed with the Duc de Choiseul at Chanteloup.

Back in London by early December, he wrote a long report on what he had seen and learned and presented it to Pitt (who was now Earl of Chatham). He noticed that the armies of the world were copying the "fopperies and absurdities" of the Prussian army and a thousand other practices that "are frivolous, whimsical, and inconvenient," indeed copying them so enthusiastically that everything else had to give way; but they had failed to copy the discoveries and improvements in tactics that had made Prussia the formidable power she now was. Frederick's system of brutal coercion had disciplined the infantry into a precision that was almost miraculous, but his frugality had kept the cavalry ill-mounted and ill-equipped. His insistence on their riding at a tremendous speed often occasioned more deaths among horses and men during an exercise than might be expected in a real action. The artillery was

> formed upon a great scale, exercised with the utmost assiduity, and provided with every utensil and store necessary for immediate and active service. Horses sufficient for the whole train are marked and registered, and distributed among the peasants, who are allowed the use of them

> upon condition that they are well foraged and always forthcoming. Inspections are made occasionally, and in case of a horse suffering by want of care, the peasant is obliged to make him good. By these means agriculture is assisted, and this numerous and expensive body maintained in the best order for draught work without trouble or cost to the state.

Nevertheless, Frederick, as secretive as he was tyrannical, kept a huge army of 160,000 men ready for instant action, at a cost of "most grievous burthens on the people." "Hence a langour of industry and manufacture, general murmur, dejection and depopulation." One could not but suspect that when Frederick died, his whole system would sink into impotence.

In Austria, Emperor Joseph II seemed to be determined "to give his court . . . as military an appearance as that of Berlin." Everything was diverted into establishing Austria as the greatest military power in Europe. Burgoyne described the great efforts to improve the cavalry, the setting up of studs, the importation of horses from Turkey, and the development of new weapons, including a "cavalry cannon" and a new type of carbine resembling a blunderbuss. Austria was clearly bent on a war of revenge against Prussia.

France, too, was busily rearming under the direction of Burgoyne's friend Choiseul, "a man of lively talents, and sanguine temper,—vigilant, secret, ambitious, enterprising"; though the minister's efforts to introduce Prussian methods of discipline had resulted in demoralization and "an incredible desertion." Nevertheless, Choiseul was an obstinate man and he had supporters among the younger nobility. Burgoyne noted that the great attention devoted to enlarging the cavalry appeared ominous. Cavalry was ideally suited not only to the defense of coastlines exposed to the superior naval power of Britain, but also to lightning raids, covering wide areas of territory, against Britain herself. He was convinced that this was in Choiseul's mind. It would be the height of folly, therefore, if England were to permit the exportation of horses, as had been reported, for France depended at present entirely on cavalry horses imported from Germany. Burgoyne's conclusion was that with Europe still in arms and ruled by restless and ambitious men, Britain had been too hasty in reducing her own defenses.

Whatever effect this may have had on Chatham, Burgoyne's painstakingly written report had no effect on national policy, and so presumably it was filed away somewhere and forgotten.[5]

A few weeks after his return Burgoyne was faced with more trouble in his regiment from Major Edward Walpole. In Portugal, as Burgoyne noted, Walpole had pulled himself together, but since then he had increasingly neglected his regiment. Finally, he had been absent for a whole year, throwing his duties onto Colonel Somerville. Now he had applied for the post of aide-de-camp to Viscount Townshend (Charles Townshend's brother), who had gone to Ireland as lord lieutenant. Burgoyne refused to recommend him, adding that if Walpole succeeded in getting his way by means of powerful influence that at least would make room in the regiment for a major "whose views of future preferment will rest upon a diligent discharge of a present trust." [6]

This incident has often been pointed out as the reason why Horace Walpole, Edward's uncle, never lost a chance of writing spitefully about Burgoyne. There may be something in the story, yet it is not quite convincing. Walpole possessed some unpleasant qualities and was not without guile. Most of his stories about Burgoyne were untrue and so most of his charges were unfair, but it is hard to believe they were so from such a petty motive; nor was Walpole so loyal to his relatives as to write deliberate untruths through private malice. Himself a writer of clear and simple prose, he despised Burgoyne's flowery pomposity and disliked him as a man, and that seems to be all there was to it.

We now come, however, to an incident in Burgoyne's life that is extremely puzzling. His parents had left Park Prospect in 1757. His mother moved into the house in Chesterfield Street, Mayfair, as has been mentioned before, which he had rented for her and which he made over to her in 1760. She lived there until 1775, when she vanishes from record. Of Burgoyne's father, whom the newspapers called "Major John Burgoyne," there is no trace for ten years; that is, until February 1767, when he was arrested for a small debt and thrown into the King's Bench prison, Southwark. There he stayed until he died on 13 July 1768.

The puzzle is that the debt was a very small one—£28 10s to a man with the surprising name of William Shakespear, plus £11 damages and costs. Such a sum Burgoyne could have paid in cash out of his own pocket, or at worst borrowed within a few hours; yet such facts as we possess seem to show that he did nothing to rescue his father during the entire eighteen months he was in jail. Of course, allowances should be made. Although the King's Bench was an unpleasant—and even dangerous—place, it was not uncommon for people of quality to go there while their relatives looked the other way and shrugged their shoulders; yet this sort of callousness is quite inconsistent with Burgoyne's reputation as a kindly and considerate man, regarded by his family and closest friends with affection. We do not know what Major John Burgoyne was like (had he been an infernal nuisance for years, incurring endless debts or blundering into ridiculous schemes for raising money?); and we do not know whether Burgoyne sent him money in jail to ensure a modicum of comfort. It is even possible that the major insisted on going to jail, where he would find plenty of congenial friends, rather than stay in the same house with his family and lose his freedom to get drunk and play cards all night. The evidence for and against Burgoyne is involved and tedious and so best dealt with in a note;[7] but it should be stressed that no explanation fits all the facts.

Meanwhile, the incident does reopen the question of who Burgoyne's real father was, for if Burgoyne knew not only that Major Burgoyne was not his real father, but that there had been some kind of sordid transaction with Lord Bingley, his behavior becomes at least understandable. This, if it could ever be shown to be true, would throw a little light on the contradictions in Burgoyne's character. Burgoyne was not exactly a snob, for he enjoyed all company, but he believed that good birth and good family were important. He could hardly have welcomed Lord Bingley as an alternative father, therefore, whatever Lord Bingley's abilities, if he knew that Lord Bingley had been a party to the transaction and, worse, came from an upstart family "of no extraction," several cuts below the Burgoynes themselves. Burgoyne's vainglory and pomposity and the affectedly "correct" style of English he always used in public could thus be seen as no more than a defense he resorted to whenever he felt the eyes of the world upon him, because he secretly knew himself to be weakest where he would have wished to be strongest. This could explain how the man who wrote *The Heiress* (though his comedies are not free of stiff passages) could write the overblown "Proclamation" to the State of New York. Everyone has a blind spot; but it was a pity that Burgoyne could not see that the proper language of a soldier, even in an age which admired the meaningless convolutions of Pitt, was the laconic simplicity of Caesar and Xenophon.

Early in 1768 Parliament was dissolved and a general election called. Burgoyne's brother-in-law, Lord Strange, was concerned over the political situation in Preston. As a cabinet minister and MP for Lancashire, he supported the administration. Of all boroughs, Preston was one of the least friendly to the government. The town corporation was strongly Tory, to the extent that during the Jacobite invasions of 1715 and 1745 they had been on the brink of joining the Stuarts. They controlled elections and always ensured that the two members returned to Parliament were men who shared their antigovernment sympathies. According to an old parlimentary decree of 1661, the vote in Preston was supposed to be held by *"all the inhabitants."* The mayor and corporation, jealous of their privileges, interpreted this to mean no more than a few hundred freeholders, for anyone not a freeholder was classed as a "foreigner." The difference was important. A "foreigner" could not open a shop, carry on any business or trade, or even turn his cattle onto the moor. Therefore he could not be considered eligible for the vote.

The corporation candidates in 1768 were two Lancashire baronets, Sir Peter Leicester and Sir Frank Standish. Lord Strange, thinking it high time to introduce a little government interest into this barbarous backwater, persuaded Burgoyne to abandon Midhurst and try for one of the Preston seats instead. As soon as he started canvassing for Burgoyne, however, he encountered such furious opposition to this "alien" that he asked a local friend, Sir Henry Hoghton, to help Burgoyne by trying for the second seat. This provoked one of the most violent elections in a century famous for the violence of its elections. True, violence seems to have been in the air in that year: There were the great riots staged by the supporters of Wilkes in Westminster and Southwark, and there were others in various parts of the country. But none quite equaled the Preston riots in intensity, length, pointlessness, or unexpectedness of result. It might be added that during all the rioting and destruction not one political issue of national importance was so much as mentioned.

First, Lord Strange baited the corporation by claiming that when Parliament had said "all the inhabitants" it had meant nothing less, and that if all the inhabitants were allowed to vote now they would return a Whig, not a Tory, member to Parliament. Next, he sabotaged the corporation's efforts to rig the voting. The previous town clerk had been a Whig, and on leaving office he had taken away with him a book containing the only full list of electors. Now he refused to give it up, and the corporation could not canvass its electors because it could not remember who they were. This plunged the town into wild rioting, and when Burgoyne set off for Preston, escorted by a guard of militia, his convoy was ambushed, and his chaise bombarded with bricks, stones, and mortal threats. He found Preston in a state of "Uproar, Violence, Sedition and Treason," for such dangerous slogans as "Bonnie Prince Charlie!" and "No King George!" were flying about in the general excitement. His meetings were broken up, the house where he dined was violently attacked, one of his supporters was killed, and he was told, by ringleaders brandishing their clubs at him, that he must either quit the town or die in it. However, he was able to muster a mob ("concourse" was his word for it) of 2,600 laborers from the estates of Lord Strange and Sir Henry Hoghton, which outnumbered the few hundred colliers and miners brought in by the corporation from neighboring villages. They paraded through the streets with colors flying and orange cockades in their hats (still the badge of Protestant factions in Ulster), fought several pitched battles, destroyed the meeting houses of the corporation's candidates, wrecked the Roman Catholic chapel and seventy private houses, burned down the mayor's house and held the worshipful mayor himself under the pump until he was nearly drowned. Hundreds of people were injured and two more killed. "There wasn't a how winda in't town!" ("There wasn't a whole window in the town!") boasted a citizen. Finally, the opposing mobs, completely out of control, degenerated into armed gangs, breaking into houses and robbing the inhabitants without discrimination. An indignant corporation supporter wrote to the *Gentleman's Magazine* (February 1768): "I have just escaped with many friends. The country is now up in arms, and the town is abandoned by our men. The cry is 'Leave not a single freeman alive!' God knows where this will end. I think tonight or tomorrow will be fatal to many. This is shocking work in a civilized country."

When the poll finally opened on 21 March, Burgoyne was the only candidate who had not fled the town, for to have followed the others, he said, "would have cast an indelible imputation upon my character." Lord Strange, who conducted operations from his fortified and guarded house, had been bringing people in from all around and lodging them in rooms and stables so that they could be classed as "inhabitants" and be eligible to vote on the day. Burgoyne went to the polls with a pistol in each hand and a guard of his dragoons, who had come up from Wimbledon—though it was said their purpose was not to protect him but to prevent the opposition's supporters from getting to the polls. The mayor predictably threw out most of the Whig votes as illegal, but accepted all the Tory ones, illegal or not, and then declared Sir Peter Leicester and Sir Frank Standish winners by 565 votes to 489. Lord Strange had kept a separate poll of the "inhabitants" and so was able to go to Parliament and demand an inquiry, claiming that *his* poll showed a Whig vote of 1,147. Parliament, which may or may not have been influenced by an administration looking for a chance to take the opposition down a peg, supported Lord Strange, reaffirmed that the franchise was "in all the inhabitants," and declared Burgoyne and Hoghton duly elected. Having delivered this slap in the face to the astounded mayor and corporation of Preston, they softened it by suggesting that the corporation prosecute Burgoyne for inciting riots. He was brought before Justice Yates at the King's Bench court in 1769. But the corporation's witnesses spoiled their case with absurd exaggerations. One even went so far as to say that Burgoyne, like some would-be Frederick the Great, had given orders to "level the Town." Burgoyne defended himself with a florid speech, in which "honour" and "reputation" were invoked every other sentence. The gist of it was that he had acted in self-defense, that every effort to cooperate with the mayor in restoring law and order had been blocked, and that he had done no worse than anyone else, he had merely been successful.

Despite this, he was fined £1,000 for the pistols, and a few of his mob leaders were fined and others jailed.

The Duke of Grafton, who was now acting as chief minister in place of Pitt (incapacitated by gout and fits of madness), promptly came to the rescue and obtained for Burgoyne the governorship of Fort William, Scotland. It was a prestigious post rarely given to anyone below the rank of major-general, and the effect of this appointment was to make Burgoyne even more unpopular than he was already. Many believed he should have joined John Wilkes in the King's Bench prison, and declared that the entire affair had been provoked by the administration to break Tory power in Lancashire. Among these was the celebrated "Junius," a satirist whose *Letters*, which once caused such a furor, are now forgotten, whose identity was never discovered, and whose name even is scarcely known today to anyone except students and readers of Byron's *Vision of Judgment*. "Junius" wrote that the governorship, worth £3,500, had been given to Burgoyne to sell, in order to pay the fine. He went on to sneer at Burgoyne as a soldier "not very conspicuous in his profession" beyond his activity at Preston and as a cardsharper and hustler. "No man is more tender of his reputation. If any man . . . were to accuse him of taking his hand at a gaming table, and watching with the soberest attention for a fair opportunity of engaging a drunken young nobleman at piquet, he would undoubtedly consider it an infamous aspersion upon his character, and resent it like a man of honour." Even Horace Walpole objected to this, saying that "Burgoyne was never supposed to do more than play very well."

The net result of all this was something nobody intended, for nobody concerned had the least interest in parliamentary or electoral reform: Colonel Burgoyne and Sir Henry Hoghton were the first MPs in England (or anywhere else, for that matter) to be elected by what was virtually a universal male suffrage, for every male freeholder and tenant was henceforth given a vote. No other constituency, not even Westminster, could boast of anything quite like this, or would be able to for more than a century. For sixty-four years Preston enjoyed "the most democratic franchise in the world," as the town historian proudly put it; indeed, when Parliament was reformed in 1832 along what were then thought to be modern lines, the vote in Preston was felt to be *too* democratic and was actually reduced.[8]

Burgoyne remained MP for Preston for the rest of his life. He built a large and handsome house, which local tradition says he designed himself, on a spot called Cooper's Hill near the village of Walton-le-Dale. Local tradition claims also that it was on this house that Benjamin Franklin installed the first lightning conductor in England. If this is true, then Franklin and Burgoyne must have been acquainted before the American Revolution, a fact not generally known. It is all the more to be lamented, therefore, that this interesting house was demolished a few years ago and replaced by a modern bungalow.

During the next six years, Burgoyne made seventy speeches in Parliament. His policy was that he would "assist Government in my general line of conduct; but that in great national points . . . I would ever hold myself at liberty to maintain my own opinion." The king, however, expected loyalty in exchange for such favors as the governorship of Fort William, rather more loyalty perhaps than a constitutional monarch had a right to expect, and when on a mere three occasions out of the seventy Burgoyne maintained his "own opinion," the king was shocked.

The most notable was during a small crisis that occurred in 1770, when a Spanish admiral high-handedly expelled the British garrison from the Falkland Islands in the South Atlantic. Distracted as it was by the grave problems in America and India, the last thing the administration wanted was a war with Spain; and when, after months of delay, the Spaniards offered a grudging apology and reparations so inadequate as to be insulting, it was content to accept them. Burgoyne was among those who thought that war, if only to remind the Spaniards whom they were dealing with, was preferable to such humiliation. In phrases remarkably similar to those used by hawkish generals in modern times, Burgoyne spoke up for national honor. "It has been the fashion to maintain . . . that military men were prejudiced judges in affairs of this nature. Sir, I disdain the idea, and denounce it in the name of my profession." A man who would wantonly promote bloodshed and war for his private advantage would be "a disgrace to his profession, to his country, and to human nature. But there are motives for which a soldier may wish for war; these are a sense of satisfaction due for an injury inflicted; a desire to make a return to our country for the honours and rewards we receive at her hands; a zeal to be the forward instrument to battle for the honour of the Crown, and the rights of the British people." When the king saw Burgoyne's name among the opposition in this debate, he thought it "so extraordinary that I almost imagine it was a mistake."

Next year Burgoyne redeemed himself by voting for the Marriage Bill. This was a measure by which the king hoped to prevent members of the royal family from marrying without his permission. To his astonishment it provoked angry opposition, on the ground that such a law would give him too much power. Who could say, it was asked, who was and who was not a member of the "royal family"? In a few generations, the royal prohibition to marry could extend over thousands of people. The Marriage Bill was passed nevertheless, and when Burgoyne voted for it the king wrote to Lord North (the new chief minister) that "had he failed to do so, I should have felt myself obliged to name a new governor for Fort William."[9]

In 1772 Burgoyne became entangled in the affairs of the East India Company. During the Seven Years' War this purely trading concern had expanded into the vacuum left by the French and, taking advantage of the disintegration of the Moghul Empire, made itself virtual ruler of Bengal, Bihar, and Chittagong. The guiding genius had, of course, been Clive. Clive, however, was a tough-minded imperialist with a streak of pirate in him, as well as a "Heaven-born General," and the following ten years were a period of misgovernment, extortion, and chaos, culminating in a famine that killed three million people—nearly a third of the total population of Bengal.

How much Clive was to blame is still a matter of controversy, but there is no doubt that some of the Company's officials and agents in India were ignorant, greedy, and vicious scoundrels, intent on amassing huge fortunes and indifferent to the fact that they were destroying a large and prosperous country in the process. By 1772 the East India Company was bankrupt, which meant that it could no longer find the £400,000 which it paid annually to the government in exchange for its monopolies. A loan was proposed to tide it over. Burgoyne opposed this, arguing that because "it is impossible to produce anything out of nothing" the Company, being bankrupt, would never repay its debt. The loan would simply disappear into the pockets of the directors. The new stockholders attracted by the loan would demand their twelve and a half percent like everyone else, without bringing in new trade, and this would impoverish the Company still further. The value of the stock would fall, which would provide a "noble harvest for the Bulls and Bears" and ruin those not let into the secret. Perhaps this was the intention behind the loan. Any minister concerned in such a scheme would deserve to be hanged, and Burgoyne was sure Lord North approved of it only because he was "unacquainted with the ways of 'Change Alley'." The proper solution was for the Company to cut down its own absurdly high rate of dividend, which, as a little schoolboy arithmetic could show, would solve all the Company's problems in a few years. But this, no doubt, was asking too much of the honorable directors.

In April 1772 Burgoyne moved for a select committee to inquire into the Company's affairs, which, he said, "through the rapacity of its servants abroad and the knavery of its directors at home" were "huddled together in one promiscuous tumult and confusion." The committee was formed, with himself as chairman, and during the next year, it interviewed hundreds of people and read thousands of papers in order to prepare its report.

It was said that Burgoyne undertook this (as it proved) thankless task at the instigation of the Duke of Grafton, whom he knew at the race track as well as in Parliament, and that he hoped for some promotion in return. It is true that Burgoyne was promoted to major-general shortly after his committee produced its report in May 1773, but the two events were not necessarily related and do not, even if they were, prove his insincerity. The sheer bulk and thoroughness of his report, published in a huge folio volume, shows that once he had embarked on his work he found himself carried away by it. He was acting independently, he claimed. Clive and others had gained huge fortunes by criminal or near criminal means; this money should either be made public or returned to those from whom it had been extorted. As a result, by 1773 Burgoyne was no longer a favorite with the administration; for after his committee began to uncover "crimes which it shocked human nature even to conceive," Lord North proposed that—there being secrets in the Company's books not fit to be made public—a secret committee should be formed to continue the investigation. When Burgoyne objected, Lord North replied contemptuously that it was not the government's purpose to snoop into petty larceny but to conduct "a great enquiry."

Burgoyne's committee continued, notwithstanding the new competition, and when it laid its report before Parliament, Burgoyne moved that the Company be brought under state control and that Clive be impeached for having illegally acquired monopolies and a private fortune of £234,000. Clive defended himself with tremendous force. He was astounded at the ingratitude of a nation to whom he had given an empire. He was more astounded at his own moderation, when he could have made himself the vastest fortune that anyone had made since the days of ancient Rome. One of Clive's supporters, Solicitor-General Wedderburn, then attacked Burgoyne. He remembered having read in a paper by "Junius" of an election carried by military force. Were there not grounds here for a prosecution against the honorable member, General Burgoyne? The reformer should reform himself. At the mention of "Junius" Burgoyne lost his temper. How he had longed to vent himself against these scandalous aspersions, he cried, "and if that wretch Junius is lurking here in any corner of this House, I tell him to his face he is an assassin, a liar and a coward!" He was too excited to notice Wedderburn's mistake. The solicitor-general, as the chief prosecutor of libels, had many times declared the writings of "Junius" to be libellous and subject to prosecution should the author be discovered. Now here was the solicitor-general hoping to prosecute Burgoyne on "evidence" from "Junius"! In the end Burgoyne lost the day. His resolutions condemning the Company's conduct were passed (for what that was worth), but those calling for the impeachment of Clive were defeated.

Burgoyne was bitterly resentful at the administration's failure to support him. It had put him in an exposed position and then basely deserted him. He had borne no malice against Clive, but had merely wished to prevent such abuses from recurring in future—a point he had to emphasize once again when Clive committed suicide in 1774. The truth was, of course, that when confronted by such a tiger as Clive the government lost its nerve and was afraid to act, while moderates began to see both sides of the question. Walpole's comment is as apt today as it was then: "The public are the victims, when great men dare, and when Government is timid, and good men tender!"

Clive is now a national hero, enshrined in children's history books beside Drake and Nelson, Wolfe and Florence Nightingale. This has been unfortunate for Burgoyne, who has often been dismissed in this affair as merely the shrillest of the cowardly and hypocritical *canaille* that destroyed one of England's greatest men. Yet it is to Burgoyne's credit that he was one of the first to speak out against the evils of Company rule in India and that many of his sensible proposals to bring the Company under state control were adopted by William Pitt the Younger in 1784.[10]

During all this, Burgoyne found time for a crowded social life. He belonged to the best clubs—Brooks, White's, Arthur's, Almack's—and as a leader of fashion he cultivated, like Beau Brummell after him, simplicity, elegance, and restraint in opposition to the flamboyance of the Macaronis (dandies). The *Town & Country Magazine* (February 1779) tells us that several styles of dress were named after him.[11] He was a frequent guest at the houses of Lord Chesterfield and Lord Ligonier, attended every race meeting, and became increasingly fond of the theater. Garrick, the two Sheridans, Henry Angelo, and J. C. Bach were among his wide circle of friends; indeed he seems to have known nearly everybody. He wrote occasional verses, including some for "The Dashing White Sergeant," which has since become a standard Scottish folk dance:

> If I had a beau
> For a soldier who'd go
> Do you think I'd say no?
> No, no, not I!
> . . .
> When my love was gone
> Do you think I'd take on
> Sitting moping forlorn?
> No, no, not I!
>
> If an army of Amazons e'er came in play
> As a Dashing White Sergeant
> I'd march away,
> March away would I![12]

Pavilion built by Robert Adam for Lord Stanley's wedding on 9 June 1774. Burgoyne was impresario of the festivities, during which his play *The Maid of the Oaks* was performed. Engraved by James Caldwell. (*From* The Works in Architecture of Robert and James Adam, *Vol. 3, No. 22; publ. London 1774-1822.*)

This rhyme was still being hawked on London streets in the 1820s, fifty years later: it is hard to think of any tribute a songwriter would desire more. Whether or not Burgoyne had a hand in inventing the famous dance is unknown, but as governor of Fort William he probably helped to popularize it.

In 1769 he moved into No. 10 Hertford Street, Mayfair, a pleasant terrace house that had formerly belonged to Lord Sandwich, where he lived for the rest of his life.[13] During his absences in the north, Lady Charlotte stayed at Kensington Palace in one of the "grace and favour" apartments reserved for important officials. Two letters from here, dated 1773, have survived. They show her character in a most amiable light. Their daughter, Charlotte Elizabeth, had died in 1764, and she was now alone. She had recently been so ill that servants had had to help her walk, and she now rather enjoyed her peaceful seclusion ("I have not seen a card at my House for two months or more"). Lady Powis and Lady Hertford, who had "scarcely been one night all summer without a party," came to play loo. Miss P. had lost £500 at cards one night, £1,500 the next, and paid it all the following morning. "Now she borrows from her sister Mary, having lost everything of her own except *Terra Firma*." In the afternoons Lady Charlotte sat in the shady part of the garden farthest from the road, although a highwayman was believed to be lurking in the bushes, waiting for nightfall. He had lately robbed Mrs. L., and so terrified her that she had dared not go out after dark since.

Lady Charlotte's correspondent was the Duchess of Argyll, who was determined to marry off her daughter Lady Betty, to Edward, Lord Stanley (Lord Strange's son and Lady Charlotte's nephew). Ambitious plans were made for the wedding. Robert Adam, who had probably been introduced through Burgoyne and had recently designed Lord Stanley's grand new house in Grosvenor Square, was commissioned to build a fantastic Corinthian pavilion in the garden of "The Oaks," with a semicircular ballroom 180 feet long, flanked by two banqueting halls. "The Oaks" itself was hastily embellished with turrets, towers, and more battlements (the demolitions contractor who knocked it down in 1957 said it was the worst built building he had ever known in twenty-five years' experience). Lord Stanley bought every orange tree in London for an "orangerie" planted at the back of the lawn, and groves of trees and shrubs were arranged to form a "natural amphitheatre." Burgoyne, as creator, impresario, and master of ceremonies, conceived the festivities as an idyllic *Fête Champêtre* modeled on the wistful visions of contemporary French artists. The date was fixed for 9 June 1774.

As the guests arrived they were welcomed by a fanfare of French horns (concealed behind bushes); they then passed through groves where dancers, dressed as swains and shepherdesses, reenacted rural pastimes—playing at ninepins, shooting arrows at a golden bird on a maypole, leaping and kicking at a beribboned *tambour de basque* that hung from a tree, and swinging joyously on swings. Punchinellos, Harlequins, and Pierrots cavorted and fell about on the grass. Music floated in the air, to the amazement of the guests (all masked and in fancy dress), from some place of concealment that no one could discover. Cupids distributed flowers to the ladies. A choir of nymphs, fauns, and sylvans sang an epithalamium to the bridal couple who, dressed as Lord and Queen of "The Oaks," were seated on thrones beneath a pediment inscribed "Sacred to Propitious Venus," while afterwards wood spirits and Druids recited a homily on the virtues of the oak tree. There were masked dances, minuets, and cotillions; but the pivotal event of the evening was a comedy, with songs, by Burgoyne himself. It was entitled *The Maid of the Oaks* and was well received—although when Garrick put it on at Drury Lane in November, some critics wrote that only the dances and the scenery (designed by the celebrated marine and battle painter De Loutherbourg) saved what would otherwise have been a dull evening. Supper was announced by the firing of a cannon, at which six tall curtains around the central chamber of the pavilion were lifted to reveal the tables spread with food, piping hot. After the meal, the curtains descended, accompanied by gasps of admiration from the company, to create the ballroom. Further entertainments included a choral concert and a corps de ballet, followed by a "Transparency" (windows lit by "Hymeneal Torches"). The celebrations ended with country dancing, illuminated by fireworks and pyramids of lights. When, in the cool air of dawn, the guests took their leave with curtsies and sweeping bows, and moved toward the lines of waiting coaches, nobody could say enough in praise of the "genius" of General Burgoyne.[14]

Few professional soldiers today would concede that a man with the talents to make a good writer and director of musical comedies could possibly make a good general, or, in fact, be fit for anything military beyond entertaining the troops. The attitudes of our forefathers toward the arts were different from ours. In 1777, three years after Lord Stanley's great wedding party, few saw anything remarkable in the fact that General Burgoyne, who had shown such skill and taste, and such a sensitive eye for detail, in bringing the dainty, flirtatious pictures of Lancret and Fragonard to life (indeed, with his powdered coiffure, graceful deportment, and melancholy, fastidious expression, he could almost have stepped out of one of them), should be leading a professional army, complete with the most powerful train of artillery ever sent abroad from England, and a horde of Iroquois through the primeval, mosquito-infested forests and swamps of North America.

CHAPTER VI

SONS OF LIBERTY

IN 1774 the thirteen British colonies in America[1] contained about three million inhabitants, of whom six hundred thousand were Negro slaves. Until the Seven Years' War (known in America as the French and Indian War), the colonies had been hemmed in by French possessions: Canada on the north, Florida on the south, and on the west by settlements and forts along the Mississippi and Ohio Rivers. Because of the continual warfare between Britain and France, the colonists were forbidden to trade with any country except Britain. Nobody minded much, for although certain commodities cost more than they would have if purchased elsewhere and although the colonists looked on this difference in cost as a tax upon them, it was "for the good of the Empire."[2] Besides, what could not be traded could be smuggled. Hence smuggling became a way of life among seafaring folk in Charleston, Boston, New York, and Nantucket. In addition, and rather more irksome, there were restrictions on manufacture: Heavy industries such as steel smelting, for instance, were prohibited.

When the Seven Years' War ended in 1763, everything changed. France lost her possessions in North America, and although Spain kept her territories beyond the Mississippi they were too far away to constitute a threat. The Americans now saw a wonderful future opening before them, if only they could be left alone to exploit the opportunities. For this they wanted three things above all: freedom to trade with whom they wished, freedom to expand westwards into Indian country, and freedom to run their internal affairs without interference by administrators sent from England.

The Administration in London had its own problems, the chief of which was an appalling national debt of £146 million. Unless public expenditure was reduced and revenue increased, Great Britain would decline into poverty and unimportance, as Genoa and other wealthy states had done before. The heaviest drain came from imperial defense, for everyone knew that France was rearming for a war of revenge, that the reconquest of her American possessions was one of her aims, and that her fleet, when combined with that of Spain, would soon outnumber the Royal Navy by a dangerous margin. Pitt's leadership had won a vast empire in a few short years; his hypnotic oratory had persuaded a new generation of officers and politicians to see themselves as latter-day Romans, but with one significant difference: In the process of conquest and rule they would bring enlightenment and the Gospel to the natives of less happy lands. Only a few old-fashioned Whigs, such as the Duke of Newcastle (who, like his mentor Robert Walpole, believed that business, trade, and "fixing" brought greater happiness in the long run than empire), viewed the entire enterprise with deep suspicion. To the empire-minded, there were sound strategic reasons for keeping a token force of regular troops in America.

Proof of this came shortly after the war, when Pontiac organized some Indian tribes into a holy war against white men and caused havoc and terror along the western frontiers. The British regular army had had to defeat him almost single-handed, for the response of the provincial assemblies in sending militia had been disgraceful. Only Virginia sent a worthwhile force and even then refused to pay for it. The reason was that during the war there had been great difficulties in paying the American troops who fought the French. Paper currency had been printed, but it had quickly depreciated in value and become worthless. Although the government was endeavoring to liquidate all war debts, it had as yet hardly begun to do so (they were not finally cleared until 1769). Therefore the Americans were reluctant to call up troops for a new war when they had not yet been paid for the previous one. Moreover, the inhabitants of the ports and coastal areas, who had seen no Indian warriors for fifty years, were not interested in wars on the western frontiers, and militia were always unwilling to travel far from their homes. The American view was that they would deal with the Indians one day. Meanwhile, if the British army wanted to fight them, let them get on with it. As for the danger from France, the Americans regarded this as a piece of British cant, for they were sure that no European power could ever conquer America again.

The British thought differently. They had a low opinion of American soldiers and militia. General Forbes described the Virginia and Pennsylvania officers who served under him as "a bad Collection of broken Innkeepers, Horse Jockeys and Indian Traders," whereas Wolfe called Americans "in general the dirtiest, most contemptible cowardly dogs you can conceive. There is no depending on them in action. They fall down dead in their own dirt and desert by battalions, officers and all." As for the famous Rogers' Rangers, admirers of

Spencer Tracy might be shocked to hear that Wolfe called them "the worst soldiers in the universe."[3] The British saw the Indian problem in relation to their concept of the Empire as a whole, and when, after Pontiac's defeat, they fixed a boundary line between Indian and white territory, they also established an Indian Service to ensure that the boundary was respected and the rights of both sides upheld. Under the direction of the two Superintendents of Indian Affairs appointed during the war (John Stuart for the southern colonies and the great Sir William Johnson for the northern), it was hoped to train an efficient corps of men who were not only familiar with Indian languages and ways (and might even take Indian wives, as Sir William had done), but were well educated—for one of the main troubles in Indian affairs was that the frontiersmen who knew the Indians best were ignorant and illiterate men incapable of learning even their own language properly, let alone of mastering the complexities of the most important of Indian arts, oratory. Such a service would have to be paid for, as would the army without which it could not function at all.

The premier, George Grenville, made various suggestions to American representatives in London as to how money might best be raised, but there seemed no method equitable to all thirteen colonies, each with its different kinds of population, trades, and industry. Voluntary contributions were unreliable, for some, perhaps most, colonies would refuse to contribute, as Maryland had refused to contribute a penny to the war against France. Eventually, a bill was proposed for raising money by means of stamps to be affixed to all legal documents, advertisements, dice, and playing cards. This would contribute rather less than a third of the £3 million per annum needed for the army and Indian Service (the bulk being met by the West Indies and the British taxpayers) and would impose a burden on the Americans of about 4s per head per year. It seemed a mild enough measure, and after Grenville had inquired in Parliament if there was any legal objection to raising revenue in this way and had been assured there was none, the Stamp Act was passed in 1765.

Meanwhile, measures had been taken to clamp down on smuggling. There seemed no reason why France and Spain, Britain's former and doubtless future enemies, should be allowed to wage economic warfare by dumping goods in America at prices so low that British manufacturers could not compete with them. Some armed frigates were therefore sent to patrol the coasts.

It was unfortunate that Grenville did not understand the realities of life across the Atlantic. He did not foresee that the Stamp Act, on account of the regulations—to say nothing of the agents—that would have to be brought in to ensure that it was carried out with a minimum of corruption, would be regarded by the colonists not as an unexceptionable measure, but as an unwarranted piece of bureaucratic interference that would throw the entire happily functioning legal system of America into confusion, and so cost everyone a great deal more, in time, trouble, and expense, than a mere 4s per head per year. Nor did he seem to know that many substantial and respected citizens of America drew a considerable part of their wealth from smuggling, for without smuggling they could not have obtained such wealth under the restrictions on trade that then existed. If these people, who were important employers as well as leaders of public opinion, should protest against this direct threat to their livelihoods, their voices would carry far and wide.

And so it turned out indeed. When the Stamp Act was announced in America, the reaction was furious. There were ugly riots in Massachusetts, New York, Rhode Island, and Connecticut. Bands of toughs calling themselves "Sons of Liberty" or "Liberty Boys" appeared in the streets, bullied stamp agents into resigning their posts, and wrecked the houses of legal and customs officers, including that of the chief justice, Thomas Hutchinson, although he personally disapproved of the Act.

The news of all this could not have reached London at a more inopportune moment. Owing to a personal antipathy between the premier and the king, Grenville's ministry had fallen, to be replaced by Rockingham's. The country was suffering a recession, and the national debt was greater than ever. The unexpected and, in the opinion of many Englishmen, illogical uproar over the Stamp Act confronted the new ministry with a serious dilemma. On the one hand, British manufacturers had millions of pounds sunk in American trade. The riots in America had brought that trade to a standstill and had within months already thrown a hundred thousand people in England out of work. If the Stamp Act could not be enforced—and every report from America indicated that it could not without sending a strong army—then it would have to be repealed. The loss of revenue expected from the stamps would be inconvenient, but the loss from the continued closure of American trade would be disastrous. However, on the other hand, the Americans were now not only demanding the repeal of the Act, but claiming that Parliament had no right to tax them, or even legislate for them, unless Americans were represented in Parliament. And as no one had made any suggestions as to how the colonies could be represented in a parliament three thousand miles distant and on the other side of a great ocean, this was tantamount to saying that Parliament should have no authority in America at all. If that was what the Americans really wanted, then repealing the Stamp Act would simply encourage them to find another grievance and agitate against that, continuing until they ceased to be a part of the British Empire. After a series of impassioned debates, the Rockingham ministry contented itself with a compromise. It repealed the Stamp Act but passed the Declaratory Act, which declared that Parliament was still the supreme authority in the Empire. This Act, which seemed so reasonable but meant so little, had the unfortunate effect of giving Parliament a principle she could not abandon without a complete loss of dignity and the American propagandists yet another, and very clear, target to aim at.

During the next few years Parliament was distracted by repeated changes of ministry. Rockingham's was replaced by Chatham's; but Chatham became ill and the Duke of Grafton officiated until his ministry was replaced by Lord North's in 1770. As those, including Burgoyne, who had opposed the repeal of the Stamp Act had predicted, American affairs did not improve but went from bad to worse. Part of the blame was put onto Lord Townshend (the same who had been Secretary-at-War when Burgoyne was in Portugal). Almost by stealth, he tried to revive the raising of revenue in America by putting duties on glass, paint, paper, and tea. The result was more riots and a proliferation of "patriotic" groups, "radical" clubs, and cells of resistance everywhere. At the same time, the customs controllers ran into more trouble, some of their frigates being seized and burned by smugglers. The culprits were never caught, for the populace hid them. The American complaint was that in Vice-Admiralty courts, which dealt with smuggling cases, there was no trial by jury and that the courts abused this advantage by making summary and unjust convictions. When it was proposed to remove those accused of smuggling to England for trial in order to obtain fairer verdicts, the Americans became angrier than ever. This, they said, was plain tyranny.

A number of leading Bostonians, worried by the increasing difficulties of trading with Britain, asked Hutchinson (who was acting as governor of Massachusetts and was officially appointed in 1771) for troops to protect their houses and stores from rioters, and General Gage, the commander-in-chief, brought some contingents back from the western forts. This was regarded as an outrage by the radicals, who stirred up mobs to jeer and throw stones at the soldiers. On one occasion, four rioters were killed when a platoon opened fire without orders; and although the soldiers were court-martialed (the American John Adams defended them) the incident was blown up into a "Massacre," with pilgrimages of mourning made to the spot each year.

The Townshend duties were hastily repealed as soon as Townshend died, except for the duty on tea of 3d a pound. Because tea was even more popular in America than in England, smugglers had cornered most of the trade. It was rumored that one trader alone, John Hancock of Boston, had half a million dollars' worth of tea hidden in warehouses about the port. It happened that the bankrupt East India Company had seventeen million pounds of tea lying unsold in its own warehouses, which it now proposed to sell in America at a price lower even than smuggled tea, thus ruining smugglers and reviving East India trade at one stroke. Any loss would be made up by the British taxpayers. The Boston merchants, egged on by the leading smugglers,[4] naturally objected, and Samuel Adams, a vociferous radical who seemed to be determined to aggravate every situation, formed Committees of Correspondence through which all the provinces could unite in resistance. To frighten the other provinces into action, Adams publicized some letters (mysteriously obtained by Benjamin Franklin, who was accused of stealing them) between Hutchinson and other officials in Boston and London. In one passage Hutchinson had written that if the "friends of anarchy" (i.e., Adams and his friends) persisted in inciting the people to violence and lawlessness "there must be an abridgement of what are called English liberties." This was taken as proof of a conspiracy by evil men to seize power and introduce arbitrary rule in the province, and, although Hutchinson protested that the letters contained nothing he had not said in public, the Massachusetts assembly petitioned the king for his dismissal. By this means Adams succeeded in widening the gulf of suspicion and misunderstanding between Britain and America, greatly lessening the chances of reconciliation and alarming the colonies. When the first tea ships arrived in Boston, Charleston, and New York, the "Sons of Liberty" boarded them and threw their cargoes into the sea. The duty on tea was a tax, they said, and Americans would not pay taxes.

The government decided to retaliate. Hutchinson, his life's work in ruins, his house destroyed, and his collection of manuscripts relating to the history of the province burned by the mob, was recalled, and General Gage, who happened to be in England, was sent out to replace him, together with a reinforcement of two thousand men. The port of Boston was closed and a number of laws passed which Parliament called "coercive" and the Americans called "intolerable." The closing of Boston was a failure, for the other provinces sent convoys of supplies to the city. Gage was unable to exercise his authority beyond the immediate neighborhood of Boston, while the governors of the other provinces found themselves practically shut up inside their residences. During the summer of 1774, the Americans formed a Continental Congress in Philadelphia, which tried to govern the provinces in lieu of the British. Incidents of terrorism became more common and more unpleasant. Unpopular officials were "rode on rails" (carried on poles whose edges were sharpened) or tarred and feathered—a cruel torture as the tar could be removed only by pulling the skin off with it. Next came the turn of "Tories"—anyone suspected of sympathizing with the British or of deploring the state of affairs. Their shops and homes were looted, their farms burned, their livestock driven off, their families harassed and stoned. Anglican clergymen who would not renounce their oath of loyalty to the king and constitution had their churches wrecked and boarded up. Some were put into common animal pounds, where the mob pelted them with red herrings in mockery of their supposed love for British soldiers. Soon quite unimportant people, such as nightwatchmen and shopkeepers' wives, were being led from town to town, covered with tar and feathers and with nooses round their necks, displaying on their backs such notices as "Tory Traitor" and "Enemy of the People." Congress disavowed such behavior and sent messages to the king assuring him of their loyalty but did nothing to stop it and condoned the persecution of anyone who put that loyalty into practice. In fact, they had no more power to prevent such excesses than had General Gage; for America, and Massachusetts especially, was drifting into anarchy.

Each side accused the other of conspiracy, both with little justification. Anglican clergy were accused of conspiring to establish a bishopric in America in order to strengthen British plans to introduce arbitrary power—although the British had no plans to introduce arbitrary power. The recent Quebec Act guaranteed, among other things, the continuance of the Catholic Church in its old privileges within the Canadian border. This was a necessary measure intended to give the strongly Catholic French Canadians, who were still resentful of British conquest, the kind of government they wanted and was considered necessary if peace and stability were to be achieved in Canada. In New England it was announced as a conspiracy between the king and the Vatican to bring papist tyranny back to North America, and there were demonstrations in which King George III, the pope, and Bonnie Prince Charlie (an improbable trio of allies) were burned in effigy. Everything the British did or proposed to do, good or bad, wise or foolish, was denounced as part of a plan to destroy the colonies and enslave the people. Adams and his friends spread wild stories that the British intended to suppress religious freedom, tax the lands, and order their troops wantonly to massacre the inhabitants.[5]

The British suspected that behind all the troubles was an evil conspiracy between smugglers and unqualified lawyers. The reasoning was thus. The Stamp Act had stipulated that, to prevent abuses, the stamps should be handled only by qualified lawyers. However, there were many unqualified lawyers in America, as there were in England, and these saw their livelihoods in danger. At the same time smugglers, who included, it was now realized, some of the most important traders in the colonies, resented the new customs controls and seized on the Stamp Act as an excuse to incite their hired mobs to wreck the houses of customs officials. Common interest in creating as much disorder as possible had brought these two unsavory groups into alliance. Such a challenge to authority attracted every kind of crackpot extremist and homespun "political philosopher," together with a parcel of bigoted, hysterical Dissenters—Muggletonians, Ranters, and such—who hated the Church of England and the throne. Since then, this gang of disreputable agitators, some acting out of ignorant fanaticism and others from personal motives of greed, had set up the cry of "Liberty" (stolen from Wilkes), provoked all the rioting and contempt for law and order, and deliberately blocked every attempt at reconciliation because they knew that the claim of Americans to be exempt from taxation had no legal basis whatever and that in force lay their only chance of success and their only safety from well-deserved punishment.

Such an explanation sounded plausible, but it took no account of the fact that not every American "patriot" was a scoundrel in search of a last refuge and that Tories were not the only Americans who were law-abiding by inclination. Many Congressmen deplored Samuel Adams and his rabble-rousing, the "Sons of Liberty," and the terrorism that forced everyone into conformity, yet they were determined to secure what they felt to be justice. Even that archvillain Hancock had refused to profit one penny by the destruction of the East India tea. On the contrary, everyone renounced tea, and from that day it ceased to be the national drink of America. In truth, the aristocratic rulers in Britain had no means of understanding America or what was happening. There were plenty of officers who had fought in America and knew American geography, but no one had any real knowledge of American society, for such knowledge could only be gained by working and living as an American. America was like nowhere else on earth, and there was nothing in Europe with which to compare it. Burgoyne once referred to Americans as "peasants," but peasants in any European sense they were not—not even the Negro slaves. There were no great estates with traditions binding lord and fief that went back to the Dark Ages; no powerful priesthood, not even an established church; no castles and cathedrals with ancient villages nestling around them. Such aristocrats as there were were self-made men or the sons of self-made men. If many American men were illiterate, American women were not. They did the reading, wrote the letters in a neat hand with correct grammar, and kept the accounts. And they knew how to manage their men better than any women in the world.

Compounding this ignorance was the attitude of the great law officers, the legal establishment of the day. Throughout the century they opposed every mitigation of the law, every reform or slightest adjustment, except toward severity, on the grounds that it would subvert the law and so bring about the collapse of civilization. The most notorious result of this was the ever increasing barbarity of the penal code.

Thus, when the Americans first broached the question of taxation and parliamentary representation, Chief Justice Lord Mansfield replied that this was a direct assault on the British Constitution, amounting to treason and rebellion; and although Burke poured eloquent scorn on this ridiculous posture, Mansfield and his colleagues stuck to it through thick and thin. By 1775 rebellion had become a fact, and Britain and America were both faced with civil war. From Boston, Gage reported that a direct clash between his garrison of five thousand men and fifteen thousand militia had only narrowly been avoided and that serious fighting could break out at any moment. If he was to maintain his position, let alone restore a modicum of law and order in America, he would need at least twenty thousand men.

There was no hope of mustering such a force within a year, and it was decided to send him three major-generals instead. There had been some difficulty in finding them, for many officers were making excuses to avoid service in America. A few felt sympathy for the Americans or had family in the colonies. The rest saw disaster ahead and did not wish to be involved. Some went so far as to resign their commissions, taking their lead from Lord Lyttleton. Lord Amherst and General Harvey, the two senior officers in the army, had both declared the notion of subduing America by force to be insane, and only their rank and prestige allowed them to remain as advisers to the king. General William Howe had made sympathetic noises on behalf of the Americans at a recent election, declaring that he would never fight against the Bostonians, who had put up a memorial to his brother, Lord Howe (killed at Ticonderoga); but under pressure he changed his mind and agreed to go. General Clinton had watched with dismay while Britain and America maneuvered into positions from which they could not retreat. There had been no need for this war, he felt, but now that it was inevitable, he could only do his duty as an officer and try to ensure, insofar as it was in his power, that the British won it as quickly and as painlessly as possible.[6]

Burgoyne was the third to be appointed. Since he had spoken so eloquently against the "narrow and rotten" system of British rule in India and was now on bad terms with Lord North as a result of that affair, it might be thought that he would naturally have taken the part of the Americans. Perhaps, as was charged against him by Horace Walpole, self-interest had something to do with his attitude, for obviously he longed for military appointment. In justice to him, however, the problems were very different. In Bengal the oppression had been real, owing to too little government control. He had never suggested that the Empire should be broken up. In America the oppression was slight, whatever the radicals might say, and could be remedied by negotiation. Yet negotiation seemed the last thing the American leaders wanted, for they made ever increasing demands and offered no concessions in return. As a result Britain was faced with a stark choice: either to keep America or to lose it. Burgoyne had voted against the repeal of the Stamp Act and for the Declaratory Act eight years before. Since then, no money had been raised for the army or the Indian Service. During the debate on whether the tea duty should be repealed (19 April 1774), he had said: "We have like an indulgent parent already ruined America by our lenity and tenderness. I am sure that the tax is not the grievance but the power of laying it. That power I shall ever aver exists in the Parliament of Great Britain." The members, who had just listened to one of Burke's greatest speeches, began to yawn and chatter at this point, and Burgoyne ended by hoping that America would be convinced by persuasion and not by the sword.[7]

By the end of the year it was apparent that if the Empire was to be preserved, it was to be by the sword. The first inkling that Burgoyne was being considered for American service came at the end of January 1775, when Charles Jenkinson, an ambitious young Treasury official, approached him outside the House of Commons and remarked that certain important people wished Burgoyne was in America. Next, he was sent for by Lord Barrington (Secretary-at-War once again) and, in a very circuitous manner, sounded out concerning his views on the American problem. Burgoyne, taking the hint, said he was anxious about his wife, "the tenderest, the faithfullest, the most amiable companion and friend that ever man was blessed with—a wife in whom during four and twenty years I could never find an act of blame!" Her health was declining. Should he die or be killed abroad, the shock might kill her or at best leave her in poor financial circumstances. "To supply the requisites of her rank, to reward the virtues of her character, I could only bequeath her the legacy of my imprudences." He asked to be excused from American service if it could be managed. After a great deal of flattery, Barrington explained that Howe, Clinton, and Burgoyne himself had been selected by the king purely on account of their military merit. This was an order. "I professed to his lordship the honour I felt in being classed with such colleagues, and I requested him to assure His Majesty . . . of my ready obedience to his commands."[8]

The truth was that Burgoyne had hoped for something better. Swallowing his pride, he approached Lord North. After a long preamble, to which his lordship listened "with attention," Burgoyne made his proposal. New York, by its geographical position and the number of loyalists it contained, was the key to America, both militarily and as a point from which to reopen negotiations. Governor Tryon was in England and not likely to return for some time to come. Furthermore, Tryon had taken part in the dispute between New York and New

Hampshire over the boundary in the Green Mountains and so, by involving himself in the factions and jealousies that divided the province, had prejudiced many people against him, through no fault of his own. "Perhaps a military man, clothed in that character only, going in his station at the head of three or four regiments, might with equal talents or with less talents than Mr. Tryon possessed, find more facility in negotiation." Burgoyne hastened to add that whereas he had no intention of interfering in matters of military command with his colleagues, in his civil capacity as governor of New York he felt he might have some chances of success. Lord North agreed but was very cautious about committing himself.

The next weeks were frustrating for Burgoyne. He pulled strings everywhere, and everywhere he was received with encouragement but no promises. He saw his old friend General Elliott, whose son he had helped in Germany. He saw Lord George Germain who, he thought, "had more information upon the subject [America], more enlarged sentiments, and more spirit than any of the ministers." His next step was to approach Lord Dartmouth, Secretary of State for America and the Colonies, often called "the American Secretary" or "Third Secretary" for short. Dartmouth's position was very difficult. His department had been created in 1768 and he himself appointed only in 1772. He was not a member of the cabinet and so had no hand in forming policy but had to carry out the decisions of his superiors. He was an intelligent man and sympathized with many of the American aspirations, but he believed that the majority were being misled by a minority, who were raising a great uproar over very little. He was worried not only by headstrong Americans but by headstrong governors, such as Lord Dunmore in Virginia, who had recently waged an unauthorized punitive war against the Indians and forced concessions of land from them in violation of the treaties. This was further proof of the urgent need for a strong Indian Service to protect both sides; yet, through lack of funds caused by the troubles in the colonies, the Indian Service was still in a rudimentary state. Dartmouth was also a deeply religious man who supported the Methodists and spent much of his spare time working in charities.

The way to Dartmouth was through his deputy, John Pownall. This man was brother to Thomas Pownall, ex-governor of Massachusetts; he was a distant relation of Burgoyne's, a professional bureaucrat, and a hard-liner in his attitude toward the colonists. At the meeting, Pownall

> entered into a long, formal and sometimes unintelligible discussion of American affairs. He talked to me as I imagined he might be accustomed to do with men really inferior to him in information, or whom he sup-

> posed to be so. Gentlemen in trade and other situations in life, which set them at a distance from great men in office . . . believing men in power to be better informed because they ought to be so, are generally patient hearers, and hence a secretary is very apt to contract an air of supercilious or ministerial importance. He was guarded—mysterious—obscure—I acquired some light into his character, but none into American affairs.

Burgoyne then saw Lord Dartmouth, who was affable, polite, and clearly better informed and more able than his deputy but who seemed to be under his thumb.

Finally, Burgoyne managed to see a certain great lord (whom he does not name), who at last explained why he was making so little progress. It transpired that Howe had also applied for the post in New York, and the king had promised it to him. Howe had given as his reason for not wanting to go to Boston his friendship for the Bostonians; but his true reason, according to Burgoyne, was that he had neither liking for Gage as a man nor respect for him as a commander-in-chief. Howe had many friends who were now intriguing for him indefatigably, and he was supported by Lord Suffolk (Secretary of State, Northern Department) and Lord Dartmouth. Burgoyne was supported by Lord North and the majority of the cabinet. The king felt that Burgoyne would make the better negotiator but did not want to go back on his promise to Howe, which he had given in an unguarded moment.

Having achieved nothing by influence, Burgoyne tried the House of Commons, where he made two speeches. The first was a rather embarrassing affair, in which he complained that his inferior station would leave him nothing but "an attentive, an assiduous, circumscribed obedience." He replied to charges in the press that the three generals had been chosen for their bloodthirsty propensities, and he appealed to the House to restore its prestige. "We sit here the mere shadows of authority, the phantom of a parliament, assembling only to lament the substance we have lost, and to propose and subtilize questions of our own impotency. . . ." He ended with a typical piece of parliamentary, jingoistic rhetoric. "Let Great Britain revert to her primitive insignificancy in the map of the world, and the Congress of Philadelphia . . . dispense the blessings of empire. Let us spare the blood of our subjects, let us spare the treasures of the state; but let us at the same time confess, we are no more a people!"

A week later (27 February 1775) he made a spirited speech calculated to bring a flush of pride to the cheeks of the ministers. "Is there a man in England—I am sure there is not an officer or soldier in the King's service—who does not think the Parliamentary rights of Great

Britain a cause to fight for, to bleed for, to die for?" He went on to say that while there was "a charm in the very wanderings and dreams of liberty that disarms the anger of an Englishman," yet the constitution and the very existence of England now depended on bringing the Americans to submission. "The trial now only is whether we have spirit to support our conviction."[9]

700 Lord North said that this speech did more essential service to government than any speech of the year and invited Burgoyne and Howe to a cabinet dinner, at which American affairs were to be discussed, but where in fact "we talked of every subject but America." The only reference to the matter during the entire evening was a remark by Lord Dartmouth (who had been invited because of the proposed agenda), who hoped Burgoyne's speech would be printed and circulated in the colonies.

Burgoyne wanted above all to avoid going to Boston merely "to make up a triumvirate of reputation," inspect a brigade, and "see that the soldiers boiled their kettles properly"; but, despite their assurances to the contrary, this was just what the administration had in mind for him. His friend the great lord told him that further efforts to change his posting would be useless.

During his round of farewells, Burgoyne saw Germain once more, and the two commiserated with each other on the inefficiency and sloth reigning in all departments. It was amazing that in this unprecedented crisis, with the entire future of the Empire hanging by a thread, there was still no single director of policy, indeed no policy at all. Burgoyne met Hutchinson and complained that Howe, Clinton, and himself had been kept hopelessly in the dark, receiving no orders, instructions, or even advice as to what was expected of them when they got to Boston and that no doubt they would be sent off without any. How were they to act, for instance, if martial law were declared? Hutchinson, who suspected what the generals were in for, thought it would be more practical for him to worry about how to act if the Americans attacked in full force.

Perhaps his only consolations were that Howe's application for New York had likewise been turned down and that he himself had been granted leave by Lord North to return to England next winter in consideration of his wife's ill-health, "unless he should have a separate command or . . . be employed in any service beyond the common routine of military business."[10] Lord North, in fact, had made a joke at the expense of the three generals, which was now going the rounds: "I don't know what the Americans will think of them, but I know that they make me tremble."

On 18 April Burgoyne wrote a letter to the king from Portsmouth which began, "Sire, Whenever this letter shall be delivered to your

Majesty, the writer of it shall be no more." His purpose was to beg the king to provide for Lady Charlotte in the event of his own death. It is a terribly stilted piece, yet there is no doubt that his affection, even love, for his wife was genuine, despite his alleged infidelities. "I do not know that Lady Charlotte ever committed a fault, except that, if a fault it can be called, of love and generosity which directed her choice to me without consulting her family. . . ."

On 20 April the generals sailed for Boston aboard the *Cerberus*, under Captain Shad (who had landed Wolfe in Quebec and afterwards brought his body back to England). "Our three generals are sailed," wrote Walpole. "Our stake is deep . . . yet it is that kind of a war, in which even victory may ruin us."[11]

CHAPTER VII

"A PREPOSTEROUS PARADE OF MILITARY ARRANGEMENT"

WHEN the three major-generals landed in Boston on 25 May they found a situation grimmer than anything they had expected. The army, together with a thousand or so loyalist refugees from the mainland and all those citizens who had not been able to get away, had been besieged in the town for over a month by an army of country people. On first hearing this news, Burgoyne is said to have exclaimed, "What! Ten thousand peasants keep five thousand of the King's troops shut up? Let *us* in and we'll soon find elbow room."[1] The story is always quoted, for it was remembered after Saratoga; yet in an American satire written later that year, entitled *The Blockheads*, the remark is attributed to Howe.

The boast, if it was made, was an idle one. Boston stood on a peninsula joined to the mainland by the Neck, which the Americans had blocked by defense works. From the south side, Dorchester Heights overlooked Boston across a small bay; from the north, across an arm of water, the city was similarly threatened by the hills of Charlestown peninsula. Fortunately the Americans had made no move to occupy either of these high points; but if they did so, and mounted cannon on them, Boston would become untenable.

The incident that had created this dangerous state of affairs had occurred on 19 April. General Gage, hearing from a spy in Congress that the colonists had a store of munitions at Concord, eighteen miles away, had sent a detachment to destroy it. Shots had been fired at Lexington, and at Concord the first British soldiers had been killed. On the march back, the column had been attacked from all sides by thousands of farmers and militia and, but for the arrival of a relief column under Lord Percy, would have been forced to surrender. As it was, 273 soldiers had been killed or wounded, and there had been very sharp fighting at West Cambridge. Dr. Joseph Warren, president of the Massachusetts Congress and already well-known to the British from his furious speeches against them, described the sortie as an "invasion" and the fracas at Lexington as a "massacre" and told hair-raising stories of how British soldiers had murdered old people and orphans in their homes and driven women in childbed naked into the streets. Whether such stories were believed or not, they added rich fuel to the emotional fire that was spreading through the populace, and soon the entire country was up in arms demanding vengeance. An extraordinary army began to gather beside the banks of the Charles River. Units came from as far as Rhode Island, Connecticut, and New Hampshire. Intermixed with the militia, farmers, artisans, shopkeepers, and fishermen was a horde of unemployed laborers, transported felons* from England who had left their masters in the prevailing anarchy, escaped Negro slaves, wild men dressed in furs and moccasins from the forests of the interior, and even a contingent of fifty Mohican Indians from Stockbridge, who had come at the request of Congress and had already killed several British soldiers with their bows and arrows.[2] Camps were improvised from whatever could be found—pieces of weatherboard, logs, turf, and rubbish—and were without tents, kitchens, or even latrines. Congress appointed Artemus Ward commander-in-chief, but many leaders from other provinces refused to recognize his authority, and some, bored with the inaction or disgusted at the drunkenness, brawling, thieving, and sickness, took their men home again. British officers could hardly be blamed for shortsightedness in supposing that this shifting swarm, resembling more a fairground mob than a military force, would scatter before the bayonets of the best infantry in the world.

Yet Burgoyne was not reassured by the state of the best infantry in the world at that moment, for the soldiers were "still lost in a sort of stupefaction, which the events of 19 April had occasioned, and venting expressions of censure, anger, or despondency."[3] Perhaps the raid had been a mistake. Since the position of the British in America was

*The number of convicts and their descendants in America at this time is debatable. Thomas Jefferson said that they were very few, scarcely more than a thousand. When researching the life of Jonathan Wild, I found that during the first ten years in which convicts were transported to America (1718–1728), an average of from four to five hundred were sent to Maryland and the Carolinas from London alone. If this rate was maintained for the next forty years, which it probably was, we have a total of about twenty-five thousand from London alone, at least half of whom remained in America, brought up families and multiplied. This excluded those transported from Southampton, Bristol, and Liverpool.

very weak, the army had to maintain its prestige. On an isolated raid such as this, the moment would always come when the column would have to turn and march back. The Americans could then claim a victory by saying that the British had been forced to retreat without achieving their objective. To this fundamental mistake had been added careless planning. The column had run out of ammunition early in the fighting, and what should have been an orderly withdrawal became, at one point, a headlong flight.[4]

In the third week of May had come news that a party of "Green Mountain Boys" under Ethan Allen and Benedict Arnold had captured the fort at Ticonderoga, on the junction of Lakes George and Champlain in upper New York, complete with its garrison, store of powder (most of which turned out to be rotten), and two hundred pieces of artillery of all calibers. Artillery was the weapon the Americans lacked above all, and by this single stroke they had reestablished the balance more nearly in their favor. Nevertheless, they were still short of trained gunners, and so it would be several months before these pieces could be put to effective use. There was, moreover, a political side to the affair which gave the British grounds for cautious optimism. New York and New Hampshire had been in dispute over their common boundaries for many years. Both claimed the territory which was then The Hampshire Grants and is now the state of Vermont. The "Green Mountain Boys" had been formed to resist by violence the New York officials sent to administer the area. After several frays, in which constables and magistrates were beaten and a courthouse burned down, Ethan Allen and his colleagues were declared outlaws in New York, with prices on their heads. With the capture of Ticonderoga, Allen's sins were forgiven in the general rejoicing, but the Continental Congress was as much embarrassed as pleased by the gift. To whom was it to belong? There seemed no way of resolving this problem that did not arouse the anger of New York or of the New England provinces. Ethan Allen was known to be scheming to set up The Hampshire Grants as an independent state or colony and might even ally himself with the British if it would help his cause. Sooner or later the quarrel would break out again, and here surely was a situation from which the British, with careful diplomacy, could derive some advantage.

The government had decided after all to send Gage 3,500 reinforcements, and when they arrived in early June they brought up his strength to nearly 5,700 men. With this force the three major-generals believed it should be possible to find a little of that much-desired "elbow-room." The difficulties, however, were formidable. As Burgoyne explained in his long letters to friends in London, the army possessed none of the requisites for moving any useful distance. There were few wagons, less horses to draw them or the artillery, and no proper boats for landing troops. Incredibly, Gage had not ordered a single reconnaissance since the day of Concord. Worst of all, there was no money. The War Office hd promised to send £50,000 for officers' pay, plus £500 equipage money for each of the generals (there were now five, including Gage and Percy). Only £10,000 had been sent, leaving £40,500 unaccounted for. "Where does this money lie, and who receives the interest?" asked Burgoyne tartly.[5] He was certain that some deputy-secretary in Whitehall had taken it down to 'Change Alley and invested it for his own profit. Yet even supposing the army fully equipped and ready to move, the prospects were daunting. "Look, my Lord, upon the country near Boston—it is all fortification," wrote Burgoyne to the Earl of Rochford. "Driven from one hill, you will see the enemy continually retrenched upon the next; and every step we move must be the slow step of a siege. Could we at last penetrate ten miles, perhaps we should not obtain a single sheep or an ounce of flour by our laborious progress, for they remove every article of provisions as they go." Howe likewise described the country for thirty miles around as "amazingly well situated" for the American manner of fighting from behind trees and fences, "being Covered with woods & small stone wall Inclosures, Exceedingly uneven & much Cutt with Ravins."[6] Nevertheless, something had to be done to make Boston secure before the Americans brought down the guns from Ticonderoga. It was proposed to advance out of the Neck, take Dorchester Heights, and then move around via Cambridge and take the Charlestown peninsula from the land side. In Burgoyne's view, "the Operation must have been very easy," and the date was fixed for 18 June.

The Americans, who knew everything that was going on inside Boston while the British knew nothing of what was going on outside it, soon got wind of the plan. Accordingly they occupied Charlestown peninsula, which had been deserted since 19 April, on the night of the 16th and dug an earth redoubt on Breed's Hill with amazing silence and speed. The British efforts to dislodge them next day resulted in a gruesome waste of lives. The British, led by Howe, lost nearly half their force and the peninsula was cleared only after two, and some say three, attacks. Burgoyne was not a participant but a spectator, for he was ordered to command the battery on Copps Hill, and it was he who, on orders from Howe, set fire to Charlestown by bombarding it with incendiary shells. He wrote a description of the next moments to Lord Stanley:

> And now ensued one of the greatest scenes of war that can be conceived. If we look to the height, Howe's corps ascending the hill in the face of the entrenchments. . . . To the left, the enemy pouring in fresh troops by

> thousands over the land, and in the arm of the sea our ships and floating batteries cannonading them. Straight before us, a large and noble town in one great blaze. The church steeples, being of timber, were great pyramids of fire above the rest. Behind us, the church steeples and heights of our own camp, covered with spectators. . . . The enemy all in anxious suspense. The roar of cannon, mortars, and musketry, the crash of churches, ships upon the stocks, and whole streets falling together in ruins to fill the ear; the storm of the redoubts, with the objects above described, to fill the eye; and the reflection that perhaps a defeat was a final loss to the British Empire in America, to fill the mind, made the whole a picture, and a complication of horror and importance, beyond anything it ever came to my lot to be a witness to.[7]

The miscalled Battle of Bunker Hill was in every sense a Pyrrhic victory. All the British gained was a defensive position they should never have lost in the first place; this, in exchange for over a thousand men and a tremendous boost to the morale of the Americans, who had proved to the world, and above all to themselves, that untrained country folk could stand and fight the awe-inspiring regulars. The most serious loss to the Americans was Joseph Warren, who, having once declared that he wished to die up to his knees in blood, had gone as a volunteer. He had been killed in the last moments of the fighting. An English officer said that he had been wounded in the head and had pleaded for his life, and that a soldier, cursing him for having done more mischief than anybody else, had run him through with a bayonet. Warren was hated for the wild accusations he had made against the army, and the story gave satisfaction to the soldiers, but it was probably not true.[8]

Burgoyne thought the tales of American courage exaggerated.

> Nothing happened there, or in any of the little affairs since, that raises them in my opinion one jot above the level of all men expert in the use of firearms; Corsicans, Miquelots, Croats, Tartars, Mountaineers and Borderers, in almost all countries, have in their turns done much more hardy things than defend one of the strongest posts that nature and art combined could make, and then run away. In short, it is as preposterous to recur to Sparta and Athens for comparisons to their courage as it is to suppose their spring of action in this revolt analogous to the spirit of Liberty that guided those states.[9]

After the battle he talked with some American prisoners and found them to be "men of good understandings, but of much prejudice, and still more credulity." He therefore recommended to Gage that they all be released without terms, in the hope that "such an act of mercy may make an impression. . . . [S]hould it fail, it will at least . . . justify acts of a different nature hereafter. . . ."[10] At the same time, he thought that the British officers, whose courage throughout had been "exemplary," had been "ill seconded by the private men. Discipline, not to say courage, was wanting." Some of the officers indeed had been accidentally wounded by their own men. It is possible that, like other watchers from a distance, he was under a misapprehension. The red lines of infantry had certainly wavered during the advances; but this had not been caused by panic but by the fact that the long grass, which had not been cut that year, concealed numerous low walls. As the infantry stumbled against them, naturally the lines broke order. The story that the officers had to prod the men forward with bayonets in the last attack would seem to have been a later American invention.

For the most part, Burgoyne had nothing to do in Boston but hover about pretending to be useful and write letters for Gage. Almost as soon as Burgoyne had landed, Gage, who had been ordered by the king to issue a proclamation offering pardon to any American who laid down his arms and went home, delegated the unwelcome task to Burgoyne. The result, which was worse than useless in that its style made the Americans laugh while its content made them angry, was one of Burgoyne's most inflated productions. It was full of phrases like "a preposterous parade of military arrangement" (the American army)—though his own piece could just as well have been called a preposterous parade of literary arrangement.[11] He became involved in a futile correspondence with his old friend Charles Lee, who, after exciting adventures in Poland as a soldier of fortune and a few years in London high society (Joshua Reynolds, the painter, being his closest friend), was now a major-general in the American army. Lee tried to embarrass Burgoyne by reminding him of Lord North's treacherous behavior over the East India affair and went on to denounce kings and courts, and the English king and court in particular, as inveterate enemies to liberty. Burgoyne, seeing the letter published in the press, felt bound to answer and defended the British Constitution as the best safeguard of liberty yet devised in the history of mankind. Lee had charged that the money raised from taxes would only go to swell the coffers of private corruption. Burgoyne countercharged that the American leaders had been determined all along on independence. If they had taken up arms merely to resist taxes, why then, "the quarrel is at an end." He proposed a meeting.

This got Burgoyne into trouble, for he had no right to make statements of policy without authority, especially if the Americans might think he did have authority. He therefore wrote to Lord North to defend himself by saying that since, in his opinion, every American leader could be bought if the price was right, he had hoped to buy Lee over to the British. He would say that the Americans were bound to lose in the end. As Lee was technically a deserter from the British army and liable to be hanged if caught, his only guarantee of safety would be to act as a secret peacemaker. A money bribe might also be offered. Congress suspected some such trick—for Burgoyne was "as cunning and subtle as the Devil himself"—and dissuaded Lee from accepting. Shortly before Burgoyne left Boston in November, Lee wrote once more to say that Burgoyne should seize this golden opportunity of making himself the "saviour" of his country and bring about a peace settlement. The idea of independence had "never entered a single American's head until the most intolerable oppression had forced it upon them." Perhaps Burgoyne alone could prevent the fatal separation, and then one day Great Britain would be "as indebted to General Burgoyne as Rome had been to her Camillus."[12]

The truth was that Burgoyne did regard himself as a potential savior of his country and was repeatedly making efforts to get himself appointed as a negotiator. He had already written to Lord North suggesting that he be given a roving commission to visit New York, or any other place not yet up in arms, to sound out the opinions of the Americans. The proposal was not a foolish one, for Burgoyne was the only officer to whom the notion had occurred that it might be useful to hear what ordinary Americans had to say. He would have made as good a negotiator as anyone available. He was shrewd when dealing with people personally, could be very persuasive, and, as the diplomatist Wraxhall observed, "no man possessed more polished manners." Lord North, however, declined his offer on the grounds that he would make too valuable a hostage should the Americans decide to hold him prisoner.[13]

Besides taking on a dispute with Washington, in which each accused the other of ill-treating prisoners, Burgoyne wrote a comedy for the officers to amuse themselves with during the lengthening autumn evenings. "General Burgoyne is our Garrick," wrote Lord Rawdon to his father from the miserable camp on Charlestown Neck.[14] The piece was called *The Blockade of Boston,* which the Americans promptly answered with a satire called *The Blockheads*. Burgoyne also wrote a verse prologue to *Zara* (a play by Aaron Hill taken from Voltaire) in which he gently reproved the New Englanders for despising "every liberal Art,/ That polish'd Life, or humaniz'd the Heart" and for objecting to women acting on the stage.[15] For the rest, he passed his time writing enormously long letters to influential friends in England, criticizing the way the war was being handled and suggesting alternative ways of handling it. Thus it was, that out of Burgoyne's hours of idleness was born the strategy that led to Saratoga.

It was clear to everyone that Boston was the worst possible place from which to open an offensive of any kind, let alone a war of reconquest. Standing as it did in the middle of a harbor, it could be defended only by holding all the surrounding coast; while the country inland was so easy to defend that it would be impossible for any but the largest army to penetrate into the province. Yet it was precisely this province which was the center of resistance and which had to be subdued if the rebellion was to be subdued.

The obvious answer was to move around and attack the province from the rear, using the long line of waterways extending from New York to Canada as a base from which to launch such an operation and to blockade the New England coast at the same time. This idea had first been put forward by Lord Dartmouth even before news of Lexington had reached England. The closure of the port of Boston had failed because the southern colonies had sent supplies. He therefore hoped that Gage would be able to detach some regiments to New York and set up a naval base there from which the fleet could patrol the Hudson, thus cutting the only roads from Pennsylvania to New England.[16] As the summer went by, further advantages of this scheme became apparent. Since the British had command of the sea, New York, being on an island, would be easy to capture and defend. Its situation midway along the Atlantic seaboard made it the ideal jumping-off-place for operations to the north or south, while the great Hudson could carry a fleet of deep-draught ships to within forty-one miles of Albany, the largest inland town in America. From the northern end of this line of waterways, which on the map seems almost to have been drawn with a ruler, reasonably large ships, such as sloops and frigates, could sail up the Richelieu River as far as Chambly, while others could be built and sailed on both Lake Champlain and Lake George. Thus any force operating along this line could be supplied almost directly from England by water. Indeed there were only four places that presented serious difficulty. The first was the Highlands above New York between Peekskill and West Point. Here the Americans could be expected to build forts to block the Hudson (as indeed they did). The next was the land bridge between Fort Edward, where the Hudson begins to bend westward, and Fort George, at the southern tip, or head, of Lake George. There was an alternative route northward along a road that led, via Fort Anne, to Skenesborough (the modern Whitehall) at the southern tip, or head, of Lake Champlain.* The third place of difficulty was the portage, or land bridge, between the northern tip of Lake George and Lake Champlain. The narrow and rapid stream joining the two lakes was guarded at its outlet by the great fort of Ticonderoga, now in American hands. The fourth place was a stretch of rapids on the

* It should be remembered that both lakes flow *northward* and are really tributaries of a slow-running river that becomes the Richelieu before it empties into the St. Lawrence. Thus the long, ribbony section of Lake Champlain between Skenesborough and Ticonderoga was sometimes called South River.

Richelieu River between St. Jean and Chambly. None of these obstacles should prove insurmountable to a strong army and fleet acting in cooperation, provided it had sufficient artillery and means of transport. Forts, or the remains of forts, existed all down the line and could be strengthened and increased in number.

There were also political considerations to take into account. Loyalists in Boston told Gage that many of the inhabitants of Albany and the Mohawk valley, although cowed at present by the rebel committees, would welcome the British with open arms. Once occupied, therefore, the country promised to be easy to hold. Again, the Champlain-Hudson valley ran along the sensitive border between New York and the New Hampshire Grants (Vermont), whose inhabitants were said to be increasingly dissatisfied with Congress over the question of their status as a separate province. A British army on the border, supported by the loyalists of Albany and the Mohawk valley and backed by promises of recognition, could well bring the Vermonters back into the British fold. Finally, in this upper corner of New York dwelt the Iroquois League of Six Nations, a confederation of Indian tribes numbering some ten thousand souls, of whom two thousand were warriors, and, beyond them, between the Great Lakes and the Ohio, a further 150,000 Indians of the "Western Confederation."[17] A British army along the Hudson and the two lakes would stand between the Indians and the rebels. At the least, this would reassure the Indians and prevent their taking up the rebel cause; at the most, it would enable the British to employ them under proper control if need be. In a letter to Lord Rochford, Burgoyne even suggested that these Indians could carry supplies of arms to the black slaves of Virginia and the Carolinas, a proposal in which he had the support of General Gage.[18] Burgoyne did not say whether the Negroes should be given their freedom in exchange for their assistance, but presumably that is how he understood it; and there is no doubt that if his proposal had been known in the South it would have been greeted with horror by rebels and loyalists alike.

For all these reasons Gage, Howe, Clinton, and Burgoyne agreed that the war should be transferred to the Hudson, and each, except Clinton, sent his proposals as to how this should best be done to friends in London.[19] The most debatable question was whether or not to evacuate Boston and occupy Rhode Island instead, as an advance base from which to attack New York, either before winter or early the next spring. Burgoyne felt that to evacuate Boston without making provision for the thousands of loyalists in the city, for which there were insufficient ships, would be fatal to the parliamentary cause, as well as inhuman. Withdrawal would also enable the Americans to enter in triumph, which would give them tremendous encouragement. On the other hand, an army in Boston would serve as an "anvil," as it were, against which to beat with the hammer blow from the west. If proper precautions were taken and raids were made along the coast to bring in supplies, Boston could be held with a relatively small force. Therefore, he hoped that a "spirited trial" would be made to possess both.

One thing was clear: any reconquest of America would have to be carried out under a minister more committed to the parliamentary cause than Lord Dartmouth and a commander-in-chief more energetic and imaginative than General Gage. Burgoyne hoped the minister chosen would be Lord George Germain, whom he believed to be the only man strong enough and well-informed enough to take the helm at this moment of supreme crisis. He therefore wrote Germain a long letter complaining of the mismanagement and inertia prevailing in Boston and including some fairly disloyal remarks about "my general and my friend," General Gage. In ordinary times, he thought, Gage was an excellent governor, but "his mind has not resources for great, and sudden, and hardy exertions, which spring self-suggested in extraordinary characters. . . ."[20] Such verbal knifing did Burgoyne no credit, although some extenuation should be made in his favor. In a desperate situation, Gage was inactive and Admiral Graves equally so. Burgoyne knew what should be done but lacked the authority to do it, or for that matter to do anything beyond twiddle his thumbs. "Major-Generals," he wrote, "are absolute cyphers. We have not even the little enjoyment of an inspection. . . ."[21]

His disloyalty was superfluous in any case, for the administration in London had already made up its mind. On 26 September orders arrived recalling Gage to London for "consultations." The king had refused to allow Gage to be dismissed, not for reasons of favoritism but because he felt it would be unjust and cruel to a man who had done his best in an impossible situation. Howe was appointed commander-in-chief in his stead. This introduced a new complication, however. The senior officer in North America, and Gage's natural successor, was General Carleton in Canada. But Carleton could not be spared at this critical time. He had already sent half his army to reinforce Gage in Boston, and news was coming through that the Americans were preparing an invasion of the province. No one knew how the French Canadians would react, but at least Carleton's prestige stood higher among them than that of any other British officer. Thus he was the only man who might be able to keep their loyalty. Therefore the command was split in two, Carleton retaining Canada and Howe all the provinces south of it from Maine to West Florida. Both were to act as civil governors as well as military commanders. There was now a further reason for transferring the seat of the war to the Hudson, for by opening a communication with Canada the command could be reunited. In his letter Lord Dartmouth promised Howe an army of twenty thousand early the next spring. Meanwhile, he was to prepare to attack New York as soon as possible, a fleet, which would enable him to do this, being on its way from England.[22]

A few days later Burgoyne received permission to return to England. In his letter of thanks to Lord North, he explained that this was doubly convenient. His wife's condition was now very grave, and he would be able to see her. Howe was keen that he should go, he emphasized, for in London he could act "in a confidential agency" to explain Howe's ideas to the ministers and to ensure that the requisitions for supplies were properly complied with. After his grim experiences of ministerial sloth that year, Howe needed a friend on the spot to goad the offices of government into unaccustomed activity. Burgoyne ended by saying that whereas he had previously not looked forward to returning to America in the spring, admiration for Howe had brought about a change of mind and he hoped to rejoin him before the opening of the great campaign the next year.[23]

Gage left on 10 October, taking with him Howe's plans for the next campaign. Burgoyne stayed on another two months. The fleet that was supposed to carry the army to New York was scattered by storms, and the attack had to be postponed until after the winter.

During these weeks, the most alarming news was coming from Canada. It seems that the Americans had anticipated just such a strategy as was being formulated by the British commanders and to forestall it launched their invasion of Canada. An army of 3,500 men under General Richard Montgomery advanced down the Richelieu River and laid siege to St. Jean. Being unable to reduce it, Montgomery sent a detachment, with one nine-pounder cannon and twelve rounds of ammunition floating perilously down the rapids, to Chambly a few miles to the north. This was a square fort with a tower at each corner, intended to be Indian-proof. Major Stopford, the commander, feared it could not withstand cannon shot and when the Americans had fired eleven of their twelve rounds, although to little effect, he surrendered. Worse, he failed to destroy his stores of powder or to spike his guns. Thus replenished, the Americans were now able to bombard St. Jean with force, and after a fifty-five day siege Major Preston (a cousin of James Boswell) struck his flag. Major Stopford's moment of panic had thus opened the way to Canada, and by the middle of November Montgomery was established in Montreal. Perhaps to the relief of Congress, Ethan Allen, the hero of Ticonderoga, had forged ahead against Montgomery's orders and been captured in a foolish attack on the city. He was now on the way to England.

Meanwhile, a parallel advance had been led by Benedict Arnold across the wilderness of Maine. After fearful hardships caused by his failure to calculate supplies properly (half his force deserted and some died of starvation), his "famine-proof" volunteers emerged at Point Levis opposite Quebec on 8 November, just as the first winter snow was falling on the city. All his boats had been lost in rapids or mountain passes on the march, however, and, as the lieutenant-governor of Quebec had withdrawn all boats to the north bank of the St. Lawrence in the nick of time, Arnold had no means of transporting his army over the river. Fuming, he sent Aaron Burr to inform Montgomery of his achievement (for there had been no coordinated plan between the two armies) and to beg him to hurry. Within a week, however, he had managed to hire from local Indians enough canoes to take his seven hundred men across, but the delay had been fatal. As Arnold was crossing, Colonel Maclean, who had brought the remnants of the British army (almost all local volunteers with no training) by forced march from Sorel at the mouth of the Richelieu, managed to slip into Quebec ahead of him and organize the defenses. Arnold gave up and decamped twenty miles west to await Montgomery. On 20 November Carleton arrived in Quebec. He had nearly been captured in Montreal and had passed the American patrols on the St. Lawrence in a whaleboat, disguised as a fisherman. His most urgent task was to send the news to England, with a desperate call for reinforcements. Doubting that a large army would be able to get through before the end of May or even the middle of June, he asked if Lord Dartmouth could send a token force to arrive at the end of April, when the ice broke and before his supplies ran out. That night, the only seaworthy frigate, the *Nancy*, with a skeleton crew and her guns removed to the walls of Quebec, sailed for England. No one knew whether she would get through, for ice was already forming on the river banks, it was snowing continuously, and there would be wild storms blowing up in the Atlantic.[24]

Burgoyne sailed for England aboard the *Boyne* on 5 December.[25] One of his last acts in Boston was to order the conversion of Old South Meeting House into an indoor exercise area for horses during the winter, essential if the animals were not to suffer. Old South was regarded by Americans as the very cradle of the Revolution (here Warren had addressed the patriots in defiance of an entire company of soldiers surrounding the pews), and since the conversion was carried out ruthlessly Burgoyne was blamed for this crass piece of vandalism. Vandalism was completely out of character for Burgoyne, for he was an amateur architect himself. The probable truth is that the damage was done after he left and in disregard of his orders.[26]

CHAPTER VIII

THE GRAND STRATEGY PREPARED

BURGOYNE arrived in London on 27 December to find that the government was making "mighty Preparations for carrying on the war in America." Lord Dartmouth had resigned on 10 November to become Lord Privy Seal. His successor was Lord George Germain, who had insisted on, and been granted, far wider powers than his predecessors and was now virtual war minister and the most important official in the kingdom.

Lord George was sixty years old. Physically, he was "of large make, though somewhat womanly,"[1] a characteristic which gave rise to rumors that he was a homosexual. This aspect is reflected in his correspondence and speeches which, though always straight to the point and written in a language which the *London Chronicle* (27 August 1776) praised as "elegance itself," are curiously rounded and feminine in style—at times almost grandmotherly. His history was unusual. Born of the great family of Sackville, he had been a distinguished soldier, noted for his courage, administrative ability, and talent for picking good officers (Wolfe had been a protégé and a lifelong devoted admirer). Then at the Battle of Minden (1759), to the astonishment of everyone, he had been charged with cowardice, ignominiously dismissed from the army, and forbidden any further employment in the king's service. The newspapers had ridiculed him as a blubbering poltroon, yet there was a political side to the affair which remained hidden. In politics he had allied himself to the crown prince (the future George III) in the feud with the king, and this had caused him to fall foul of the Prussians and their allies, whom the crown prince hated.

The disobedience to orders for which he was court-martialled may therefore have been due not to his cowardice but to his carrying a quarrel too far. Whatever the truth, the crown prince was convinced that Lord George Sackville was the victim of a monstrous injustice and determined, when he became king, to extend him his protection and discreetly arrange his return to office. Nevertheless, during the next years Lord George, who changed his name to Germain to comply with the terms of a will, remained in the wings of the political scene and busied himself with his estates, being almost a model of what an old-fashioned country squire should be. He took pains to see that no tenant was unemployed, that every house was repaired at his expense, that the sick received free medical treatment, that the talented young were provided with an education, and that everybody attended church on Sundays, where he often conducted the choir himself, and was not abashed to stand up and point out the moral lesson of the sermon when he thought the congregation might not understand it. Lord George's hour came with the American war, for, as much by temperament and upbringing as out of loyalty to his king, he believed that the rebellion struck at the heart of the constitution and that the only practicable policy was to put it down by force—the sooner the better—and redress the American grievances afterwards. Thus the king saw in him a dependable servant and loyal ally, and he gave his full support to Germain's measures and plans.

The overriding problem was manpower. Though press gangs conscripted for the navy in their brutal and arbitrary way, there was no conscription for the army. Despite every effort and every trick thought up by unscrupulous recruiting officers, recruiting brought in at most a hundred a week and often as few as thirty; in Ireland a good week brought in three and a bad week none.[2] Nor did Germain have power, as a modern government would have, to prohibit recruiting by such rival institutions as the East India Company, which would have increased his forces by several thousand men. Hence, the government was forced to seek help abroad or abandon the conflict. Catherine the Great of Russia, who had assured the king of her support, now sharply refused his request for soldiers. Four German principalities, however (Waldek, Brunswick, Hesse Cassel and Hesse Hanau), were willing to send a total of nineteen thousand men in exchange for a payment that finally came to over £5 million. The Americans were outraged that Britain should employ foreign troops to settle her domestic problems and maintained that this put the civil war onto the same footing as a war between sovereign states. If the British treated Americans as foreigners, then foreigners they would become. The opposition in Parliment, led by Fox, likewise declared this move a further proof that the king and his friends were conspiring to overthrow the constitution and reestablish absolute monarchy in England. In reply the government wanted to know: If the Americans objected to being treated as foreigners, why as British subjects had they refused to pay taxes in the first place, why had they been negotiating with France and Spain since June for recognition as an independent state, why did they even at this moment have agents in Paris negotiating the purchase of arms, and why did their commanders, such as Washington, insist on being treated with the same formality as was due to officers commissioned by the king? Thus each side became more firmly convinced than ever that the other was conspiring to overthrow the constitution and abolish liberty.

To Lord George Germain, who had no doubt that Parliament's cause was right, the purchase of foreign troops was merely the welcome solution to an otherwise insoluble problem. During his first months in office, he worked with indefatigable energy to conjure up the forces Howe and Carleton would require. His new powers brought a flood of new and complex problems to his American office; for now he had not merely the colonies (including the West Indies) to run as before, with all their multifarious routine matters—land grants, the appointment of officials and judges, the settlement of religious disputes between Protestants and Catholics, Indian affairs, epidemics, and slave uprisings in Jamaica—but also a war of unprecedented difficulty at a three-thousand-mile distance. It was no longer enough to discuss strategy; he had to plan it and organize the forces and supplies to carry it out. To do this he had to prod the Treasury, the Admiralty, the War Office, and the Board of Ordnance, all prickly, resentful, and hidebound, into continuous activity and ensure that they actually delivered the money, the ships, the men, the transport, and the supplies, every article of which he had to order himself, even such items as jigs, tools, jars of grease, and cakes of soap. Yet, his office being relatively new and junior among government departments, he had a staff of thirteen: two undersecretaries, eight clerks, two porters, and Mrs. Muley, the "Necessary Woman." Moreover, while even a minor government department today would employ several times that number in typists alone, his office had to copy out every letter in careful copperplate handwriting, never less than twice and sometimes as many as twelve times. He had besides to attend meetings of the Privy Council and cabinet, debates in Parliament, and the king's levees at St. James's Palace. Indeed, a perusal of any one of the several hundred volumes of his correspondence will show that the accusations of sloth, ignorance, and incompetence thrown at him after the war by such political enemies as Lord Shelburne (who said his "was a very idle office") must be dismissed as mere party political nonsense.[3]

Carleton's dispatches from Quebec had arrived, despite every hazard, on Christmas Eve. His proposals tallied well with the plans of Howe and Burgoyne, for he had always believed that the forts of Crown Point and Ticonderoga on Lake Champlain should have been extended into a line of fortifications linking New York and Quebec, so that in the event of a war an army of ten or fifteen thousand could be rapidly transported from one province to the other. This, of course, had not been done. Nevertheless, he believed that Canada was the most advantageous place from which to get at the back of the colonies, and he hoped the government would send him ten to twelve thousand men early in the spring. Such a force, equipped with frigates, "might greatly change the face of things on this continent."[4]

At the same time, and this was most important, he asked for three hundred "batteaux" (flat-bottomed boats) and some gunboats to carry his army across Lake Champlain, after he had driven the Americans from Canada, and to attack Ticonderoga.

This fitted perfectly with Germain's own ideas, for since the summer he too had decided that the war should be shifted to the Hudson, in order to "pour an army from Quebec on the back of the colonies."[5] Both Gage and Howe had sent estimates of the troops required, varying between 35,000 and 24,000 men altogether. In his latest letter, dated 9 October 1775, Howe had drastically reduced this total to about 18,000 men: 12,000 for advancing up the Hudson toward Albany, with the primary object of opening a communication with Canada; 3,000 for the defense of New York itself; 3,000 regulars, plus 3,000–4,000 Canadians and Indians, to push down from Canada toward Albany.[6] Germain, however, knew that he could do better than this, for he would be able to supply the generals with more men than they had asked for. Carleton would get his 10,000, while Howe would get the 20,000 already promised by Lord Dartmouth. In the event, Germain was able to exceed even this, for a total of 33,800 men were sent to America in 1776.[7]

It is no wonder, then, that after his first meeting with Germain Burgoyne wrote to the Earl of Huntingdon, "I partake of all well wishers to the cause of the Constitution in this important contest . . . in the satisfaction of seeing the affairs of America in the able hands of Lord George Germain; and when I consider the resolution with which . . . he is supported from the throne, I derive great confidence in the prospect of the next campaign."[8] Lord George asked Burgoyne to draft a memorandum on the next campaign, based on the assumption that Canada had fallen, which Burgoyne submitted under the title "Reflections on the War in America."[9] After dealing with the need for a more effective blockade of the New England coast, Burgoyne recommended that the regulation proportion of one light infantry company per regiment be increased as a permanent feature of the army. Light infantry and artillery were the only means of dislodging the Americans, who were so adept at fortifying posts and fighting from behind every tree. He warned too against underestimating American soldiers and militia. His most important suggestion was for a two-pronged campaign, with one army advancing from New York and the other from Montreal, to form a junction in Albany. The loss of Quebec would be no obstacle, for the fleet could push straight past it toward Montreal, as had been done in 1759, leaving the city to be starved or battered by artillery.

It has been said that in advocating a two-pronged advance toward a middle point, instead of a single drive from New York with a large army, Burgoyne allowed personal ambition to distort his military judgement. He wanted the command of the northern army in order to claim at least half the credit in the hour of victory. We do not have Burgoyne's original paper, only some brief extracts quoted by de Fonblanque, who merely says that Burgoyne stressed the formidable objections to a single advance from New York owing to the difficulties of local means of supply and transport. But, it is asked, since the Hudson could carry the fleet to within forty-one miles of Albany itself, what difficulties of transport could he have had in mind? Moreover, a strategy in which two armies converge to a middle point is always risky, since the enemy has interior lines of communication and can concentrate against each army in turn. Those who have written thus do not seem to have considered the circumstances in which the paper was drafted. The reconquest of Canada was paramount, and an army of at least ten thousand would be required for it. Why not use this army, then, in pursuing the Americans southward? Such a move would also place the British between the rebels and the Indians at the beginning of the campaign. Thirdly, the peculiar lie of the Hudson-Champlain line would make it impossible for Washington to take advantage of his interior lines of communication, for the British would have command of the water. Wherever he tried to make a stand, even on the formidable Highlands, he would always be in fear that a second army would be on his back immediately. Thus, in Germain's words, the rebel army would be caught "between two Fires."[10] Howe had written that in his view the only hope of subduing the rebellion lay in forcing Washington to a pitched battle, which he would certainly lose. What better way of bringing this about, therefore, than by the strategy proposed? Washington would either have to stay in Pennsylvania and watch the British achieve all their objectives or stand and fight and be destroyed. In short, the plan offered every advantage:

1. It would introduce mobility into the war.
2. It would cut off the rest of the provinces from New England and allow the British to reduce the two halves one at a time.
3. When the British harassed the frontiers, the inhabitants would be forced to flee to the rebel army for protection, thus increasing instead of reducing that army's problems of supply.
4. It offered the best chance of forcing Washington to battle.
5. Ships patrolling the Hudson and the lakes would prevent Washington from attempting to reenter New England, for Howe would be warned at once and be able to meet him with his entire army.
6. Alternatively, it might trap Washington in New England itself.
7. It would give comfort to the loyalists in upper New York and aggravate, to the British advantage, the tense situation between the New Yorkers and the Vermonters.
8. It would reassure the Indians, instead of leaving them on the far side of the rebel army.
9. The forts and posts along the line, once established, would be easy to supply.
10. It would provide the best base from which to mount operations southward—or in any direction desired.
11. It would reunify the two commands at present at New York and Quebec.
12. Finally, it was practicable. In 1690, Frontenac, the French governor of Canada, had tried just such a plan and had failed only because of insufficient strength. In the French and Indian War (Seven Years' War) armies of seventeen thousand men had operated successfully in the same area.

A single advance from New York offered few of these advantages, besides posing serious difficulties. America being a country of small settlements, armies larger than about twenty thousand could not operate unless supplied entirely from England itself, for even with a friendly population such a number could not live off the land. An army of thirty-five thousand would therefore be forced to keep to the Hudson, thus exposing its flanks and rear to an ever increasing danger of attack. First, the Highlands would have to be taken, doubtless at the cost of heavy casualties. Then Albany would have to be reached, and beyond that Ticonderoga. Nor would the capture of Albany necessarily force Ticonderoga to surrender, although at present Albany was its supply base; for Ticonderoga could find alternative supplies from the Mohawk valley or New Hampshire. After Ticonderoga, the lakes would have to be crossed and Canada retaken. During all this time, Washington would have his rear secure and could avoid battle if he chose. The loyalists and Indians would be behind the Americans, and the Canadians would be under American authority so long that they might decide to join the rebels aginst Britain. In other words, a single advance from New York posed almost the same problems as confronted the British in Boston or any other city on the coast, such as Philadelphia: It would lead on and on into nowhere.

Indeed there were so many factors in favor of a two-pronged advance that Burgoyne's private ambitions one way or another were irrelevant to its acceptance. The only question was whom to appoint to command the army to relieve Carleton. Clinton, being senior to Burgoyne, was next in line for so important a mission; but he had been ordered by Lord Dartmouth to lead an expedition to South Carolina, and it was too late to make a change. Burgoyne, who was in London and had been the most enthusiastic and inventive propounder of this plan from the beginning, was the natural and obvious choice. Accordingly, he was ordered to prepare to take command of the expeditionary force that would sail for Canada at the end of March 1776.

Burgoyne could have had little time or incentive for a gay social life in London, for it was one of the worst winters remembered. Deep snow covered England. The Thames froze solid, London Bridge was blocked, and reports came in of stagecoaches buried beneath drifts, their horses, drivers, and passengers frozen to death, while the convoys preparing for America at Deptford, Gravesend, and Chatham were icebound. The exquisite beauty of the Georgian metropolis, with its forest of snow-encrusted church spires, was little compensation for the misery and hardship of the inhabitants. Queen Charlotte gave £500 to the distressed poor of the capital, for the price of coal had soared to £1 17s per ton, and Lady Dartmouth followed in her humble way with a gift of £100 to the poor of Blackheath, notoriously the coldest of the nearby villages. The war, too, was casting a shadow over society. The huge Rotunda at Ranelagh Gardens was dark and deserted, the owners being unable to provide candles or fires. The Pantheon in Oxford Street had switched from balls to lectures and recitals, and Mrs. Cornelys, the leading impresario of masquerades, was bankrupt. People no longer approved of her extravaganzas. Gone were the cardinals and bears, the men dressed as walking trousers and bouquets of flowers, the Golden Room and the Skeleton Room (wherein a skeleton was propelled from a closet at the jerk of a lever). Costumes of shepherdesses and country bumpkins, alluding to the innocent pleasures of a life close to Nature, were now preferred, and ladies who persisted in wearing the towering elaborate wigs of the year before were patriotically satirized. At Mrs. Hobart's masquerade at Richmond, for instance, a Mr. Baker appeared "dressed as a lady in a modern headdress, four feet in height, and adorned with large Portugal Onions, roots of celery, radishes, carrots with an endive in the centre of the cap, and several other kinds of garden stuff; the wearer supported the character with great humour, though several ladies were put out of humour to find themselves the ridicule of young men, as well as old dowagers and old maids, that have no hair on their heads." Yet after the amateur dramatics of Boston, Mrs. Siddons at Drury Lane and Sheridan's new comic opera *The Duenna* at Covent Garden must have been a sumptuous relief.[11]

Burgoyne resumed his duties as an MP, attending the Commons on 20 February for Fox's debate on "the ill success of His Majesty's Arms in North America." Fox made one of his best speeches, saying that the aim of the present ministry was "the total destruction of the Constitution of this free form of government"; yet the uninterrupted disasters that had resulted from their policy of coercion revealed that they were incompetent even to do that. In the debate, Burgoyne spoke up for the army and, in contrast to what he had written privately to Lord Rochford, praised the courage and discipline of the troops at Bunker Hill so emotionally that he was reprimanded by the Speaker.[12] The opposition press treated him roughly, as did Horace Walpole, who claimed that Burgoyne had subtly blackmailed the government, offering his silence on the mismanagement at Boston in exchange for the Canadian command, promotion, the increase of his regiment (plus salary and perquisites), and other favors.[13] Walpole was mistaken on every point, yet such is the skill of his writing that the unpleasant picture of Burgoyne remains even after Burgoyne is proved innocent of all the charges.

Burgoyne's chief attention, however, was occupied by the preparation of the army for Canada. Three infantry regiments were to go from England (the 21st, 29th, and 31st Foot) and six from Ireland (the 9th, 20th, 24th, 34th, 53rd, and 62nd Foot), one, the 47th foot, being transferred from Boston.[14] Their strength varied between 450 and 550 men, making a total of about 5,000. In addition there were to be three German infantry regiments, two cavalry, and a battalion of grenadiers, coming to 2,868 men. For artillery, there were to be four companies of British, totaling 464 including officers, and one of Hesse-Hanau, who were reputed to be the best gunners in the world. Thus Carleton was to have about 8,300 reinforcements, which, with the 1,500 he had already and the 3,000 or more to follow in July, would bring his army up to 13,000 before the autumn. The force, moreover, contained some of the toughest and most experienced troops in the British army, while many of the Germans, it was assumed, would be veterans of the campaigns of Frederick the Great. Each regiment could take 60 women, 42 servants, 86 tons of baggage, 4 wagons for personal baggage, 16 horses with harnesses, 700 blankets, 27 "water-decks of painted Oil Cloth," 60 watch coats for guard duty at night and a strictly regulated quantity of other "Necessaries." Burgoyne and his two aides-de-camp were to be allowed forty tons of baggage between them, which was nearly half that of an entire regiment.[15]

Much more important were the frigates, gunboats, and three hundred "batteaux" Carleton had requested in order to facilitate amphibious warfare on the St. Lawrence and to carry the army across Lake Champlain and attack Ticonderoga when the Americans had been driven from Canada. Germain had ordered four hundred to make sure, but no one seemed to know what "batteaux" were. The Ordnance Board appointed Lieutenant-Colonel Gabriel Christie to find out and supervise their construction. He was a veteran of the French and Indian War and, owning a large house at St. Jean now in rebel hands, was anxious to return to Canada. On 11 January he sent details and drawings of two types of "batteaux," both with pointed bows and sterns, the larger capable of carrying thirty barrels of provisions and twenty men. However, he thought it would be a waste of precious shipping space to build them on the spot and carry them over, since they could be "run up" almost anywhere in the forests of Canada. As a result of his opinion the order was not followed through earnestly, and only ten were built, with parts for fourteen more.[16] He had forgotten, or not understood, that the entire purpose of Carleton's request was that, besieged in Quebec, he would be unable to build any boats, and once in pursuit of the Americans he would have no time, even if he had the skilled artificers. Moreover, as Christie ought to have known, boats should be made of seasoned wood if they are to be trusted in active service, whereas to "run them up" in the forests would necessitate their being made of green wood. Similar trouble occurred over the gunboats, or "Carvel Boats," each to carry a single eighteen-pounder or nine-pounder cannon. As late as 12 March, a Captain Debbeig discovered by chance, when calling at the Admiralty, that the gunboats being built had neither masts, sails, anchors, nor cockles. Sir Hugh Palliser, one of the Lords of the Admiralty, explained that Germain had merely ordered gunboats and that without a *proper* order from his lordship these secondary parts could not be provided.[17] This sort of thing was partly due to growing friction between Germain and Lord Sandwich, First Lord of the Admiralty, although both ardently believed in a maximum effort to finish the war.

Yet despite these and countless other such difficulties, the convoys began to assemble at Spithead, Plymouth, and Cork in February. At Chatham, Captain Douglas, commander of the small emergency relief force ordered to reach Quebec as soon as possible, had worked day and night to fit out his ship, the *Isis* (fifty guns), for, as Sandwich wrote to him urgently day after day, the fate of Quebec, even of the Empire, depended upon him. He needed no encouragement, for he thought the American rebellion "atrocious—the most insolent, the most ungrateful, that ever reared its opprobrious head against an indulgent parent state,"[18] and sailed as soon as the ice melted at the end of February, disappearing into the winter storms of the Atlantic. Three other warships and six transports were to rendezvous with him in the St. Lawrence.

Burgoyne was distracted from his task by ill health, and in March he had to undergo the horrors of an eighteenth-century "chirurgical Operation."[19] He was more concerned, however, about his wife, whose condition had grown alarmingly worse over recent weeks. In an age when diagnoses depended largely on guesswork, without even thermometers, it was considered unseemly to discuss the symptoms of disease, and so we know nothing of her case. In February, however, her parents died within two days of each other, to be followed a week later by her favorite sister, Lady Margaret, and by the news that her other sister, Lady Mary, would not survive a week. It happened that in the same week Burgoyne received his orders to embark with the first division of Brunswick troops. He was to sail on the *Blonde* under Captain Philemon Pownoll. "It seems he is rich," added Germain, "and you need not fear putting him to expense." Burgoyne's promotion to lieutenant-general, in keeping with his duties of second-in-command under Carleton, had come through with permission to antedate it as far as he wished. "The King enquired anxiously about Lady Charlotte and you," ended the order, "and I trust I did not inform him wrong when I said she was something better." Burgoyne replied, asking for a postponement of his departure.

> Her piety, resignation and fortitude, of which no woman ever had more, are not proof at once, and her body not at all, against these combined sorrows, and in my soul I believe that my immediate separation, against which, however, she would not say a word, would convey her to the family grave before it is closed. In this situation, my Lord, were the common duty of a foreign war only concerned, I should think myself justified in petitioning his Majesty to withdraw from the campaign. I would ever relinquish all I hold or could ever hold from the Crown, rather than forsake the duty I owe to a wife who has never given me a moment's pain, except upon a bed of sickness or in an hour of parting.[20]

It may seem odd that Burgoyne should think a foreign war of less importance than a colonial rebellion. To his generation, the modern idea of a total war in which states fight to the death was unknown. Wars were fought over issues of slight concern to the people at large; peace treaties were signed long before a collapse, and, after an exchange of territory and the surrender of a few forts, life went on much as before. The American War of Independence was, in this respect, rather different: It was not only among the first of modern wars, in that guerrilla tactics played an important part in the winning of it, but was one of those few wars (the Spanish Civil War is another) in which the issues over which the two sides fought, or imagined they fought, are still alive and likely to remain so for the foreseeable future.

The movements of fleets, when all depended on the chance of a favorable wind, could not be subject to the private affairs of generals, however, and on 31 March Burgoyne went to Portsmouth. His instructions were that if Quebec had fallen and Carleton was dead (though news had come of the repulse of an American attack on 31 December in which General Montgomery had been killed, it was still possible that Quebec might be starved into surrender), he must decide what action to take. Most important was to ascertain the disposition of the Indians and secure their goodwill through the agents. The Canadians presented a more difficult problem. The punishment of a few of those who had flagrantly gone over to the Americans "cannot fail to have a good Effect, but your Discretion, & Genl. Carleton's Knowledge of their Character & Temper, will suggest the best means of giving every possible Countenance and Encouragement to those who have manifested their Attachment. . . ."[21]

There was another problem brewing over seniority. Carleton was the ranking officer on the continent, and it had been intended to appoint him commander-in-chief once a communication had been opened with New York. However, a new factor complicated the situation. General Howe's brother, Admiral Lord Richard Howe, was to take charge of the fleet in American waters and the two brothers were to act, in addition to their warlike roles, as peace commissioners. Their powers were strictly limited, so much so that their authority to pardon, which was about all they had, was thought by many likely to cause more harm than good. Modern historians likewise have maintained that the Howes could hardly have been expected to achieve much by carrying a sword in one hand and an olive branch in the other. It should be remembered that by this time the government profoundly distrusted, and with reason, the Continental Congress, and believed that wider powers would simply encourage Congress to play for time while it organized more thoroughly for resuming the war. The peacemaking powers were not therefore an olive branch; they were strictly limited to be consistent with the government's policy of subduing the rebellion and bringing its leaders to book first and dealing with American grievances after. Carleton, as governor of Canada, could not have independent authority to negotiate. What was to happen, then, when the two armies joined, if Howe's authority in America had to remain supreme? Germain wrote to Howe to say that if Carleton was dead, he was to take over as commander-in-chief for the whole continent and could, therefore, appoint Clinton (the next senior officer) to Canada or leave Burgoyne there as he thought fit. Germain said nothing about what he should do if Carleton was still alive.[22]

When Burgoyne greeted the German regiments at Portsmouth, he found himself in the middle of a ludicrous crisis. The Germans were fussy about their boots, none more so than the Brunswick Dragoons, who wore enormous affairs reaching high up their legs to give them an impressive, though ponderous, air of martial dignity. The original supply had disappeared in Holland and an emergency replacement had been ordered. When unpacked these turned out to be five thousand pairs of "Dancing Pumps, and so small that no use cou'd be made of them."[23] This was serious, for the dragoons had come without their horses, it being hoped they would find mounts in Canada; now they could neither ride nor march. On top of this, the fleet could not sail, despite a favorable wind, as the sailors on the transports (owned by merchant contractors) were striking over a wage dispute. This was eventually settled and the fleet, thirty sail with naval escort under Captain Dalrymple, put to sea on 4 April.

As Burgoyne went aboard the *Blonde*, he was surprised to see a young midshipman standing on his head on the yardarm, arms outstretched, swaying perilously high above the water. "Oh, that's only young Pellew at his antics again," explained Captain Pownoll. "If he falls he'll but go down under the keel and come up on the other side." Pellew had run away from school to escape a beating and was determined to go to America, where his grandfather owned most of the land on which Annapolis was built. He was to attract Burgoyne's attention again and in later life was to become one of Nelson's most distinguished admirals. Perhaps indeed Lord Exmouth (for he was made a peer) inspired the creation of "Captain Hornblower," for their adventures were remarkably similar.

Burgoyne wrote a last letter to Germain, asking him to reassure "His Majesty, that no private Misfortune shall interfere with the trust reposed in me, and that every faculty I am Master of shall be exerted to my last Breath, to forward his Service."[24]

On the same day the six regiments in Ireland, under Brigadier-General Simon Fraser, a good-natured professional soldier who was to become Burgoyne's closest friend in America, set sail in forty-six transports from Cork. Here, too, there was trouble, for the navy, with its usual contempt for merchant seamen, weighed anchor without warning. In the resulting panic, valuable stores were left on the quayside, two transports collided and became entangled, and three ran aground.[25]

No sooner had the armies sailed than news arrived that the Americans had solved the problem of whether or not the British should evacuate Boston. General Knox had brought fifty-eight guns across the snows from Ticonderoga and General Thomas had started to bombard the city with them from Dorchester Heights. Two weeks later, on 17 March 1776, Howe sailed for Nova Scotia with his army and fifteen hundred loyalists crammed into seventy-eight ships. All his artillery, wagons, and powder were left behind for the Americans, to whom wagons, guns, and powder were almost as valuable as life itself. The shortage of wagons alone was to affect British operations for the rest of the war. Yet Howe had neglected to take any of the precautions Burgoyne had specified as essential to the security of the city. Dorchester Heights had not been occupied, nor any raids carried out along the coast. The whole strategy for 1776, which depended on an early start, was now thrown out of gear, for an attack on New York would be unthinkable for at least four months. Worse still, the Americans now had a superb advance base, impregnable to attack from the sea, from which to mount naval operations of their own and send raiders to intercept British transports on their way to Halifax or Quebec.

His task in Boston completed, General Thomas went north to Quebec with a strong reinforcement to instil new energy into the siege of the only city in British hands on the North American mainland. Everything now depended on whether Captain Douglas and his nine ships could get through to Quebec before starvation forced Carleton to surrender or an overwhelming attack carried his defenses.

CHAPTER IX

PRECIPITATE FLIGHT OF THE REBELS

THE *Isis* had aboard the grenadier company of the 29th Regiment (about forty men) under Lord Petersham, who at twenty-three had already been a professional soldier for seven years. On 11 April they found their way blocked by an icefield in the Gulf of St. Lawrence. While they were searching for a way through, the wind rose to a gale. Wrote Captain Douglas in his report,

> We now thought it an enterprize worthy of an English ship of the Line in our King and Country's sacred Cause, and an Effort due to the gallant Defense of Quebec, to make the attempt of pressing her, by Force of Sail, thro' the thick, broad and closely connected Fields of Ice, (as formidable as the Gulf of St. Lawrence ever exhibited), to which we saw no Bounds towards the western Part of our Horizon.[1]

Choosing a spot where the ice was only twelve feet thick, he rammed the ship against it. The shock dented the bow but split the ice. They worked their way in, watching anxiously as strips of wood torn from bow and hull floated away in the passage left behind them. They continued thus, during nine days of "unspeakable Toil," for 180 miles. Snowstorms smothered them; ice weighed down the sails. Often they were stuck fast, when "it was a Pleasure to see Lord Petersham, exercising his Troops, on the Crusted Surface of that Fluid thro' which the Ship so recently had sailed." They at last broke out into clear water and after two more weeks of blizzards and gales reached the rendezvous at Isle aux Coudres, some seventy miles below Quebec. To their joy, the frigate *Surprise* and sloop-of-war *Marten* appeared on the same day, having followed through the gap left by the *Isis*. They had on board the light infantry company of the 29th and one hundred marines. Three days later the *Triton* arrived with her five transports bringing the stores and the rest of the 29th Regiment. They had come by another route and miraculously seen no ice at all! As the little fleet worked its way up the swollen river, deftly avoiding the ice packs that bore down upon them, smoke signals rising from cape to cape encouraged them in the hope that Quebec must still be holding out. Douglas ordered the *Surprise*, by far the best sailer, to go ahead as fast as possible, and at sunrise on 6 May she announced her presence in Quebec Basin with a triumphant cannon shot. "The News reached every Pillow in Town, people half-dressed ran down to the Grand Battery to feast their eyes with the sight of a ship of war displaying the Union Flags."[2] While the *Surprise* opened a cannonade against the American battery on Point Levis, the *Marten* and the *Isis* disembarked their troops. By one o'clock, General Carleton with one thousand men led a sally against the Americans on the Heights of Abraham, "to see what these mighty Boasters were about; they were found to be very busy with their Preparations for a Retreat."[3] Deserted by their commanders, Generals Thomas and Wooster, the besiegers fled "as if the Devil was after them," leaving everything behind, tents, baggage, wounded, matches still burning beside the cannons, their breakfasts on the tables, even their weapons, while the *Marten* and the *Surprise* continued upriver, bombarding the Americans who were trying to escape along the bank and driving them into the forests.

Carleton issued a proclamation that all those of "His Majesty's deluded subjects" who should be taken prisoner were to be treated kindly. He was not concerned with reckless pursuit but with ensuring that when Burgoyne's army arrived, it would be able to sail past Quebec and deploy ninety miles west at Trois Rivières. "To carry on transportation of army supplies Etc.," he insisted to Captain Douglas, "it is necessary to have absolute command of the river." The army would ascend a stretch of river called the Rapids of Richelieu, where the ships would have to be lightened by disembarking the troops and be shepherded over the rapids by the navy. Furthermore, there were five rivers and innumerable streams emptying into the St. Lawrence on the way, in any of which the Americans could hide and ambush the force as it went by, preoccupied as it would be with the difficulties of getting its heavy equipment and supplies up the river. The troops, marching by land, would have to reembark at each river crossing, for the Americans burned the bridges as they retreated. The most hazardous point would be the rapids, where, if the Americans made a surprise attack, the warships could not be brought into action. By 27 May Carleton had a ship stationed at the mouth of every river, so that as contingents of troops arrived the ship could carry them across, land them again, and replenish them with enough supplies for the march to the next river. This would leave the main fleet free to carry the stores and to put down the artillery, with all speed, wherever it might be needed to repel an American counterattack.[4]

Meanwhile, Burgoyne and his army were approaching the end of their seven-week journey. No convoy of sailing ships could achieve more than three-quarters the speed of a single ship, for the task of keeping them together was prodigious. The prevailing winds in the North Atlantic being westerly, the convoy was required to zigzag its way across three thousand miles of ocean against the elements. The tacking operation had to be rigorously enforced. After maintaining one course for half a day, the commodore in the van would fire a gun, one shot for a turn to starboard, two for a turn to port, and his signal would be repeated by the men-of-war all down the line. Painfully and slowly the transports would heave around ninety degrees, the warships harrying them like dogs driving cattle through a gate. Flag signals were still experimental, and merchant captains, who despised the navy and were by nature "fractious" (as Burgoyne had written at Portsmouth), could not be trusted to take notice of them. Guns were therefore surer, and any ship that got above her station was fired at—not a mere warning shot across the bows, but a cannon shot straight into her, until she became obedient.[5] Yet even despite this the fleet came close to total disaster on the night of 7–8 May when passing Cape Race, Newfoundland. The captain of the *Woodcock*, on which Lieutenant Digby of the 53rd Regiment was sailing, was becoming worried at not having heard the signal gun and was deciding to turn anyway "when the sailors on deck cried out we were most on shore, and we could easily perceive the breakers at a small distance, on which the vessel was put about with the greatest dispatch, and all our guns fired at once as signals for the rest of the fleet to keep off. Some we saw much nearer land and feared they would be lost, in short it was a scene of the greatest confusion, every ship getting from shore as well as possible." Next morning, three transports, with three complete companies of soldiers, were missing. They had last been seen among the rocks and were feared lost.

The soldiers were appalled. Newfoundland was a name to inspire dread, for its inhabitants, the Eskimo, were known to be a surly, intractable people of hideous appearance, who refused all contact with Europeans, except to attack ships in distress and murder, even devour, their crews. Digby makes the curious observation that the faces of the men, unlike all other Indians, were bearded up to the eyes, which suggested to him that they were not Indians at all but the descendants of Basque fishermen.

Burgoyne had seen no more of America so far than the view of surrounding hills from a Boston rooftop, which was scarcely more instructive than the view from a rooftop in Plymouth. The first intimation of the "real" America, a new world whose scale was outside anything in his experience, came in May as they approached the Gulf of St. Lawrence and "Discovered at a distance numerous Islands of Ice, some three times higher than our main top mast head and formed in the most romantic shapes, appearing like large castles, when the Sun shone on them, all on fire."[6] It was customary on passing the Isle aux Oiseaux to fire a cannon for the sport of watching the birds rise and darken the sky with a swarm nine miles across; and again, when part of the convoy was nearly driven against the shore of Anticosti, the soldiers were amazed at the dense herds of seals crowded onto the rocks along the waterline as far as the eye could see in either direction. Sergeant Lamb of the 9th tells us in his journal that several of the recruits on this voyage, who had never been further than their villages before, were driven mad by the sight of endless ocean day after day and threw themselves overboard.

On 26 May the fleet was met by the *Surprise* and told that Quebec was still in British hands and the Americans in full retreat. Burgoyne begged Captain Dalrymple to let him take the twelve fastest ships on ahead so that they could push past Quebec and cut the Americans off before they reached Sorel, for in this way not one would escape; but Dalrymple believed his orders would not allow him to disperse the convoy. Burgoyne therefore changed to the *Surprise* and sailed on alone.[7]

The spectacular, but ultimately wearing, succession of harsh and savage landscapes changed, with the proximity of civilization, into smiling scenes of meadows, orchards, villages, and churches until, on 29 May, the *Surprise* passed the dangerous "Traverses" and dropped anchor in the Basin of Quebec.[8] Hearing that Carleton was upriver with a "few Troops to keep the Rebels in Awe," Burgoyne and his aides-de-camp rode next morning in cabriolets along the riverbanks, "over a most romantic wild country," in search of him. They found him at the town of Champlain.

General Guy Carleton was Irish by birth and three years younger than Burgoyne. He had been the benevolent dictator of Canada since 1770, and his rule depended on complicated maneuvers and intrigues. He had but one aim in view: to win the trust of the originally hostile French Canadians (whose Catholicism, no doubt in reaction to Protestant rule, was of an almost Spanish fervor) and so develop Canada into a permanent and stable province of the British Empire. Thus his leniency toward the French was resented by British settlers as inexplicable partiality against themselves, and his Quebec Act, guaranteeing the privileges of the Catholic Church, was denounced by the less perceptive Protestants in England as a piece of chicanery little short of treason. Yet it was perhaps this policy which saved Canada for the British. In the wake of Montgomery and Arnold, Congress had sent a commission under Benjamin Franklin to try out the Canadians and reassure the priesthood that the Church of Rome was not the enemy of Americans. Franklin's task was made impossible by the bigotry of New Englanders who, like the citizens of London, still thought of the pope as a creature with horns, hooves, and tail, and were still denouncing Carleton as his puppet. With the arrival of the first British ships, Franklin abandoned his fruitless task and hastened back to Philadelphia, though a Jesuit in the commission, Father Carrol, bravely stayed behind another three weeks. Indeed the American army had not been popular, even with those Canadians who had first welcomed it. The main reason was that the Americans had omitted to bring silver coinage and so had had to pay for everything in paper money. If this was refused, they had taken what they needed by force. The inevitable protests had brought down stronger measures; hostages had been taken and threatened with execution. This was no way to win over a population whose friendliness was vital to American success, yet it is hard to see what the Americans could have done. Their troops were unpaid and could not raise credit. They had no food, tents, blankets, shoes, stockings, or coats. There was bad discipline, for most of the officers were untrained, uneducated men who had been elected on the strength of their popularity. Entire battalions packed up and went home when the termination of their enlistment contracts approached, and those who remained were decimated by malaria and smallpox. It was obvious to the Canadians that when the avenging British army appeared this rabble could not hold Canada for long. On 3 May the American commander, advised by Franklin, decided to withdraw to St. Jean on the Richelieu River and build defenses there; but, calculating that they still had a month before they need expect the British army, he determined to make a last attack on the city. Three days later the *Surprise* appeared on the river and the rout began.

The main convoys arrived at Quebec on 1 June, but Carleton ordered them to continue to Trois Rivières. Thanks to Carleton and Captain Douglas, Burgoyne found a system for transporting his entire army already arranged and waiting, and the regiments were able to advance up the St. Lawrence, without stopping, as though up a scaling ladder, and to pass the rapids, under the "careful & judicious inspection of Captain Ludwidge on the 'Triton,'" with clockwork precision.[9] Burgoyne supervised the British regiments in their march along the north bank, and Major-General Adolf von Riedesel led the Germans, with contingents of Canadians, along the south bank. The entire operation, barely mentioned in history books, was one of the most efficient carried out in the American war.

Burgoyne had been giving some thought to the problem of encouraging bravery and good service among the soldiers. In those days medals had not been thought of, and the only award to a brave soldier was a payment of money, usually £1. From time to time the king would present an exceptional soldier with a pension, a house, or a market stall free of license, but the system was random and inadequate. Burgoyne's proposal, therefore, was something of an innovation. He published in General Orders on 5 June that the companies should be divided into three classes.

> The general rule for forming these classes is length of service, but distinguished valour, sobriety, the sentiments and conduct of a man of honour, must be preferred to length of service when joined with an inferior degree of Military Virtue. The second class shall, on all occasions, give place and pay a deference to the first and the third to the second.

He expected his officers to take great care in ranking the companies and to "distinguish the most worthy by a superior degree of indulgence and esteem: the natural goodwill which men of honour feel for each other, though in different ranks of life, will sufficiently enforce this piece of justice." By this means he hoped that those punishments, "as painful to order as disgraceful to receive, may be in a great measure, if not entirely, avoided."[10]

If Burgoyne was pompous and long-winded on public occasions, as when speaking in Parliament or writing proclamations to the American people, he always struck the right note when dealing with his officers and men. Lieutenant Digby, for instance, compared him with Carleton, who, although respected as a "very able General and a brave Officer," was excessively cold, rigid, and formal in his manner, even among his friends. For this reason,

> he was far from being the favourite of the army. Genl Burgoyne alone engrossed their warmest attachment. From having seen a great deal of polite life, he possesses a winning manner in his appearance and address, far different from the severity of Carleton, which caused him to be idolized by the army, his orders appearing more like recommending subordination than enforcing it. On every occasion he was the soldiers' friend, well knowing the most sanguine expectations a general can have of success, must proceed from the spirit of the troops under his command. The manner he gained their esteem was by rewarding the meritorious when in his power, which seldom failed, from the praise which they received, to cause a remissness in duty [to be] odious and unmanly, and a desire of emulation soldier-like & honourable.[11]

This is almost a description of what a model corps commander should be: perceptive, considerate, just, yet never sacrificing his authority to popularity. Unlike some abler generals, such as Wellington, he never called his soldiers "scum," and for this reason they did not behave like scum and loot, rape, and murder at every village they came to. I have already suggested that Burgoyne's pomposity was a defense against the world, owing to his unease over his social origins; yet these origins could also explain—because he was not really a snob by nature—why he was so perfectly at ease among his social inferiors and military subordinates.

Brigadier-General Fraser was establishing the advanced corps at Trois Rivières when, at dawn on 4 June, a Canadian arrived to say that three thousand Americans had crossed the St. Lawrence in fifty batteaux and were now less than two miles away, coming full tilt at the British along the riverbank.

When General Sullivan had arrived at Sorel with his reinforcements, he had found the American army in chaos and General Thomas, the hero of Dorchester Heights, dead of the smallpox. His second-in-command was General William Thompson, about whom Patrick Henry had coined the immortal phrase, "This is a *man!*" Thompson, a boastful loudmouth given to sending gasconading letters to Washington and the general staff, declared that had he been in charge Canada would never have been lost and that he would drive the British back into the ocean if he were given the chance. He was given the chance; and now, with great energy but little intelligence, he was blundering through the woods to destroy, as he thought, a handful of Canadians, light infantry, and grenadiers.

The result was exactly as Carleton had planned. The 9th and 47th Regiments were disembarked immediately, and Major Williams of the Royal Artillery, surprised to hear Fraser begging him for God's sake to get what artillery he could on shore, unloaded two six-pounders and eighty rounds in twenty minutes. The *Marten*, in the van of the fleet, pulled in close to shore just as the first Americans came in sight, advancing at the double along the strip of open land between the river and the forest. As they passed, the *Marten* opened fire. The Americans in front wavered and then ran for the woods, followed by the rest. Fraser was not to be caught by surprise, however, and had already deployed the 62nd Regiment along a road through the forest, against whom the Americans, advancing "with great resolution," collided and were beaten back within minutes. It was now the turn of the British to advance, which they did along the riverbank, while Major Williams and his guns, moving forward continually between rounds, forced the Americans to keep under cover and off the main road west that led to their landing place. Yet the bulk of the Americans got away, taking all but two of their batteaux with them. General Thompson and a few others reached the landing place too late and had to run back to the woods. After wandering in a swamp for twenty-four hours, they were attacked by swarms of black flies. These insects, which are still the scourge of this part of Canada in early summer, can bite away all the exposed skin of a victim and even blind him if he cannot find protection. It is hardly surprising that in their wretched state the Americans ran to the road and surrendered. Brigadier-General Nesbitt, heedless of their condition and of the order to treat prisoners humanely, force-marched them in the blazing sun for six miles to headquarters. There, however, they were met by General Carleton and General Burgoyne, "who treated them very politely and ordered them refreshments, which General Burgoyne himself served." Thompson then "accosted Gen. Burgoyne and the rest of the Field Officers in the following manner: 'General and fellow soldiers! The fate of the day has made me your prisoner; however, we are both subjects of the same King, therefore let us shake hands together!' and advancing up to Gen. Burgoyne, embraced him; at the same time telling him, that as he and the troops had come hastily on the expedition, they might be in want of some provisions, and that they were welcome to some hams and other refreshments, that he, Gen. Thompson, had on board his batteaux."[12]

Two hundred and eighty Americans were captured and at least sixty killed. Burgoyne's comment was that their attempt "was founded in rashness and executed with timidity, two principles which compounded make a consummation of preposterous conduct."[13] Perhaps he should have seen the fact that the Americans were able to attack at all, when their main army was in flight, as an ominous sign of the future; but the British were riding on the crest of the wave, and the warning was lost upon them. The advance from Quebec had been brilliantly organized and faultlessly carried out. The soldiers looked with pride at eighty ships, men-of-war, frigates, sloops, schooners, and transports, their great lines of white sails moving slowly through the heart of Canada, between forests unchanged since the creation, cultivated valleys, clean brightly painted villages, and apple orchards all in flower, beneath a blue summer sky and majestic clouds. It was a sight to fill the Canadians and Indians with wonder and the Americans with astonishment and fear—the awesome power of the British Empire.[14]

At the very moment that Carleton might have pushed his success home and destroyed the American army, he did not move. Two days were spent brigading the army; thus it did not resume its advance until the 13th.* Nevertheless, they crossed Lac St. Pierre, where delays could

* Brigading means putting the regiments into marching and battle order. Each regiment consisted of eight companies of the line, called *battalion companies*, and two *flanking companies*, grenadiers on the left and light infantry on the right. This arrangement, however, was not always desirable. Carleton, for instance, separated the flanking companies from all ten regiments and formed them, together with the whole of the 24th Regiment, into an Advanced Corps under Fraser. The battalions (i.e., regiments shorn

usually be expected because of currents that ran sometimes at over seven knots, and reached Sorel in one day, to find the Americans gone, the town in flames, the guns spiked, and all stores removed.

Carleton arrived next (15 June) and ordered Burgoyne to pursue the Americans up the Richelieu with a detachment of four thousand men and artillery but warned him *not to press too closely*, for he himself intended to sail around to La Prairie (opposite Montreal), march across the neck of land to St. Jean, and cut them off. Burgoyne and his force covered fifty miles on the 15th, but the broiling heat and the tiredness of the men, after weeks cramped onboard ship, persuaded him to switch to night marches. In their haste, the Americans had failed to destroy a bridge, so Burgoyne was able to cross the river to the west side and reach the burning fort of Chambly on the night of the 18th.

During all this time, the American General Sullivan had been performing the almost impossible task of keeping together an army deserted by nine-tenths of its officers, shattered in morale, and ravaged by an epidemic of smallpox (to say nothing of malaria). On his return, barely two thousand out of five thousand men were fit for more than light duty. Disease had wiped out some regiments entirely and reduced others to less than a score of men. Isle aux Noix, on the river above St. Jean, was being used as a hospital with one surgeon to look after two thousand sick, wounded, and dying and soon became a scene of horror avoided by the retreating soldiers. Yet there were many who did not desert or panic, and they saved the army. Starving and ragged, weak with fever, they hauled the precious batteaux, with their loads of sick, wounded, and stores, up the river and over the rapids to St. Jean, sometimes standing up to their waists in water for twelve hours at a time. Most astoundingly of all, the Americans managed to evacuate the hospital on the island, transferring the men from the boats onto the three captured British schooners (*Liberty, Enterprise,* and *Royal Savage*) that constituted the American navy and sailing them to the safety of Ticonderoga. It may be wondered what other army in the world, at that time, would not have simply left them to their fate.

Meanwhile, Benedict Arnold, who had been wounded in the attack on Quebec in December, was at Montreal. A force of Indians, with

---

of their flanking companies) were themselves formed into two brigades, the first under Brigadier-General Gordon, the second under Brigadier-General Nesbitt (the same who had captured Thompson). The battalions could be changed about from brigade to brigade, but usually each brigade consisted of three, and at most four; those battalions not brigaded were stationed in rear camps and assigned to transport or garrison duties. Obviously the Advanced Corps was the place every ambitious officer desired to be, for it was here that he would find the best chances of action, extra pay, and promotion. The artillery was usually divided into two parts, the battalion pieces (distributed at two six-pounders per battalion) and the heavy pieces in the "Park." Carleton, however, formed the battalion pieces into two brigades of their own so that they could be concentrated where needed quickly, while keeping the Park separate as usual.[15]

units of the 8th Regiment, which had been isolated in its posts along Lake Ontario through the winter, had appeared at a place called the Cedars, not far from Montreal, and captured four hundred Americans. Arnold had been able to negotiate an exchange of these for four hundred of the British captured at Chambly and St. Jean the previous autumn; for the British commander, Captain Forster, was unable to feed so many prisoners and was not certain that he could prevent their being ill-treated or killed by the Indians. Now, in the middle of this delicate business, Arnold had to pack up and take the remainder of his army south with all speed. This was the moment when Carleton should have appeared at La Prairie, chased them through the forest to St. Jean, and forced the entire invading army, caught between Carleton and Burgoyne, to surrender with its guns, boats, and, not least, Benedict Arnold himself. Carleton, however, was lying windbound at Varennes, some ten miles away; and, instead of disembarking the Advanced Corps and sending it by the coast road to La Prairie and thence to St. Jean, Carleton waited for the wind to change. Thus Arnold and his young aide, General James Wilkinson, were able to reach St. Jean unharried, while Wayne sent a covering force to help them. It was the report of this which made Burgoyne suspect that the Americans were about to attack again. He therefore redeployed his advanced guard and reduced his speed even further, assuming that Carleton or Fraser were already at or near St. Jean.

This gave Sullivan time to evacuate his entire army from St. Jean and Isle aux Noix and Arnold time to dismantle a British row-galley (a small ship especially designed for maneuverability on Lake Champlain) on the stocks and pack her, with her working drawings, onto his batteaux, although at the sacrifice of some of the loot he had brought from Montreal. Arnold then rode with Wilkinson to see where the British were and discovered them two miles away, advancing cautiously. The two men then returned at the gallop while the Americans set fire to the village, including Colonel Gabriel Christie's fine house, and the fort. Arnold shot his horse, cursed Wilkinson when he hesitated to do the same, and made a point of being the last American to leave Canada, just as he had been the first to set foot there the year before. The remainder of the loot he sold in Albany for his private profit, much to the indignation of his fellow officers.

Burgoyne arrived in St. Jean just as the flames were getting under way and Arnold's boat was disappearing out of musket range up the river. There was no sign of Fraser or Carleton. Having no buckets, the soldiers could do little to put out the fires until a heavy thunderstorm damped them. The Advanced Corps from La Prairie arrived the next day (the 20th), and Burgoyne published the following order, with a special order of rum:

> The expedition on which Lieut. Gen. Burgoyne has had the honour to be employed being finished by the precipitate flight of the rebels, he shall think it his duty to make a faithful report to his Excellency the Commander-in-Chief, of the zeal and activity shewn in the officers and men under his command, to surmount the difficulties of the march and come into action. Those are principles that cannot fail to produce the most glorious effects whenever the enemy shall acquire boldness enough to put them to the proof.[16]

In a letter to Clinton he described the American retreat as "unsoldier-like and disgraceful."[17] The fact remained, however, that they had saved the bulk of their army and most of their batteaux, burning all those they could not take with them. By failing to pursue them after the skirmish at Trois Rivières, and then from Varennes to St. Jean, Carleton had lost the greatest advantages of victory. All the courage of Captain Douglas in the Gulf of St. Lawrence and the skill spent in bringing the army from Quebec to Trois Rivières, had gone for virtually nothing. Now the army was faced with the task of building a fleet of ships and batteaux to carry them across Lake Champlain to Ticonderoga. The Americans still had three schooners on the lake and would be able to build more while the British built their fleet. A report had lately arrived that General Howe had left Halifax and must by this time be in New York. If the junction with him were to be effected before winter, there was not a moment to lose.

CHAPTER X

"ALL MY PLANS HAVE BEEN DISAPPOINTED"

BURGOYNE set up headquarters at Chambly, where the rapids empty into a tranquil basin, greatly used today by water skiers. He designed the building himself in a style described as "quite Arcadian." It had a domed roof, arched windows, and a colonnade "something like the Pantheon" and was covered with green boughs for coolness. The setting, too, was typical of Burgoyne's taste. So romantic was the view across the water of the burned-out fort, resembling an antique castle, with the gleaming guns of the Park artillery ranked beside it, and of the smoke from campfires rising above the forest trees, and so peaceful the murmur of the rapids, that everyone called HQ "the Bower."[1]

The officer who acted both as Burgoyne's second-in-command and as commander of the Royal Artillery was Major-General William Phillips. A veteran of the Seven Years' War and a close friend of Clinton, he believed that the officers who had served in Germany were a race superior to all others, especially to those who had fought only in America. At Minden he had brought up his guns at the gallop, an unprecedented feat which contributed to the victory and to some extent compensated for the disgrace incurred by Lord George Sackville (Germain). In the Royal Artillery he is remembered also as the founder of the band, and in accounts of the Burgoyne campaign, fictional or otherwise, he is usually portrayed as an irrepressible, stentorian-voiced, red-faced fire-eater who terrified the men but got things done. In fact, however, he was rather fat and easygoing. As a friend wrote to Clinton in 1760, Phillips "gives orders by a single nod of his black head or the wave of his lily-white hand . . . and is persuaded the order is obeyed. Not at all."[2] He had, moreover, an abrasive, sneery side to his character, which caused Thomas Jefferson, who knew him as a prisoner and quarreled with him, to call him "the proudest man of the proudest nation on earth."[3]

The commander of the Germans was Freiherr Adolf Friedrich von Riedesel. He had been a soldier since boyhood and had likewise fought at Minden. A thoroughly competent and honest officer, he was known affectionately by the British (although he was only thirty-eight) as "Old Redhazel." His wife was a lady of petite appearance but strong character. She arrived with their children not long before Saratoga, determined to share all dangers with him. Her memoirs of the American Revolution are a classic.

As soon as he had finished the drawings for his headquarters, Burgoyne rode to Montreal, where more than two thousand Indians, some from as far away as Lake Michigan, were assembling for a "talk" with General Carleton on whether or not to take up the hatchet against the king's rebellious subjects. "Talks" were bewildering and exhausting affairs that lasted from dawn to sunset for several days at a stretch, for oratory was the national art of the tribes, or "Nations" as they were called, of the Northeast. The Iroquois League of Six Nations in particular had evolved a complicated procedure of debating and voting by which the interests of tribes, clans, families, sachems (civil chiefs), war chiefs, warriors, and women (who, owning all the property, had the last say in everything) were balanced against one another, and agreements were sealed by the exchange of symbolically decorated belts called "wampum." At such conferences, Europeans had to listen patiently to reams of epic poetry and wait long periods while the Indians sat in silence, locked in mysterious contemplation. Carleton had neither the time nor the inclination for this sort of thing and ordered Burgoyne to go in his stead. It was likely to be a tense and dangerous occasion, and Carleton advised Burgoyne to play it as coolly as possible.

The British employment of Indians in the War of Independence was then, and remained for over a century, a powerfully emotional subject. General Gage's excuse that the Americans had used them first was a lame one, for there was no comparison between the fifty Mohicans at Boston, who had been civilized and Christianized for a century, and the thousands of painted savages from the frontiers who were now expected to burn and kill everything and everyone in their path. The ghastly episode at Lake George, when fifteen hundred British troops, with their women and children, had surrendered to Montcalm in 1757 and then been massacred by his Indian allies, was in everybody's memory. So, naturally, when the Indians first appeared in the camps of Burgoyne's army they aroused a certain nervousness. Young officers fresh from the drawing rooms of Mayfair (though Eton and Westminster provided as good a preparation for living among these savages as could be found anywhere on earth) were fascinated and repelled by their strange allies. They admired their warriorlike dignity but despised their capriciousness and drunkenness; they wondered at their skill in finding their way through dense and trackless forests and were amused by the sight of grown men dancing naked, except for daubs of blood and paint and birds' heads tied to their genitals; they were nauseated by the stench of the bear grease they used to repel mosquitoes and were chilled by their weird and terrifying singing.[4]

The British always intended to incorporate the Indians into the Empire, and for this they had set up their Indian Department and Indian Service. In Sir William Johnson they had an agent of genius who was so free of racial arrogance that he married two Mohawk women. His Canadian deputy Colonel Daniel Claus even proposed a scheme by which garrison children could be sent to live in Indian villages in order to learn their language and ways before going on to grammar school.[5] Already certain Indian chiefs, such as Thayendanagea and Oteronghyanento, were being commissioned into the British army.[6] Thayendanagea was to rise to lieutenant-colonel. In fact, the British were groping their way toward the imperial system of native regiments officered by British and a few natives later adopted in India, Africa, and the Far East. Whether they would have created in America anything so remarkable as the British Indian Army in India is another question, for the character of the American Indian and the hatred of the white population might well have prevented it. Nevertheless, in the short period between Pontiac's war and the American Revolution, the British set up the beginnings of a service that was unique in its time for the clarity with which it saw the problems confronting it. Their achievement has been consistently ignored or underrated by all but a few American historians.

Sir William died in the year before the Revolution, and neither his nephew and successor, Colonel Guy Johnson, nor his son, Sir John Johnson, inherited his abilities. They were both strongly loyalist. In 1775 Colonel Johnson fled to Canada from his home near Amsterdam, by the Mohawk River, to be followed the next spring by Sir John.

The Indians themselves, deprived of the one white officer who, they said, had never deceived them, were in turmoil, beset on all sides by cajolements and threats from colonists and British alike to take part in a quarrel they did not understand. For the first time since its foundation by Hiawatha two hundred years before, the Iroquois League was divided. The Mohawks took the British side and followed the Johnsons out of America. The Oneidas and Tuscaroras remained neutral but with sympathies toward the rebels. The Senecas, Onondagas, and Cayugas were unable to make up their minds. The Americans meanwhile set up their own Indian Commission under General Philip

Schuyler (who was related to the Johnsons by marriage) in order to rally the undecided Indians to the cause of Congress. After the first conference at Albany, however, an epidemic broke out among the warriors, who regarded it as a divine punishment for betraying their oath of loyalty to the king; nor had they been able to obtain any promises from the Americans over the restoration of stolen Indian lands. Accordingly, the survivors joined their brethren in Canada.[7]

General Carleton believed that Indians should be used only when incorporated into the regular army. Thus, when Colonel Guy Johnson offered his warriors to help against the American invasion of Canada, Carleton refused. Unfortunately, he refused in a tactless way, for he insisted on keeping the Indians waiting near Montreal, against the advice of the chiefs, who feared the city would expose their warriors to too many temptations to drunkenness. Carleton meanwhile received positive orders from Lord Dartmouth, through Gage, to employ Indians. He compromised by sending thirty warriors under a British officer to St. Jean, where they drove off the first American attack. This delayed the invasion by a fortnight and so probably saved Canada. Nevertheless, the Indians lost several men and were so disgusted by the refusal of Major Preston to send troops to support them and by the lack of appreciation for their service that they went home. At the same time Carleton dismissed Colonel Claus, whom he disliked, and replaced him with Major Campbell, for reasons of politics. This was another mistake. Campbell could speak no Indian and the Iroquois would entrust no confidential matters to interpreters. Guy Johnson and Claus sailed for England to complain and to ensure that the post of superintendent (Guy had not yet been appointed) was not wasted on someone who had cornered the patronage but whom the Indians would not respect. They took with them Captain Joseph Brant-Thayendanagea (Sir William's brother-in-law and the most influential man among the Iroquois) and Ensign Oteronghyanento. During two interviews with Lord George Germain, whom he called "Brother Gorah," Thayendanagea explained the Iroquois position. The Proclamation after Pontiac's war in 1763 had established a line beyond which no European could build a house or plough a field. Since then the frontier had been a scene of uninterrupted skirmishes, massacres, murders, thefts, frauds, and broken agreements instigated by white settlers determined to get land come what may. Despite this, the king, by virtue of his office, loved all his subjects equally. He represented a supreme authority to whom Indians could appeal for justice if treaties were not upheld, and he had shown that at least his intentions were honorable. On the other hand, the rebels offered nothing beyond the certainty that as soon as they had the chance they would drive the Iroquois off the remaining "small Spots" of land remaining to them. Therefore, with reluctance and misgivings, Thayendanagea would advise the Six Nations to assist the king in subduing the rebellion, for in so doing lay their only hope of survival.[8]

Johnson (now appointed superintendent) and the two Mohawks left England and joined Howe on Staten Island in July. The Indians returned to Canada through enemy territory, and Johnson stayed with Howe. Howe himself had spent so much time among the Indians as a young officer that his friends had called him "the Savage," and he was naturally sympathetic to the Indian predicament. He would have preferred them to stay neutral, he wrote; but since this was clearly impossible, the young warriors must be made to understand that by treating with the rebels they were facilitating a rebel victory, which would "finally lead to the Misery and Destruction of the whole People."[9]

This then was the situation that confronted Burgoyne when he sat amid the great concourse of Indians and was offered the pipe of war. He declined it politely. Nevertheless, he concocted a plan which, with the support of Sir John Johnson and others, he now submitted to Carleton. He himself would take three battalions of regulars, some Canadians, and fifteen hundred Indians up the St. Lawrence to Oswego on Lake Ontario and then descend the Mohawk valley toward the Hudson. Such a threat to their rear would interrupt the Americans in their building of ships and defenses at Ticonderoga and might even cause them to abandon it; "for I cannot suppose," he wrote, "that any General would have remained at Ticonderoga, Fort Edward or any other post above the junction of the Mohawk & Hudson Rivers."[10] This would not only render Carleton an easy passage south, so that the time lost in shipbuilding might yet be recovered, but would doubtless assist Howe's advance up from New York by spreading panic and confusion among the Americans. Carleton agreed and gave Sir John Johnson a commission to raise a regiment of loyalists on the way, for Sir John had assured him that most of the population of the Mohawk valley would welcome the British and give them supplies. Then Carleton procrastinated and finally canceled the project on the grounds that there were no provisions to spare. Burgoyne offered to find provisions himself, but Carleton would not budge. This was all the more frustrating because Burgoyne knew that Germain had sent enough supplies to feed twelve thousand men for seventy-five days, in case the Americans should have destroyed or carried away all stores. The army was already able to live off the land, however, and this food was now surplus and more than enough to supply such an expedition. Carleton closed the subject by sending home all but 460 Indians.[11]

Immediately after this, Burgoyne received a letter from Congress setting forth the reasons why the Americans had decided not to honor the exchange of prisoners Benedict Arnold had agreed to with Forster at the Cedars. Shortly after that affair Father Carrol, the Jesuit member of Benjamin Franklin's commission in Montreal, had returned with a story that the Indians had massacred one hundred American prisoners. This number had quickly been reduced to twenty-eight and then to six, but he claimed other prisoners had been ill-treated and even shot at by the savages. Finally, Arnold had no authority to make exchange agreements. The truth, however, would seem to be that no prisoners were killed at all. Nor is it certain that any were ill-treated. In a letter discovered after the war, General Thompson had written shortly before his capture that reasons must be invented for refusing to honor the treaty, otherwise the Americans would leave Canada empty-handed.[12] Why Congress wrote to Burgoyne instead of Carleton was not explained, unless it was that the Americans were irritated by Carleton's lofty refusal to acknowledge any communication from Montgomery or Arnold during the siege of Quebec. Congress had just signed the Declaration of Independence (4 July 1776) and were determined to be treated with respect. It happened that shortly after the arrival of this letter, Brigadier Gordon was shot and killed by Whitcomb, an American scout. The British regarded the deed as murder, and Carleton published an order that henceforth no messages, flags of truce, etc., would be accepted from assassins, traitors, or rebels. He was especially angry over the fact that at the Cedars Captain Forster had bought the American prisoners from the Indians with hard cash. Nevertheless, he released all the prisoners just the same and provided them with clothes and food as well, telling them in his farewell speech to be careful not to come that way again, lest he should not treat them so kindly in future. The Americans, alarmed at the moral effect this might have, publicized widely the insulting parts of his order, as though it had been his reply to Congress (which it was not) and as a proof of the hopelessness of trying to be reasonable with the British. They suppressed all mention of the cash paid for the American prisoners and of the Gordon incident. At the same time, they continued to whip up emotions over the "Massacre of the Cedars." To Carleton, however, the entire episode was proof of the kind of trouble to be expected from using Indians. Even when the proportion of Indians to regulars was small, there were problems. A party of regulars, Canadians, and Indians on one occasion came upon a boatload of eighteen Americans. In the shooting, an Indian was killed. When the Americans surrendered, the Canadians shot all but two of them, to the indignation of the regulars. The Indians then demanded one of these two as "a Sacrifice for the ——— of their Deceased Friend." Brigadier Fraser offered a Negro instead, but only on condition that he could buy him back immediately. This was agreed, and Fraser kept the Negro as his personal servant.[13]

Throughout July, August, and September the British and Americans were racing each other to build their fleets. On each side the labor was immense. The British had trouble trying to bring the two schooners, sent in parts from England, up the Richelieu from Chambly to St. Jean past the rapids. An attempt was made to transport the *Maria*, named after Carleton's wife, by road, but heavy rain soon defeated that by turning the road into mud. Both ships had to be dismantled again and drawn up the rapids on rafts. By the end of August, however, the army had completed in St. Jean both the schooners, a huge "radeau," or floating battery patterned on a Thames barge, called the *Thunderer*, an American "gondola" captured during the advance, twenty gunboats (twelve of which had been brought in sections from England), each with a heavy cannon firing over the prow, and four longboats with field cannons strung aboard, besides over four hundred "batteaux."[14] Meanwhile, 120 miles away at the southern end of Lake Champlain, the Americans, driven and inspired by the versatile Benedict Arnold, had completed eight gondolas from his designs, each with a gun firing over the prow and a six-pounder on each side; four row-galleys based on the British ship brought from St. Jean on the last day of the retreat; a cutter; and a schooner of about the same size as the *Maria* and *Carleton* (eighty to ninety tons). Named the *Revenge*, she was but lightly armed owing to a shortage of cannons. Arnold had planned in addition a thirty-six-gun frigate, but lack of men, arms, and facilities had made this impossible. That he was able to achieve what he did was remarkable enough and owed much to the administrative ability of General Horatio Gates, whom Schuyler had sent to take charge in Ticonderoga. This much-maligned man, born the son of a servant in England and godson to Horace Walpole, lacked a martial appearance, to the extent that the American soldiers nicknamed him "Granny," and he had a weakness, at least equal to Burgoyne's, for political intrigue. Nevertheless, the Americans were lucky to have him as Arnold's superior, for it was he who provided Arnold with the men, materials, and shipyards with which to build the fleet, often in the teeth of irrational opposition. Reports came that Howe had landed on Staten Island on 2 July, and in September came the grimmer news that he had brilliantly defeated Washington on Long Island and was already preparing to attack Manhattan. Gates had no illusions about Arnold's fleet, which was hopelessly inferior to the British one, but he knew that every week's delay made less probable the junction of Howe's army with Carleton's before winter. If the newborn republic could survive its first winter, it could probably survive anything.

The same sense of urgency afflicted Burgoyne. With the support of Phillips (who thought further delay madness),[15] he urged Carleton to send a strong force of light infantry, Canadians, and Indians down the

St. Jean, on the Richelieu River, Canada, the British headquarters from which Burgoyne launched his invasion of New York in 1777. (*From Anburey's* Travels Through the Interior Parts of America.)

lake shore. They should endeavor to get behind Ticonderoga to the spot called "The Landing Place," where Lake George empties into the narrow stream that links it with Lake Champlain. Another force should go to Skenesborough and destroy the shipyard there. At the same time, as much of the army as possible should be embarked on the "batteaux" and held in readiness to move closely behind the fleet, thus narrowing every delay to the minimum.[16] Carleton would have none of it. Instead, he insisted on waiting another month while a large warship, the *Inflexible*, was brought up from Montreal and reassembled at St. Jean. A team of sixteen shipwrights under Lieutenant Schanck of the navy completed the job in twenty-eight days. In his report Captain Douglas wrote that "The achievement almost exceeds belief."[17]

Carleton then put himself in command of the fleet, and in the flagship *Maria* (Captain Pringle, the same who had taken Carleton's dispatches to London the previous autumn) he led them south in the first week of October. Burgoyne was ordered to remain with the army on the Richelieu River, where he waited for news in anxious suspense, sharpened by the knowledge, which he had just received from London, that Lady Charlotte had died at Kensington Palace on 7 June.

Carleton found the Americans waiting in the channel between Valcour Island and the west shore and attacked them from the south to cut them off from Ticonderoga. The heavily outgunned Americans lost two ships but were able to slip past the British under cover of darkness. However, the rest of their fleet was either captured or burned by Arnold himself, who escaped with his men through the forest to Crown Point, despite parties of Indians sent forward to stop him. As soon as he received news of the victory, Burgoyne embarked his army and set sail. Stopping at Rivière au Sable (today the sightseeing spot called Ausable Chasm), he issued an order warning his soldiers that "It is a part of Magnanimity to spare publick demonstrations of Triumph upon the present Occasion." This was, after all, a civil war.[18] His brigades landed at Crown Point on 18 and 19 October.

The fort, which had been built in 1759 by General Amherst, stood on a peninsula and commanded a splendid view of the lake. Needless to say, the barracks were still burning and all the stores destroyed. However, two days later the sky was darkened by vast flocks of migrating pigeons, thousands of which settled on the trees, barrack buildings, and tents. Across the bay, herds of deer wandered along the shore beside the edge of the forest. Thus the provision boats and carts of the army were loaded to bursting with unexpected stocks of meat.[19]

The question now was whether or not to attack Ticonderoga. The season was drawing on. The first snow had fallen three weeks before, and sudden squalls were making the lake dangerous; one had nearly turned the *Carleton* on her beam ends. The lake usually became impassable after the middle of November, and all the signs pointed to an early and severe winter. Therefore any move would have to be made and concluded within three weeks.

Ticonderoga, from the Indian *Cheonderoga* meaning "clashing waters," had been built by the French in 1775 and was first called "Fort Carillon" after the sound of the rapids nearby. It had been the scene of a famous and bloody British defeat in 1758, but after its capture the next year had been allowed to fall into disrepair. Now, under the supervision of the Polish volunteer Kosciuszko, the Americans had extended the old "French Lines" and built two new forts, one on a hill a little way inland called Mount Hope and another on the recently named Mount Independence across the narrows of Lake Champlain. The walls and ramparts of Ticonderoga, which was itself a strong, star-shaped fortress of classic Vaubanesque type, still carried 144 cannons; yet despite its sobriquet of the "Gibraltar of the North," Ticonderoga had a flaw which Montcalm had observed twenty years before and which had caused him to dislike the place as a deathtrap. On the west side of the outlet from Lake George, there rose Sugar Loaf Hill, eight hundred feet in height and with slopes that in many places were nearly perpendicular. John Trumbull, the artist, who was at this time serving as Gates's adjutant-general, tried to convince Gates, Wayne, and others that Sugar Loaf Hill was a serious danger, but he was ridiculed "for advancing such an extravagant idea." He fired a twelve-pounder at it from Mount Independence and a six-pounder from the fort itself, yet when the shot fell near the summit, thus proving that any shot fired *from* the summit could easily reach the fort, Gates replied that no one could get guns to the top of such a hill. Trumbull took Benedict Arnold, "Mad Anthony" Wayne, and a few others to the top of the hill and showed them that a causeway for transporting artillery could be built up the far, or northwestern slope. Trumbull then drew up a proposal which said that while the existing fortress and surrounding strong points required at least ten thousand men and one hundred heavy guns to defend them, a fort on the top of Sugar Loaf Hill would require no more than five hundred men and twenty-five guns; not only that, but such a fort would be nearly impregnable, would completely dominate the river, and would provide a viewpoint from which the country could be watched for fifteen or twenty miles in all directions. He sent copies of his report to Gates, Schuyler, and Congress in order to make sure it was not ignored.[20]

When Carleton, Burgoyne, and Phillips surveyed Ticonderoga from a ship just out of cannon range, they saw the several forts, redoubts, and earthworks fully manned, abatis (trees cut down and tangled together, their sharpened branches pointing toward the enemy) in position with ground cleared in front, apparently hundreds of can-

Ticonderoga, by James Hunter, prior to its attack by the British on 6 July 1777. The boom and chain can be seen across the lake, and the "Old French Lines" to the right. The officer wears the blue of the Royal Artillery. (*Courtesy of the Trustees of the British Museum.*)

nons, and the new flags of thirteen stripes flying above every headquarters. They estimated the garrison at between nine and twenty thousand (it was in fact thirteen thousand).[21] Burgoyne and Phillips urged that a trial be made of the defenses. If the garrison were in a state of panic and if the lines of retreat were left open, the Americans might be frightened out of the fort. Should that happen, the campaign the next year would be already as good as won. If not, then the British needed to do nothing but withdraw to Crown Point for the winter. Carleton said that he saw little object in wasting lives but agreed to hold Crown Point as an advance base for the resumption of the offensive next year. Thus reassured, Burgoyne decided to leave for England. Carleton gave him some memorandums for delivery to the government, containing a list of reinforcements and additional supplies for the next campaign. He asked Burgoyne to amplify this last memorandum in particular detail, from such knowledge of the requirements as he had collected during the campaign. Carleton mainly asked for a reinforcement of four thousand men and a corps of boatmen, essential in a country of so many lakes and rivers. Of next year's strategy he merely observed: "With a reinforcement to the above amount, and well composed, a large corps may be spared to pass Lake Ontario, and to operate upon the Mohawk River. Another corps might possibly be employed to penetrate to Connecticut River."[22]

The fact that Carleton makes no mention of the intended junction with Howe on the Hudson does not mean, as is often supposed, that he was against the operation or did not think it would happen, but simply that he took it for granted. Here, he was merely approving the Mohawk expedition which he had set aside that year and suggesting in addition a move toward Rhode Island, should Howe decide to land there.

In Quebec, Burgoyne received a disgruntled letter from Phillips saying that Carleton had changed his mind again and decided to abandon Crown Point. "I stand alone and unable to bear up against the sloth and changes of this atmosphere. . . . You will scarcely suppose that there is neither reconnoitring post nor scout sent forward, but as the whim of a drunken Indian prevails." Yet two deserters from Albany had just reported that thirteen British ships had already passed the Highlands and were sailing up the Hudson. Howe's army might appear over the hill at any time. "I shall be very happy, as a citizen, if Howe succeeds, even to Crown Point, but, as an officer, I wish this army might have been allowed the share in the war which it should, in my opinion, have had." Phillips complained that Burgoyne's original plan for the fleet and army to move together down the lake had been rejected, and that Ticonderoga had not been attempted. Even a failure would have severely shaken the enemy. As it was, the army was "distressed and hurt at the languor which governs every movement." He ended, "I do most sincerely hope you will come out to us. The next year must divide this army, and we will go together if it be possible. Take care of our cause in England."[23] Phillips was either absurdly optimistic or very ignorant of American geography in supposing that Howe and all his army could reach Crown Point within a week or two; yet the remark shows how fixed in everybody's mind was the hope of a junction of the two armies before winter.

On his way to Quebec Burgoyne had stopped at various places to order the construction of a chain of posts for the supply of Crown Point through the winter.[24] Carleton's decision, therefore, seemed all the more reprehensible. Burgoyne wrote a letter to Clinton in which he guardedly revealed his feelings. He began by excusing his departure for England. "A secondary station in a secondary army is at no time agreeable; but many circumstances combine in the present instance to make it uncommonly dissatisfactory. My private motives are yet more forcible—a mind sunk at times in distress, a constitution unfitted to severity of cold, a few duties yet remaining to the memory of Lady Charlotte. . . ." He wrote of himself, yet again, as "an unconnected Cypher in the world—the partner lost which made prosperity an object of solicitude—my prospects are closed. Interest, ambition, the animation of life is over."[25] Clinton had lost his own wife some years before and had been so shattered that for a time Phillips had been concerned for his sanity. Burgoyne was, therefore, sure of a sympathetic reader. Nevertheless, Burgoyne was writing according to the fashionable conventions of the time, and he knew perfectly well that neither interest nor ambition were over by any means. The clue to what he was really after comes in the next paragraphs. "All my plans have been disappointed," he wrote, meaning that Carleton had rejected every one of his suggestions from the Mohawk expedition onward. He conceded that "odd & misplaced" as such an action must appear, Carleton had sound reasons for taking charge "of the naval department only," although it would not be proper to explain what those reasons were. This seems to mean that Burgoyne was prepared to defend Carleton in public for leaving the army behind when he sailed off in search of Arnold but that secretly he still did not agree. Crown Point, however, could have been made tenable "if Carleton had called on his own good sense and not been guided by the drawings and technical reasonings of dull, formal, methodical, fat engineers." Now the army was back where it had started and faced with another shipbuilding competition against the Americans during the winter. This could only encourage the rebels and have the worst possible effect on public opinion in England. "I much honour Carleton's abilities & judgement; I have lived with him on the best terms & bear him real friendship—I am therefore doubly hurt that he has taken this step in which I can be no otherwise of service to him than by silence."

The truth was that Carleton's direction of the campaign had been disappointing. Twice, the opportunity of a decisive victory had been thrown away. He had treated everyone with haughty indifference and condescended to explain any of his often baffling decisions. He had offended a number of officers, including Captin Gordon, the chief engineer and reputed to be the most skillful in the British army, who was threatening to resign (and later did) because Carleton had dismissed his recommendations as "impertinences."[26] Yet Carleton had seized on the recommendations of engineers to justify his withdrawal from Crown Point. To judge by the tone of Phillips' cryptic remarks and of Burgoyne's letter to Clinton, it would seem that "a tribe of gentlemen," as Burgoyne called them later, had discussed with Burgoyne what to do about Carleton, lest this year's shambles be repeated next year, and asked him to broach the matter in London. For the moment, Burgoyne was unable to make up his mind. There was no knowing, for instance, whether Carleton was in or out of favor in London. His wife, Lady Maria, had arrived with an Order of the Bath for her husband, in recognition of his defense of Quebec. This suggested that his standing was high, in which case silence would be the only politic course to take. On the other hand, Burgoyne knew that some ill-feeling had arisen between Carleton and Lord George Germain, for he himself had had to exercise considerable tact to avoid offending either party. What he did not know was that during the summer this ill-feeling had grown to uncontrollable hatred.

CHAPTER XI

HIGH COMMAND

THE quarrel between General Carleton and Lord George Germain caused endless mischief. Once these two officials had begun to insult and obstruct each other, relations between Germain and the other generals, which needed to be clear and straightforward during a war fought across three thousand miles of ocean, becme confused by suspicion, and out of this confusion grew the misunderstandings that led to the blunders that resulted in the disaster of Saratoga.

Why two such intelligent men of the world should have quarreled in the first place is a mystery. Horace Walpole says that Germain hated Carleton as one who, so he supposed, had been unfavorable to him over the Minden affair; for although Carleton had been in Canada at the time, he was a close friend of the Duke of Richmond, who was a personal enemy of Germain's and an outspoken leader of the opposition.[1] There may be some truth in this, in that Carleton possibly resented taking orders from a man who had been court-martialed for cowardice, but the notion seems to have occurred to Germain, if it occurred at all, after, not before, the quarrel had begun. Carleton was the aggressor, even if Germain regarded him with distrust from the beginning.

To start with, there was trouble over the northern army's quartermaster-general. Carleton appointed his own brother, Major Thomas Carleton. Germain appointed Lieutenant-Colonel Christie, the same who had canceled the order to build batteaux in England. When Christie arrived with Burgoyne, Carleton refused to allow him to take up his duties, so that during the critical days when the army was disembarking its stores, it was without a quartermaster-general. When Christie complained and abused Carleton to anyone who would listen, Carleton wrote to London demanding Christie's recall and set Burgoyne to tell Christie that any more such conduct would bring severe retribution on his head. Burgoyne tried in vain to calm Christie, pointing out that there must be a history behind all this. There was indeed, for Christie had opposed Carleton's Quebec Act and other measures. Christie then wrote a long letter to Germain denouncing Carleton as incompetent. Carleton, he said, pursued an incomprehensible plan and consulted nobody. He rarely gave orders and, when he did, usually countermanded them. He lost invoices and bills of lading; stores were either sent to the wrong units or left in the open; officers sailed up and down the rivers searching in vain for their tents, powder, wagons, guns, and provisions; Carleton had wasted precious days before ordering the construction of boats, then had foolishly tried to take the schooners overland in rainy weather; finally he had ordered fortifications to be built in useless places and employed Cnadians in useless tasks. Much of this criticism was probably spite, for such chaos is familiar to everyone who has served in any army; but some of it does seem to have been pertinent, since similar exasperation can be sensed in Phillips' letters to Burgoyne and Fraser.[2]

Meanwhile, in London, Germain was encountering his own troubles with Carleton. Having received from him only the briefest account of the expulsion of the Americans, Germain answered (14 May), in a letter otherwise highly flattering, with a mild regret that Carleton had sent no details of strengths, dispositions, etc., so that government could send its instructions.[3] This elicited no reply, although the complaint was reasonable in that Germain was trying to coordinate strategy between the armies on the Atlantic side and in Canada. Then in August there arrived a letter from General Howe, dated 7 June, expressing his concern over what would happen when his army joined Carleton's on the Hudson. Would he retain control over his own army, or would Carleton, the senior officer, have first call on reinforcements and authority over promotions? He suggested that the two armies should behave as allied armies do when camped side by side, each retaining autonomy over its internal affairs.[4] The problem, all questions of jealousy aside, was that Howe and his brother Admiral Lord Howe had recently been appointed peace commissioners. Therefore Howe's authority in America had to remain sacrosanct if he were to conduct negotiations. Another difficulty was that Carleton was deeply offended because he had not been invited to join the Peace Commission. Perhaps Germain had had a hand in this; although when it was formed nobody in London knew if Carleton, besieged in Quebec, was still in command, or a prisoner, or dead, and there was no time to wait. The Administration devised a rather too clever solution to Howe's problem. Since Carleton, they reasoned, was civil governor as well as military commander, he had no authority to cross the American border. His fine record as governor showed how urgently he was needed to restore good government in his province. Therefore Carleton should hand over the command of the army, once it had crossed the border, to Burgoyne. Moreover, since there was some doubt as to what was the border, the line would have to be readjusted. Ticonderoga, for instance, which had always come under the orders of the commander in Quebec, should now be considered as part of America. The implication of all this was that Burgoyne, being Howe's junior, could put himself under Howe's orders without embarrassment. The letter informing Carleton of the government's decision was sent on 22 August 1776.[5] Even if it was politically justifiable, there is no doubt that Germain regarded this solution with relish, for it was obvious that Carleton was not going to like it. By the same packet* he wrote to Burgoyne, saying that although Carleton would be properly honored for his defense of Quebec and subsequent victory over the Americans, Germain had been against awarding him the Order of the Bath until he had done something more positive to deserve it. He was not surprised by the Christie affair, but he would not allow a good officer, appointed by himself, to be ruined by the personal whim of any commander.[6]

Early in November there arrived a letter from Sir Guy Carleton (as he now was) dated 28 September, in which he at long last explained why he had not answered Germain's request for information. He had had no time to write lengthy letters, he said, because he had been very busy driving the Americans out of Canada, "a task which was happily executed long before I could profit by any Instructions your Lordship might think necessary to favour me with." He had hoped that his Lordship would have known that the next step was to build a fleet, including the three hundred batteaux he had particularly requested last November. Yet only ten had arrived so far, with parts for fourteen more. He supposed, he added with true Irish sarcasm, that the rest had fallen into the hands of the Americans or were still somewhere on the Atlantic, held up by contrary winds.[7] This was no way to write to the Secretary of State, and it ended any hope of proper relations between the two men.

Shortly after this the officer entrusted with the important letter of 22 August, telling Carleton to surrender his command to Burgoyne, reap-

* Dispatches for America from government offices were sent to the Admiralty, "to go as soon as may be." This often meant two to eight weeks' delay before they left England. Sometimes they were returned to the department, as the Admiralty assumed they no longer served a purpose. Sometimes they were sent so late that they caused more confusion on arrival than if they had never gone. There were nine packet boats intended to provide a monthly service, but storms, etc., caused further delays (PRO CO 5/136, p. 163; CO 5/253, p. 123). Carleton, for instance, once went ten months, from October 1777 to July 1778, without orders or news from England, and this at a time of supreme crisis, during which Burgoyne surrendered. Howe resigned, he himself resigned, and France entered the war! Uncertain communication was the worst single hazard faced by the British in the American Revolution.

peared with the news that he had been unable to reach Quebec owing to ice in the St. Lawrence estuary. This, said the *Morning Post*, "has distressed Administration more than all the unlucky accidents that have befallen them during the whole of the American campaigns."[8] No doubt it had. The tantrums that would follow when Carleton learned, a year too late, of the change in his status, were unpleasant to imagine, for he would pass the winter in the happy belief that he was to lead the next year's victorious invasion of New York. At about the same time came news that Howe had defeated Washington on Long Island and Manhattan. All England rejoiced, though Germain knew that these victories should have been won at the beginning, not the end, of the year; nor could he help noticing that Howe had allowed the entire American army to escape each time he had routed it. Clinton's expedition to South Carolina had failed miserably, owing to storms at sea, Lee's clever defense, and the inability of Clinton and Admiral Parker to agree about anything. Finally came news that Carleton had destroyed Arnold's fleet, captured Crown Point, and then inexplicably taken his army back to Canada, while Burgoyne was coming home without leave. So much for finishing the war in one campaign. Germain must have wondered what manner of generals these were whom the king had in his service.

Naturally, when Burgoyne arrived in London late at night on 9 December he found the town buzzing with rumors about himself. Some newspapers said he had quarreled with Carleton over "an etiquette" (i.e., who was to command where), others that he had arrived in very bad health, or in very good health.[9] The often repeated story that he was out of favor at court because he was associated with Carleton's behavior and had to beg an audience with the king is not true and owes its existence, like so much of the misinformation about this period, to Horace Walpole.[10]

Burgoyne had certainly been worried that his return might be coolly received, and from Portsmouth he wrote to Germain protesting his ardor for the king's service. He explained that Carleton had wanted him to come (as Howe had done the year before) to expound the plans for the next year in person.[11] During the voyage he had written the report Carleton had desired of him. Carleton's original memorandum had consisted of a few short sentences on a small piece of paper. Burgoyne's "Memorandums & Observations relative to the Service in Canada" is sixteen foolscap pages long and very detailed.[12] Besides supporting Carleton's requests with facts and figures, Burgoyne set out in detail which regiments (totaling three thousand men) should be kept for the defense of Canada when the invasion of New York was resumed the next spring. This has encouraged historians to suppose Burgoyne already saw himself standing in Carleton's shoes. Perhaps he did, but it should be remembered that Burgoyne was merely doing what he had been ordered to do.

These papers, together with Carleton's latest dispatch (dated 22 October), Burgoyne presented to Germain at noon on 10 December. The dispatch merely said, without apology or explanation, that cold weather would make it impossible to reestablish Crown Point. The army had, therefore, gone back to Canada. The Americans would probably build another fleet during the winter. The sting was in the tail, for it ended:

> I cannot omit on this Occasion, mentioning to your Lordship the great Satisfaction I have received from the Services of General Burgoyne, not only from the Zeal and readiness with which he concurred with me in promoting His Majesty's Service, but from the attention and assiduity which he showed in discountenancing & preventing all faction and party in this Army; Dispositions which, your Lordship must be sensible, when unfortunately they are encouraged by Persons eminent by their Stations, are capable of defeating the most zealous Endeavors, and of rending abortive the best concerted plans of Operation; the candour and fairness, therefore, of General Burgoyne's Conduct in this particular, as well as his alacrity upon all occasions, deserves this acknowledgment in return.[13]

It would be hard to decide whom this must have embarrassed more. Without permission, Carleton had dragged Burgoyne into his feud with Lord George; he had accused Lord George of subverting the campaign by planting troublemakers in the army and had hidden behind Burgoyne while saying it. Finally, he had implied that Burgoyne, too, was aware of Lord George's malpractice and justly despised him for it.

Many historians have written that when Burgoyne reached London and saw that Carleton had fallen from grace, owing to his abandonment of Crown Point, he forgot his vows of silence and intrigued against his chief in order to supplant him. The charge was first made after Saratoga. Burgoyne hotly denied it as "abhorrent to the honour of an officer and the liberality of a gentleman."[14] Yet his refutation was vague and unconvincing, and because we have evidence to suggest that Burgoyne did criticize Carleton, it is usually accepted now that the charge was true. Carleton's letter, I think, explains why he did it, and to a great extent it exonerates him, for what loyalty could he owe to a man who had compromised him so unscrupulously?

Carleton's character was baffling. An Irish Protestant, of all Protestants the most anti-Catholic, he had protected the Catholic Church in Canada for the wisest of political motives. He had treated Montgomery contemptuously, yet buried him with full military honors. Regarding the rebels with disdain, he had twice sent all his prisoners home.[15] His defense of Quebec and his advance from Quebec to Trois Rivières had been masterly. Yet he had let the entire American army escape to fight another day; then, having gone to such pains to build a fleet to carry his army over Lake Champlain, he had left the army behind, against the advice of all his officers, when the hour came to move. He had consistently rejected or ignored every proposal made by Burgoyne, Phillips, or anyone else, and he had needlessly offended many officers over trivialities. He would stand no interference with what he regarded as his private empire and was quarreling with Germain not only over Christie, the use of Indians, and other matters, but also over the appointment of judges and civil officers. Humane and visionary, reserved and distant, he could be petty and vicious when he thought himself threatened. Perhaps, therefore, he was suspicious of Burgoyne's too polished manners and decided to forestall any intrigue by setting Burgoyne and Germain at odds. To Germain, who knew only some of the facts, it all added up to the conclusion that Carleton was too slow and had bungled the campaign. Burgoyne, at the interview, seems to have confined himself to a few remarks about Carleton's rejection of the plan for the Mohawk expedition.[16]

There is one curious fact about this quarrel: Neither Carleton nor Germain ever got their facts right about the other. Germain blamed Carleton for not using Indians and for withdrawing from Crown Point, yet in both decisions Carleton was more in the right. Indians were too dangerous, and Crown Point could never have been kept up, on the enemy's doorstep as it were, through a Canadian winter. Burgoyne's proposal to establish "posts" across 120 miles of blizzard-swept ice was simply naive. Germain never learned that Carleton's fatal mistake had been not in October but in June, when he had delayed after Trois Rivières and allowed the Americans to escape from Canada, for it was this which led to all subsequent British misfortunes: the delay on the lake and the failure to reach Ticonderoga until too late, which in turn fatally delayed and hindered the campaign the following year. Conversely, Carleton always assumed that Germain was the man responsible for not sending the batteaux. Had he known it was Christie, he would have had just the reason he needed for getting rid of him. Burgoyne's misfortune in all this was that he was directly in the line of fire between his two superiors. One false step could incur the enmity of either, and both were powerful enough to wreck his career.

Why did Carleton bungle the campaign? Some have put it down to incompetence, without explaining how we are to square that with the brilliance of his performance up to Trois Rivières. Others have said that he let the Americans escape deliberately. He did not wish to inflict too crushing a defeat on them, so the argument goes, and thereby push them over the brink of irreconcilable war. After the Declaration of

Independence, he realized that he had miscalculated and, appalled by the enormity of his blunder, tried to shift the blame onto Lord George by means of one trumped-up excuse after another, such as the failure to send batteaux and the presence of "traitors" in his army.[17] A similar motive was attributed to Howe when he failed to capture Washington's army on Long Island and Manhattan.[18] It makes more sense applied to Howe, for he was a peace commissioner anxious to lose no chance of negotiating. Carleton, surely, would have been more likely to induce a mood for negotiation in Congress by capturing the American army than by letting it go. Moreover, such a motive is inconsistent with his attitude to rebellion, for he had "always believed," he wrote once, "that the American leaders had from the beginning been intent on keeping the war aflame by any means, for therein lay their only hope of safety."[19] An explanation not offered so far is that he was so hurt on learning that he was not invited onto the Peace Commission (of whose existence he heard just before the Battle of Trois Rivières) that he lost interest in the war and sulked, like Achilles in his tent. This is borne out by his temperamental behavior at the time of Saratoga.

The king, far from refusing to see Burgoyne, was anxious to see him as soon as possible; indeed, Germain had to ask to see the king first, in order to relate his own version of what had passed at the meeting with Burgoyne.[20] Burgoyne therefore attended the levee at St. James's next morning (11 December) and had a long conference with the king that afternoon. Two days later the king wrote to Lord North of his decision. Carleton was *not* to be dismissed, for that would be unjust and cruel. "Perhaps Carleton may be too cold or not so active as might be wished, which may make it advisable to have the part of the Canadian army which must attempt to join Gen. Howe led by a more enterprising commander." He concluded, "Burgoyne may command the Corps to be sent from Albany and Phillips must remain with Carleton in Canada."[21]

Burgoyne may or may not have been told of this decision. Many people were complaining against him for supporting Carleton, saying that in not criticizing his chief he had thrown away an opportunity for promotion he would not find again.[22] Burgoyne knew how ministerial decisions changed from day to day and did what he could to keep in the ministry's favor. It happened, for instance, that the Duchess of Northumberland died, and her son Lord Percy went up to the House of Lords. This left a vacant seat in the Commons, which Burgoyne determined to fill with an Administration supporter, his aide, young Lord Petersham. He achieved this by a piece of election rigging so blatant that it would make any modern practitioners of political sabotage and "dirty tricks" green with envy. The procedure was that the vacancy would be proclaimed from the hustings and one hour allowed for voting. Burgoyne contrived to have the election held even before the duchess was buried, so that the opposition had no time to campaign. Then he bribed the high bailiff of Westminster to bring the time forward by half an hour, from noon to 11:30, without informing the opposition. Finally he ensured that voting tickets were sent only to his own supporters. Presenting himself and Lord Petersham at the hustings beneath the portico of St. Paul's Church, Covent Garden, and bringing with him his officers and voters, Burgoyne was able to declare Lord Petersham the winner by noon. At that moment, however, the opposition, in the person of Sir Watkin Lewes, appeared puffing and blowing, having just learned what was going on, and demanded fair play. The high bailiff had prudently posted a cordon of constables around the hustings. Lewes' supporters, having no tickets, were legally not "voters" but a "mob," and the constables refused to allow them to reach the poll. A riot threatened. A deal was done. Since the tickets were presumably "lost in the mail," the high bailiff allowed the opposition to vote but charged a shilling a head. After a few minutes, however, the writ and returns were snatched up, taken into the church, and counted behind locked doors. Lord Petersham was again declared duly elected. Opposition newspapers cried that if this kind of unconscionable fraud were permitted in violation of the law and of the wishes of the electors, English citizens had no longer even the shadow of the rights of election left to them.[23]

After Christmas news arrived that Clinton was coming home in a huff. He was indignant that his account of the Carolina expedition had been published in an edited, and so distorted, version, and he wanted to vindicate himself. Germain commented to his deputy, Knox, "Burgoyne will not be sorry to see he is not the only General, second-in-command, that takes that liberty, without the King's leave."[24] Burgoyne, however, had just had another audience with the king, during which he had humbly laid himself "at his Majesty's Feet" for active employment and was now off to Bath for a cure. He begged Lord George for his patronage in obtaining a command and said he would be available at one day's notice.

Clinton was a threat, for it was very probable that the administration would give him the important Canadian command to quiet him down. Indeed, on 24 February the king wrote to Lord North to say that Germain was going to propose Clinton for Canada and Burgoyne for New York under Howe, adding "I thoroughly approve of this."[25] Accordingly, Burgoyne submitted to Germain on the very day that Clinton arrived (28 February) a long memorandum entitled "Thoughts for Conducting the War from the Side of Canada."

It turned out that Clinton, who wanted the Canadian command very much, was diffident about asking for it and was satisfied with an Order of the Bath (or "Red Ribbon") instead. On 1 March the command was given to Burgoyne.[26] No doubt his "Thoughts" decided the government in his favor, yet it has been said that Burgoyne was the worst possible choice for command in such a theater of war. He was a dashing cavalryman through and through, yet he was to lead an army, consisting entirely of infantry and artillery, in a slow and laborious progress through forests and swamps, over rivers and innumerable obstructions, far from any base of supply. Clinton certainly possessed some of the patience and foresight required for this type of warfare; yet it may be wondered how he would have managed with Carleton. Carleton was cold, condescending, and prickly. Clinton was shy, and almost paranoiacally touchy, always imagining insults where none existed. Neither was tactful. Whoever went to Canada would have to tell Carleton that he was to lose his army, and it would not have been long before Carleton and Clinton were either not on speaking terms or formed into a close alliance against Germain. On the other hand, Burgoyne was just the man to handle this sort of situation perfectly. Perhaps this consideration partly influenced the government in its decision. Besides, Howe had particularly asked that Clinton return to him in New York.

Burgoyne's "Thoughts"[27] said very little not said before. The facts and figures concerning the regiments to be left in Canada and the force to go down to Albany (at least eight thousand men) he had already given in detail in his "Observations" on Carleton's memorandums. He reemphasized, too, the need for a "weight of artillery" to blast aside any obstacles the Americans could put across the land roads. This would be especially necessary for taking Ticonderoga, which he supposed garrisoned by twelve thousand men. He doubted that any fleet the Americans might have built for the lakes would be very formidable, but should their navy be strong on Lake George, there was the alternative route south, a bad second best, via Skenesborough, Fort Anne and Fort Edward. Anticipating possible trouble from Carleton or, more likely, his staff, Burgoyne was anxious to be held free from any blame for anything that went wrong before the army crossed the border.

Howe had recently written (30 November) that if the action along the Hudson were successful he intended in the autumn to take a strong force southward to capture Philadelphia.[28] Therefore, Burgoyne summed up:

> These ideas are formed upon the supposition, that it be the sole purpose of the Canadian army to effect a junction with General Howe, or after cooperating so far as to get possession of Albany and open the communication to New York, to remain upon the Hudson's River, and enable that general to act with his whole force to the southward.

Some historians have said that this paragraph is ambiguous; but if it is read, as it was intended to be, with Howe's letter of 30 November in mind, it is perfectly clear.

In the same letter Howe had mentioned transferring an army of ten thousand men to Rhode Island, whence they could advance up the Connecticut River. Carleton had also mentioned the possibility that part of his army could advance down the Connecticut, and Burgoyne, therefore, suggested that the junction with Howe might be effected on that river instead of the Hudson. After giving details of the Mohawk expedition, which Carleton had finally approved, Burgoyne suggested that if the government felt the Canadian army was not strong enough to carry out such operations, the entire force could be transferred by sea to New York. Indeed, the commander should be allowed latitude to do this anyway, should he find the circumstances of the war radically changed when he arrived in Quebec. This should be done only as a last resort, however, since it would require a large force to be left for the defense of Canada, which would deplete the numbers sent to Howe. Nor did he think it would be as effective as an invasion from Canada via Ticonderoga. Some have said that to send the army by sea to New York was the most sensible idea in Burgoyne's paper and that it is strange that the government should have rejected it. Yet it would have required a large concentration of ships in Canada, ships which were already destined elsewhere. The army was in Montreal and could hardly have reached New York before August or even September. Finally, the British would have been left with a single advance from New York, the disadvantages of which were only too well known, and a dangerously exposed Canada.

Burgoyne's "Thoughts" and his earlier "Observations" were read by a senior military officer, either General Harvey or Lord Amherst, who submitted his own comments to the king on 5 March. In the main, he approved of everything, though he thought the numbers for the Mohawk expedition were "but Small."[29] He thought not employing Indians a "mistaken Idea of Humanity" and insisted commanders should be "put out of Doubt" on this question. He disliked the idea of going around to New York by sea. The king summed up these opinions in a short directive of his own, which set the seal of royal approval, as it were, on the entire venture.[30] He wrote that Burgoyne was to be ready to sail on the *Apollo* on 20 March. This had already been arranged by Lord Sandwich, to Burgoyne's delight, since his friend Philemon Pownoll was to be the captain. When the Admiralty, owing to some bureaucratic mix-up, suddenly changed its mind and put him on another ship, Burgoyne had to resort to some bureaucratic bullying and blackmail ("There have never been more pains," he wrote, "to obtain the protection of the God Apollo!") to change it back again, and he sent Pownoll a silver drinking cup to celebrate his victory.[31] They would now be able to drink the ladies' health every day of the voyage, he added, and exercise his aide Sir Francis Clerk's talents for mixing the "negus," a drink compounded of sherry, sugar, hot water, and spices.

For the next three weeks Burgoyne occupied himself with preparations for the expedition. Phillips had ordered some more gunboats. He hoped that this time they would be standardized and not the assortment of all shapes and sizes of the previous year (Phillips had sent plans to make sure) and that they would be made of seasoned, not green, wood. In the Battle of Valcour Island, gun platforms had split or shattered after a few rounds, which had nearly lost the British the fight.[32] Indian presents were a problem; for the year before some fool had sent hundreds of blankets of a dun color which the Indians had regarded as grossly insulting, being a mark of slavery.[33] One thing Burgoyne did not lack was a wealth of new inventions. Lieutenant Twiss of the Engineers had designed a boat which anticipated the landing craft of World War II. It had a "mantelet or draw-board," pierced with loopholes for musketry, raised over a square prow, to enable troops to land in the face of enemy fire. Phillips had ordered a number of these in June 1777, but Major Blomefield, also of the Engineers, had been unable to find any material, in the course of experiments on Woolwich Common, that would resist musket shot at close range.[34] Blomefield himself had given thought to the problem of transporting boats overland. Accordingly, he had constructed a huge "Machine" with eight wheels "for carrying great Weights with the least degree of friction possible," which he hoped would transfer all the boats from Lake Champlain to Lake George in a few days. Burgoyne approved it and it was packed on board the man-of-war *Proteus*. It happened, however, that in the autumn the American ship *Alfred*, under the celebrated Captain John Paul Jones, had captured seven British transports, including the *Mellish* carrying twelve thousand uniforms for Burgoyne's army. The king had insisted that these be replaced immediately and ordered that they be taken on the *Proteus*, who could defend herself against anyone. The space being already occupied by Blomefield's "Machine," the uniforms were left on the quayside. When the king learned this, to "his great Chagrin & Surprize," he ordered the *Proteus* to be stopped. Angry letters flew to and fro, but the "Machine" was too complicated to unload. Thus Burgoyne's soldiers had to go without new uniforms and were forced to cut off the tails of their jackets and the brims of their hats for patching, so that they all resembled light infantrymen. Colonel Congreve, father of Congreve, the inventor of rockets and common matches, devised a gun carriage which could be dismantled and carried on horseback through forest trails. Several of these were allotted to Fraser's Advanced Corps,[35] the first occasion on which this familiar piece of equipment was used in any army in the world. Finally, Lieutenant Schanck of the navy had been experimenting with his famous "sliding keel," which could retract into the hull of the boat and enable it to sail from deep into shallow water. Unfortunately he had been too busy building ships to perfect this useful invention in time for the campaign.

So far everything had been straightforward. The campaign was simply to pick up where it had left off and accomplish what it should have accomplished the year before: that is, the junction with Howe and all the benefits flowing therefrom.

The manner in which this grand strategy was hopelessly spoiled is one of the great puzzles of history and has never been satisfactorily explained. The participants, the king, Germain, Burgoyne, Howe, Clinton, and Carleton, knew they were standing for a moment at the center of the world's stage and needed no reminding of the importance of their roles. Howe, indeed, longed to be rid of his. They assumed they were acting in a great epic and were not to know that later generations would read it as a period farce, complete with crossed letters, thwarted ambitions, jealousies, and misunderstandings. After Saratoga, the truth, if anyone knew it even then, was effectively buried by the determination of everyone to put the blame onto everyone else. Inevitably a vast amount has been written on the subject, different historians attributing blame according to their several points of view. Each has contributed a new fact here, a new explanation there, so edging us gradually nearer to an understanding of what must have happened. Similarly, the account which follows contains facts and certain items of evidence which have so far been overlooked.

Trouble first arose from Howe's letter of 30 November 1776, for if he were to operate on the Hudson, in Rhode Island, and in New Jersey he would need, he said, a reinforcement of fifteen thousand to bring his present strength of twenty thousand "effectives" up to thirty-five thousand. Congress, he added, had just voted fifty thousand for the American army. Germain, alarmed, could promise only eight thousand, and on 14 January he wrote to tell Howe that since his returns showed Howe's strength to be twenty-seven thousand, surely this would bring his total up to the required thirty-five thousand.[36]

Meanwhile Howe, who had obviously had doubts about his request, sent another plan, dated 20 December and called his "2nd Plan," requiring no reinforcements at all. However, it was a complete change from everything that had been agreed on for the past year and a half. He said that since his success against Washington and pursuit of the shattered American army across New Jersey had disposed the inhabitants of Pennsylvania to peace, he would take advantage of this by making Philadelphia the prime object of the next year's campaign. This would mean reductions elsewhere. Only two thousand would be left in Rhode Island (captured by Clinton shortly before his return to England), five thousand in New York, and three thousand to "act defensively" on the Hudson below the Highlands, their real purpose being to protect New Jersey on the northern side. Burgoyne could hardly reach Albany before September, he said, and the decision as to what the Canadian army should do thereafter could be left until then.[37]

Howe had no sooner sent off this letter than Washington recrossed the Delaware, wiped out a German regiment at Trenton and then inflicted a sharp defeat on the British at Princeton. The numbers involved were small, but the moral victory was enormous. Tom Paine's pamphlet "The American Crisis," with its stirring opening "These are times to try men's souls," had just appeared, and the Americans were "all liberty mad again."[38] Washington had declared to the world, in effect, that the Revolution was still on and that, far from being a desperate bid for power by a small gang of self-seekers, it was a great popular movement.

Yet the warning was lost on Howe, who persisted in supposing the Pennsylvanians disposed to peace. He had changed his mind about the war. Success lay, he now thought, not in defeating Washington in battle but in occupying large tracts of territory, and, above all, the rebel "capital," Philadelphia. Thus, at the very moment when he should have turned back to the Hudson as still the best, if not the only, hope of reconquest, he lost interest in it.

General William Howe, tall, dark, and thick-set, had none of Burgoyne's volubility and quick intelligence, less still his taste for literature, and he found the labor of thinking out strategy and dealing with the massive correspondence of a commander-in-chief not only uncongenial but painful. Lee, in an acid letter, described him as

> the most indolent of mortals . . . scarcely ever read the letters he signed . . . naturally good humoured, complaisant, but illiterate and indolent to the last degree . . . confounded and stupefied by the immensity of the task imposed upon him. He shut his eyes, fought his battles, drank his bottle, had his little whore, advised with his counsellors, received his orders . . . shut his eyes, fought again. . . .[39]

In battle, on the other hand, Howe was "all fire and activity," totally fearless, as cool as Caesar, and, like Burgoyne, adored by the soldiers. Yet he did possess considerable intelligence of a sort and he had undoubted skill as a tactician, which makes his conduct of the war all the more baffling.

Howe's new plan of 20 December reached London on 23 February.

On 3 March, at the very time Burgoyne's "Thoughts" were being approved by the king's military advisers, Germain wrote to Howe: "I am now commanded to acquaint you that the King entirely approves of your proposed deviation from the plan which you formerly suggested, being of the opinion that the reasons which have induced you to recommend this change in your operations are solid and decisive."[40]

Although Howe made no such promise, Germain seems to have assumed he would return to the Hudson after capturing Philadelphia, thus securing both the rebel "capital" and the Hudson-Champlain valley in a single year. That Howe had waived his request for reinforcements meant that Germain would not have to face Parliament with yet another plea for more men, at a time when the nation believed the war to be as good as won. The trouble he was having with Carleton and Clinton probably made Germain more amenable to any suggestion from Howe. How else are we to explain the haste with which he approved Howe's change of plan, before even examining its consequences? Whatever his reasons, Germain committed himself and in doing so left himself no room for maneuver. It was his first and worst mistake.

In the same letter he informed Howe that instead of the eight thousand reinforcements offered in his last letter, only five thousand could be sent; but since the new plan required no reinforcements, presumably this would not put Howe to any inconvenience. When Howe read Germain's two letters of 14 January and 3 March and realized that Germain had included sick, wounded, killed in battle, and prisoners with the Americans as part of the "strength" of his army, thus arriving at his total of twenty-seven thousand instead of the actual twenty thousand, he suspected Germain of playing with figures for political reasons. His admiration for Germain, which had been strong, turned to distrust and contempt.[41]

The last week of March was a crowded one for Lord George and General Burgoyne, the more so since it was Easter week and all business had to be concluded before the government offices began their holiday on Saturday. On Wednesday 26 March, Burgoyne attended the king's levee at noon, had a final conference with the king afterward, and received his instructions. These were verbal, for the orders he took were in a sealed letter to Carleton. The only written orders he ever received were an extract Carleton gave him just before the start of the campaign.[42] This letter, dated 26 March, was from Germain. It informed Carleton of the letter of 22 August of the previous year (enclosing a copy), which had never been delivered. Germain then repayed Carleton for some of the abuse he had received during the last year by observing that as a result of the withdrawal from Crown Point, a number of insurgents had been freed to reinforce Washington's army, thereby enabling the rebels to achieve their success at Trenton. There was a grain of truth in this, although it was rather unfair to claim that it was only the arrival of Gates with seven hundred men from Ticonderoga that had inspired Washington to cross the Delaware. "Upon these accounts," Germain continued, "and with a view of quelling the rebellion as soon as possible, it is become highly necessary that the most speedy junction of the two armies should be effected. . . ."

The body of the letter dealt with the distribution of the forces in far greater detail than Burgoyne's "Thoughts." Not 3,006 but 3,770 troops were to be kept in Canada, though this included the 8th Regiment stationed at the western posts and some reinforcements. The force under Burgoyne was to be the same as it had been the year before: an Advanced Corps (the 24th Regiment and light infantry and grenadier companies from all regiments) of 1,568 men; a 1st Brigade of three regiments (the 9th, 21st, and 47th, less 50 men from each to stay in Canada) making 1,194; and a 2nd Brigade (the 20th, 53rd, and 62nd Regiments, less 50 men each) again making 1,194; all the Germans except Hanau Chasseurs and a detachment of 650; artillery as specified by Carleton and Phillips, plus some Canadians and Indians. The Mohawk expedition was to consist of one battalion of British regulars (200 men), a battalion made up of Sir John Johnson's volunteers and 133 other American loyalists, 342 Hanau Chasseurs, and as many Indians as possible. The expedition was to be commanded by Lieutenant-Colonel Barry St. Leger. Both these forces were to proceed by their different routes to Albany and put themselves under the command of Sir William Howe. Germain then continued:

> I shall write to Sir William Howe from hence by the first packet. But you will nevertheless endeavour to give him the earliest intelligence of this measure, and also direct Lieut. General Burgoyne and Lieut. Colonel St. Leger to neglect no opportunity of doing the same, that they may receive instructions from Sir William Howe. You will at the same time inform them that until they shall have received orders from Sir William Howe, it is his Majesty's pleasure that they act as exigencies may require and in such manner as they shall judge most proper for making an impression on the rebels, and bringing them to obedience, but that in so doing they must never lose view of their intended junctions with Sir William Howe as their principal objects.[43]

That night, it is said, Burgoyne played cards at Arthur's with Charles James Fox; and when he remarked that he hoped to have brought America to her senses before he returned to play again, Fox replied, "Burgoyne, be not over-sanguine in your expectations: I believe when you next return to England you will be a prisoner on parole."[44]

He left for Portsmouth on Thursday 27 March, staying with friends on the way, and arrived at Plymouth on Easter Sunday. There was no hurry, for storms were driving ships back into port.[45] This goaded Germain into writing sarcastically to his deputy Knox the following Wednesday, "I am sorry Burgoyne cannot avail himself of this fine wind. . . . I didn't know two winds were necessary before they could put to sea." Burgoyne, however, *was* availing himself of this fine wind, for next day the *Apollo* set sail for Quebec.[46]

Germain had promised to write to Howe by "the first packet" in order that the movements of the two armies should be properly coordinated. He never did so; or rather, he merely sent Howe a copy of the orders to Carleton, with no instructions as to what Howe was to do about them. As a result, Howe was left free to pursue his new plan of attacking Philadelphia, which lay in the opposite direction to Albany.

Many have been the explanations offered for Germain's behavior. One is the story of the "pigeon-holed dispatch." According to Lord Shelburne, Germain did write a letter to Howe but, being in a hurry to leave for the country, would not wait to sign it. When he returned to London he had forgotten about it, and the letter, duly docketed but unsigned, lay in a pigeonhole until it was discovered after the war.[47] This story is generally disbelieved, for other explanations have been offered on evidence more solid than that of Lord Shelburne, who was both a leader of the opposition and a notorious liar. Shelburne said he heard the story from one of Germain's deputies, but when the papers of William Knox, Germain's first deputy-secretary, were published in 1909, they were found to contain a story which appeared to show the incident in a truer light. He writes that when Carleton's orders were ready and Germain, who was about to leave for his home in Sussex, came downstairs to sign them, Knox pointed out that no letter had been written to Howe

> to acquaint him with the plan and what was expected of him in consequence of it. His Lordship started, and D'Oyley [the second deputy-secretary] stared, but said he would in a moment write a few lines. "So," says Lord Sackville, "my poor horses must stand in the street all the time and I shan't be to my time anywhere." D'Oyley then said he had better go, and he would write from himself to Howe and enclose copies of Burgoyne's Instructions, which would tell him all that he would want to know, and with this his Lordship was satisfied, as it enabled him to keep his time, for he could never bear delay or disappointment.[48]

Yet all D'Oyley would seem to have written was a brief covering note enclosing "Burgoyne's Instructions" (i.e., Germain's letter to Carleton of 26 March), along with some routine papers, for Howe's information. Howe received this package by the warship *Somerset* in June.[49] Thus, after Saratoga he was able to say that he had never been ordered to advance toward Albany; on the contrary, by Germain's letter of 3 March he had had the royal approval of his own plan to attack Philadelphia. Therefore, not only was he in no way to blame for the disaster at Saratoga, but also he was astonished that Burgoyne or anyone else had ever expected him to act along the Hudson. He had written twice, he said, first on 20 December and again on 20 January. Any doubts left by his first letter should have been removed by his second. In this, which he called his "3rd Plan," he proposed to attack Philadelphia from the direction of New Jersey with his main army, while a contingent went around by sea and attacked the city from the Delaware side. The rest of the letter (20 January) concerned reinforcements, of which he now demanded not fifteen thousand, or none, but twenty thousand! As for Burgoyne and the Hudson, they were not mentioned at all. *Since both these letters,* said Howe, *were answered by Germain's letter of 3 March,* Burgoyne had had an entire month in London during which to acquaint himself with the changed plans and therefore had no possible excuse for claiming that he expected Howe to meet him at Albany.[50]

Howe's defense has been the basis of the case against Burgoyne ever since. Historians have played several variations on the theme, but the theme itself can be reduced to this: Neither Germain nor Burgoyne ever defined exactly what they meant by a "junction" with Howe; therefore, they must have meant not a "junction" in the obvious sense of two armies meeting, but something else. It could be argued, for instance, that once over the Canadian border Burgoyne was technically under Howe's command and that, although the two armies would still be more than a hundred miles apart, they would be theoretically "in cooperation." From this rather strained argument it is concluded that Burgoyne always supposed he was strong enough to reach Albany unassisted by a corresponding move northward on the part of Howe. Once Burgoyne was in Albany, the Hudson could be "opened," in some mysterious way, to New York, while Howe amused himself in New Jersey or Pennsylvania. When things began to go wrong in August, after the Americans had decided to fight back instead of to surrender, then and only then did Burgoyne complain that Howe had done nothing to support him and that this, not his own incompetence, was the cause of all his troubles. After Saratoga Germain used this argument to shift the blame from himself back onto Burgoyne, and some historians have inclined more and more to the view that Germain, not Burgoyne, was in the right. After all, it is said, Germain had approved Howe's plan to attack Philadelphia for good reasons. Howe would still be between Washington's army and Burgoyne, and the capture of Philadelphia would bring under British control a wide corridor extending from Virginia to Canada. Thus, it is said, Germain did not thoughtlessly approve two plans that were contradictory, as he was accused of doing, for the plans were consistent. Weight is added to this argument by the fact that when Germain returned to London on 7 April, he had a conversation with General (by this time Sir Henry) Clinton, who was just about to return to New York. Clinton was skeptical, if not alarmed. The capture of Philadelphia, he maintained, would achieve nothing and lead nowhere; it would tie down a large part of the army holding it and completely undo the entire grand strategy that had been so carefully thought out. Surely, countered Germain, Howe would be finished in Pennsylvania in time to support Burgoyne in the autumn? No, answered Clinton, for only a small part of Howe's army would be free to return to the Hudson. Germain was noncommittal.[51]

The problem boils down to a single question: Did Burgoyne, or did he not, expect Howe or a large part of Howe's army to advance up the Hudson and join him in Albany? Most historians now believe he did not, rather that he always expected to reach Albany on his own. I think they are mistaken.

Firstly, if Burgoyne omitted going into the deeper purpose of the campaign (cutting the colonies in two, etc.) in his "Thoughts," it was because they were so familiar by then as to need no repetition. If, when he wrote "junction," he had meant something else, he would have said so. The entire idea was a pincer movement (as such an operation is now called), and there is no such thing as a pincer movement with only one claw.

Be that as it may, let us look at the documents:

1. In his notes on Burgoyne's "Thoughts," the king's military adviser (Lord Amherst?) had concluded that Burgoyne must "force down to Albany and join *att that Place"*; to which the king himself had echoed that the force from Canada must join Howe *"at Albany."*[52]
2. On 25 March (the day before he wrote his order to Carleton) Germain wrote to Lord Townshend, Master-General of Ordnance, concerning forty-six artillerymen intended for Rhode Island but accidentally posted to Canada instead. Germain asked that they nevertheless embark for Canada, "from whence they are to proceed . . . by way of Lake Champlain, until they join the army under General Howe, when they will receive his Orders for joining their respective companies. . . ."[53]
3. On 19 April Germain wrote to Howe concerning the 342 Hanau Chasseurs that Howe had requested. These had likewise gone to Canada by mistake but "would make Part of the Detachment ordered down the Mohawk River to Albany and join your Army."[54]
4. There is a whole body of correspondence concerning the brigadier-generals in Burgoyne's army, Fraser, Hamilton, and Powel. Their rank was purely "local"; that is, in Canada they were ranked as brigadiers but on the Army List they were still lieutenant-colonels. Howe

wanted these officers to revert to their real rank when the two armies joined in order to prevent clashes of precedence with officers senior to them in his own army. Indeed, by the letter of the regulations, they should revert to their rank of lieutenant-colonel the moment they crossed the Canadian border. Burgoyne naturally fought for his own officers and wished them to keep their local rank of brigadier-general as long as possible, at least until the two armies physically joined. Letters about this passed among Burgoyne, Howe, Germain, and Lord Barrington (Secretary-at-War) right through the campaign (references to this subject can be found in every one of Burgoyne's letters from May onward).[55] The fact that the officers were to join Howe's army and put themselves under his command is taken for granted throughout.

5. When Burgoyne arrived in Canada on 6 May, he wrote to Fraser saying, "the military operations, all directed to make a junction with Howe, are committed to me."[56]
6. Finally, there is a letter from St. Leger to Burgoyne. It is dated 11 August, when his force was delayed at Fort Stanwix on the Mohawk, and expresses anxiety over a strong American force coming to attack him. A diversion from Burgoyne, he said, would draw some of them away and "greatly expedite my junction with either of the Grand Armies." Obviously, St. Leger expected Howe's army as well as Burgoyne's to be in the vicinity of Albany. He could have received this notion only from Burgoyne or Carleton.[57]

Of the above letters, neither Germain's to Lord Townshend nor St. Leger's to Burgoyne has been published or mentioned before in discussions of this problem, so far as I can find, but they provide strong evidence in Burgoyne's favor. In all these references to a junction, for instance, there is no word that Burgoyne was ever expected to go further south than Albany itself. How then could Burgoyne, *in* Albany, be expected to form a junction, or "open a communication," with the New York army when that army was still below the Highlands 125 miles to the south? How could those forty-six artillerymen rejoin their units in Rhode Island or the Hanau Chasseurs join Howe's army in order to proceed to Philadelphia, where Howe wanted to use them, if the way had not been cleared for them? Howe, of all people, should have asked himself these questions, but they never seem to have occurred to him.

It has been said that since Burgoyne was at Germain's elbow during those weeks when Germain was answering Howe's correpondence, he must have been fully aware of everything that was going on. The fact is, however, that no one was at Germain's elbow. On the contrary, Germain seems to have spoken with the generals only at occasional and rather formal interviews. Clinton, for instance, had dined with Burgoyne in March and yet was astonished when he later learned of Germain's (and Howe's) change of plan. If Burgoyne had known that the

Hudson was no longer the important operation and that the old plan had been radically changed, he would have discussed it with Clinton, Howe's second-in-command and the most likely man with whom he would effect a junction in practice; yet he did not.

There is one remaining detail, not mentioned in previous discussions of Saratoga but worth dealing with here. In one of his speeches before Parliament during the inquiry into Saratoga, Burgoyne, defending himself against the charge that he was over-artilleried and so hampered in his movements, said that he took along some heavy guns in case he should have to spend the winter at Albany "without communication with New York."[58] At first sight, this sounds as if he had inadvertently let the cat out of the bag and that he had all along expected to reach and hold Albany alone. Yet, in the context of all that has been said, this surely means that, a junction with Howe's army having been effected and Howe having turned south to attack Philadelphia, an American countermove might sever the communication once again during the winter, a contingency he ought to be prepared for. Alternatively, Howe might never be able to get through to Albany at all, being blocked at the Highlands, and Burgoyne would need heavy artillery if he was to keep the city.

From all this it appears inescapable that Burgoyne left England in the belief that a cooperating action between the two armies, with a view to an eventual junction, as had always been intended and ought to have been achieved in 1776, was still the basis of the plan for 1777 and that Germain gave him no reason to think otherwise.

Why, then, did Germain not inform Burgoyne of the radical change of plan? Howe pointed out that his two letters of 20 December and 20 January (his "2nd and 3rd Plans") were answered on 3 March, which should have given ample warning to all concerned. This has been regarded as conclusive evidence against Germain and against Burgoyne too if Germain informed him of the letters.[59] Here, in fact, Howe made a mistake, whether deliberate or accidental, which has misled historians ever since.

The letters in and out of Germain's office were numbered in series according to correspondent and subject matter each year. Thus his letter to Howe of 3 March is endorsed "No. 5. Answer to No. 3 and 4. Approving plan of operations as altered in No. 4." Neither "No. 3" nor "No. 4" is the 20 January letter. "No. 3" was a letter from Howe, dated 20 December, concerning American strengths. "No. 4" was the letter, also dated 20 December, already referred to, wherein Howe first proposed an attack on Philadelphia as his primary object. The 20 January letter, the one which was supposed to have removed all doubt, has no series number or date of receipt. Moreover, it is heavily creased and tattered (indeed, it is hardly legible), as though it had been carried in a gentleman's pocket for a long time.[60] I have found no answer or reference to this 20 January letter anywhere in Germain's files. When, therefore, did it arrive and why was it not receipted and endorsed, as were all the other letters, especially important letters such as this?

Reports in the *New Daily Advertiser* and *London Chronicle* of 1 April 1777 say that an important dispatch from Sir William Howe in New York was brought to London by a messenger from Cork, in Ireland, where the ship carrying it had been blown by the same storm that had delayed Burgoyne's departure, and that it was delivered to Stonelands in Sussex, where Germain was spending his Easter holiday. If this was Howe's letter of 20 January, then a great deal that has so far appeared mysterious is explained.*

Firstly, it means that when Burgoyne left England, Howe's "2nd Plan" of 20 December was the only one that had arrived. Germain may or may not have told Burgoyne about it; the question is immaterial. It will be remembered that in that letter Howe proposed to attack Philadelphia with his main army, leaving five thousand in New York and three thousand on the Hudson below the Highlands, to "act defensively." In his answer on 3 March Germain had promised five thousand reinforcements. This would have brought the total on the New York side to thirteen thousand, of whom eight thousand at least could have been expected to fight along the Hudson, quite sufficient to prevent the Americans from concentrating against Burgoyne while threatened so dangerously in their rear. This was not as good as Burgoyne's original plan, but it would do, and, if Burgoyne was told of it, there is no reason to suppose he was alarmed.

The incident of Germain's hurry to be off on his holiday and D'Oyley's perfunctory covering note, which told Howe nothing, now becomes more understandable. This was Easter week, and everyone knows the increasing desire to get things out of the way that besets people when holiday time draws near. It had been a week of extraordinary pressure. Germain, besides finalizing the orders and coping with the vast amount of last-minute details, had had to attend several

* A reader familiar with these papers might object that the lack of a series number on Howe's letter of 20 January proves nothing since *private* letters were often not so numbered. The fact is, some were, and some not, but they *were* given receipt dates on the back and usually copied into the entry book, neither of which was done for this letter. The objection would not alter the fact that Germain's letter of 3 March did *not* reply to Howe's letter of 20 January, as Howe later claimed it did. True, in the House of Lords papers there is a chronology of Howe's correspondence with Germain, in which this letter is said to have been answered on 3 March; but that statement, together with all the papers, came from Howe himself as part of his defense. Nevertheless, even if the hypothesis—that Howe's letter of 20 January did not reach Germain before 1 April—is put aside on the grounds that one cannot prove a negative, I must reiterate that we are still left with the difficulty of explaining away the six items of evidence, listed earlier, showing that a junction of the two armies was expected by Burgoyne when he left England.

meetings with the other Secretaries of State, a Privy Council, and two levees.[61] On Good Friday afternoon (28 March), as Germain was leaving at last, Knox pointed out the lack of a letter to Howe. D'Oyley, equally anxious to be away, scribbled his note and left. The clerks fair-copied it and sent it post haste to the Admiralty, knowing that the convoys were due to leave at the first change of wind. Perhaps Germain intended to write to Howe at greater length when the reinforcements left the next month. But on Easter Monday, 31 March, Howe's new plan of 20 January arrived, which made it only too clear that Howe had lost all interest in the Hudson and Burgoyne's army.

It has been said that if Germain was not culpable in failing to write to Howe, he was certainly culpable in not writing at once to Burgoyne to warn him of what had happened. Yet consider Germain's dilemma. If he did write to Howe, he would have to send an order as detailed and peremptory as the order to Carleton, telling Howe exactly which troops to take to Philadelphia and which to send to the Hudson. But he had already persuaded the king and the ministers to approve Howe's decision to attack Philadelphia and had written to Howe on 3 March transmitting that approval. The new plan was merely an extension of the old. How could he explain to the king and government a sudden reversal of policy and write Howe a letter that would almost certainly provoke that general's indignant resignation, especially since Germain knew that he had let Howe down over the matter of reinforcements? On the other hand, what could he tell Burgoyne? To call off the whole campaign just as it was getting under way? To capture Ticonderoga, or at most Fort Edward, and wait there through another winter? After the previous year's failures, such a prospect was unthinkable, for by the next year, while the British had dithered about, the Americans would have grown immeasurably stronger and France might well have entered the war. Against this was the hope that if Howe made an early start and if Burgoyne was strong enough and brilliant enough to force his own way to Albany in the meantime, all might yet be well. True, there might be a risk to Burgoyne's army, but surely it would be better to risk even Burgoyne's army than to order a standstill now, which would throw away the last chance of success and be tantamount to admitting to the king, the government, Parliament, and the nation that the Secretary of State could not control the generals and did not in fact know what he was doing. Germain, therefore, not knowing what to do, hoped for the best and decided to do nothing. This would explain his curious, rather self-defensive conversation with Clinton on 7 April, and why Howe's letter of 20 January was not receipted or even copied into the entry books, why, indeed, Germain carried it about until it was so worn as to be scarcely legible. Thus it turns out that there may well have been a missing dispatch after all, though it was never the one Lord Shelburne or Knox imagined.

After Saratoga, Burgoyne conceived the notion that his army had been deliberately hazarded in order to prevent an overwhelming concentration of American forces against Howe. Historians, finding no word of proof that Germain had intended any such thing, have dismissed Burgoyne's accusation as nonsense.[62] Yet, if the interpretation given here is correct, Burgoyne was partly right: Germain did hazard his army, though for quite a different reason.

This brings us to the heart of the matter. Germain was unable to control the generals not merely because he lacked the personal force of William Pitt, but because the administration, being weak, had no means of disciplining the senior officers of the army. The generals had friends in, or belonged to, great families. Carleton had the Duke of Richmond. Clinton had the Newcastles and Lincolns. Burgoyne had the Derbys and their allies. Howe belonged indirectly to the royal family itself. The generals had seats in the House of Commons or House of Lords. If they were crossed they could abandon their posts of duty and come to London to make trouble for a government which had difficulty in finding generals to fight the war at all. Hence all those comings and goings across the Atlantic, those speeches in Parliament, backstairs intrigues, and letters to the newspapers, actions no longer permitted to officers unlucky enough to serve in those few countries which have at last learned the lesson that generals must never be allowed to meddle in politics. The generals went to war not in a spirit of loyal service to their king and country but, despite all their talk of "honour" and "duty," in the manner of men doing their country a great favor.

So it came about that on the night of 8 April 1777, the man-of-war *Somerset*, carrying her precious packet of papers which was to change irrevocably the course of history, weighed anchor off St. Helen's, Isle of Wight, and set sail for Halifax and New York.[63]

CHAPTER XII

"THIS ARMY MUST NOT RETREAT"

BURGOYNE reached Quebec on 6 May. This was the anniversary of the relief of the city, which everyone regarded as a good omen.

Carleton, infuriated by Germain's orders, hid his feelings and declared that he would provide everything for Burgoyne's army "with the same care and attention as if I was to command it myself."[1] Nevertheless, Burgoyne wrote to Fraser that night, "My situation is critical and delicate in many respects here. It has been still more so on the other side of the water, all which I shall take the first secure occasion to communicate to you."[2] In the same letter he told Fraser about the intended junction with Howe. This brings up a curious point. A few weeks later Burgoyne discovered a paper being handed about which published "the whole design of the campaign as accurately as if it had been copied from the Secretary of State's letter." He wrote to General Harvey saying that he had kept the plan even from his own "family" (i.e., staff) and wondered how the secret had got out. Yet he had told Fraser on the very first day, it appears. Burgoyne, forgetting this, asked Harvey to find out who in Germain's office was leaking information. He had forgotten also that the the complete plan had been published, briefly but accurately, in the London newspapers several times and that copies of these must have come over with the convoys. In the end it made no difference, for the Americans remained ignorant of British intentions. Many believed that the entire northern army would be taken around to New York by sea, as indeed Burgoyne had once suggested. This too had been published in the newspapers.[3]

It had been the mildest winter in living memory. Crown Point could have been held after all, though Carleton could not have foretold this in November. Nevertheless, it meant that the moving of the army toward St. Jean had gotten off to an early start. Burgoyne decided that he would open the campaign without waiting for the convoys of reinforcements and supplies following him from England. Difficulties arose immediately. He had specified two thousand Canadians to assist the army in its transportation. Carleton had ordered a *corvée* (under an old French feudal law men could be drafted into public service) of three hundred only, for he had not dared insist on more. Even these were surly, uncooperative, and deserting daily. When Burgoyne complained, Carleton replied, in effect, "I told you so." "If Government laid any great stress upon Assistance from Canadians, it surely was not upon any Information proceeding from me." There was no remedy, for "these People have been governed with too loose a rein, for many years, and have imbibed too much of the American Spirit of Licentiousness and Independence. . . ."[4]

Burgoyne moved to Montreal on 14 May, where he discovered that no provision had been made for horses to draw the field artillery and supply wagons. As no contract was placed until 7 June, by which time the army was already on the move, he has been severely criticized for this—yet he was by no means entirely to blame. In fact a letter from Burgoyne to Carleton, dated 20 May, shows that he had already asked Carleton to order seven to eight hundred horses and that Carleton had objected that so many were unnecessary. Burgoyne then wrote rather sharply to Carleton pointing out that although this number was not needed for attacking Ticonderoga, it would be needed afterward, and that it was only sensible to have the horses now on short call. After a week's delay Carleton replied, promising to order the horses and even another *corvée* if Burgoyne insisted, but he did nothing. On 5 June Burgoyne received a letter from Phillips (dated 4 June) saying that the horses had not been ordered. Since no horses or wagons were likely to be found in America north of Albany, the matter was very urgent. However, Burgoyne had already written to Fraser, requesting him to send the Advanced Corps to establish rendezvous posts along Lake Champlain as far south as the River Bouquet. In the same letter he mentioned that one thousand or more horses, together with the officers' horses, would go in convoy through the forest and meet the army when it reached Crown Point. This shows that he was still under the illusion that Carleton had attended to the matter. Without waiting for Carleton, therefore, he contracted for five hundred wagons and one thousand horses. As he explained in a coldly formal letter to Carleton, this was less than half the number required. Only fourteen days' supplies could be carried at a time, instead of the thirty days' stipulated, and there would be no transport for tents or soldiers' baggage. Carleton ignored this letter, the matter was dropped, and Burgoyne was subsequently blamed by historians for lack of foresight. The truth seems to be that although he had made a point, in his "Thoughts," of being held free of responsibility for anything that went wrong before crossing the American border, when it came to the time Burgoyne was too polite, or too mindful of his own delicate political situation, to bully Carleton as he should have done. Instead, he took Carleton on trust, with fatal results.[5]

There was confusion about the Indians. Lieutenant-Colonel St. Leger was ordered to take on at least one thousand Indians for his Mohawk expedition, but no one told him which nations they were to come from, where he was to find them, or how he was to supply them. He wrote to Commissary-General Nathaniel Day, an old and close friend of Burgoyne's, suggesting Niagara as the obvious rendezvous and asking for more information. Day replied that Niagara could not and would not supply so large a force. As for information, since he had no authority to correspond with St. Leger, he could not be expected to answer questions.[6] Colonel Daniel Claus, who had returned from London, was to lead St. Leger's Indians. However, he found that the Indians who had been under his care for the past fifteen years, and whom he could depend on, were all to go with Burgoyne, while he was to lead various groups of Iroquois whom, except for Thayendanagea, he hardly knew.[7] This was asking for trouble. Worse, two French Canadians of doubtful honesty and loyalty were to be in charge of Burgoyne's Indians. One was de Langlade, who was collecting warriors from the territories of the Great Lakes; he was the man who had planned and carried out the ambush and defeat of Braddock's column at Fort Pitt in 1755, a disaster from which the young Washington was one of the few officers to emerge with honor. The other was Luc de Chapt de la Corne Saint-Luc, who had led Montcalm's Indians during the hideous massacre at Lake George. After the war Sir William Johnson had dismissed him and replaced him by Claus. Sailing to France, Saint-Luc had been shipwrecked on the coast of New Brunswick and walked back to Quebec, a distance of seventeen hundred miles, in deepest winter. This feat had made him a hero in the eyes of the *habitants*. On the eve of the American invasion, Carleton had sacked Claus and replaced him with Major Campbell, Saint-Luc's son-in-law, to please the French and prevent Saint-Luc from stirring up trouble among his Algonkian and Ottawan friends. Notwithstanding this, when Montgomery's army arrived Saint-Luc changed sides and then, foreseeing that the Americans would not be in Canada long, he changed back again, but was taken prisoner and removed to Albany. From there he had escaped and returned, via New York, to Quebec at the end of May. Instead of punishing him for treason, Carleton put him in charge of Burgoyne's Indians. The strangest thing was that the officer who was most needed in Canada, Colonel Guy Johnson, was absent. After Carleton's interference, he had gone to London to obtain his commission as Indian Superintendent. Now he had it, and his authority over the Iroquois at least would be unquestioned. Yet Howe insisted on keeping him in New York, where he had nothing to do and was out of touch, at this most critical moment, with the warriors he should have been leading.[8]

On the same ship as Saint-Luc arrived Sir John Johnson, who had spent the winter in New York with his brother-in-law. He brought with him a letter from Howe, dated 5 April. It said that since Howe expected to be in Pennsylvania by the time the northern army crossed the border into New York, he would not be able to furnish much assistance to it, or even communicate with it, as soon as he would wish. However, he would leave a corps below the Hudson Highlands, which the Americans had now "obstructed with several forts." Despite these forts, he hoped a communication by shipping might be opened with the northern army eventually.[9] According to his own testimony after Saratoga, Burgoyne was not alarmed by this letter. He assumed Howe would soon receive Germain's orders, which would remove all further misapprehensions. Furthermore, in obedience to instructions, he had written to Howe three times explaining the plan, from Plymouth, Quebec, and Montreal. Howe, for his part, never admitted receiving any such information. In a letter to Germain, he mentioned in passing one letter from Burgoyne which he said did "not contain anything more material" than remarks about the lateness of reinforcements and supplies. In a letter to Burgoyne, however, he did acknowledge receiving all three letters but said merely that he would "observe their contents."[10] From this, historians have assumed that Burgoyne was lying when he told Parliament that he had informed Howe of his plans. It is evident, in my view, that Burgoyne was telling the truth but that he told Howe only twice, in his letters from Plymouth and Quebec. The letter that contained nothing material was from Montreal, dated 16 May, and in saying that he told Howe three times Burgoyne was merely making an honest mistake. It should be observed too that Sir John Johnson came from New York under the impression that a junction was to be formed between the two armies, for otherwise he would have told Burgoyne and St. Leger (on whose expedition he was to lead a corps of loyalists) differently.

The brigading of the army presented no problems as it was almost the same as the year before, except that the two British brigades were to consist of three battalions each to make them "square." The 1st, under Brigadier-General James Hamilton, was to consist of the 9th, 47th, and 53rd Regiments, and the 2nd, under Brigadier-General Watson Powel, of the 20th, 21st, and 62nd Regiments. The Advanced Corps was the same as before: that is, the 24th Regiment in the center, the light infantry companies of all the regiments in Canada (except the 8th) on the right under Major the Earl of Balcarres, and on the left the grenadier companies of the same under Major Dyke Acland. The German "Reserve," under Lieutenant-Colonel Breymann (whom von Riedesel called "chivalrous" but others called a drunken brute), was to act in conjunction with the Advanced Corps when necessary, for the army was not large enough to spare a proper reserve. The two German brigades of the line were under von Specht and von Gall; while a corps of Brunswick Dragoons was under Lieutenant-Colonel Baum. Being without horses or jackboots, which mercifully had never arrived, they were allowed to wear leggings, though were still burdened with their huge helmets and long swords.

One thing the northern army did not lack was artillery, for Germain had sent a huge "battering train" to Canada the year before in case Quebec had been taken by the Americans. During the winter Carleton and Phillips had chosen from this 138 pieces, of which thirty-seven were heavy guns (twenty-four- and twelve-pounders), forty-nine medium guns (six- and three-pounders), and fifty-two howitzers and mortars, a howitzer being simply a long-barreled mortar mounted on a traveling carriage. This powerful train was intended to reduce Ticonderoga, for there was to be no repeat of the disaster of 1758, when Abercrombie's men had been slaughtered owing to insufficient artillery. Consequently, all but a few light pieces assigned to the Advanced Corps (four of which were to be slung on horseback on the new Congreve carriages) were to be transported by ship. Phillips was nominally in charge of the artillery, but Burgoyne, waiving army regulations, appointed him as his own second-in-command and the duty fell upon Major Griffith Williams. In command of the German gunners was Captain Pausch, who later wrote an excellent memoir of the campaign.

We do not know the exact strength of Burgoyne's army, for figures given by different officers vary; but roughly there were between 3,250 and 3,724British regulars, between 2,900 and 3,020 Germans, and a little over 500 artillerymen, including 100 Germans. If we add to this the 150 Canadians and the 400 or so Indians who appeared at the River Bouquet when the campaign opened, we have a total fighting strength of a little under 7,800 men.[11] If we further add officers (who were not counted on all returns) and noncombatants, such as musicians, cooks, batmen, and civilians (including women), we have a total "ration strength" of something over 10,000 people. Yet the core of this army, the 6,500 or so regular infantrymen, was far short of what Burgoyne had stipulated: 8,000, including 1,000 reinforcements sent from England.

Nevertheless, if the army was deficient in numbers it was not so in ability and experience. Three of the regiments had long and glorious histories. The 20th, 21st, and 24th had been at all of Marlborough's greatest victories, Ramillies, Blenheim, Oudenarde, and Malplaquet; and some had fought at Fontenoy, Dettingen, Culloden, Minden, the taking of Quebec, and the siege of Havana. The 20th had once been commanded by the great Wolfe, when Lord George Sackville (Germain) had been its colonel. At Minden, by a mistranslation of the German orders, it had recklessly attacked a strongly defended position and fought off repeated charges by an entire brigade of French cavalry sent to brush it out of the way. It was to save his old regiment from annihilation that Lord George Sackville had been ordered to advance and had failed to do so. Notwithstanding the loss of half its officers and men and a complete lack of support from the British commander-in-chief, the regiment had attacked again and driven the French cavalry back in rout. This had tipped the scales at the critical moment and resulted in the defeat of the entire French army. Exclaimed the French general bitterly, "I never thought to see a single line of Infantry break through *three* lines of Cavalry, ranked in order of battle, and tumble them all to ruin!" It had been an impossible victory, the sort of feat people had in mind when they called the British infantry the best in the world; and veterans from that desperate campaign, looking with pride at the names embroidered on their standards, could be forgiven for regarding the coming adventure with contemptuous confidence.

As for Burgoyne's officers, for so small an army the concentration of talent and privilege was remarkable. Of the British officers alone, more than thirty were to become generals in later life. Four (Burgoyne, Phillips, Lord Petersham, and Acland) were already members of Parliament. Several were peers, of whom Lords Torpichen and Napier were still in their teens. The adjutant-general, Major Robert Kingston, had been a founder member of the 16th Light Dragoons and was with Burgoyne in Portugal. With Burgoyne also were young Edward Pellew, RN, the future Lord Exmouth (one of Nelson's best admirals) and the engineering genius Lieutenant Schanck, whose gun platforms were later to revolutionize naval warfare and of whom I have already spoken. With such regiments and such officers, Burgoyne had every reason to feel proud.

Between the British and the Germans, however, there was a certain mutual contempt. The German officers were mostly veterans of the campaigns of Frederick the Great and Prince Ferdinand, but the ranks were heavily weighted with most unmilitary men—schoolmasters, tavern keepers, old tramps, violinists, and such, who had been high-handedly rounded up and packed off by their princes. The British regarded their German allies as brave, but stolid and slow. They all looked alike (a complaint, incidentally, which the Germans themselves made about the Americans). They sang marching songs, mostly indeed hymns and psalms, which filled the British with a sense of deep melancholy, and they were prone to the most peculiar outbreaks of collective depression, standing together and weeping that they would never see their beloved and beautiful homeland again. Some declared they were going to die; they then lay down, became ill, and died. No one could suggest any cause but homesickness. The Germans, for their part, regarded the British as overbearing, conceited, and yet withal amateurish in soldiering and slovenly on parade.

Of the American loyalists Burgoyne entertained high hopes. Their commander was Colonel John Peters, a Yaleman and a judge, who had been a member of the New York Provincial Congress. Believing the rebellion to have been the result of a conspiracy between dissenting clergymen and smugglers,[12] he had broken with his family, who were all strongly prorepublican and patriot, and come to Canada after the mob had burned down his house. The most important of the Americans, however, was the tall, handsome, and ebullient Philip Skene. A veteran of the last war, both in the West Indies and on Amherst's campaigns, he had obtained the grants on large tracts of land south of Ticonderoga. He had built a village, sawmills, and a stone house for himself near South Bay, which he renamed Skenesborough, and imported settlers from his native Scotland to live there. He had also bought a barge, in which he liked to travel about on the lake, rowed by Negro slaves in wigs, gloves, and full livery. He kept his mother's corpse lying on a table in a room of his house, for under the terms of an annuity she was to receive money so long as she remained "above ground." During the dispute between New Hampshire and New York, he had played a double game, befriending Ethan Allen (who admired him) and his "Green Mountain Boys" and betraying them to the New York authorities. When Allen and Arnold captured Ticonderoga, Skene was in London obtaining a newly invented post for himself as "Governor of Ticonderoga." Thus his schooner, which Arnold commandeered and renamed *Liberty*, had the honor of becoming the very first ship of the United States navy. Skene returned to America, against the advice of everybody, to take up his governorship and was arrested on landing. He was exchanged, despite his vociferous loyalism, and after a spell with Howe he returned to London. Now he was a sort of political adviser to Burgoyne, for he claimed great knowledge of the country through which the army was to pass. He believed the inhabitants loved him, when in fact they hated him. He liked to be addressed as "Major," or "Colonel," or even "General," though his real rank seems never to have been higher than that of captain.

During the weeks of preparation, the weather had been atrocious. The early spring, which had been so encouraging at first, had been followed by almost continuous rain for three weeks. Roads turned to quagmires, streams to rushing torrents. Bridges were swept away and movement was impossible for days on end. Being made of unseasoned wood, the hastily built carts warped and split. Lieutenant Hadden tells us that on the short journey from La Prairie to St. Jean more than half the wagons of his detachment were broken.[13] Nevertheless Burgoyne, working with energy and enthusiasm, overcame all obstacles and had the army ready to move by the middle of June. On the 10th he received his written orders from Carleton, and the next day he rode to St. Jean "without a stop." On this same day the forward units of the Advanced Corps arrived at the mouth of the River Bouquet. On the night of the 12th, Phillips gave a banquet to all the officers, and next morning the royal standard was hoisted aboard the *radeau Thunderer* and saluted by all the guns of the ships and forts. This flag, normally flown only when a member of the royal family is present, had been ordered to be displayed at three separate places in America at the commencement of the campaigns, as a sign to all loyal subjects that the king had not forgotten them and was about to reassert his authority on their behalf. After a review, Carleton left for Quebec and Burgoyne rode down the length of the entire army, answering the cheers of the soldiers by smiling and raising his hat. "Ah, my brave Springers!" he called out to the 62nd as he passed. It was a Devonshire word (most of the men coming from that county) for an ambitious young man nothing can stop, and, if tradition is to be believed, it was adopted henceforth as a regimental nickname.

The fleet had been augmented by a new warship, the *Royal George*, even larger than her sister *Inflexible*, and, of course, by the American gondola and cutter taken the year before. Scouts had reported that the Americans had built no ships on Lake Champlain during the winter. The guns were therefore taken out of the British ships to make room for stores. The two warships were to tow a pontoon bridge designed by the ever inventive Schanck to connect Crown Point with the eastern shore, at exactly the place where the bridge crosses today.

Burgoyne boarded the *Maria* and left Isle aux Noix on 17 June, reaching the Bouquet River on the 20th. On emerging from Cumberland Bay, the first rendezvous, the fleet ran into a storm. The batteaux bobbed up and down on the chopping waves, taking in dangerous quantities of water. The Germans, unable to get around the cape or see the fleet through the veils of driving rain, were scattered and forced back to shore. With evening, calm returned, and Burgoyne landed to address a party of four hundred Indians who were awaiting a word from the general. They were mostly Iroquois or Iroquois-related tribesmen from Canada and were commanded by Major Campbell and Captain Alexander Fraser, a nephew of the brigadier-general. He was universally liked and admired by the army and had raised and trained a corps of sharpshooters picked from the British regiments, with whom these Indians were supposed to cooperate. During the winter he had gone native, entertaining his fellow officers to suppers of "wild meats"; but he still found the Indians difficult to control. Of the large body of Western Indians under Saint-Luc, there was as yet no sign.

The Iroquois, resplendent in full war paint and regalia, admired those who were well-dressed and eloquent. Burgoyne did not disappoint them. Standing in a clearing in the forest, on a spot where Willsboro Public Library stands today, he treated them to a resounding speech full of fire and wind. Then he got to the heart of the matter. "This war to you, my friends, is new; upon all former occasions in taking the field you held yourselves authorized to destroy wherever you came, because everywhere you went you found an enemy. The case now is very different."

They were to kill, he explained carefully, only when ordered by their British officers. "I positively forbid bloodshed, when you are not opposed in arms. Aged men, women, children and prisoners, must be held sacred from the knife or hatchet, even in the time of actual conflict. You shall receive compensation for the prisoners you take, but you shall be called to account for scalps." These, he repeated, were to be taken from the dead, not from wounded or prisoners. Their rewards, their zeal, and the worth of their services to the king, their "never-failing Protector," would be judged according to the strictness with which they obeyed these orders.

The warriors chorused their approval with cries of *"Etow! Etow!"* and an old Iroquois chief was elected to make an answering speech.

> We receive you as our father, because when we hear you speak, we hear the voice of our great Father beyond the great lake. We rejoice in the approbation you have expressed of our behavior. We have been tried and tempted by the Bostonians; but we have loved our Father, and our hatchets have been sharpened by our affections.

Having promised to obey all orders they received or should receive, the old chief sat down to renewed cries of *"Etow! Etow!"* That night the Indians formalized the proceedings with a dance of war, which Burgoyne and his officers watched with mixed amusement and uneasy, prickling apprehension.[14]

On 25 June the fleet sailed southward in full array along the lake. It was a brilliant, thrilling spectacle. In front paddled the canoes of the Indians, Colonel Peters' Tories, who had dressed themselves as make-believe Indians for this campaign, and the Canadians in white summer smocks. Next, in gunboats, came the grenadiers of the Advanced

Corps, sitting upright in rows, their muskets and bayonets gleaming, the reds, yellows, and greens of their tall, miterlike helmets denoting their different regiments. Then came the main body of the army: in the middle the fleet of ships, their white sails barely catching the faint breeze, the senior officers standing in their pinnaces where all could see them, Burgoyne in full dress prominent on the *Maria*. On the right, in a flotilla of batteaux, rowed the British battalions, covering the mirror surface of the lake with lines of scarlet; on the left the Germans, with lines of light blue, dark green, and black. Martial music, sounding clear over the water, raised the spirits of the troops to the importance and excitement of the occasion. Behind sailed more boats of all shapes and sizes, carrying stores, cattle for food, farriers, clerks, drivers, the army's women, cooks, sutlers, and mechanics. Ahead, extending to the horizon, the water shimmered under the summer sky; on either side, it reflected the trees lining the shores of the lake and its islands. Wrote Sergeant Lamb of the 9th, "It looked like some stupendous fairy scene of a dream, which the waking fancy can scarcely conceive."[15] More prosaically, Burgoyne's aide, Sir Francis Clerke, observed that in the intense heat, the loss of the British uniforms (due to Blomefield's "Machine," it will be remembered) had turned out to be a blessing in disguise; for the shortened coats and brimless hats were not only more efficient in this country, they also gave the soldiers "a lively, smart appearance."[16]

Lord Balcarres, leading his light infantry in a rush against the crumbling walls, had found Crown Point deserted, and the army landed in stages between 26 and 27 June.

At Putnam Creek, Burgoyne stopped to issue a "Proclamation" to the inhabitants of New York, New Hampshire, and New England. After listing all his titles, by which he set himself up as a heaven-sent target for American satirists, he expounded the justice of the parliamentary cause and the wickedness of the rebellion, "the completest system of Tyranny that ever God in his displeasure suffer'd for a time to be exercised over a froward and stubborn Generation." He appealed to all those inhabitants who doubtless abhorred this usurpation to stay quietly in their homes, not to remove their cattle, hide their forage, break up bridges and roads, or block up streams. Everyone coming to his army would be protected, for he was "at the Head of Troops in full powers of Health, Discipline & Valor." As for those who disregarded his offer, trusting to distance to protect them,

> I have but to give stretch to the Indian Forces under my direction, and they amount to Thousands, to overtake the harden'd Enemies of Great Britain and America, (I consider them the same) wherever they may lurk. . . . The messengers of Justice and of Wrath await them in the Field,

> and devastation, and famine, and every concomitant horror that a reluctant but indispensible prosecution of Military duty must occasion, will bar the way to their return.[17]

On 29 June the army moved off again, landing next day on both sides of the lake a few miles north of Ticonderoga. Burgoyne issued a final General Order before the campaign was to start in earnest. In previous orders he had already informed the troops that they could not have been chosen to his better satisfaction. He had reminded his officers of the American skill in "Little War" and of the consequent care to be taken in clearing ground around the camps and posting sentries in concealed positions. Officers must inculcate into the minds of their men "a reliance upon the bayonet," which "in the hands of the Valient is irresistible. The Enemy convinced of this will place their whole dependence in Intrenchments and Rifle Pieces; It will be our glory, and our preservation, to Storm when possible." [18] Now, he told them:

> The Army embarks tomorrow, to approach the Enemy. We are to contend for the King, and the constitution of Great Britain, to vindicate Law, and to relieve the oppressed—a cause in which his Majesty's Troops and those of the Princes his Allies, will feel equal excitement. The Services required of this particular expedition, are critical and conspicuous. During our progress occasions may occur, in which, nor difficulty, nor labour, nor Life, are to be regarded. This Army must not retreat.[19]

Early on 1 July the forward units of the army rounded a bend in the lake and saw before them, just as the morning mists were evaporating in the heat of the ascending sun, the squat gray fortress of Ticonderoga. Cleared of all trees and undergrowth, the low promontory on which it lay appeared, in contrast to the dense forest that everywhere else came down to the very water's edge, as bald as the crown of a monk's head. The ground was zigzagged with trenches and earthworks. The muzzles of hundreds of artillery pieces poked through battlements and walls of fascines. Before the lines had been placed the inevitable tangled abatis of sharpened tree trunks and branches, the barbed wire of the eighteenth century. Above the fortress, and over the height of Mount Independence across the channel, flew the thirteen stripes of the United States of America. Stretched over the channel floated an enormous boom of chains and logs, the work of months of labor, and behind it a pontoon bridge. Ticonderoga, the "Gibraltar of the North," was the first, and as the army supposed the most formidable, obstacle barring the way to Albany, the junction with General Howe, and the strangling of the newborn republic while it was still in its helpless infancy.

The British believed that the Americans had between six and twelve thousand men in Ticonderoga. In fact there were little more than three thousand, many of whom were sick or without coats, packs, or shoes. Of the nine hundred militia, only ninety had bayonets. The new commander, Major-General Arthur St. Clair (whom Burgoyne called "Sinclair"), had been at the fortress barely two weeks, and he had even less knowledge of British strengths and intentions than the British had of his.

Some modern historians have claimed that Burgoyne knew all this from Carleton's spies but preferred not to inform his officers. Thus we have here, it is implied, yet another example of his vanity and stupidity. The intelligence reports, however, may be read in the files. There are seven of them, and they are consistent in stating that whereas the garrison at the end of March numbered between one and two thousand men, most of whom were militia, fifteen regiments raised in New England were on their way and would bring the strength up to at least twelve thousand men (two reports say twenty thousand). Only one informer doubted that the Americans would be able to raise more than six thousand.[20] In the event, small numbers of reinforcements did arrive, the last being twelve hundred who entered the fortress on 4 July, while Burgoyne was mounting his attack. Burgoyne was right in taking no chances. If he had told his officers that Ticonderoga was weak and it had turned out to be strong, his army would have had little confidence in him afterward.

General St. Clair owed his unenviable appointment to a quarrel in which he was not concerned. General Gates, it will be remembered, was of British servant-class origins. He was naturally happiest, therefore, among the republican-minded New Englanders and Bostonians, and he resented being under the orders of General Philip Schuyler, an aristocratic patroon of New York, whom he regarded as little better than an amateur. American generals were no more ashamed than their British counterparts of abandoning their posts of duty to air their grievances or further their careers. Gates had gone to Congress to tell tales against Schuyler. On being deposed as a result, the outraged Schuyler had likewise left his headquarters and gone to Congress to get himself reinstated.

Meanwhile, the care of Ticonderoga, the greater part of whose garrison had been withdrawn south, was left to Major "Mad Anthony" Wayne, who spent a miserable winter trying to keep seventeen hundred sick, cold, hungry, and dispirited men from packing up and going home. He hardly blamed them, for Ticonderoga, he wrote, "appears to be the last place of the world that God made, and I have some ground to believe it was finished in the dark." Nevertheless, aided by his engineer, Colonel Jeduthan Baldwin (who had himself complained of "this Retreating, Raged, Starved, lousey, thevish, Pockey Army in this unhealthy Country"[21]), he had managed to set the men to work on new blockhouses and abatis and to begin the bridge and boom before he left in April. Gates, on returning to power, had preferred to stay in Albany, where he could keep an eye on political developments. In June, Congress had changed its mind and reinstated Schuyler. In disgust, Gates went to Philadelphia, where Congress was sitting once again, to charge Schuyler with incompetence and treason. Schuyler meanwhile had appointed St. Clair, who had been with Howe, Carleton, and many of Burgoyne's older officers at Wolfe's capture of Quebec, to reorganize Ticonderoga in expectation of a British invasion.

The Americans could agree on strategy still less, however. Washington believed that the British lacked the power to take and hold the Hudson-Champlain line. He therefore suspected the Canadian army would join Howe by sea, for the region around New York was in his view the vital theater of the war. All he had to do, he said, was to keep Howe south of the Highlands, and the outcome of the war would be assured in favor of the Revolution. Consequently, Washington refused to send the requested ten thousand to Ticonderoga, which Wayne had in any case told him was strong enough to look after itself. Gates believed that Burgoyne and Howe should attempt to join at Albany but hoped Howe would not have the sense to see this; he was the only American commander to assess the situation correctly. Schuyler believed that the main British effort would be along the Mohawk and told St. Clair to regard any move on Ticonderoga as a feint. It made little difference, for St. Clair had but three thousand men to hold two thousand yards of defense works, not including Fort Ticonderoga itself, the new star fort and redoubts on Mount Independence, or the fortifications a mile or two away on Mount Hope. His chief scout, Whitcomb (the same who had shot Brigadier-General Gordon the year before), had been prevented by Captain Fraser's Indians from reconnoitering the British army, so St. Clair had no means of judging if this was a main force or a subsidiary one. Worst of all, despite Trumbull's warnings of the previous autumn, nothing had been done during all the squabbling to fortify Sugar Loaf Hill.

Burgoyne landed the Advanced Corps on the western shore, three miles below the fortress, to make a feint against the intrenchments and to work around as far as possible to the right. Breymann's Reserve was landed on the eastern shore with orders to approach, and if possible make its way around the far side of, Mount Independence. Burgoyne himself transferred to the *Royal George*, which he stationed in the middle of the lake, whence he could best control the two wings of his army. A boom was cast in front of the fleet to prevent any attack by fireships. As the Advanced Corps neared the American defenses, their marksmen experimentally shooting at any Americans who exposed their heads, the Americans opened an answering fire with all their muskets, rifles, and cannons, along the entire length of the line, against the express orders of St. Clair. Nevertheless, they captured an Irish light infantryman of the 47th, who had been so surprised he had fallen flat on his back. As he was taken, he swore, "By Jasus! I killed the man in the sally-port! A fair shot!" That night they got him drunk with a fellow Irishman pretending to be a loyalist, and he told them all they needed to know about Burgoyne's army and its purpose. Obviously this was no feint, and St. Clair realized that he was in a corner. If Ticonderoga fell, the only men who stood between Burgoyne and Albany were seventeen hundred Continentals (as soldiers of the American army were called) and one thousand New York Militia under Schuyler. Nor was there any artillery, for the few cannons there were had no carriages and were lying about in the streets of Albany. Nevertheless, St. Clair still hoped that the British would make a frontal attack on the lines, just as they had done at Bunker Hill. If they did that, the fort might hold.

Burgoyne intended no such thing, for he too had seen Bunker Hill. On 2 July a corps under Fraser took Mount Hope and cut off communications with Lake George. Breymann, on the left, was encountering trouble, however, for a narrow strip of swampy ground, actually the mouth of a creek, was forcing his brigade further and further inland in search of a place to cross, before they could continue their advance toward Mount Independence.

Burgoyne, meanwhile, had devised his trap. He ordered his chief engineer, Lieutenant Twiss, to go with an escort and climb Sugar Loaf Hill, in order to see if artillery could be mounted on its summit. Phillips had no doubts, for, he said, "Where a goat can go a man can go, and where a man can go he can drag up a gun." Twiss reported that a causeway for cannons could be built up the far slope, out of sight of the Americans, in twenty-four hours. Throughout 4 and 5 July, soldiers and pioneers, supervised personally by Phillips, cut down trees, cleared away bushes and rocks, beat logs flat into the ground, and then, using teams of oxen, hauled two light twenty-four-pounders, some medium twelve-pounders, and some eight-inch howitzers to the top of the mountain. What the Americans had thought to be impossible to do in ten months, at leisure, the British had done in two days in the face of the enemy and, moreover, in complete secrecy. It now only remained for Breymann, reinforced by a brigade under von Riedesel, to find a way to Mount Independence and the trap would be shut. By the evening of 5 July, however, his men, cutting their way through an undergrowth more impenetrable than any human defense, had still found no crossing.

How the secret of the guns on Sugar Loaf Hill was inadvertently revealed to the Americans is not certain. Some say Indians lit a fire on the hill. James Wilkinson, who was now St. Clair's second-in-command, says that the British guns bombarded ships in the channel, but this was so contrary to Burgoyne's orders that it is hardly credible. In his novel, *The Guns of Burgoyne*, Bruce Lancaster has a gun fired accidentally by a recruit, which is as plausible an explanation as any. Burgoyne, perhaps out of chagrin, does not mention the subject. Whatever the truth, from the moment St. Clair examined the heavy guns through his telescope, he knew that he had the choice between sacrificing his army for the sake of his honor or his honor for the sake of his army. Wisely, he chose to save his army, for the fort was lost whatever else might happen. That night the British were surprised by a sudden bombardment from the American cannons and later by the outbreak of several fires inside the fort. Here accounts differ. American reports mention only one fire, started foolishly by the drunken de Fermour, the French volunteer in command of Mount Independence. Digby, however, writes, "I never before saw such great fires," and says that his superior officers imagined the whole thing was a trick to lure them into an attack by moonlight. With the first glimmerings of dawn, all doubts were removed. Three deserters came in and said the garrison had escaped. Half had sailed up South River (as the upper part of Lake Champlain was called) toward Skenesborough, taking the sick and stores; the rest had gone from Mount Independence along the road to Castleton. Fraser, without awaiting orders from Burgoyne, took the fortress, and then led as many of his corps as he could find across the bridge. Four American artillerymen, who had been left as a heroic rearguard to prevent just such a crossing as this, were found in drunken sleep beside their guns. Fraser marched off at full pace in pursuit of the fleeing Americans. Burgoyne sent von Riedesel, with the Reserve and a regiment of Brunswickers (about one thousand men all told) to support him.

Burgoyne then ordered the gunboats to form up and attempt to shoot through the giant boom and the bridge, mounted on twelve sunken piers, behind it. The Americans had assumed these two barriers would prevent pursuit for at least a day. The gunners blew asunder both obstacles in half an hour, making a gap wide enough for the largest ships to sail through. Taking the best-sailing gunboats and ships with him, Burgoyne led the pursuit up the lake. Through the hot summer morning and into the afternoon, they sailed along the narrow, sluggish waterway. At times the lake was so narrow that the overhanging cliffs nearly touched their yardarms. Lieutenant Hadden could not understand why the Americans had not left detachments along the cliff tops; for, concealed in the bushes, they could have halted the fleet completely and escaped long before any landing party could have

Fort Anne. Both the blockhouse (right) and Philip Skene's saw-mill were burnt on the approach of Burgoyne's army. (*From Anburey's* Travels Through the Interior Parts of America.)

climbed up to them. Then, at about four o'clock, Burgoyne and his ships sailed into the wider space of South Bay, resembling rather a Scottish loch with its surrounding forest-covered hills and purple blossoms by the water's edge, where they saw the American ships at anchor and the American soldiers on shore happily preparing their first meal of the day. According to Dr. Thacher, their surgeon, the Americans had had a pleasant voyage upstream, cheering themselves with "the many dozens of choice Wines" they had found among the hospital stores[22] and encouraging one another over the futile efforts Burgoyne must be making to break through the obstacles back in Ticonderoga. It was over in a few minutes. All the American ships and boats were blown up, burned, or captured, and the Americans fled into the woods, leaving their sick behind.

Burgoyne landed his first troops south of Skenesborough in an attempt to cut the road to Fort Anne. Unfamiliar with the jumble of hills and tngled undergrowth, they lost their way and were unable to prevent the Americans from setting fire to Skene's warehouses and sawmills. The fire spread to the forest, and soon the whole side of the hil was ablaze.

In the hurry, there had been no chance to muster the battalions in their proper order, and precious time was lost while Burgoyne collected 190 men of the 9th Regiment and sent them, under Colonel Hill, down the forest track to Fort Anne. When darkness came they had to sleep on the ground where they could. After a forced march all the next day through stifling heat and swarms of the horrible black flies, they came in sight of Fort Anne at sunset. They found several boats stuck in the narrow, bending stream called Wood Creek and loaded with more sick and women, whom they had to send back to Skenesborough under escort, thus adding to their own, and Burgoyne's, problems.

The fort was a small, decaying structure, surrounded by a palisade long overgrown with shrubbery and ivy. Early the next morning an American deserter came in, saying that there were one thousand panic-stricken men in the fort, anxious only to save themselves. Colonel Hill sent a messenger back to Burgoyne asking for reinforcements in case of a trap. Burgoyne had, in fact, already sent the rest of the 1st Brigade (batallion companies of the 47th and 53rd Regiments), headed by a party of Indians under Captain John Money, deputy quartermaster-general. Meanwhile, Colonel Hill found that his suspicion was justified, for the "deserter" managed to escape and, half an hour afterward, the British were attacked by a large force of Americans, including one thousand New York Militia under General van Rensselaer who had just arrived from the south. Told by their spy that Colonel Hill's detachment numbered barely four companies, they hoped to execute a sharp revenge for the disgrace of Ticonderoga. The fighting, although small in scale, was extremely fierce and lasted three hours. The British made one counterattack, in which they took some prisoners and two regimental colors. After that, their inferior numbers told against them, and they were forced to withdraw up the side of a steep hill. Then both the British and the Americans ran out of ammunition at almost the same moment and both waited in a silence broken only by the rumble of approaching thunder. After a few minutes, an Indian war whoop was heard through the trees, and the Americans disappeared into the forest. From the British ranks three cheers rose above the groans and cries of the wounded. They believed they had inflicted two hundred casualties on the Americans; the real number is unknown. The war whoop, it turned out, had been given by Captain Money. His Indians had refused to advance any further at the sound of the firing, and he had come on alone. After watching the fight for some time and seeing the Americans out of ammunition, he decided that such a trick might throw them into confusion.

The surgeon being dead, Colonel Hill ordered Sergeant Lamb to remain with the wounded. He wrote:

> It was a distressing sight to see the wounded men bleeding on the ground, and what made it worse the rain came pouring down upon us like a deluge, and still to add to the distress of the sufferers there was nothing to dress their wounds . . . so I took off my shirt, tore it up, and with the help of a soldier's wife—the only woman who was with us, and who kept close by her husband's side during the engagement—made some bandages, stopped the bleeding of their wounds, and conveyed them in blankets to a small hut about two miles to our rear. . . .[23]

The entire detachment, with the reinforcements, was ordered back to Skenesborough. Burgoyne established headquarters in Skene's stone house. On 9 July, Fraser and von Riedesel appeared after their circuitous march through the hills of Vermont. They had caught up with St. Clair's rearguard at Hubbardton, where the track they were following joined the old road from Crown Point to Castleton. The fighting began when the infantry came upon part of Colonel Nathan Hale's 2nd New Hampshire Regiment cooking breakfast beside a stream. The Americans fled pell-mell into the forest. The main body of the Americans, two brigades totaling about two thousand men, under Colonels Ebenezar Francis and Seth Warner (one of Allen's "Green Mountain Boys" and a survivor of the Canadian campaign), were posted on high ground behind hastily erected wooden breastworks. Fraser had but 850 men. Nevertheless, he led them up the slope, and there they stayed, pinned down by a murderous rifle fire. This was Lieutenant Digby's first "serious engagement," and he confessed that for a few moments "the idea . . . of conveying me before the presence of my Creator had its force"; but, he was pleased to add, he did not deviate from his duty as a soldier, for "a proper resignation to the Divine Being is the certain foundation for true bravery."[24] Lord Balcarres, attempting to turn their left flank with his light infantry, was wounded and later counted thirty shot holes through his coat and trousers. Major Acland took his grenadiers further out to the right still, in an attempt to cut off the Americans from the road to Castleton. His men had to climb the rocky, precipitous face of Zion Hill. It was a nerve-racking moment, for any man who slipped would have fallen hundreds of feet to his death. On the summit, they found the way clear, until a party of sixty Americans came toward them, their rifles clubbed (pointed down) in surrender. When they were ten yards from the waiting grenadiers, who had been ordered to receive them, they suddenly lifted their rifles and fired from the hip, killing many men and wounding Acland. The vengeful grenadiers chased them down the far slope, caught them, and, when they surrendered, bayoneted them to death. While the British were extending their right to turn the Americans left, the Americans, who had more men, were trying to turn the British left and probably would have succeeded but for the arrival of the Germans, who came marching up the track from Ticonderoga singing psalms. Curiously, the Americans were also singing psalms to keep up their own spirits. Soon after this, Colonel Francis, who had behaved with extraordinary courage, was killed, and his men broke and ran. Warner, in raging despair, led off his regiment eastward into the Vermont hills. Later that day, a British officer leading a company into the forest to shoot some of the cattle that had run there during the fighting stumbled into Colonel Nathan Hale and his men wandering among the trees. He told the colonel he was surrounded by an entire brigade and tricked him into surrender. At the end of the year, Hale was exchanged on parole and returned to his home, where Gates tried to have him arrested for cowardice and treason.

With his forces reunited in Skenesborough, Burgoyne ordered a *feu de joie* in celebration of these victories, divine service for the army to give due acknowledgment to God for their success, half a pint of rum to every man, and a holiday on Sunday 13 July. He published a further proclamation, inviting all Americans to apply to "Colonel" Skene for enrollment in the loyalist regiments, and on 11 July he wrote a long dispatch to Germain recounting the marvellous events of the past week. In a letter of the same date to Lord Hervey, Burgoyne wrote that the American defense of Ticonderoga "convinces me that they have no men of military science. . . . [T]hey seem to have expended great treasure, and unwearied labour of more than a year to fortify, upon the supposition that we should only attack them upon the point they were best prepared to resist."[25]

In a private letter to Germain (also 11 July), he related that "some hundreds" (actually about six hundred) of Americans had come in volunteering to serve in his army, some for this campaign and some for the duration of the war. This showed, he thought, the "great effect" worked by his proclamation from Putnam Creek. He was no more than amused, therefore, to see that a parody of his proclamation, written by Francis Hopkinson (a lawyer and signatory of the Declaration of Independence who wrote occasional verse and satires), was being distributed through the country by the Committees of Correspondence. Burgoyne had begun his piece,

> The Forces intrusted to my Command are designed to act in concert and upon a common Principle with the armies and fleets which already display in every quarter of America the Power, the Justice, (and when properly sought) the Mercy of the King.

Hopkinson, therefore, began:

> When the Forces under your Command arrived at Quebec, in order to act in concert and upon a common Principle with the numerous armies and fleets which already display in every quarter of America the Justice and Mercy of your King, we, the Reptiles of America, were struck with unusual Trepidation and Astonishment.[26]

Yet it must be confessed that no one was able to produce a parody funnier than the original.

While the pamphleteers reproved Burgoyne for threatening them with thousands of savages and wondered how so cultivated a man could descend to such barbarity, Burgoyne himself was already having doubts about his Indians. Many of them, instead of coming forward with the army, had stayed in Ticonderoga to loot and get drunk. He was disgusted by the sight of scalps drying in the wind at the Indian camp, like skins on a gamekeeper's gibbet.

> If, under the management of their interpreters and conductors, they are indulged, for interested reasons, in all the caprices and humours of spoiled children, like them they grow more unreasonable and importunate upon every new favour; were they left to themselves, enormities too horrid to think of would ensue; guilty and innocent, women and infants, would be a common prey.[27]

He had been assured that the "Outawa" and other Western Indians, who were on their way with Saint-Luc, were "more brave and more tractable." Yet at this stage the Americans might have been surprised to hear that Burgoyne thought the warriors so useless. In a letter to John Stark, a hero of Bunker Hill who had returned to his Vermont home in anger at being passed over for promotion, one Cogan wrote that during the disorderly retreat from Hubbardton, "the Indians took & killed a vast number of our men."[28]

Nothing, however, could dull the startling brilliance of General Burgoyne's performance. Whatever might be said of his ill-judged and verbose proclamation from Putnam Creek, a week afterward the same commander had taken Ticonderoga, the "Gibraltar of the North," with the deft skill of a professional wrestler throwing a challenger from the crowd to the floor. Indeed, the very suddenness of his success had brought him too far too fast and, since he had always intended to go to the Hudson by the more commodious and practicable route of Lake George, it had brought him to the wrong place. The next moves, therefore, required the most careful consideration.

CHAPTER XIII

"A GLORIOUS SPIRIT IN OUR GENERAL"

THE loss of Ticonderoga stunned the Americans. How could the "impregnable Bastion" have been abandoned without resistance? The New York Council of Safety called the measure "highly reprehensible and probably criminal." Even Washington found the event so baffling as to defy conjecture. While he, however, preferred to learn more facts before passing judgment and wrote an encouraging letter to Schuyler to say that "our affairs are not desperate, and our exertions ought to be in proportion to our misfortunes and our exigencies," the majority clamored for the arrest and punishment of the two commanders of the Northern Department. "I believe we shall never hold a post," wrote John Adams, "until we shoot a general." A rumor spread about to the effect that Schuyler and St. Clair had been bribed with silver bullets fired into the fortress by British marksmen. General Gates was happy to encourage such nonsense and found supporters among those Congressmen who had at one time or another been offended by Schuyler's grand manner and lofty hauteur. Forgetting his own failure to heed Trumbull's warnings about Sugar Loaf Hill, Gates declared amid enthusiastic applause that he, or indeed any patriotic general, could have saved Ticonderoga. A movement began for his appointment to replace Schuyler. Schuyler, to whom the thought of treason had never occurred, much though he despised the New Englanders, found himself proclaimed a traitor. What made the accusation worse was that he was as much in the dark as everyone else about St. Clair's conduct, for St. Clair and his army were still somewhere in Vermont. Nevertheless, sending out desperate calls to all and sundry (few replied) for men, supplies, cannons, muskets, and ammunition, he went to Fort Edward. The arrival of van Rensselaer's militiamen checked the British at Fort

Anne. While the fighting was in progress, Schuyler assembled one thousand axmen and the next day sent them to cut down trees and destroy all bridges as far as they could along the forest track to Skenesborough. Sergeant Lamb, hiding in his log cabin with the wounded, heard them at work day and night, but he was not discovered. In addition, Schuyler ordered the commander of the rear guard, General Fellows, to bring back all cattle, horses, carriages, food, and everything else that might be of use to the enemy. He issued a proclamation forbidding anyone to assist the invaders under pain of treason. The British, he said, were "forcing Slavery on the United States of America, & under the specious Pretext of affording you Protection. . . ." He reminded the people that in New Jersey loyalists and those who came for pardon were treated no better than the rebels, that is, "with the worst wanton Barbarity, & such as hath not even disgraced Barbarians." The British "cruelly butchered without distinction of Age or Sex, ravished Children of ten to Women of eighty years of Age. . . ."[1]

On 14 July St. Clair rejoined Schuyler at Fort Edward. All his militiamen had deserted on the way. With his Continentals, however, Schuyler now had about 4,500 men to oppose the British. Unfortunately, several New England regiments chose this of all moments to claim that their period of service was up. The very people who accused Schuyler of treason packed up their stores and departed. This left him with under three thousand men, with no "tents, houses, Barns, Boards, or any Shelter" and with only five rounds per soldier.[2] Since Fort Edward was useless, he decided that the best thing to do was to retreat to the high ground at Saratoga, where he owned land and could count on the support of most of the inhabitants. He wrote asking Washington to bring his army north, for with their combined forces they could fall on Burgoyne, who at Saratoga would have his lines of communication stretched to the limit, and cut him to pieces. Washington, however, realizing that his own troops were in little better condition than those in the north, feared that a forced march from New Jersey to Albany across Howe's front was beyond the capacity of his army, so he told Schuyler he would have to manage on his own. He did, however, send some artillery and appoint the redoubtable Benedict Arnold (who was engaged in a dispute with various authorities over his alleged embezzlement of public money but had covered himself with glory harassing a British raid on Danbury, Connecticut) as Schuyler's second-in-command. Arnold's prestige would be worth five thousand men.

To Burgoyne, the advance to Fort Edward presented the unpleasant prospect of a struggle along twenty-three miles of winding, swampy track through dense forest, unusable all along its length by any kind of wheeled carriage. Nevertheless, and despite the worst Schuyler's men might do, he calculated that the journey would take a fortnight.

Alternatively, he could withdraw the entire army to Ticonderoga, wait for the boats to be transferred to Lake George, and then go by water to Fort George. From Fort George to Fort Edward there was a sixteen-mile road via Glenns Falls. This was his originally intended route, being shorter (from Ticonderoga), easier, and less exposed to flank attack. The news from Ticonderoga, however, was discouraging. Only three hundred of the one thousand horses hired in Montreal had arrived, and the transport of boats and stores over the bridge of land was behind schedule. Heavy rain had turned the clay soil into what Major Williams of the Royal Artillery called "slippery sludge," so that it required all of his artillery horses to pull a single medium twelve-pounder. "I hope this will be the last water business I ever have to do with," he wrote to Germain, "for I honestly confess that I never met with so much fatigue. . . ."[3] If it took three days to get seventeen guns ready for embarkation, how long would it take Burgoyne to embark the entire army?

Next, Burgoyne was uncertain of the state of Fort George. It was protected in front by water, on both sides by marshland, and behind by a steep hill. If the Americans decided to hold out there come what may, which they might do after Ticonderoga, then he would be delayed until he could get his guns onto the hill behind. During this time, the Americans could destroy the road to Ford Edward even more effectively than they were destroying the road to Fort Anne now, and he might not reach Fort Edward within a month. On the other hand, to continue on his present route would threaten the garrison from the rear and oblige them to retreat without a shot.*

Finally, he did not place complete trust in loyalist assurances that the inhabitants of Vermont would come pouring in to join him. On the contrary, they might come pouring over to attack his supply lines. If he could create the impression that he was about to turn his entire army eastward by means of a feint (which he called a "jealousy"), the militia of the eastern provinces would keep their distance.

By 11 July he had made up his mind. The infantry was to cut its way to Fort Edward via Fort Anne, while the artillery and heavy supplies were to go by Lake George and Glenns Falls. Von Riedesel and the Germans were to be stationed at Castleton, as a threat to Vermont. For

* In *General Burgoyne in Canada and America* (Gordon and Cremonesi, London, 1976, p. 135) the military historian Michael Glover writes that the chief factor weighing in Burgoyne's decision to take the overland route was the intelligence reports that the Americans had built row-galleys on Lake George; by capturing Fort George from the rear, therefore, he would deprive these galleys of their base. While it is true that one report did mention such galleys "a-building," I do not think this was the decisive reason. Burgoyne did not mention it later, either in his dispatches to Germain or in his defense before Parliament. As things turned out, there were no American row-galleys on Lake George, all boats having been burned by the Americans themselves after the withdrawal from Ticonderoga, and Burgoyne probably knew this before making his decision.

the next two weeks the soldiers and pioneers labored unceasingly to clear the route. For some stretches of road, trees had been cut down across it at twelve-yard intervals and in such a way that their branches were entangled. Forty bridges, some over ravines thirty feet deep, had to be built and a log causeway laid down over a swamp two miles in length. Once again the army performed the impossible, as it had done in building the fleet the year before and by 22 July the road was ready. Burgoyne, however, now had to wait because the supplies and artillery were not ready in Ticonderoga. Major Blomefield and his hoped-for "Machine" did not arrive until 23 July. Indeed, since nothing more is heard of this "Machine," which had caused so much trouble, it presumably either broke or was found to be too heavy for the mud. Meanwhile, twelve special carriages, "resembling a Waggon without the Body,"[4] had had to be built for transporting the gunboats and batteaux.

The two corps moved south more or less simultaneously: Burgoyne and the main army leaving Skenesborough on 25 July and the boats sailing up Lake George on the 26th.[5] By the 30th, Burgoyne had established his headquarters in a building called "the Red House" near Fort Edward. American snipers (many of them in fact Oneida and Stockbridge Indians) had begun to make themselves felt; "scarce a day passed without firing," wrote Burgoyne. So far, they had managed only to wound a few loyalists and Indians. During the march, however, an incident occurred which, some authors have claimed, was to have a decisive effect on the campaign.

On 20 July, Saint-Luc, de Langlade, and the Western Indians arrived at Skenesborough, but instead of the five hundred "brave and tractable" warriors Burgoyne had been counting on, there were barely more than 150. A possible explanation of this may be seen in a letter from Major de Peyster in Michilmackinac. He informed Carleton that de Langlade had reported the theft of a great part of the money and gifts intended for purchasing the Indians' assistance. De Peyster, however, was certain that de Langlade had embezzled it.[6] Hence, de Langlade had been able to enroll only a ragbag of desperate characters, adventurers, and outcasts from their tribes many of whom had come for the chance to murder and loot without risk. Saint-Luc encouraged them in this, for since his imprisonment by the Americans, he had never ceased to declare, *"Il faut brutalizer les affairs!"*

Burgoyne, however, had no intention of brutalizing affairs, and accordingly treated the Indians (doubtless to Saint-Luc's disgust) to the same speech as he had delivered on the bank of the Bouquet River. At first he thought of sending the entire Indian corps into Vermont, but reports that Schuyler and Arnold were fortifying in Saratoga persuaded him to concentrate his forces on the Hudson. On 25 July his anxieties over the Indians were justified.

A party of assorted Indians had been raiding as far as New Perth (now Salem, Washington County, New York). On the way back they had passed the cabin of a Tory family called Allen who were cheerfully awaiting the arrival of the British. The Indians, more interested in looting the house than in the political differences between white men, killed all eight of them, including the children, and took the scalps to Fort Edward. Here, the American rear guard was preparing to withdraw, for Fraser's Advanced Corps was already at Pitch Pine Plains nearby, and Burgoyne himself was in Fort Anne. In the skirmish, the Indians killed and captured some Americans, including two women. One of these, a young person called Jane McCrae, they killed, and returned to Fraser's camp with her scalp added to their collection. It turned out that she was betrothed to Lieutenant David Jones, a loyalist serving with the Advanced Corps.

The murder of Jenny McCrae has become part of the folklore of Washington County. Many different versions of the story, including a full-length romantic novel, were written in the following century. On certain points, however, the more sober accounts agree. Jane McCrae, daughter of a Presbyterian minister, belonged to a family divided by the Revolution. Three of her brothers were rebels, one a colonel in the militia with Schuyler. Two were loyalists, as was Jane herself. She became engaged to David Jones, a local man who was likewise a loyalist. In October 1776 he and his brother fled to Canada and joined the corps under Peters. Jones was now hoping to be reunited with his fiancée. Jenny probably had the same idea, for instead of going south she went north to visit her friend, Mrs. McNeill, a stout Scots widow of Fort Edward. More importantly, Mrs. McNeill was not only an outspoken Tory but a cousin of Brigadier Fraser. After this, the stories differ. Some say that in the shooting the two women hid in the cellar, from which the Indians dragged them out by the hair. The Indians then put Jenny on a horse but, finding Mrs. McNeill too fat, stripped her naked and forced her to walk behind. On the way back the party met some Indians sent by Jones for the precise purpose of finding Jenny and bringing her to him. The chief who had captured her refused to give her up, and to settle the argument he either tomahawked her or shot her and took the scalp back to the army to claim the reward. Others, basing their story on a version told by Mrs. McNeill herself in old age, say that Jane, being on horseback, was accidentlly shot by Americans aiming too high.[7]

There was, however, one eyewitness, Samuel Standish, a soldier captured by the Indians. He gave a brief account of the episode when applying for a pension in later life.[8] In 1830, however, he was visited by the American historian Jared Sparks, to whom he gave a much fuller and more vivid description. As this version has never, as far as I can discover, been published before, and since it clears up many discrepancies in other versions, it is worth quoting at some length. Standish told Sparks:

> One morning very early, as he was standing on a piquet guard under Lieut. Van Vechten, he heard a firing very near him, & suddenly several Indians appeared in the bushes. He discharged his piece, & ran down the hill towards the fort, which was half a mile distant. No sooner had he reached the bottom of the hill than three Indians sprang out of the bushes, fired upon him, & wounded him in the foot. One of them came up to him, caught him by the neck, threw him on the ground, & pinioned his arms. He then pushed him violently, & motioned to him to go up the hill with all speed. They arrived at the top of the hill at the place where he had stood centinel, near a large pine tree & a spring of water. Several Indians were gathered round the spring, and in a few minutes he saw Jenny McCrae and Mrs. McNeill walking up the hill with a party of Indians. They came near the spring and stopped. In a short time violent language passed between the Indians, & they got into a high quarrel, beating each other with their muskets. In the midst of the fray, one of the Chiefs in a rage shot Jenny McCrae in her breast, & she fell & expired immediately. Her hair was long & flowing, and the same chief took off the scalp, cutting so as to unbrace nearly the whole of that part of head on which the hair grew. He then sprang up, tossed the scalp in the face of a young Indian standing by, brandished it in the air, and uttered a savage yell of exultation. When this was done the quarrel ceased, & the whole party moved off quickly, for the fort had already been alarmed. They went as soon as possible to Genl. Fraser's camp, which was then five miles distant on the road to Fort Anne.[9]

At the British camp, the chief presented Jenny's scalp to the horrified David Jones. Presumably, therefore, the Indians had misunderstood their mission, supposing Jenny to be an enemy whom Jones wanted taken dead or alive, and had simply quarreled over who was to collect the reward. Standish's story contains other interesting details: Jenny was obviously willing to go with the Indians; there were no horses to be seen; Mrs. McNeill was not naked, then or at the British camp, where as a prisoner Standish saw her again; the quarrel between the chiefs was not between the murderous Le Loup ("the Iroquois Wolf"), or Wyandot Panther, and the mild, virtuous Duluth sent to rescue Jane (as is given in nearly all versions), but between an Ottawa and a Caughnawaga; he suspected that some of the Indians were in fact white men, American Tories in disguise. Standish himself was interrogated kindly by Fraser and sent to Ticonderoga as a prisoner, whence he escaped after two months. Jones tried to resign his commission, was refused, and later deserted, retiring to Canada. He never married. The bodies of Jane, Van Vechten, and others killed in the fighting were buried, not by weeping American soldiers, but by loyalists who remained behind after the rebels withdrew.

Burgoyne was told of this affair the same evening, and wrote back to Fraser:

> The news I have just received of the savages having scalped a young lady, their prisoner, fills me with horror. I shall visit their camp tomorrow morning; I beg you to desire Major Campbell to have them assembled—none absent—I would rather put my commission in the fire than serve a day if I could suppose Government would blame me for discountenancing by some strong acts such unheard barbarities.[10]

The next morning he ordered the culprit to be arrested and charged with murder, promising that the chief would be hanged on conviction. The chief protested that the girl had been shot by Americans. Saint-Luc pointed out that if an Indian chief were hanged as a common British criminal, all the Indians would desert immediately. He implied that either they would rejoin their Oneida brethren at present fighting for the rebels, or they would burn and massacre every settlement they came to on the way home. Reluctantly, Burgoyne pardoned the Indian. Fraser shrugged off the affair by saying, "This is a conquered country, and we must wink at these things."

Great importance has been attached to this incident. It is said that a tremendous propaganda campaign was now started, portraying the "massacre" of a virtuous young lady in such harrowing terms that thousands of local farmers, hitherto indifferent to the war, rushed off "to go agin Burgoyne," and that it was even proposed to turn Jenny McCrae into the "Yankee Joan of Arc" Tom Paine had been looking for—but because she was a Tory, this would have been rather difficult. In fact, there is little evidence for such statements, for the contemporary American newspapers, where one would expect to find such a campaign, hardly mention the affair at all. The murder of Jenny McCrae, indeed, seems to have made little impression until Gates took it up just before Saratoga, and she does not seem to have become a legend until the early nineteenth century.

A great deal more has been written on Burgoyne's "fatal decision" to take the land route to Fort Edward instead of the water route by Lake George. I have already given his reasons for so deciding, and they would appear to be valid enough. Many of his officers agreed that, despite the grueling labor involved, the land route was indeed shorter.[11] Burgoyne's loudest contemporary critics, such as the historian Stedman, were not there at the time and never saw the country. Some, notably loyalists who saw treachery and corruption everywhere, claimed that Burgoyne's true reason for taking this route was that

Skene, who perceived the great advantages that would come to himself from a road built across his land, persuaded or bribed him to do so. This is hard to believe. Burgoyne was an ambitious man, as his critics never ceased to point out. If that is true, then his entire future, to say nothing of that of the Empire, was at stake. Such trifling favors as Skene might have offered could not have weighed much against the rewards and favors Burgoyne could expect from a grateful country in the event of his success. It would appear, therefore, that he was decided not by Skene's reasoning but by his own. Indeed, now that he was at last in supreme command, the stubbornness that had always underlain his polished manners began to show itself more plainly. Fraser observed this when he wrote from Skenesborough to Robinson (Lord North's undersecretary at the Treasury): "Our Genl is really a fine agreeable manly fellow, but hates lines of resistance, when they interrupt his projects, and they will occur here frequently."[12]

Two other charges against Burgoyne are not so easy to counter. The first is that a great part of the delay in Ticonderoga was due to Burgoyne's insistence on bringing up to Ford Edward a "huge Train" of artillery. It consisted of forty-two pieces, including four medium twelve-pounders and two light twenty-four-pounders (French guns of a special construction which were so light, Burgoyne argued, that despite their power they were to all intents and purposes fieldpieces). He needed these heavy guns, he said later, in case the Americans dug themselves in behind river fords or on islands, particularly those at the mouth of the Mohawk River, or built strong redoubts across narrow defiles; finally, he would need them should he have to spend the winter at Albany cut off from Howe. It should be remembered that at this period artillery was acquiring the same kind of prestige as air support was to do in the Second World War, Korea, and Vietnam. Indeed, Lord Townshend, Master-General of Ordnance, complained that the call for cannons was becoming so habitual "that the smallest Body of Infantry wish not to move without them."[13] Nevertheless, Burgoyne obviously felt slightly uneasy about this afterward, for in his speech before Parliament he resorted to a little verbal conjuring to pretend that he actually had less guns than the customary allotment to an army of his size, which was not true.[14] Nor could he answer the accusation that the delay occasioned by his bringing up his guns gave the Americans time to recover, block the roads, and build the defenses he would now need the artillery to batter down.

This brings us to the second charge, which is that he would have had neither a need for artillery nor any supply problems later if, on reaching Skenesborough he had immediately sent a flying column to Fort Edward. Schuyler's men could not then have cut down any trees, destroyed any bridges, or taken away any provisions. At Fort George the Americans had four hundred carts, sixteen hundred horses, and piles of stores guarded by only seven hundred frightened militia. All these would have been captured, the road from Fort George protected, and the army's shortage of horses ended. Both Digby and Hadden remarked on this at the time, Hadden believing that seven hundred picked men, assisted by the horse-carried three-pounders, would have done the job and completely broken the American will to resist.[15] But because Burgoyne insisted on keeping the entire army based at Skenesborough and employed on repairing the Fort Anne road, the Americans had time to recover, destroy the Fort George-Fort Edward road as well, evacuate their horses and stores, and destroy or remove everything in the settlements they left behind. Neither Digby nor Hadden, however, suggests how such a flying column could have been fed and supported. Burgoyne was extremely short of men at this moment. He had assumed, first, that Ticonderoga would be garrisoned by troops from Canada, but Carleton stuck to the letter of his orders (one feels with a certain secret satisfaction) and refused to allow this. Thus four hundred men had to be left at Crown Point and another 910 in Ticonderoga. Secondly, Fraser's Advanced Corps, from whom such a flying column would have had to be taken, was exhausted after the useless battle of Hubbardton, besides being depleted by 150 casualties and a large detachment left to protect the wounded, whose evacuation was not completed (owing again to lack of transport) until after the army left for Fort Edward. Hadden indeed complained that Fraser had no business chasing the Americans through Vermont at all, but should have been in his proper place, on the right at Fort Anne. But this is to say that, in the excitement of discovering that the Americans had slipped out of the trap he had so carefully prepared, Burgoyne should have had the almost supernatural prescience to have recalled Fraser at once, instead of sailing to Skenesborough in the hope of cutting off the Americans and catching them between his own and Fraser's corps.

Thirdly, the Germans were at Castleton, fourteen miles to the east. Reports came that Warner had collected five thousand men at Manchester, Vermont, and was advancing north. Von Riedesel sent detachments to Rutland, Wells, and Tinmouth, and after some skirmishing, Warner retreated to Arlington. The battles at Trois Rivières and Trenton, however, had taught Burgoyne that the Americans were able to rally and counterattack at the very moment when all seemed lost, and this threat, or the possibility of a more dangerous one, was not to be ignored. He probably felt, therefore, that with only two thousand men in Castleton, three thousand in Skenesborough, and supplies so uncertain, he did not dare risk dividing his force any further for the moment. Von Riedesel complained in his journal that he requested permission to send a strong detachment into Vermont to find much needed horses for his dismounted dragoons, but that Burgoyne refused, "pretending" that the army was about to move south.[16] This was written some years after, when relations between the British and Germans had become sour. The truth is, Burgoyne did intend to move the army on 22 July (he personally rode to Fort Anne and beyond to inspect the route) and was only held up by the delay in Ticonderoga. Fourthly, Burgoyne was short of horses. Now, Digby writes that when the army set off at last for Ford Edward, it had nearly as many horses as men, which raises doubt as to just how short of horses Burgoyne really was. Digby must have been mistaken, however, for even if his own unit was plentifully supplied, there were at least three thousand men at Skenesborough, which was twice as many as there were horses for the entire army (1,500), Ticonderoga, Crown Point, and Castleton included. Fifthly, Hadden's suggested seven hundred men, even picked men, would not have been enough. Schuyler still had three thousand in Fort Edward, after the New England regiments went home. The arrival of a small, isolated, detachment of seven hundred redcoats might, instead of demoralizing them, have reinspired them with fighting spirit. In that case, the near defeat at Fort Anne would have been repeated as a complete one, with disastrous consequences to Burgoyne's entire campaign. Finally, Hadden thought that Burgoyne should have marched the bulk of his army straight to Fort Edward, regardless of the road. But this would have meant relinquishing the feint toward Vermont, which Burgoyne wished to maintain in order to keep the enemy militia on that side at a safe distance from his vulnerable left flank.

If all this seems rather technical and detailed to the general reader, it is given here because, as I have said, a great deal has been written against Burgoyne on this matter, and most of it has been allowed to stand unanswered. Burgoyne made many mistakes, and it is a biographer's duty to admit them; it is also my task to clear him from blame he does not deserve.

When Burgoyne moved down to Fort Edward, Schuyler and Arnold fell back to Stillwater, which the engineer Kosciuszko (later to become famous, first as the Liberator and afterward as the Dictator of Poland) thought a better situation for defense. Schuyler's wife and servants bravely stayed behind to burn the corn standing in his fields; but their example did not prevent alarm and consternation from spreading through the inhabitants of the Hudson valley, who now abandoned their homes and fled southward. Long cavalcades of wagons formed in the path of the retreating American army, adding to the confusion. An eyewitness, Simeon Bloodgood, remembered the carts piled with furniture, horses panting under two or three riders, the trail of straggling country folk on foot, the burning cabins, the sudden panic and screams of terror when parties of Indians appeared out of the woods and opened fire. "Every one for himself was the constant cry." His mother walked twenty miles, leading wagon horses, carrying an infant in one arm, and a club in her hand, yet "not a person in the throng offered to assist her."[17]

Burgoyne arrived in Ford Edward to find the farmhouses, barns, and haystacks burned, the corn spoiled, the livestock driven off. This he stigmatized as "an act of desperation and folly" which might retard him but could not finally impede him.[18] Many of the local farmers were Tory, however, and they now came out of hiding with their families, destitute, terrified of the Indians, and begging for food. He could not refuse them, yet he had but four days' supplies in hand. Scores of his carts had again been broken on the march from Skenesborough, and he had moved too late to prevent Schuyler's men from blocking the road from Fort George. Until his carts were repaired and the road cleared, supplies, instead of flowing from Lake George as intended, would come down in a tiny irregular trickle. Nothing barred his way to Albany, and messengers arrived to tell him that St. Leger was already on the Mohawk. It was imperative to reach the junction of the two rivers soon in order to favor that column's advance. The Hudson valley extended before him, lush, fertile and inviting after the wild forests and mountains behind, yet he could not move forward at the very time when everything depended on speed and decisive action.

Under these circumstances, it was only natural that Burgoyne should turn his thoughts to the powerful army in New York. His last letter to Howe had been on 2 July, just before the attack on Ticonderoga. He was then under the impression that Ticonderoga would be garrisoned by troops from Canada. After saying that he was glad of this, because it would enable him to keep his army complete, he went on: "The enemy do not appear to have the least suspicion of the King's real instructions relative to the campaign after the reduction of Ticonderoga. I shall implicitly follow the ideas I communicated to your Excellency in my letters from Plymouth and Quebec."[19]

As I have said before, we do not know what those letters from Plymouth and Quebec contained, but in the context of the previous allusion to the king's real instructions, it is hard to see what else it could have been but an exposition of the great plan. Since Ticonderoga, Burgoyne had "spared no pains to open a correspondence with the Commander-in-Chief"; he had sent ten messengers by different routes, but not one had returned.[20]

Then, on 5 August, a messenger from Howe arrived at last. Written on two thin strips of paper which had been rolled onto a quill, the letter said:

New York: *17 July:*
DEAR SIR,

I have received yours of the second instant on the 15th, have since heard from the rebel army of your being in possession of Ticonderoga, *which is a great event, carried without loss*. I have received your two letters, *viz.* from Plymouth and Quebec, your last of the 14th May, and shall observe the contents. There is a report of a messenger of yours to me having been taken, and the letter discovered in a double wooden canteen, you will know if it was of any consequence; nothing of it has transpired to us. I will observe the *same rules* in writing to you, as you propose, in your letters to me. Washington is waiting our motions here, and has detached Sullivan with about 2500 men, as I learn, to Albany.

My intention is for Pennsylvania, where I expect to meet Washington, but if he goes to the northward contrary to my expectations, and you can keep him at bay, be assured I shall soon be after him to relieve you. After your arrival at Albany, the movements of the enemy will guide yours; but my wishes are, that the enemy be drove out of this province before any operation takes place in Connecticut. Sir Henry Clinton remains in command here, and will act as occurrences may direct. Putnam is in the highlands with about 4000 men. Success be ever with you, Yours etc.

WILLIAM HOWE.[21]

From this it was obvious at the very least that Sir William Howe himself would not be coming to meet Burgoyne in Albany with ten thousand men. But was there any other meaning veiled behind Howe's laconic sentences? Burgoyne was expected to reach Albany; Howe did not wish him to turn toward Connecticut until the rebels were "drove" out of New York. Clinton was to act as occurrences directed. Clearly, Howe could not imagine Burgoyne able to drive the rebels out of New York by himself. According to Burgoyne's last information, which was when he left England,[22] five thousand men were to be left in New York City and three thousand on the lower Hudson, while a reinforcement of five thousand was promised for early summer. Out of this thirteen thousand, Clinton should be able to detach eight thousand, which was more men than Burgoyne himself had, in order to attack the Highlands and move up the Hudson. Burgoyne had twice told Howe of his plans and had reminded him of the fact in his last letter. Howe had now acknowledged these letters and said he would observe their contents. Perhaps, too, Germain's instructions concerning the plan had not arrived by 17 July, when Howe had written; in that case, they had either arrived since or would soon do so.[23] There could be no question, then, that Howe was, or would remain for long, ignorant of the plan for a junction, and presumably Clinton would attack when the right moment presented itself. Thus on a second reading Howe's letter did not appear so disappointing after all. Meanwhile, Albany beckoned in the distance. Burgoyne's triumphs had been spectacular, and though there were difficulties now, a renewed effort could overcome them. If he could reach Albany *first,* not only would Clinton's task in breaking through the Highlands be made infinitely easier, but Burgoyne would become the hero of the hour.

Next day, therefore, he sent off by the same messenger a cheerful letter to Howe, relating his successes and distributing praise to all his men, even the Indians. He did not see how he could reach Albany before 23 August. The message intercepted in the canteen, he explained, had not been from him to Howe but was part of a trick which might have succeeded but had not.[24] When, after the war, Clinton wrote a long book justifying his part in it, he said of this letter that it showed Burgoyne to be in the highest spirits, "and did not contain an expression that indicated either an expectation or desire of cooperation from the southern army." Historians have agreed with Clinton and gone further by regarding this letter as a proof that he actually did not desire cooperation and had never intended it.

Meanwhile, Burgoyne kept these letters secret and returned to the practical problems of resuming his advance to Albany. The difficulties of bringing supplies down from Ticonderoga had, if anything, increased, for he needed to assemble a fleet of batteaux to carry these same supplies down the Hudson. This meant that precious boats needed for ferrying supplies over Lake George had to be lifted onto carriages (which themselves had to be brought over the lake) and pulled by oxen from Fort George over a road that was still potholed and treacherous. A recent spate of rainstorms had once again turned the roads into mud. It never seemed to be possible to bring up more than a two-day supply at a time, one day of which was always consumed before the next consignment arrived. The remaining seven hundred horses contracted for had still not appeared, and Carleton apparently could not be bothered either to ascertain what had become of them or even to call the contractor to account. Yet so acute was the shortage of carts that even if Burgoyne had relinquished his artillery, as his critics later said he should have done, the 273 horses thus freed would have had no carts to pull. Thus the accumulation of stores was painfully slow. "At this moment," he told Phillips, "one month's provision would be worth £100,000 to Great Britain!"[25] At the beginning of the campaign, Burgoyne had ordered that officers should restrict their baggage to a minimum. "Minimum," however, was a vague word, and many young officers, new to campaigning, could not see how they could appear as gentlemen without their boxes of wigs, jars of hair powder, and libraries of books. After some sharp insistence, these items had been sent back, and now many officers managed without beds and slept in the tents with their soldiers. The Germans, feeling this was not their war, had been more reluctant to obey, and angry complaints had passed, to be as angrily contested. Despite this, after Saratoga a ministerial pamphleteer paid to discredit Burgoyne described his baggage train as "a mark of Eastern Pomp."[26]

This brings us to a famous story always offered as an example of Burgoyne's self-indulgence and hypocrisy: that while telling his officers to live rough, he kept no less than thirty carts for his own private luxuries.[27] The origin of this story is a General Order issued by Phillips on 19 August, expressing his "utter astonishment" that thirty carts laden with baggage "said to be the Lieutenant-General's" were on the road from Lake George, despite all the previous orders that nothing but provisions was to be carried on carts. Phillips ordered an inquiry into how such a thing could have happened. Since, he said, he was "perfectly acquainted with His Excellency's sentiments upon this subject, that he would on no account suffer his private conveniency to interfere with the public Transports of Provisions," he was sure "his Excellency will mark the strongest resentment of this very indecent disobedience of General Orders."[28] In other words, some officer in the rear had not dared to assume that "His Excellency" was not an exception to General Orders and was about to learn his mistake. The story itself owes its existence to some historian who read the original source carelessly because that is what he wanted to believe. Nevertheless, it is true that not only Burgoyne but also all the officers liked to enjoy themselves in the evenings, no less than the soldiers, and did so according to the conventions of eighteenth-century military life. Officers' and soldiers' wives were allowed to come on campaign, for the modern recourse of separating men from women on every pretext would have been regarded by our ancestors as a barbarity. "One proof of the spirit of our Army," wrote Sir Francis Clerke to his father on 10 September,

> is that the Ladies do not mean to quit us. . . . [W]e have frequent dinées, and constantly musick; for my part, & I know it is your opinion, this campaigning is a favourite portion of Life; and none but stupid Mortals can dislike, a lively Camp, good Weather, good Claret, good Musick and the Enemy near. I venture to say all this, for a little fusillade during dinner does not discompose the Nerves of even our Ladies.[29]

By this time, Burgoyne had acquired a mistress. According to Baroness von Riedesel, she was the wife of a commissary officer; according to the *Town & Country Magazine*, the wife of a Virginian planter taken prisoner in Ticonderoga.[30] Some authors have described her as beautiful and one has even gone so far as to call her "Fanny Loescher," but this appears to be based on nothing more substantial than a historical novel of the 1930s. The fact is, we know nothing about her at all. While again it is true that Burgoyne liked to dine formally and in the style expected of an eighteenth-century general and that none of his officers, British, German, Canadian, or American, were averse to sharing his table, as they did nightly, stories that his tent was of double oiled layers of silk, that his larder contained fourteen different kinds of fresh, smoked, and pickled meats, that his wines were carried in two carts equipped with special springs, and that, in short, he dallied in luxury while his men nearly starved appear to date only from the second half of the twentieth century. Against them we have the testimony of Lord Harrington, Lord Balcarres, Major Kingston, Lieutenant Digby, and Sergeant Lamb, who wrote that His Excellency happily shared the hardships of his soldiers. From time to time his Indian scouts brought him a trout or two caught in Saratoga Lake, and we do know that he enjoyed, or pretended to enjoy, rattlesnake soup, which was available in unlimited quantities.

Lack of men, partly due to Carleton's refusal to relieve the garrisons at Crown Point and Ticonderoga, compelled Burgoyne to give up the communication through Skenesborough, and the slowness with which supplies could be brought down from Lake George inspired him to consider other means of replenishing his stores and increasing his number of horses. He took up von Riedesel's proposal for a raid into Vermont. While the original plan had been for a march eastward from Castleton in order to get behind the enemy at Manchester and Arlington, Burgoyne felt this would detach the corps too far north to enable it to rejoin his advance on Albany. He therefore ordered a raid eastward to Arlington itself and, if possible, Rockingham on the Connecticut River. He suspected that Warner would retreat in front of the corps and offer no serious resistance. From Rockingham the corps was to turn west and join Burgoyne at Albany. Such an expedition would find mounts for his Brunswick Dragoons, recruit more loyalists, and obtain substantial quantities of draft horses, oxen, carts, and provisions, for he dared not begin his final advance on Albany with less than thirty days' supplies in hand. There were other advantages as well. There was at present an American brigade in Vermont which Schuyler was planning to send to attack St. Leger. This would keep them where they were. It would also keep reinforcements from coming to Albany from New England, because the Americans would suppose Burgoyne was about to invade Massachusetts.

The only problem was whom to detach. The Germans were on the left, and by the dictates of military etiquette the honor should be theirs. Fraser complained that Germans were the slowest troops in the world and quite unsuitable but refused to make a formal objection to Burgoyne. Burgoyne was strongly criticized for sending Germans on this expedition, but he had little choice. The Germans were still resentful at remarks that had been passed about the Trenton affair and had tried to restore their national pride by claiming that only their arrival had saved Fraser from defeat in Hubbardton, a claim that had brought some sarcastic replies. Burgoyne probably felt that to override military etiquette on this occasion would cause a great deal of bitterness, whereas to send the Germans would do much to restore their morale. At the same time he had too few British troops to spare for such a detachment, for he would need all he had for the assault on the American defenses at Stillwater, where the main fighting and heaviest casualties were to be expected. Finally, it was the Brunswick Dragoons who needed mounts, not the British infantry.

The Germans could speak no English, so it would be necessary to send a corps of loyalists with them. Unfortunately, the loyalists had also been grumbling that they were not treated with enough respect and that Burgoyne was deliberately holding back the commissions he had promised them. One group had actually deserted, and it was only with great difficulty that Burgoyne managed to persuade them to come back. How much of all this was Burgoyne's fault and how much was inevitable is hard to say, for our only source is a highly biased American account written after Saratoga. Nevertheless, there is no doubt that at this period in their history, the British were the most bumptious and arrogant people on earth, treating all allies with crass insensitivity.

The Indians were even more troublesome. On 4 August they had called another conference to complain about the restrictions imposed upon them. Burgoyne told Saint-Luc that he would rather lose them all than connive at their enormities; an Indian chief replied, "Death in the Pot!" (that is, he considered the entire campaign ill-omened).[31] Nevertheless, the expedition would need Indians, and the conference came to an end with nothing decided.

To bring himself onto a parallel with Arlington, Burgoyne moved the entire army south as far as the Batten Kill, a wide stream emptying into the Hudson from Vermont, opposite Schuyler's estate in Saratoga. On 11 August he sent a mixed corps of 800 men (200 German infantry, 175 Brunswick Dragoons, 300 Tories and Canadians, 50 picked British marksmen under Captain Fraser, a squad of Hesse-Hanau gunners with two three-pounders, and some Indians under Saint-Luc) into Vermont. At the last moment he changed their orders. He had heard that the Americans had a large magazine and a corral of horses in Bennington; Lieutenant-Colonel Baum (the commander) was to go there instead, mount his dragoons and continue to Albany as before. He was, however, to avoid a major action. As the expedition set off, Fraser's Advanced Corps crossed the Hudson over a bridge of boats and occupied Schuyler's houses, barns, and barracks.

Secrecy, speed, knowledge of the country and its people, and flexibility of maneuver were essential to the success of Baum's raid. To this end, the corps marched in parade-ground order along a main road, behind a military band playing loud and stirring music. Every ten minutes or so, the column stopped to redress the lines. The Indians fanned ahead and destroyed every farm they came to, spreading terror and alarm miles beyond them. Baum was ordered to find out the sentiments of a people torn by the complicated and constantly changing loyalties of a civil war in which he himself had no concern and since neither he nor his senior officers could speak English, Philip Skene was sent along as adviser. All this would probably have sealed the fate of the expedition whatever happened, but at that moment Burgoyne suffered from two of the many strokes of sheer bad luck that were to dog him for the rest of the campaign. First, there was a tremendous thunderstorm followed by torrential rain so fierce that the troops in camp were driven out of their tents. The bridge of boats was swept away. Edward Pellew once more distinguished himself by diving into the river and rescuing a valuable boatload of provisions.* The Advanced Corps had to be brought back in boats under conditions of extreme danger from the racing waters. The other piece of misfortune was more complicated. It may be remembered that John Stark, the Vermonter hero of Bunker Hill, had been sulking at home in protest against being passed over for promotion. On 18 July, however, the New Hampshire Congress persuaded him to lead their people once more into battle, on condition that he need obey no orders but their own. The country folk, led by parsons, doctors, and solicitors, flew to arms behind his prestigious name. As Baum set forth, it happened that Stark was in Manchester with eighteen hundred men. He received orders from Schuyler, whom he loathed both personally and as a New Yorker, to proceed to Stillwater. Hearing that Burgoyne's entire army, as it was believed, was on the march again and that a party of Indians had been seen at Cambridge, he refused to obey Schuyler and marched to Bennington, sending orders to Seth Warner and other local leaders to meet him there. His intention was to get behind Burgoyne's army and harass its rear, regardless of what the Continental army at Stillwater might wish. Thus it was pure accident that brought him face to face with Baum's Germans, who were at that moment approaching Bennington in search of horses. In response to the local people's demands for instant attack, Stark promised that if he did not give them fighting enough by sunset the next day, he would never call them out again.

* Pellew had behaved with great bravery during the naval battle at Valcour Island the year before.

Meanwhile, as the Germans and their auxiliaries plodded forward, Skene excelled himself. He welcomed scores of rebel soldiers pretending to come in for pardon, signed them up, told them the strength, disposition, and route of the column and let them go again, instructing them only to wear white papers in their hats as a sign for the Indians to spare them. When many of these men said they preferred to stay and fight the Yankees, he allowed them to do that as well. As Hadden wrote, "He acted like a ——!"

When Baum learned that he was confronted by nearly two thousand men, he took post on a hill, threw up some breastworks, and sent back for reinforcements. Burgoyne, awakened from his sleep, sent off the German reserve under Breymann. These crawled forward through the rain, likewise stopping every few minutes to dress their lines and straighten their heavy helmets. As Breymann's men advanced at half a mile an hour, occasionally speeding up to two miles an hour, Baum's force was attacked and wiped out. The pretended "loyalists" signaled for the battle to begin by shooting selected German officers in the back. The Indians, led by Saint-Luc, fled at once. Captain Fraser, the only intelligent officer on the expedition, managed to extricate most of his sharpshooters, but Baum and all but nine of his Germans were killed or taken prisoner. Stark, who had fought both at Bunker Hill and with Wolfe on the Plains of Abraham, said this was the hottest battle he had ever seen. "It represented one continued clap of thunder." Indeed, the smoke of the battle was seen from the heights of Stillwater, thirty miles away.[32] Curiously, nothing was seen or heard by Breymann. Skene, who had escaped, told Breymann to advance. The relief column arrived just as Stark's victorious army was scattering over the battlefield in search of plunder. The Americans retreated in confusion, but were saved by the arrival of Seth Warner and his brigade. By sunset, Breymann was in full flight, his men lumbering down the road, his cannons left behind for the enemy.

When the news reached Burgoyne, he personally waded across the Batten Kill at the head of the 47th Regiment, but as the remnants of the relief column came drifting in, it became obvious there was no one to save. He was too busy to notice when Saint-Luc arrived, declaring that his Indians were sick of the absurd restrictions and that it was in any case hunting time soon. Within an hour all the Western Indians had left; they were followed during the next few days by hundreds of the Iroquois. In all, Burgoyne had lost over nine hundred officers and men, four cannons, hundreds of muskets, all the powder and stores of the column, and three-quarters of his Indians. Nor had he acquired any new horses or provisions. Yet before he had time to weigh the consequences of this disaster, a message came from St. Leger. Carleton had told him that Fort Stanwix would be weakly defended by sixty militiamen and that there were no proper defense works. Instead, St. Leger had found the fort repaired and strong, with glacis, ditches, and bastions "pinched out" at the corners of the walls. The garrison contained six hundred men, amply provided with food and munitions. St. Leger's light cannons were useless. Ignorant of the strength of the garrison, St. Leger had stupidly paraded his regulars in front of the fort, thus informing the defenders that they were besieged by a force smaller than their own. He had thrown copies of Burgoyne's proclamation into the fort, and his nine hundred Iroquois had set up a chorus of blood-curdling yells; but these had merely steeled the garrison, under Colonel Peter de Gansevoort, in its resolve never to surrender. A relief column under Nicholas Herkimer, eight hundred men with four hundred oxcarts, had come from Fort Drayton; and Sir John Johnson's loyalists and Joseph Brant-Thayendanagea's four hundred Mohawks and Senecas had ambushed and destroyed it, killing Herkimer, at Oriskany. Nevertheless, without cannons St. Leger could not reduce Fort Stanwix quickly, and he was alarmed by the approach of a strong force of Continentals under Benedict Arnold. What was he to do? He hoped a diversion by Burgoyne would draw Arnold away and facilitate his own junction "with either of the Grand Armies" (i.e., with Burgoyne or Howe, whom St. Leger supposed to be in the region of Albany).[33] Burgoyne wrote back to say that he gave permission for St. Leger to do what was best, regardless of orders: He could continue the siege, come to Burgoyne across country if possible, return to Canada and come down via Ticonderoga, or bypass the fort and continue along the Mohawk, provided he could place firm trust in Johnson's assurances that all the inhabitants were loyalist.[34].

Burgoyne by now suspected what those assurances were really worth. The tempting picture of a frightened people longing to take up arms against their oppressors, as given by local "advisers" like Skene and Johnson, had turned out to be dangerous nonsense; yet these advisers still enjoyed the confidence of government. Burgoyne's awakening was sudden and dramatic and was followed by a growing realization of the implications of Howe's letter. On 15 August he had supposed that a German brigade would be able to march almost at will through Vermont, help themselves to thirteen hundred horses, and bring them back unmolested, in strings of ten so that each man could lead ten horses! Five days later (20 August) he was writing to Germain:

> On this side I find daily reason to doubt ... the professing loyalists. I have about 400, but not half of them armed, who may be depended upon; the rest are trimmers, merely actuated by interest. The great bulk of the country is undoubtedly with Congress, in principle and in zeal; and their measures are executed with a secrecy and dispatch that are not to be

equalled. Wherever the King's forces point, militia, to the amount of three or four thousand assemble in twenty-four hours; they bring with them their subsistence, etc., and, the alarm over, they return to their farms. The Hampshire Grants [Vermont] in particular, a country unpeopled and almost unknown in the last war, now abounds with the most active and the most rebellious race of the continent and hangs like a gathering storm upon my left.[35]

After lamenting his lack of communication with Howe and summarizing Howe's letter, he went on:

No operation, my Lord, has yet been undertaken in my favour: the highlands have not even been threatened. The consequence is, that Putnam has detached two brigades to Mr. Gates [who had just replaced Schuyler], who is now strongly posted near the mouth of the Mohawk-River, with an army superior to mine in troops of Congress, and as many militia as he pleases. He is likewise far from being deficient in artillery, having received all the pieces that were landed from the French ships which got to Boston.

The rest of the letter is so remarkable that it is tempting to wonder if recent events had not unbalanced Burgoyne's mind:

Had I a latitude in my orders, I should think it my duty to wait in this position, or perhaps as far back as Fort Edward, where my communication with Lake George would be perfectly secure, till some event happened to assist my movement forward; but my orders being positive to "force a junction with Sir William Howe," I apprehend I am not at liberty to remain inactive longer than shall be necessary to collect twenty-five days' provision, and to receive the reinforcement of the additional companies, the German drafts and recruits now (and unfortunately only now) on Lake Champlain. The awaiting of the arrival of this reinforcement is of indispensible necessity, because from the hour I pass the Hudson's River and proceed towards Albany, all safety of communication ceases. I must expect a large body of the enemy from my left will take post behind me.

He dared not delay after the arrival of the recruits lest the lateness of the season and the increasing numbers of the enemy prevent his retreat to Ticonderoga, should that be necessary.

When I wrote more confidently, I little foresaw that I was to be left to pursue my way through such a tract of country, and hosts of foes, without any co-operation from New York; nor did I then think the garrison of Ticonderoga would fall to my share alone, a dangerous experiment would it be to leave that post in weakness, and too heavy a drain it is upon the life-blood of my force to give it due strength.

> Yet I do not despond.—Should I succeed in forcing my way to Albany, and find that country in a state to subsist my army, I shall think no more of a retreat, but at the worst fortify there and await Sir William Howe's operations.
>
> Whatever may be my fate, my Lord, I submit my actions to the breast of the King, and to the candid judgement of my profession, when all the motives become public; and I rest in confidence, that whatever decision may be passed upon my conduct, my good intent will not be questioned.
>
> I cannot close so serious a letter without expressing my fullest satisfaction in the behaviour and countenance of the troops, and my compleat confidence that in all trials they will do whatever can be expected from men devoted to their King and country.

The key sentence in Germain's instructions to Carleton (26 March) had been

> . . . you are to give him [Burgoyne] orders to pass Lake Champlain, and from thence, by the most vigorous exertions of the force under his command, to proceed with all expedition to Albany, and put himself under the command of Sir William Howe.

This was clear enough. A later paragraph, however, had said that until Burgoyne and St. Leger

> . . . shall have received orders from Sir William Howe, it is his Majesty's pleasure that they act as exigencies may require, and in such manner as they shall judge most proper for making an impression on the rebels, and bringing them to obedience; but that in so doing, they must never lose view of their intended junctions with Sir William Howe as their principal objects.

Any officer seeking for latitude in his orders could surely have found it there. Burgoyne read his orders a hundred times, so he said, and came to the opposite conclusion. In his two letters of 5 April and 17 July, Howe had said that the movements of the enemy must guide Burgoyne's after reaching Albany. Therefore Burgoyne claimed that the instruction to "act as exigencies may require" applied only after his arrival in Albany. This was how he understood it, he said, and how both Carleton and Howe understood it as well.[36]

It should be mentioned first that the copy of Germain's letter which Carleton gave him when the campaign opened—and which constituted the only written orders Burgoyne ever received—begins "Upon these Accounts, and with a view of quelling the rebellion as soon as possible, it is become highly necessary that a most speedy junction of the two armies should be effected." This, and Carleton's deletion of all references to the forces to be left in Canada, does change the balance of the letter when it is read and makes the whole seem more peremptory than the longer version that is usually published.[37]

Although this is a minor point, even minor points can weigh a great deal with minds under stress. The grand strategy of a junction of two armies had been Burgoyne's particular obsession since 1775. It had offered every promise of success, where nothing else had offered even hope. Now, it was collapsing piece by piece around him. First, the problems of supply had led to the wretched affair at Bennington, which had been followed by the stalemate at Fort Stanwix. But none of these would have mattered had even the faintest gesture of aggression been made below the Highlands. Had General Howe pushed resolutely toward Albany in June or July, as had been planned and as Burgoyne had done, no amount of minor mishaps or even mistakes could have prevented the two generals from dining together in Albany by the middle of August; and if no one had considered deeply what to do next (a favorite point of criticism made against the plan), that, too, would not have mattered, for Great Britain would now have had all the cards in her hand.

Then again, suppose Clinton had already opened, or was about to open, his attack: For Burgoyne to sit where he was, or to retreat, would have exposed his colleague to terrible danger and himself to justifiable accusations of cowardice or incompetence. Thus, in Burgoyne's agitated mind sensible reasons intertwined themselves with foolish ones. The idea that he might get to Albany first developed into the idea that he might have to get there alone. Pride, contemplating the alternative of disgrace, then hardened this idea into a determination to get there whatever happened and at whatever cost. No one could afterward say he had not done *his* duty.

The dignified style and serious content of official papers and histories conceals, and so makes us forget, that the motives of statesmen and generals, no less than of scientists and philosophers, are often as personal, irrational, and at times even childish as those of ordinary men and women. The language of an Act of Parliament, a Treaty, or a military report may be elaborate, but the thought is always simple.

The news, brought by a party of Mohawks under Thayendanagea himself, that St. Leger had returned to Canada and was coming to join Burgoyne via Ticonderoga only strengthened Burgoyne's resolve. The tale was unedifying enough. While the Indians had been ambushing Herkimer, de Gansevoort had sent out a foray to lay waste their camp and take all their possessions. This had thrown the Indians, despite their victory, into a hysterical rage. At that moment, an Indian-speaking simpleton called Hon Yost had appeared, to say that General Benedict Arnold was approaching with an army more numerous than the leaves of the maple trees above. In fact, Hon Yost was a Tory condemned to death, to whom Arnold had promised a pardon in exchange for this service. Some Oneidas, also sent by Arnold, then arrived and confirmed the story. Arnold himself was still some forty miles away with only three thousand men, but the trick worked. After excited counsels among themselves and with St. Leger's officers, hampered by the fact that Claus and Thayendanagea disliked each other, the Indians departed. St. Leger then had to withdraw his men by night, leaving the camp untouched and the fires burning, in order to deceive the garrison. During the retreat a number of Indians, to the despair of the British officers of the Indian Service and of Thayendanagea himself, turned on the Europeans, murdered some, and stole all the provisions they could. The American story that St. Leger and Sir John Johnson almost came to blows in mutual recrimination is probably untrue, for they remained friends for years after. Claus attributed the failure to the casualness of General Carleton, who had given misleading intelligence about the state of Fort Stanwix. This may be true, but it is also true that the Indian Service was not yet strong and experienced enough to put down the incessant quarreling among the different tribes of Indians. Nor was St. Leger, brave as he might have been, equal to his difficult task.[38]

On the American side, Gates's intrigues with Congress had at last prevailed, and he was sent to replace Schuyler, arriving on 19 August. Schuyler, far from showing resentment, offered his services and advice in any way that might be needed; but Gates treated him with studied rudeness and kept him out of staff conferences. Schuyler then retired to Albany, where he supervised the melting down of window leads for bullets. One of the first matters Gates attended to was a letter from Burgoyne protesting over the treatment of Germans and loyalists taken prisoner in Bennington. Some had been killed in cold blood after surrendering, and loyalists had been tied together and dragged through the local towns, buffeted and kicked by the inhabitants. "If Duty & Principle, Sir, make me a public enemy to the Americans, . . . I seek to be a generous one." He also added that he wished to impugn no guilt to Gates personally. Gates replied that it was strange to see "the famous Lieutenant-General Burgoyne, in whom the fine gentleman is united with the soldier and the scholar," paying savages for the scalps of Europeans and went on to cite the case of Jane McCrae, "a young lady lovely to the sight . . . dressed to receive her promised husband," and a hundred more men, women, and children murdered by the Indians. The stories about Bennington were false, and if Burgoyne spoke of generosity, "Inclosed are letters from wounded prisoners in my hands, by whom you will be informed of the generosity of their Conquerors." In his indignant reply, Burgoyne protested that Jane McCrae, whose "fall wanted not the tragic display you have laboured to give it," was an isolated example, abhorred as much by himelf as by anyone. He knew of no others, he said.[39] There were, as we know, quite a number of others. Americans indeed claimed there were over six hundred, but this, considering the thinness of the population between St. Jean and Fort Edward, seems hardly possible. The modern reader, accustomed to a world in which civilians are massacred wholesale, may be surprised that our eighteenth-century ancestors, whose world was so coarse and callous in many ways, should have made such a fuss over the death of one girl, and a Tory to boot; yet their sense of horror was genuine. They took civilized standards, individual life, and the rights of property very seriously and so, pardoxically perhaps, did not think it inconsistent that the theft of an article worth more than a shilling should be punished by death. No one thought it more than proper that Burgoyne was now permitted to send to those officers who were prisoners in Gates' hands all their personal belongings and even their servants. At this time, too, Burgoyne gave permission to the officers' wives to stay with the army and face the perils ahead with their husbands, if they wished. There were at least half a dozen of them. Lady Harriet Acland had arrived, in advanced pregnancy, to nurse her husband through the wounds he had received in Hubbardton, and Baroness von Riedesel appeared with her three little daughters and an old manservant. The family lived in a room at the Red House, where, she said, she spent as happy a time as she remembered in her life, surrounded by people who loved her. Sometimes there was nothing to eat, but on other days they picknicked on the grass, in glorious weather and beautiful countryside. Bear meat she found very good, and at night, while the gentlemen played cards, she put the children to bed. Her maids, detailed by Burgoyne from among the army's women, slept "in a sort of Hall."

Burgoyne now had to consider the best way of advancing on Albany. If he went down the left, or eastern, side of the Hudson, the numerous creeks emptying into the river would force him to make wide detours and leave his batteaux unprotected. Moreover, his left flank would be constantly exposed to attacks from Vermont. Finally, he would have to cross the Hudson somewhere, as Albany stood on the western bank. If he crossed over immediately, he would cut off his communication with Canada, but the road on the other side was protected on the right by a long bluff of hills and thick forests, while the river protected his left. He decided, therefore, to cross at Saratoga. The army had to wait three more weeks while it brought up enough provisions for thirty days and gathered its strength for the final push. The reinforcements (not the one thousand originally promised, but only three hundred German recruits) at last arrived and were given a brief training. Captain Fraser's sharpshooters were augmented by another eighty-five men. Of the

Indians there were about eighty left. Since Burgoyne had refused to pay for scalps after Bennington,[40] these Indians had not stayed on for any mercenary motives. They were probably Iroquois Mohawks, of all the nations the ones most committed to the cause. The 62nd Regiment was brought down from Ticonderoga, and the 53rd, under Brigadier-General Powel, was sent back. The garrison at Fort Edward was transferred to Diamond Island on Lake George, where Burgoyne felt it would be safer.

Then, on 13 and 14 September, Burgoyne took his army across the Hudson. When the rear guard was over, he ordered the bridge to be broken up. Some called this step rash, thinking Burgoyne should wait until news came from Howe or Clinton in New York. Others said that if he did that, he might have to wait until Doomsday and that every passing day reduced the chances of success, which at present were good. "In my opinion," wrote Lieutenant Digby,[41] "this attempt showed a glorious spirit in our General, and worthy alone to be undertaken by British Troops, as the eyes of all Europe, as well as Great Britain were fixed upon us. . . ."

CHAPTER XIV

"OH FATAL AMBITION!"

THE news of the fall of Ticonderoga reached London in August. According to Horace Walpole, the king rushed into the queen's bedroom crying, "I've beat them! Beat all the Americans!"[1] He immediately wished to confer on Burgoyne an Order of the Bath. Burgoyne, however, had already warned Lord Derby that should this particular order be offered, he did not want it. Walpole said this was out of pique at not being given it earlier. More likely, Burgoyne was being careful. Carleton had been knighted the year before against the wishes of Germain, who had said prizes should be given after, not during, campaigns. All over England church bells rang and prayers were read out at service calling on God to protect General Burgoyne and his brave army and to punish the ungrateful rebels; all over New England ministers called on God to protect them from General Burgoyne and smite the savage invaders. In Paris, where it was believed that God looked down on all Protestants with equal displeasure, the news put Foreign Minister Vergennes, who had been cautiously steering France toward a war of revenge against Great Britain, at a non plus. He had recently connived at aid to the Americans to the extent of authorizing a shipment of royal cannons to Boston, the very pieces that now awaited Burgoyne on the heights of Stillwater. The complete collapse of American resistance in the north, however, suggested that perhaps France was tying herself to a useless, even dangerous, ally. Vergennes decided to delay further negotiations until more news came of Burgoyne.

To Lord George Germain, the news came as a relief. On 8 May another letter had come from Howe, dated 2 April. It said that since Howe had not received the reinforcements he needed, his original plan of a land march on Philadelphia, supported by a flank attack from the sea, was impracticable. Therefore, he intended to move the entire army by sea, landing it at the mouth of the Delaware. Enclosed was a copy of Howe's letter to Carleton (5 April) saying that Burgoyne could expect no aid from New York this campaign.[2] Germain answered this on 18 May, saying that while the king approved this change of plan, he hoped "it might be executed in time for you to co-operate with the army ordered to proceed from Canada and put itself under your Command." He added that the king approved of Howe's letter to Carleton.[3]

This letter has been held up as the supreme example of Germain's imbecility. Why had he waited so long to warn Howe and why, when he did so, did he phrase his warning so feebly, and at the same time approve Howe's letter to Carleton? If the interpretation given in Chapter XI is correct, however, then the letter falls naturally into place. It will be remembered that because the first letter from Howe (20 January) that referred to a movement on Philadelphia by sea arrived not before but *after* Burgoyne's departure, Germain, rather than cause confusion and embarrassment all around, and risk prolonging the war, by sending counterorders, decided to let well enough alone and trust that Burgoyne could reach Albany unassisted. This new letter from Howe (2 April) merely proposed that the entire army, instead of a part of it, was to go by sea. Since Britain had command of the sea, such a move might mean that Philadelphia would be captured sooner than by a land attack and that Howe could then sail part of his army back to New York and up the Hudson. Howe's letter to Carleton merely relieved Germain himself of the responsibility of writing to Burgoyne. Everything depended on when Howe began his campaign. Unfortunately, Howe was incapable of hurry. Week after week went by without news and Germain's anxiety mounted. Then, almost simultaneously, came reports that Burgoyne had taken Ticonderoga and that Howe had moved at last. The letters from the two generals, however, were somewhat contradictory, as might be expected. Burgoyne (11 July from Skenesborough) spoke of concentrating all his forces for the advance to Albany and the junction with Howe;* Howe (16 July from New York) made no mention of a junction at all. Germain told the king that he would not bother His Majesty with Burgoyne's letter just now; at the same time he inadvertently left Howe's letter out of the papers as well. Nevertheless, on 3 September he wrote to Howe, taking care not to acknowledge the receipt of Howe's letter, to say that he was glad there now existed "the fair prospect of a junction" earlier than Howe himself had expected."[4]

* Unless, of course, these references to a "junction" were added by Burgoyne after his return to England. For further discussion of this problem of whether Burgoyne forged part of his evidence offered in defense, see Chapter XVII and notes. As I say there, I am not sure he did forge the letter in the form that it was published but suspect that Germain may have "lost," or quietly suppressed, another letter of the same date in which a junction was mentioned. Otherwise, why did Germain not wish to show the letter to the king?

Clinton, meanwhile, arrived in New York on 5 July to find that Howe had spent June marching about New Jersey in order to prove what he wanted to believe: that a land advance on Philadelphia was impossible without the reinforcements he had been denied. Now the fleet was assembling to carry the entire army southward. For three weeks Clinton pleaded with Howe, in vain, to change his mind and cooperate with Burgoyne. Howe blocked all arguments with the reply that his plan had been approved by government. The temperaments of the two generals grated on each other, and the arguments degenerated into a review of all their old private resentments.[5] Clinton's frustration was heightened by the knowledge that nearly every officer in the army agreed with him, though only Colonel Stuart (Lord Bute's son) foresaw real danger to Burgoyne. Deaf to the sound of grinding teeth, Howe sailed away on 23 July. The fleet, commanded by his brother Lord Howe, appeared in the mouth of the Delaware but, instead of landing, put to sea again. Washington, fearing a trick, hovered by the Hudson. Clinton still hoped it was a trick, for Howe had left him with but 7,700 men ("a D...d starved deffencive") with which to cover Manhattan, Staten Island, Long Island, the Highlands, and a large area of surrounding territory. Of these men, three thousand were loyalists and one thousand were sick. On 10 August he received news that Howe was making for Chesapeake Bay. Clinton accordingly sent a cyphered message to Burgoyne to say that he could make no diversion in his favor but would try something when reinforcements arrived. Howe was going to Chesapeake, "the worst move he could make at this time."[6] No sooner had this gone off than Burgoyne's "high spirited" letter (6 August) arrived from Fort Edward. This set Clinton's mind at rest, for if Burgoyne were doing well and expected, as he said, to be in Albany by the twenty-third, Clinton's letter would at least inform him of the situation in New York. Unfortunately, the message never reached Burgoyne, although Clinton supposed it had. Thus Burgoyne continued to assume Clinton had a large force in New York and Clinton assumed Burgoyne knew he had not.

Howe landed at Head of Elk, at the top of Chesapeake Bay, on 25 August. Germain's letter of 18 May, reminding him of his duty to cooperate with Burgoyne, had reached him at sea. Now on 30 August, almost at the same time as Germain, in London, was writing to Howe of the fair prospect of an early junction, Howe wrote to Germain to say that such a junction was obviously out of the question.[7]

There have been many explanations offered for Howe's behavior, none of them entirely convincing. It used to be thought that it was Charles Lee who first put the idea of moving south into his mind. Lee had been captured in December by a company of Burgoyne's 16th Light Dragoons (under Lee's old comrade from Portugal, Colonel

Harcourt). Fearing he might be hanged, Lee tried to ingratiate himself by submitting a paper to Howe, dated 29 March 1777, in which he said that the British would be better to concentrate on the southern colonies, where resistance was less organized. Modern research, however, has shown that Howe had made his decision before meeting Lee. In any case, Howe's plan was very different. Alternatively, it has been suggested that Howe was jealous of Burgoyne, though others have objected that Howe was too inactive by temperament to be jealous of anyone. I think the truth is that while Howe was not jealous of Burgoyne personally, he did resent being involved in a strategy that was not his own. From the moment Burgoyne "took over" the Hudson plan, Howe liked it less and less and reacted to every mention of it with stubborn, silent evasion. A junction with Burgoyne's army created, besides, problems of precedence among the officers of both armies which made it more trouble than it was worth. Certainly he resented the way in which Germain had sent to Canada artillery and reinforcements he felt were rightfully his, just as Carleton resented Germain's supposed favoritism toward the army in New York. Yet, even so, why did he ignore Burgoyne's two letters from Plymouth and Quebec? The probability here is that once he had made up his mind on his own strategy, he closed it to anything that did not fit in. Burgoyne's plan did not fit in; and when Burgoyne's letters arrived, followed by the copy of Germain's orders to Carleton and Burgoyne, Howe presumably ignored their implications, assuming that his own letter to Carleton of 5 April would take care of the matter. Once he had decided that Burgoyne was irrelevant, he came to assume that Burgoyne could make his own way to Albany unassisted. In his letter of 16 July to Germain (the one which Germain did not show the king), he said that if Washington turned north and attacked Burgoyne, "the strength of Burgoyne's army is such as to leave me no room to dread the event." Moreover, if that happened Howe would follow him, and Washington would be trapped between the two armies. On the other hand, if Washington followed Howe southward, Burgoyne would meet no opposition at all.[8]

Why General Howe should have supposed all this is hard to understand, although there are historians who say he had every right to suppose it. Yet, it must be asked, if Howe believed he could not reach Philadelphia overland with fifteen thousand men, by what reasoning did he suppose Burgoyne could cross twice that distance with only seven thousand and hold off Washington's entire army besides? If he was at sea somewhere off the Delaware coast, how could he turn around and reach the Highlands in time to be of use to Burgoyne? It has been said that Howe was banking on loyalists to help Burgoyne.

Indeed he was, but he was also banking on loyalists to help himself, so the discrepancy remains.

Whatever Howe's reasons, the result was calamitous. He took his army clean out of the war for five weeks, at this most critical of times. When they arrived at Head of Elk, the men were weakened after days of sitting cramped on deck beneath a broiling sun. Nearly all the horses of his cavalry, Burgoyne's 16th Light Dragoons, had had to be thrown overboard when a storm had broken their legs or backs. He was now further from Philadelphia than he had been the previous March. The people of Maryland, unlike those of New Jersey, were almost universally hostile. The British forces were now hopelessly separated, and it was Washington, not the British as Germain had intended, who commanded interior lines of communication across all the continent from Wilmington to Stillwater. Hence Washington could deploy his forces north or south as he pleased, without fear of interception by the weak garrison in New York. Moreover, the removal of the main British army to Chesapeake lifted the threat of a strike across Connecticut toward Boston. Scarcely able to believe his good fortune, Washington declared, "Now let all New England rise and crush Burgoyne!"

In General Gates the New Englanders had the commander they had wanted. To encourage them further, Washington sent substantial reinforcements to Gate's army. Among them, a brigade under General Lincoln was ordered to advance north through Vermont, get behind Burgoyne's army, and cut his chain of posts. Washington also sent the corps of riflemen under the famous Daniel Morgan. Their Pennsylvania flintlocks (also called Kentucky rifles) were far superior in range and accuracy to the short rifles used by Captain Fraser's marksmen or von Riedesel's Jägers. Morgan, a cousin of Daniel Boone, had marched with Arnold to Quebec, been captured, and exchanged. Since then he had, by his exploits, turned himself into a living legend. His men were unencumbered with heavy packs and accustomed to covering hundreds of miles in a single forced march, always refusing wheeled transport as a hindrance.

Thus it was that when Burgoyne and his army crossed the Hudson and set off on their desperate adventure, Gates already had 4,500 men, with fresh regiments coming in daily. Kosciuszko, thinking Stillwater too vulnerable, found the ideal spot for defense works a few miles north on Bemis Heights, named after a local tavern keeper. Here he built a system of earthworks and breastworks behind a deep ravine which ran into the Hudson. In plan, his lines formed three sides of a square, each about three-quarters of a mile long. The eastern line ran along the ridge where the heights dipped down several hundred feet toward the river, while across the flat meadowland between the foot of the heights and the water along which ran the road to Albany, he built a number of trenches and breastworks, heavily defended with cannons. The highest point of his camp was the northwest corner, where stood a small house belonging to a farmer called Neilson.

Burgoyne's army advanced toward these defenses in three columns. On the right, Fraser's Advanced Corps and Breymann's Reserve (which had been reconstituted since Bennington) threaded their way through the wooded heights overlooking the valley. The main army, consisting of the regiments of the line and the Park artillery, marched along the road to Albany, making a splendid sight with bands playing, colors flying, and guns gleaming with polished brilliance. Burgoyne had combined the two British infantry brigades into one, consisting of the 9th, 20th, 21st, and 62nd Regiments. The 47th was deployed along the riverbank to cover the stores and baggage being carried down the Hudson on a flotilla of batteaux. In the rear came the wagons of the hospitals and kitchens, the herds of cattle, the supernumeraries (cooks, mechanics, etc.), and a crowd of women on foot. The officers' wives rode in little carts. Finally marched a rear guard of Germans.

On 15 September they reached a place called Dovegat, the modern Coveville, where, during the night, Major Acland's tent caught fire when his dog overturned a candle. Acland, only barely recovered from his leg wounds, was pulled out by his servant, but he plunged back into the flames to find his wife and was badly burned. She, however, had crawled out safely on the other side and treated the entire incident with cheerful stoicism. Acland nevertheless led his grenadiers off through the forest the next morning, his head and hands swathed in bandages. By sunset the army reached Sword's Farm, less than four miles from the enemy lines. Early the following morning a party of soldiers looking for potatoes, in disobedience to Burgoyne's orders two days before that no one was to go foraging until the morning fog lifted, was ambushed by a group of Morgan's riflemen and lost nearly thirty killed, wounded, or taken prisoner. That night, Burgoyne wrote in General Orders:

> To the great reproach of discipline, and of the common sense of Soldiers who have been made prisoners, the Service has sustained a loss within ten days that might in Action have cost the lives of some hundreds of the enemy.
>
> The Lieut. General will no longer bear to lose his men for the pitiful consideration of potatoes or forage.
>
> The life of the Soldier is the property of the King, and since neither friendly admonition, repeated injunctions nor corporal punishments have effect, after what has happened, the Army is now to be informed, and it is not doubted the Commanding Officers will do it, solemnly, that the first Soldier caught beyond the advanced Centries of the Army will be instantly hanged.[9]

Burgoyne was finding it increasingly difficult to persevere with his mild principles of discipline. Toward thieves and looters (especially of American property) he had always been implacable, and several had been sentenced to a thousand lashes, a punishment from which no one survived. On the other hand, he was still lenient toward offenses due to thoughtlessness or oversight. As I have mentioned in the opening chapter, an officer who had momentarily abandoned his post to attend to some private matter was let off with a reprimand.

At Sword's Farm, a road branched westward and upward into the forest-covered hills. From here to the American lines, the heights formed a sort of plateau gouged out by two curvaceous ravines. Part of this plateau had been cleared for farming and was crisscrossed with paths. About two and a half miles west, the road from Sword's Farm formed a T-junction with another road from the north which continued down to Neilson's Farm. This was the route Burgoyne ordered Fraser and his corps to take. He himself would follow, with the six British battalions of the line (the 9th, 21st, 62nd, and 20th in that order, for that was their order of seniority), until he was midway between Fraser and the river. Then he would turn south and follow a short road that led to the first of the ravines barring the way. This, several hundred feet deep, resembled more a forest canyon than a ravine and was hence called the Great Ravine; but Burgoyne himself, with two thousand men, had already reconnoitered this part of the ground on the 16th[10] and had sent out a detachment to build a bridge across the creek. The German battalions and the Park artillery under Phillips were to advance along the road to Albany beside the river.

Baroness von Riedesel tells us that on the eve of battle Burgoyne was cheerful and confident of victory. Historians have sneered at such shallow optimism. However, that his confidence was shared by the army is shown by Digby, Hadden, and the other diarists, as well as by Sir Francis Clerke's letter to his father:

> Immediately after, we shall try the Countenance of Mr. Gates; they pretend to be in spirits and threaten to give us a drubbing, but on the approach of the red Coats I rather believe it will be as usual, they will find out that they can take up better ground in their rear. . . . As we advance we shall be compact, and the Distance from the Lakes encreasing, we cannot expect to keep up the Communication, therefore we set our faces forward, and mean to bite hard if any thing dares to show itself. As to numbers of our foes, I believe them great, mais n'importe, what are we not equal to?[11]

Unaware that events in the world beyond, linked through the personage of Lord George Germain as the "One Great Director" of the war, were combining together and multiplying the odds against him,

Burgoyne believed that, even if the Americans in front outnumbered him and were strongly posted, he had a good chance of forcing or turning their lines, and that after that the way to Albany would be open once again.

Burgoyne's generalship has been severely criticized by some historians, mainly American. It is said that by dividing his small army into three, he fatally weakened it and made communication between the wings impossible in such thickly forested country. He should have concentrated his entire force and attacked on the flat ground beside the river, using his heavy artillery to batter down the defenses there. Deprived of his Indians he had to advance blindly in the forest, along the river at least he could have seen where he was going. Against this opinion, we have the authority of the great Sir John Fortescue, historian of the British army. After describing Kosciuszko's entrenchments, Fortescue writes:

> Burgoyne, however, was a better soldier than the Pole. He remarked very quickly that there was a hill on the American left which commanded the whole of their position, but which was still unoccupied. Could he but seize this hill by a vigorous attack, he could haul his heavy guns to the summit and rake the American trenches from end to end. For this object accordingly he laid his plans.[12]

This, of course, is in flat contradiction to the critics. Unfortunately, I have found no evidence that Burgoyne was able to form such a clear-cut plan. Though I am reluctant to dispute with so distinguished an author, whom I greatly admire, it does seem that Fortescue confused this battle with the second battle on 7 October, when Burgoyne certainly had some such idea in mind. Nevertheless, Burgoyne's tactics do not appear to have been so blind and foolish as they are often thought.

To start with, Burgoyne did not know the exact position or extent of the American lines, for his Indians and auxiliaries were never able to get within sight of them. Yet he must have known that the lines slanted upward for about three-quarters of a mile and that the ground continued to rise to the west of them. Suppose, however, he had ignored that fact and attacked along the riverbank with his entire army, as Nickerson and others say he should have done. One has only to stand on the heights overlooking the Albany road to see the fatuity of the idea. First, his approach would have been slow, for bridges would have had to be built over the streams opening into the Hudson from the ravines. Second, he would have had to attack where the enemy were strongest. Third, while he was busy crossing the streams, the Americans could have swept around through the forest and, driving Fraser's corps from the ridge, pinned the entire army against the river, firing from high, rocky, forested ground with the sun behind them!

Burgoyne divided his army because he had no choice. He surmised that Gates, whom he regarded as an able administrator but a timid tactician, would keep his men behind their lines and wait for the British to be massacred by superior fire power. If he did not know of an actual "hill" (though there is a rise about a quarter of a mile west of Neilson's Farm, well within range of Fraser's six-pounders, from which he could have enfiladed most of the American line, which slopes *downward* east of the farm) he did suspect that there probably was one.* The obvious thing was for Fraser to feel his way toward it, while von Riedesel on the left kept the Americans busy in their camp. Burgoyne meanwhile would come out of the forest somewhere near the westernmost corner of the defenses and prevent a sally toward Fraser. Then, perhaps, the two corps could unite on the flank or in the rear of the American camp. This, according to an American author of the last century, was the plan as told afterward by Phillips to Benedict Arnold.[14]

There is also another piece of circumstantial evidence to support this view of Burgoyne's intention. It will be remembered that when Burgoyne returned from his European tour, he presented Pitt with a copy of a paper which Frederick the Great had written for his generals. It concerned the lessons of the Seven Years' War, which Frederick called the "new war of positions." There is a passage exactly relevant, wherein Frederick pointed out what could be done when attacking an enemy of superior numbers strongly fortified on elevated ground. "You must immediately look for and seize a higher spot on the flank, which the enemy in nine cases out of ten will have neglected." He added that such high spots could always be detected by a skilful eye.[15] This was the maneuver that had conquered Ticonderoga and which might well succeed now. Moreover, Burgoyne's reading of his opponent's character was correct; for if Gates had had his way, the Americans *would* have stayed behind their lines. Fraser's corps would then have reached the raised ground, where the Americans had in fact begun to dig a few trenches, and placed his six-pounders upon it. Since the forest had been cleared in this area, he would have had an open field of fire across which to send his shot bouncing along the rear side of the defenses that sloped down the hill, and Burgoyne would have been perfectly placed to storm the lines as the Americans withdrew. Penned up in their camp, the Americans could well have sufferd a catastrophic defeat. It has been said that Gates was the only general on either side who could have lost the war in an afternoon; if that is true, then Burgoyne could have won it.

Burgoyne's mistake, if it can be called such, was to take no account of

* Burgoyne may not in fact have been so ignorant of the American positions as is sometimes believed. On 17 September, Fraser paid £5 13s 4d to "men who brought in an exact account of the rebel army, cannon & dispositions."[13]

the character of Benedict Arnold. That restless, conceited, but able and very brave man foresaw precisely this danger and badgered Gates to take, almost literally, the bull by the horns and attack the British in the forest, where their terrible bayonet charges and heavy guns could not be fully effective. Reluctantly, Gates allowed Morgan's corps, supported by Dearborn's light infantry, to move forward in search of the enemy.

Burgoyne, meanwhile, had led his four battalions across the Great Ravine and to the head of a second ravine called Mill Creek (or Middle Ravine). Here they emerged from a thin pine wood onto a clearing. This was part of a farm belonging to one Freeman, now dead, whose sons were loyalists in Canada.[16] Burgoyne ordered Freeman's log cabins and huts, which stood in the clearing, to be occupied by a piquet. The fighting began when a part of Morgan's corps, crossing the clearing, saw the piquet, opened fire and, pursuing them toward the pine wood, found themselves face to face with a line of redcoats. Some of the British infantry opened fire when they realized these unkempt figures in coonskins and fringed hunting jackets were not Indians and accidentally killed some of their own piquets running toward them. Burgoyne ordered a signal gun to bring his men to their senses, and when its booming echoes died away Morgan's riflemen had vanished into the woods on the far side of the clearing. In the long silence that followed, the British heard a faint and strange squawking from the enemy wood. It was Morgan, rallying his scattered men with a "turkey call," an instrument for decoying wild turkeys. Realizing the Americans had come out to fight instead of staying behind their breastworks, Burgoyne deployed the 21st, 62nd, and 20th Battalions in line from right to left, with artillery in the gaps between them. The 9th was ordered back into reserve. A sudden outburst of firing from the high ground to the west indicated that Fraser was now engaged. Burgoyne had arranged for three guns to be fired in quick succession as a signal for the entire army to advance, since the wings could not see each other. After the tense quiet that always precedes an infantry attack, the three guns boomed, and the lines of British infantry, with drums beating and bayonets pointing forward, began their advance across the clearing. They were met by a murderous fire from the wood. Gates, at the frantic request of Arnold and all his officers, had consented to send out regiments of Continentals to support Morgan; the first two of these, from New Hampshire, were already in place, while a number of Morgan's men had climbed into the trees, whence they could better pick off the British officers striding forward in front of the lines. One by one the officers fell this way and that, and great gaps appeared in the ranks. The advance stopped, and the men, breaking formation, retreated toward their pine forest. Brigadier Hamilton formed them up again in a V-shaped line centered upon Freeman's farm buildings just as the Americans in turn came charging out of their wood. The action now became general as the British artillery was brought to bear on the wood opposite. This was Lieutenant Digby's first experience of a "real" battle, as opposed to a skirmish, and he was as astonished and shaken by the sight as every novice has always been: "such an explosion of fire I never had any idea of before, and the heavy artillery joining concert like great peals of Thunder, assisted by the echoes of the woods, almost deafened us with the noise."[17]

Over this clearing the fight swayed back and forth for nearly four hours. The weight of numbers against the British began to show its effect; for Gates now had seven thousand men in his army, and as each American regiment retired to lick its wounds another moved in to take its place. Gradually, too, they extended their line to the right and left and threatened to surround the British brigade on three sides. Groups of American riflemen, indeed, actually got around to the rear. The worst casualties were suffered by the artillery, who lost all their officers except Lieutenant Hadden and thirty-six out of their forty-eight men. Several times the guns were captured and turned around, but the Americans, lacking linstocks and horses, were unable to fire or remove the guns before being driven off. Of the 62nd Regiment, in the center, barely sixty men out of its original four hundred were left standing.[18] Phillips, who had ridden through the woods from the river, saved the regiment by personally leading the 20th in a bayonet charge from its left flank. Burgoyne himself went from company to company to rally the brigade, again calling "Well done, my brave Springers!" to the 62nd as he passed. Sergeant Lamb wrote, "He shunned no danger; his presence and conduct animated the troops, for they greatly loved the General. He delivered his orders with precision and coolness, and in the heat, danger and fury of the fight, maintained the true characteristics of the Soldier—serenity, fortitude, and undaunted intrepidity." Digby supports this by saying that General Burgoyne was everywhere and did everything that could be expected of a brave officer. His aide, Captain Greene, was wounded by an American marksman who, from his richly embroidered saddlecloth, mistook him for Burgoyne, and this started a rumor in the American camp that the British general was dead.

During all this time, Fraser's corps, exchanging fire with Learned's brigade, dared not move to aid the hard-pressed center for fear of losing its advantageous position on the highest ground. At length Burgoyne sent orders to von Riedesel, who had been kept waiting near the river, to bring up a regiment and hit the Americans on their right flank. The Germans arrived with artillery in the nick of time, and under their fire the Americans collapsed. The British made one more bayonet attack just as the sun set, but the wood now contained only dead and dying. The Americans had disappeared.

The British spent an anxious night resting on their arms. They could hear the cries and groans of wounded men in the dark of the forest, but were under pain of death not to go beyond the sentries. More harrowing were the sudden outbursts of yelps and snarls as packs of wolves ran through the undergrowth, fighting over corpses and attacking those who were still alive but unable to defend themselves. With dawn, Burgoyne wished to resume his attack, for he was sure the Americans were too disorganized to hold their lines. His guess was right, for chaos reigned in the American camp. No food had been issued the previous day, and the men were down to a single round of ammunition each. Had Burgoyne's army come charging through the morning fog, after the first volley the Americans could have done nothing but break and run. Fraser, however, said the soldiers were too exhausted, and Burgoyne accepted his advice.[19] Thus once again he was cheated of total success. Technically, since he held the field, he could claim the battle of 19 September as a victory, though like Bunker Hill it was a Pyrrhic one. He had lost over five hundred men killed, a high proportion of them officers, and he had still not beaten through the American lines. Indeed, he had not even seen them. He decided to attack once again, on the twenty-first, before it was too late.

When the twenty-first dawned, however, wet, cold, and foggy as usual, the army was still not ready for an attack. Indeed, the eight hundred or so wounded were not yet in the hospital, the stores and cattle not securely defended, and the brigades, with the 62nd Regiment decimated and the 20th and 21st terribly mauled, not yet reformed. Burgoyne postponed the attack one more day, probably with growing doubts as to its feasibility. The battle had shown the very superior numbers of the Americans, and there was no knowing how fast their strength was increasing. Moreover—and this was the most unwelcome truth of all—the Americans had been as stubborn and brave as his own British regulars, whom everybody conceded were no ordinary soldiers. If Gates was soon to have twelve thousand men behind strong, well-laid, and *hidden* defenses, with ample supplies and open lines of communication, what could Burgoyne do with 4,300, cut off from all communication, with barely a month's supply in hand and hardly any time to reach Albany before the weather made campaigning impossible? Historians, secure in their studies, have sneered at Burgoyne for casting his eye desperately toward New York and complaining bitterly that no hint of cooperation had come from that powerful army. But how many in his situation would not have felt as he did?

That night, indeed, a messenger arrived from General Clinton, bringing the first word from the outside the army had received for a week, and the first from New York since July. It was in code, and to the uninitated read as a rambling, inconsequential, piece of banter:

> While you my dear Burgoyne are reaping laurels I am forced to sleep. You must know my temper too well to doubt that I do not concede them *to you* with good will, & are convinced that I take my share in your success . . .

and so on for twenty-one lines.[20] The key to the cypher was a sheet of paper with a hole cut in the shape of an hourglass, which, when placed over the original, revealed the meaning hidden in the prose. Burgoyne had lost his key and had to cut another from memory. After several tries, he was able to isolate the following message:

You
know my
good will, & are
not ignorant of my
poverty. If you think
2000 men can assist
you effectually
I will make
a push at
Montgomery
in about ten days
but ever jealous of
my flanks; if they make
a move in force on either
of them, I must return to
save this important post.
I expect reinforcements
every day. Let me know
what you would
wish.[21]

Forts Montgomery and Clinton* were the strongest of the forts which the Americans had built during the past year to guard the Highlands, and if Burgoyne knew little of their situation or size he had reason to suppose they were formidable. Two thousand men were a curiously small number with which to storm such obstacles, but presumably

* Fort Clinton was named after George Clinton, who had just been elected governor of New York. It was commanded by his brother, General James Clinton. They were both distantly related to Sir Henry, through a former royal governor of New York. In overall command of the Highlands was General Israel Putnam, the hero of Bunker Hill, and a veteran of the French and Indian War.

Sr H. C to Burgoyne 1777

While, you my dear Burgoyne are reaping laurels, I am forced to sleep. You know my temper too well to doubt that I do not cede them to you with good will, & are convinced that I take real share in your success. You're not ignorant of my hopes of being able to work at last upon —'s poverty. If you think the young man more tractable, I'll try him. Surely 2000 men can assist Sir W. importantly just now! I'll send him them, for you effectually secure me to the Northward. With what I shall have left, I will make no scruple of asserting they should Mr Putnam make a push at me, "il laisse sur les ongles". ~~Indeed~~, excepting at Fort Montgomery, I believe they have few troops near me. I think in about ten days the Corps shall sail. Vaughan leads them. He's well, but ever jealous of reputation, does not like keeping guard here. Both my flanks, if they make a decent defence, are secure, for I think a move in force on either of them not probable. Now talking of them I must return to my old argument & say, that tho' to save this important post, is a great object, we have greater. I expect reinforcement by the middle of October: Recruits arrive every day. Let me know about that time where a push will help you & what you would think of reinforcing Rhode Island, as Pigot ~~[illegible]~~ wish to make an excursion in that quarter.

, you
know my
good will, & are
not ignorant of my
poverty. If you think
2000 Men can assist
you effectually
I will make
a push at
Montgomery,
in about ten days
but ever jealous of
my flanks, if they make
a move in force on either
of them I must return to
save this important post.
I expect reinforcement
every day. Let me know
what you would
wish

Sir Henry Clinton's coded letter, with cypher. (*Courtesy of the Sir Henry Clinton Papers, William L. Clements Library, The University of Michigan, Ann Arbor.*)

the five thousand reinforcements would reach Clinton very soon. Burgoyne did not want to fail; and the more his difficulties thickened about him, the more unthinkable appeared the consequences of failure. How many times had he said "Britons do not retreat"? Frederick the Great and Wolfe had snatched victory in circumstances even more adverse than his own. Here was a sudden ray of hope, and by its light the prize of Albany glittered temptingly once again in the distance.

He therefore sent the messenger back that night, after diverting the attention of the Americans with an artillery bombardment, with the following note:

> I have lost the old Cypher, but being sure from the tenor of your letter you meant it to be so read, I have made it out. An Attack, or even the menace of an Attack, must be of great use, as it will draw away part of this force, and I will follow them close; do it, my dear friend, directly.[22]

With this he sent a verbal message to give Clinton a truer picture of the situation. His army had salt provisions for no more than thirty days, and his communication with Canada had been cut. Nevertheless, he believed he could still force his way past Gates to Albany and unite with the New York army.[23]

Burgoyne meanwhile decided to fortify his position and wait for further news from Clinton before attacking again. He ordered redoubts, some of earth and some of wooden breastworks, to be built in a rough semicircle from a position north of Freeman's Farm down to the river, placing his headquarters in the middle. A pontoon bridge was laid across the Hudson, over which patrols were sent to reconnoiter the east bank and see if a clearer picture of the American defenses could be formed. At the same time, he tried to reestablish contact with the north, sending two letters to General Powel at Ticonderoga. There is something odd about this, however, for at Saratoga a passing Indian was shot by an American officer, who found both letters in the warrior's pouch. The first letter described the battle of the nineteenth as a victory; but in the second (dated 21 September) Burgoyne made the curious remark that had the action been fought nearer the river, so that the left column could have been brought into action sooner, not a man of the enemy would have escaped.[24] Although the first letter has since been quoted as evidence of Burgoyne's foolish optimism, it would seem that by sending both letters by one Indian (perhaps without clear instructions) Burgoyne intended the letters to be intercepted and by this remark hoped to persuade Gates to keep his force concentrated near the river. It is certainly true that Gates always feared that that was where the main attack would come, and it was this fear, and his consequent reluctance to advance his troops into the forest, which was the source of his quarrel with Benedict Arnold.[25]

Burgoyne continued to send messengers to Clinton. On 23 September he sent what was more or less a duplicate of the one two days before, adding, "I have beat the Enemy, but as the Night stopt the pursuit the Victory was not decisive."[26] On the 27th heartening news was brought by some loyalists who slipped into camp. Howe had scored a decisive success in the south, and Washington's army was on the point of dissolution.[27] That night, Burgoyne sent Captain Scott into the forest toward New York. His written message simply mentioned the Bennington affair and the fact that he could not keep up his communication with Canada. His instructions were to push for a junction with Sir William Howe, and he wished Sir Henry Clinton to make a diversion in his favor. The verbal message stated his true position. He was down to five thousand troops, having lost five to six hundred on the nineteenth, with many sick. The rebel army was about twelve thousand, with four thousand more hovering in his rear. He believed he could still force his way to Albany if a communication could be opened with New York. In that case he could hold his present position until 16 October. However, once in Albany he would have to be supplied through the winter. If this were not possible, he would have to make good his retreat before the ice set in; that meant that he would have to move before the twelfth. "Genl. Burgoyne begs Sir Henry Clinton will give him an Answer, conveying the plainest and most positive Meaning, how he should act for the good of the Service. . . ."[28]

The next day, however, a German officer captured in Bennington arrived under a flag of truce to discuss the exchange of an American colonel. He brought the disturbing news that Lincoln had attacked Ticonderoga, destroying the ships, taking many prisoners, and releasing three hundred American prisoners kept in a barn. Lincoln had also attacked Fort George and Diamond Island, and although he had been beaten off the island with loss, he had destroyed several boats on the lake. Now Lincoln was on his way back to join General Gates. Burgoyne's position was clearly becoming more dangerous every day. That night he sent Captain Campbell to Clinton, with a message even more strongly worded than the previous one. His provisions would last only until 20 October. He wished to receive orders as to whether he should attack or retreat. He would never have allowed his communication with Ticonderoga to be cut had he not expected a cooperating army from Albany. He wanted a positive answer as soon as possible, especially as to whether or not Clinton, once in Albany, would be able to supply him or keep open a communication with New York through the winter.

Besides the diversions Burgoyne had to stage to keep the Americans busy while his messengers stole out of camp, every night was punctuated by constant alarms as bands of auxiliaries, called "Cowboys" if they were Tories and "Skinners" if they were rebels, skirmished in the surrounding forest. Sentries were beng picked off and groups of Indians, who had now joined the Americans, sometimes penetrated into the camp itself from the rear. One old American backwoodsman who saw his own son in a redoubt feeding some of Burgoyne's horses shot him dead. Food was becoming noticeably short, for many wagonloads of flour had been spoiled by the frequent rainstorms. The entire army slept, when it slept at all, in its clothes, and, to add to its discomforts, the wolves who came down from the neighboring hills to feed on the dead had increased to thousands. Fraser, thinking at first that the noise was due to fights among the officers' dogs, issued an order that any loose dog in camp would be hanged, but a party sent out next night discovered the truth. Meanwhile, the stench of corpses which hung over the camp was frightful. Desertions, especially among the Germans, became frequent for the first time, and Burgoyne, with uncharacteristic harshness, gave his remaining Indians permission to kill and scalp any deserters they caught. Yet perhaps it was not so harsh, for Burgoyne knew that none of his Indians would venture from the camp unsupported.

Still Burgoyne hesitated. His knowledge of Clinton's cautious nature must have told him that no move would be made in New York until his replies were received there. Clinton's letter had taken eleven days to reach him. His own replies could not possibly get through before 1 October, supposing they got through at all. Clinton's offer to move on 21 September therefore had to be disregarded. Yet he persuaded himself that Clinton might appear behind Gates's army at any moment. Indeed, under the pressure of the repeated and ever more serious disappointments since the arrival of Howe's letter on 5 August, Burgoyne's mind, as I have said before, seems to have gradually lost its balance. Concerning his thoughts at this time, he wrote later to Germain that he was afraid to retreat lest Gates be freed to concentrate against Clinton or Howe. This was reasonable enough and perhaps even a justification for his staying where he was; but then he went on to say:

> . . . I reasoned thus. The expedition I commanded was meant at first to be *hazarded*. Circumstances might require it should be *devoted*. A critical junction of Mr. Gates' force with Mr. Washington might possibly decide the fate of the war; the failure of my junction with Sir Harry Clinton, or the loss of my retreat to Canada, could only be a partial misfortune.[29]

"Devoted" was his word for "sacrificed." I have already suggested that Burgoyne's guess that his army was being hazarded was not far from the truth, but not by any means for the reason Burgoyne had come to imagine. Germain may well have not informed Burgoyne of Howe's change of plan and thereby deliberately hazarded his army because he preferred such a calculated risk to the obvious dangers of calling off the entire plan. He did not intend Burgoyne to lead a "forlorn hope" (as such suicide missions were called) so that Howe himself would not be overwhelmed by superior numbers. Furthermore, how could Burgoyne reconcile this notion with the news of Howe's victories (he had fought Brandywine and captured Philadelphia) and the impending collapse of Washington's army? The probable truth is that Burgoyne was guided no longer by reason but by emotion.

On 4 October, with no news from Clinton and the situation becoming more dangerous every hour, he called a council of his staff officers, the first since the campaign opened. He proposed that, with eight hundred men posted to guard the supplies, he would lead the rest of the army in a final attack on the enemy's left and try to get at the rear of the American defenses. Von Riedesel suggested a retreat to Fort Edward. Fraser supported him. Phillips abstained from voting. No decision was taken (which was why Burgoyne, who knew politics, had held no previous councils), but on the sixth an inspection of the British camp was made to calculate how many to leave for its protection. Burgoyne then decided to move the next day.

There is some controversy over his plan. Von Riedesel writes that he intended merely a reconnaissance in force, with a foraging expedition at the same time. The foremost American historian of this campaign, Hoffman Nickerson, writes that Burgoyne's plan was very vague and that although there was "some talk afterwards" of enfilading the American lines with artillery fire from a hill on the American left (just as Fortescue says Burgoyne had intended on the nineteenth), this was nonsense, as "no such hill exists." Two such hills do exist, as I have observed before, and Burgoyne's engineers, despite the danger, had almost certainly discovered them by 5 October. Moreover, if Burgoyne intended a mere foraging and reconnaissance sortie, why did he take fifteen hundred picked men, the best remaining to him, supported by two twelve-pounders, two howitzers, and six six-pounders, together with Fraser, Phillips, von Riedesel, and the cream of his officers? His plan, then, seems to have been to take post on the American left, stay there overnight with the cannons in position, and launch a combined attack the next morning from the left, and from the front with two thousand of the troops who had been kept in camp to guard the supplies. Burgoyne seems to have supposed, despite the events of the nineteenth, that Gates would still prefer to wait behind his lines and allow Burgoyne to move around as he pleased. It was Burgoyne's worst misjudgment.[30]

It is true that in the American camp a serious quarrel had broken out between Gates and Arnold. Gates, perhaps out of jealousy, had pointedly made no mention of Arnold in his report of the battle of the nineteenth. Arnold had resigned his command in protest but still lingered about the camp gathering supporters. Whether or not Arnold had really been on the field is uncertain. Wilkinson, in his *Memoirs*, says that neither Arnold nor (incredibly) any other American general officer had been on the battlefield during the entire day. Neilson, the owner of the farm, later told the historian Jared Sparks that he had seen Arnold inactive in camp throughout the battle.[31] On the other hand, Arnold had certainly ordered several regiments out against Gates' wishes and so saved the day. Now the army was split into two factions: Arnold and most of the officers and soldiers on one side; Gates and his staff on the other. Gates, however, was no longer worried by temporary unpopularity, for he might soon become the first American general to win a decisive victory. The British, with no other way out, might try to regain all by some rash stroke; "that failing, their utter ruin is inevitable." Nor did he doubt that Burgoyne was the man to make that rash stroke: "Despair may dictate to him to risk all upon one throw; he is an old gambler, and in his time has seen all the chances."

On 7 October, Burgoyne led his column, fifteen hundred strong with artillery, out of the camp toward the northwest of the American lines shortly after noon. He had started out late not, as some have said, through laziness and stupidity, but because he had calculated that, in the event of a reverse, darkness would cover his retreat. Thus the morning had been spent in councils and in instructing the Indians who were to go out, as usual, as a screen in front. Unfortunately, during this time of waiting an artilleryman saw his chance to desert and warn the Americans of an impending attack. Furthermore, although Burgoyne was in no hurry, it is hard to see why he finally advanced in such a leisurely fashion. When the column reached a clearing, it stopped, set up light cannons, and opened fire on an American piquet a few hundred yards away. The troops sat down, while the foraging parties moved about gathering corn. Burgoyne then ordered the column to move on toward the high ground not far ahead. By this time, however, the Americans had had sufficient time to call out and deploy their entire army. With the first reports of a British move, Gates had once again sent out Morgan and Dearborn with fifteen hundred men. On the insistence of Arnold, Lincoln, and others, Gates sent out more brigades, totaling over six thousand men, in support, saying "Let Morgan begin the game."

Thus Burgoyne was suddenly and violently attacked by battalion after battalion of Americans charging with yells and cheers out of the forest and across the clearing. The Indians and Captain Fraser's marksmen were scattered to the winds, the grenadiers on the left were cut to pieces, and Acland, again shot through both legs, was taken prisoner. Wilkinson saved him from being shot point-blank by a boy who had followed with the militia. The British and German line was now in danger of being cut off from the camp and of being surrounded on the right flank by Morgan's riflemen. Two cannons had already been captured in wild hand-to-hand fighting, during which Major Williams had been taken prisoner, and the Germans in the center were beginning to break and run. Arnold, meanwhile, had appeared on the scene, in disobedience to Gates's orders, waving his sword above his head as he rode through a hail of fire between the two armies. Placing himself in front of a Massachusetts brigade, he took command of the attack against the right. It was then, on Arnold's advice, that one of Morgan's riflemen (to whom Morgan in turn said, "That gallant officer is General Fraser. I admire him, but it is necessary that he should die—do your duty!") shot and mortally wounded Fraser, who was at that moment trying to redeploy his men.

Burgoyne ordered a retreat. He himself, shot through waistcoat, collar, and hat, yet unscathed, rode back to tour the redoubts and instruct the captains that they must expect an assault and must hold to the last man. The officers noted that the general's face was lined with anxiety. Covered by the light infantry, the column poured back to camp, leaving all its cannons behind. Arnold now led the advance against Freeman's Farm, where Lord Balcarres had taken post with such men as he could muster in the confusion. Thanks largely to the cannons, the Americans were beaten back, and it looked as if the fighting was over. Arnold, however, noticed that between the Balcarres redoubt and the redoubt on the extreme right, held by Breymann and his Reserve, stood a pair of cabins in a dip, manned only by Canadians. He therefore led a charge against the cabins and, when the Canadians fled, continued around to the rear of the German redoubt. He was wounded once more in his leg. Almost at the same time, however, Breymann was killed (perhaps by one of his own men, for he had slashed at his men with his sword to make them fight), and the Germans fled or surrendered. By now, darkness was coming on, and the battle ended at last.

Burgoyne's gamble, played with a clumsiness untypical of him, had cost him another five hundred men, half of them taken prisoner, and a score of his best officers, including Major Acland, Major Williams, Captain Blomefield, and Captain Money. His aide, Sir Francis Clerke, was dying in Gates' headquarters, where the commander was haranguing him on the justifications for the Revolution. When Clerke, who had more serious things to think about, showed signs of polite boredom,

The scene at Bemis Heights after the battle of 7 October 1777. The little procession is the burial party for Brigadier General Fraser. The engraving was done from an original sketch by Burgoyne's aide, Lieutenant Sir Francis Kerr Clarke, who was captured in the battle and later died of his wounds. (*From Anburey's* Travels Through the Interior Parts of America.)

Gates exclaimed, "Did you ever see such an impudent son of a bitch?" Fraser had been taken to the house used by Baroness von Riedesel, where she had been preparing a supper for him, Phillips, and Burgoyne. He was laid on the table and told by the surgeon that he had not long to live. He died the next morning. During the night, the baroness heard him exclaim, "Oh fatal ambition! Poor General Burgoyne! Poor Mrs. Fraser!"[32]

During the night, Burgoyne countered the loss of the Breymann redoubt, which exposed his right wing to the enemy, by withdrawing north across the Great Ravine. The next day, the two armies faced each other, offered battle and exchanged fire, during which Lincoln was badly wounded, but neither dared to move.

Captain Fraser's men, who as usual had recovered quickly, returned from their morning scouting to say that a strong American force was making a wide circle through the forest, which would soon put them in command of the road back to Saratoga. With great reluctance, Burgoyne gave the order to prepare a retreat. One duty remained, however. Fraser has asked to be buried in the Great Redoubt, a strong fortification overlooking the Hudson, and Burgoyne was determined to honor the memory of his friend, come what may. At sunset, the burial party ascended the hill. While Mr. Brudenell, the chaplain to the Royal Artillery, read the prayers and delivered a sermon with unaltered voice, cannon shot from an American battery, who did not realize what was happening, struck the earth all around them and covered them with dust. It was a scene, wrote Burgoyne, that would "remain to the last of life upon the mind of every man who was present." Von Riedesel called it "a real military funeral—one that was unique of its kind."[33] Nevertheless, the Germans grumbled that this sentimentality was wasting precious time in which they could have been making good their escape.

Several hundred wounded were left behind in the care of Dr. John Mcnamara Hayes, to whom Burgoyne gave a letter expressing his confidence that Gates would show them the same consideration and humanity that Burgoyne himself would have shown, had the fortune of war reversed their roles. Then at nine o'clock the army set off on its long and hazardous march toward Ticonderoga. Although it was two hours before the rear guard could get under way, the operation was carried out so silently that the Americans heard nothing. At that moment it began to rain.

CHAPTER XV

HAVOC AND DESOLATION

AFTER the defeat of Breymann's corps, feelings ran high between the British and the Germans. British officers remarked, "First Trenton, then Bennington, and now *this!*" Lieutenant-Colonel von Speth, with fifty men from von Riedesel's regiment, sought to retrieve national honor by recapturing the redoubt during the night after the battle, but, tricked by a pretended Tory, lost his way. Burgoyne made some scathing remark, which was reported back to von Riedesel. For this neither the baron nor the baroness ever forgave him. A German officer wrote to his family in disgust at the "confounded pride and arrogant bearing of the English, who treat everyone that was not born on their ragamuffin Island with contempt,"[1] and it was only natural that his colleagues should have sought to blame their misfortunes on the British general. Sixty Germans expressed their opinion by deserting in a body.

Now, it happens that the two most detailed accounts of the retreat to Saratoga were written by von Riedesel and his wife many years later when national pride and the memory of certain things Burgoyne had said about the Germans in his letters and parliamentary speeches had crystallized their feelings into hard resentment. Thus we are told that when von Riedesel reached Dovegat at two o'clock in the morning and received from Burgoyne an order to halt, he was astonished at such stupidity. If the general had abandoned his precious guns, carts, and boats, and made a forced march all night, the army could have reached Saratoga at dawn, crossed the Hudson unopposed, and been clear on the road to Fort George by noon. The Baroness even went so far as to say that Burgoyne "lost his head." He was so set on the "Order" promised him if he achieved his junction with Howe that he could not bear the thought of retreating and with childish petulance jeopardized the entire army by halting on every absurd pretext. He even insisted on counting the guns![2] This is the version of the story that has passed into standard history books, where we read that Burgoyne, as slow in retreat as in advance, "clung to his guns with an almost mad perversity."[3] Then there is a story that Burgoyne in desperation turned to Skene, saying, "You brought me to this pass. Now tell me how to get out of it!" To which Skene replied that he should march off by night, scattering his baggage at intervals. The rebels would be so busy plundering that he would get clean away.

In fact, however, Burgoyne was determined to keep his army together, which was extremely difficult at night on such a narrow road and under a continuous downpour. The guns stuck in the mud, the carts and wagons slithered into holes, their horses too weak with hunger and fatigue to pull them out, and the boats became almost unmanageable in the swollen torrent of the river. He knew that a corps of the enemy under General Fellows was entrenched on Saratoga Heights in front of him and that other corps might be posted at the crossings at Batten Kill and Fort Edward. His rear guard was constantly harassed by skirmishers, for the Indians had discovered his retreat, and shooting continued all night. Thus the army was overextended, and von Riedesel was in danger of being ambushed. Moreover, as the rear guard crossed the half a dozen creeks on the way, they had to break up each bridge behind them. Hence the orders to halt. As for the guns and supplies, he needed them for several reasons. The cannons, especially the twelve- and twenty-four-pounders, were better than any the Americans had. If he left them by the roadside, the Americans would soon turn them around and use them against him. Suppose he found his way across the river blocked by the enemy: He not only would have no guns to force the crossing, but also he would find those very guns blasting his own position to pieces. Nor was it possible to destroy the guns. There were no tools for knocking off the trunnions (the only foolproof method) and spikes could be removed very easily.[4] Hence, again, his "counting" the guns was not an act of wanton sulking but a necessary precaution to discover what fire power remained to his army, whether any guns could be abandoned, and to ensure that each gun had its proper ammunition and store of dry powder ready for instant use. It was the same with the wagons. While the army was at Dovegat, columns of Americans were seen advancing along the east bank, some of whom opened fire on the boats. Burgoyne thereupon ordered every cart carrying anything but essentials, such as food and powder (medical equipment having been left with the hospital at Freeman's Farm), to be burned, so that the horses could be freed for drawing the artillery and few remaining carts more rapidly.[5]

As the army was about to set off at three in the afternoon, Lady

Harriet Acland sent a note to Burgoyne asking permission to join her husband, now a prisoner with the Americans. Baroness von Riedesel tells us that the night before Lady Harriet had been told that her husband had been mortally wounded.

> At this she became very wretched. We comforted her by saying it was only a superficial wound and that, since nobody could nurse him better than herself, she ought to go to him at once. We were sure no one would refuse her. She loved him very much, although he was a plain, rough man, who was drunk nearly every day. Yet he was an excellent officer. She was the loveliest of women. Thus I spent the night, at one time comforting her and at another looking after my children, whom I had put to bed.

Burgoyne, needless to say, consented, but, he tells us,

> The Assistance I was enabled to offer her was small indeed; I had not even a cup of wine to offer her; but I was told she had found, from some kind and fortunate hand, a little rum and dirty water. All I could furnish to her was an open boat and a few lines, written upon dirty and wet paper, to General Gates, recommending her to his protection. Mr. Brudenell . . . readily undertook to accompany her, and with one female servant, and the major's *valet-de-chambre* (who had a ball which he had received in the late action then in his shoulder), she rowed down the river to meet the enemy.

Burgoyne goes on to say that the Americans, suspecting treachery, kept her waiting in the boat, despite the rain, for "seven or eight dark and cold hours"; but the Americans, probably with truth, said she was delayed only a few minutes. Nevertheless, Burgoyne admitted that Gates received her

> with all the humanity and respect that her rank, her merits and her fortunes deserved. Let such as are affected by these circumstances of alarm, hardship and danger, recollect that the subject of them was a woman; of the most tender and delicate frame; of the gentlest manners; habituated to all the soft elegancies, and refined enjoyments, that attend high birth and fortune; far advanced in a state in which the tender cares, always due to the sex, become indispensably necessary. Her mind alone was formed for such trials.[6]

Lady Harriet had ridden with the army in a little tumbril and had made herself much loved by the soldiers for the kindness, cheerfulness, and presents she distributed daily among the wounded. Gates himself, for all his pretended dislike of the upper classes, was bowled over by her: "She is the most amiable, delicate piece of Quality you ever beheld!" he told his wife. Nor did he find her husband plain and rough, rather "a learned, sensible man, though a confounded Tory."[7]

The bridge over the Fish Kill, bordering Schuyler's estate, had been destroyed, and the army—the women too—had to wade across up to their shoulders in water. Burgoyne left the artillery and Hamilton's brigade (the remains of the 20th, 21st, and 62nd Regiments) on the south side of the stream. The sick, wounded, and women were sheltered in some barracks Schuyler had built for the militia before his retreat; the officers and their wives took refuge in the house; the soldiers, too exhausted even to light fires, threw themselves down onto the soaking ground and lay in the rain. When Baroness von Riedesel, who had been riding in a cart, demanded angrily of Phillips why the army had stopped (the exhausted soldiers could have answered her question), she tells us that Phillips replied, "Poor woman! I admire you! Drenched to the skin as you are, you still have the courage to go on in this rain. If only you were our commanding general! But he says he is tired, and wants to spend the night here and give us our supper!" One cannot help suspecting, however, that with her imperfect grasp of English she misunderstood what Phillips said and years afterwards put into his mouth what she would have liked him to have said. Phillips never expressed disapproval of Burgoyne to anyone, then or later, and it is hard to believe that even in an overwrought state he would have been so unguarded. However, she then goes on to say, "In fact, Burgoyne liked having a jolly time and spending half the night singing and drinking and amusing himself in the company of the wife of a commissary, who was his mistress."

This remark has given rise to one of the most widely quoted stories about Burgoyne: While the wretched soldiers lay all night out in the rain, "Gentleman Johnny" held a wild party in Schuyler's house, which blazed with lights and resounded to the noise of laughter and breaking glasses, until he and his officers drowned their misery in drunken oblivion. It originated with von Eelking, the von Riedesels' first editor and translator, who read the passage carelessly and commented on it thus because, again, that is what he wanted to believe. Receiving the approval of Mr. Nickerson's authority, it now takes its place, along with the story of the thirty carts and Burgoyne's mad clinging to his guns, among the legends of Burgoyniana to be found in history books. It is tiresome to have to refute so much nonsense, but it must be done. The baroness did not say he threw a party *that* night, but that he liked to enjoy himself *at* night, of which she disapproved, at least as far as Burgoyne was concerned. If Burgoyne had not been able to find even a glass of refreshment for Lady Acland that afternoon, how could he have thrown a drunken party that night? Nor is such behavior consistent with the behavior of the other officers, such as Balcarres, Harrington, or the sober Kingston. What did happen that night was that one of the barracks accidentally caught fire, and all the officers and men nearby worked desperately to rescue the wounded inside.[8]

The next morning, Burgoyne withdrew Hamilton's brigade and the cannons (there were now twenty-seven) across the Fish Kill and moved the entire army onto the heights overlooking both Schuyler's estate and the Hudson. The enemy brigade under Fellows had hastily retreated over to the east bank of the Hudson at Burgoyne's approach. Burgoyne sent Colonel Sutherland with engineers, Captain Fraser's marksmen, some Tories and Canadians under Captain Mackay, and the 47th Regiment to the ford at Fort Edward to ascertain if a crossing might be possible there. Sutherland reported back to say that he had crossed and found Fellows' camp so badly sentried that he had ridden right around it without being seen. A surprise attack would scatter them. Burgoyne refused permission, for he had intelligence that Gates' entire army was now approaching up both sides of the river, and he did not wish Sutherland's corps to be isolated and destroyed. Besides, he had seen an opportunity of giving a more serious check to the Americans. General Gates, having been timid, had suddenly turned bold. The report that Sutherland's detachment was building a bridge at Fort Edward intimated that Burgoyne was close behind and waiting to cross. He therefore ordered five brigades to pursue Burgoyne closely, in the hope that they would catch him at the vulnerable moment of crossing the Hudson. The ground from Saratoga Heights to the Fish Kill was open grassland rolling downward, ideal for the close-order tactics at which the British infantry excelled but which they had never been able to employ on this campaign. Burgoyne calculated that the Americans would cross over the Fish Kill under cover of the early morning fog. This fog lifted every morning at the same time. If, therefore, they were over the stream when that happened, he would have them with their backs to the water facing a bayonet charge of all his infantry, supported by all his twenty-seven guns. To clear his field of fire, he now ordered that the remainder of Schuyler's buildings, including his beautiful house, be burned. It was a gamble, but Burgoyne probably had the Battle of Cannae in mind, when Hannibal had used a similar fog to surprise and destroy a hugely superior Roman army. He therefore recalled Sutherland and the 47th, leaving the Canadians and Tories to finish the bridge.

Three brigades of Americans did indeed cross the Fish Kill under cover of the fog, believing that Burgoyne was further north at Fort Edward. They met a deserter who told them that Burgoyne was waiting for them with his entire army; but Gates regarded this as a bluff by which the British hoped to cover their escape. Then, however, a second deserter, a German this time, confirmed the story. Gates urgently ordered a retreat. Just as the Americans wheeled about, the fog lifted dead on time, and they saw the British in line of battle on the slopes above, preparing to charge. The guns roared. The Americans fled pell-mell into the water but made their escape. Thus Burgoyne's last throw came within a hair's breadth of success, a success which, but for one deserter, would have saved his army at the eleventh hour and been hailed afterward as a brilliantly planned and executed victory. It was, said Burgoyne, "one of the most adverse strokes of fortune of the entire campaign," and his disappointment must have been the sharper for knowing that once again his estimate of Gates' character had been correct. Perhaps the worst part of the incident was, however, that no sooner had Sutherland and his infantry returned to Saratoga than the Canadians and Tories under Mackay decided to escape to Canada while they could and left the bridge unbuilt. General Fellows thereupon placed himself beside the ford, with cannons.

That evening Burgoyne held a conference with Phillips and von Riedesel. Burgoyne made various suggestions, some of them admittedly wild. One was that the army cross the Hudson by night and make a rapid circuit south, bypassing the Americans and reaching Albany. Von Riedesel advocated abandoning everything and slipping out by the only road still open, the north road, and crossing at a ford he knew of four miles above Fort Edward. Burgoyne did not like this idea, for he had received news, through the few prisoners taken, that Clinton had at last moved and, not only that, had captured the supposedly impregnable Highland forts. He was now approaching Albany, it was said. While the conference was going on, however, Burgoyne suffered a further setback in that the Americans raided and captured nearly all the remaining boats before their supplies had been unloaded.

During the next day, the situation became, in Lord Petersham's words, "as bad as possible." The forest to the west swarmed with "Skinners" and Indians who had changed sides, supported by the whole of Dearborn's and Morgan's rifle corps. To the south Gates sat with his main army, and to the east Americans lined the entire far bank of the river. The last to arrive was Stark, the victor of Bennington who crossed the Hudson from the Batten Kill and posted his Vermonters on the north road, thus cutting the only remaining escape route. Stark had previously joined Gates on the eve of the battle of 19 September; but, not wishing to take orders from a Congress general (Vermont had just created itself and was very prickly about its independence), he had marched away again. Now, with rather ill grace, Stark had returned to be in at the death. Indeed, the spectacle of a dying British army attracted thousands of men from miles around. They proclaimed themselves soldiers, though they were little more than spectators. Meanwhile, the American artillery kept up a ceaseless bombardment of the British camp. "Camp," however, was a euphemism for a long, bare, undulating hill on which stood only a few clumps of trees. The men and women huddled in the open, without tents or bedding, or behind the few remaining carts, which had been turned over for breastworks. The wounded and sick lay wherever dips provided cover from the incessant cannon balls and red-hot shells. The oxen and cattle wandered about and began to die, for there was no grass on the upper part of the hill where the army lay, and the stench of their corpses mingled with the smoke of the campfires rolling low over the ground in the cold air. Snipers perched in surrounding trees and shot anyone who moved during the day; at night parties of raiders infiltrated between the piquets and shot the sentries. The fetching of water was so hazardous that eventually no one would go except a woman, who dared the Americans to shoot at her. They did not, and she became the army's heroine. Curiously, in the midst of all this hunger and danger, the soldiers kept a veritable zoo of pets they had caught in the forest: deer, racoons, foxes, a porcupine, and even a giant bear, which a German sergeant, who had probably been a bear keeper in Europe, led about on a chain. There were still a few houses standing on the eastern slope facing the river, and in the cellar of one of these, later called "Marshall's House," Baroness von Riedesel hid with her children and servants, and those army women who also had children. When she first moved in there, she was shocked that the women had relieved themselves in the corners and made them clean the place thoroughly, herself washing the floors and walls with vinegar. The seriously wounded lay in the rooms above, and she found that the hardest thing to bear was the stink of their wounds. Major Blomefield, for instance, had had part of his mouth shot away and was continually spitting out pus to stop himself from choking. A soldier, who had just had his leg amputated, was hit by a cannon ball which tore off his other leg and threw him from the table to the floor, where he died a moment after. Discovering that some of the wounded officers had had no food for two days, the baroness buttonholed Lord Petersham and sent him to Burgoyne. The general came and "pathetically" thanked her "for teaching him his duty." When she pointed to the young officers, saying it was all a disgrace, Burgoyne asked them why they hadn't come to him, seeing that his kitchen was open to everyone at all times. They were not accustomed to going to the general's kitchen for food, they answered. It is obvious that the good baroness completely missed the courteous irony in Burgoyne's expression of gratitude. She was right to complain, of course, and it was not her fault that she could not catch the subtleties of English upper-class usage. Nevertheless, if, as a distinguished modern historian tells us, Burgoyne did not think it worthwhile to waste his celebrated charm on Baroness von Riedesel, it is not hard to understand why.

During the next two days, plans for escape were again discussed, but, after one attempt to probe for a route to the north had ended in failure, they were dropped. By the next day (13 October) it became clear that a march to Lake George was a mere dream, for barely three days' provisions remained to the army. Burgoyne therefore summoned a second council of war, this time including captains commanding corps. He began by declaring that, since he had never asked their advice on this campaign, he and he alone was responsible for their unhappy predicament. He could see little possibility of retreat or movement in any direction, though he expressed "his readiness to undertake at the head any enterprise of difficulty or hazard that should appear to be within the compass of their strength or spirit." Since he believed that capitulation had been in the minds of most or all of them, he wished to put to the vote the question of whether an army of 3,500 men with plentiful artillery could ever be in such a situation as justified capitulation (at that moment a cannon ball whizzed down the table but did not hit anybody), to which the council answered "yes." He then asked if this was such a situation, to which the answer was again "yes."* The council then voted to capitulate upon "honourable terms," and Burgoyne sent a message to Gates.

Next morning, Major Kingston, Burgoyne's adjutant-general, met Gates' adjutant-general, the young Lieutenant-Colonel James Wilkinson, "a youth in a plain blue frock, without any other military insignia than a cockade and a sword." After a brief *contretemps* over dignity (Kingston resented being "hood-winked," that is, blindfolded), they proceeded to Gates' headquarters while Kingston "expatiated with taste and eloquence upon the beautiful scenery of the Hudson river and the charms of the season." Kingston delivered to Gates the following statement:

> After having fought you twice, Lieutenant-General Burgoyne has waited some days, in his present position, determined to try a third conflict against any force you could bring to attack him.
>
> He is apprised of the superiority of your numbers, and the disposition of your troops to impede his supplies, and render his retreat a scene of carnage on both sides. In this situation he is impelled by humanity, and thinks himself justifiable by established principles and precedents of state, and of war, to spare the lives of brave men upon honourable terms. Should Major-General Gates be inclined to treat upon that idea, General Bugoyne would propose a cessation of arms during the times necessary

*The one dissenter was the seventeen-year-old Midshipman Edward Pellew, the future Admiral Lord Exmouth, who said he had never heard of sailors surrendering and offered to lead his party of seamen through the forest, confident he could "bring them off." Two days before, Pellew had led a raid across the Fish Kill and recaptured a batteau with five-hundred barrels of provisions. Burgoyne kindly took him aside from the conference and explained that since the entire army could not be "brought off" in that way, it would be unfair and demoralizing to the soldiers if the sailors were allowed to escape. American loyalists, of course, whose fate after capture might be grim, *were* allowed to leave.

to communicate the preliminary terms by which, in any extremity, he and his army mean to abide.

Gates immediately pulled from his pocket a paper containing his own proposals. These amounted to unconditional surrender, although certain privileges such as parole would be granted. Kingston protested that Burgoyne would never agree and was led back to the British camp, all the time reminding Wilkinson of what British infantry had done at certain battles, such as Minden.

Burgoyne called another conference and was pleased to hear that the officers unanimously rejected Gates' proposals. Burgoyne then pointed out that in war it is the defeated party who usually offers proposals for surrender in the hope that they might be accepted. The fact that Gates had made proposals of his own suggested that something was troubling him. The most likely possibility was that Clinton was advancing rapidly and that Gates was afraid he might have to withdraw before Burgoyne surrendered. If that was so, then the British still had time to play with. Accordingly, he sent Kingston back with answers to Gates' proposals and a list of counterproposals. Gates' articles and Burgoyne's answers ran as follows:

I. General Burgoyne's army being exceedingly reduced by repeated defeats, by desertion sickness, &c. their provisions exhausted, their military horses, tents, and baggage, taken or destroyed, their retreat cut off, and their camp invested, they can only be allowed to surrender prisoners of war.

ANSWER. Lieutenant-General Burgoyne's army, however reduced, will never admit that their retreat is cut off, while they have arms in their hands.

II. The officers and soldiers may keep the baggage belonging to them. The generals of the United States never permit individuals to be pillaged.

ANSWER. Noted.

III. The troops under his Excellency General Burgoyne will be conducted by the most convenient route to New England, marching by easy marches, and sufficiently provided for by the way.

ANSWER. This article is answered by General Burgoyne's first proposal, which is here annexed.

IV. The officers will be admitted on parole; may wear their side arms, and will be treated with the liberality customary in Europe, so long as they, by proper behaviour, continue to deserve it; but those who are apprehended having broke their parôle, as some British officers have done, must expect to be close confined.

ANSWER. There being no officer in this army under, or capable of being under the description of breaking parôle, this article needs no answer.

v. All public stores, artillery, arms, ammunition, carriages, horses, &c. &c. must be delivered to commissaries appointed to receive them.

ANSWER. All public stores may be delivered, arms excepted.

VI. These terms being agreed to and signed, the troops under his Excellency General Burgoyne's command may be drawn up in their encampments, where they will be ordered to ground their arms, and may thereupon be marched to the riverside, to be passed over on their way towards Bennington.

ANSWER. This article inadmissable in any extremity. Sooner than this army will consent to ground their arms in their encampment, they will rush on the enemy, determined to take no quarter.

VII. A cessation of arms to continue till sun-set, to receive General Burgoyne's answer.

In his counterproposal, Burgoyne insisted that the soldiers did not lay down their arms *in their camp* and were allowed to march out in proper military order. He also proposed that they be given a free passage to England from Boston, on the promise that they would not take up arms against the United States during the present contest. He also insisted, when Kingston met Wilkinson at sunset, that "If General Gates does not mean to recede from the 6th article, the treaty ends at once. The army will to a man proceed to any act of desperation, rather than submit to that article."

Gates rejected these proposals indignantly. Then, the next morning, just as the shooting was about to start, he sent a messenger accepting them, on condition that the business be concluded by two o'clock in the afternoon and that the soldiers lay down their arms by five o'clock. It was then ten o'clock in the morning, and Burgoyne, convinced that Gates felt himself under some kind of threat, insisted that since these negotiations were mere preliminaries to a treaty, which would have to be drawn up by officers delegated from both sides, four hours was not long enough. Again Gates agreed. Burgoyne suspected that Gates was banking on a surrender by noon the next day (16 October), and once more felt stirrings of hope. Perhaps Clinton was nearer than anyone supposed.

While the delegates haggled and the guns stayed silent, the British and German officers strolled by the river and up onto the heights of Saratoga. In the stillness of the afternoon, they surveyed the infinity of hills and mountains extending into the hazy distance, ridge upon ridge covered in gorgeous array of umber, russet, deep red, black and gold; for the autumn of northeastern America was now at its most majestic, providing an appropriate backdrop of sumptuous melancholy beauty for the last act of this extraordinary drama.

By evening, all was settled with the exception of one detail: Burgoyne insisted that the word "Capitulation" be replaced by the word "Convention." Captain Craig, one of the British delegates, wrote a letter to Gates saying that if this were done Burgoyne would sign.

That night, however, a loyalist stole into the camp with stirring news. Clinton had not only captured the Highland forts and inflicted a crushing defeat on the Americans, but also he had reached Esopus, only fifty-five miles from Albany. That was eight days ago. He must therefore be in Albany itself by now. The next morning Burgoyne called another council to discuss whether, in the light of this information, some means might be found of withdrawing from the treaty—or of postponing it. The majority voted that no honorable means could be found and that further delay might lead to worse conditions. Burgoyne, who was perhaps rather enjoying his new role of tricky lawyer, sent a demand to Gates that, since negotiations had been opened on the understanding that American numbers were vastly superior to his own and since he had received intelligence that Gates had detached a large proportion of his force southward, two British officers should be allowed to inspect and count the American army. Gates was exasperated, for he felt that Burgoyne was making fun of him. At the same time he, too, had received reports of Clinton's success, together with an exaggerated estimate of Clinton's numbers, and was uncertain how long he could remain where he was. Finally, he had been given an intercepted message from Clinton to Burgoyne, which began with the French phrase *"Nous y voici,"* and said that he would soon be at Gates's rear. Some said the British were within twenty miles of Albany.

Meanwhile, Burgoyne held a last council. Again, the officers gave a majority opinion that the loyalist's information, being mere rumor and hearsay, was not to be believed. In any case, Clinton could never dislodge Gates in two days, by which time there would be no food or water at all. The officers commanding the 47th and 62nd Regiments believed that their men would not fight any more unless attacked first, that procrastination would simply sign the death warrant for all the loyalists still with the army, that there was no more ammunition to fight with, and that further resistance, let alone a desperate attempt to break out, would sacrifice hundreds of lives for nothing.

At that moment, Colonel Sutherland returned from Wilkinson. He carried in his hand the letter which Captain Craig had written, saying that Burgoyne would sign the surrender if the word "Convention" was substituted for "Capitulation." Gates had agreed to this and Burgoyne was bound in honor to sign. Gates gave Burgoyne one hour to do so. Burgoyne signed with no more ado.*

*The full terms of the surrender, entitled "Articles of Convention between Lieutenant General Burgoyne and Major General Gates," are given in Appendix II.

That night, Captain Campbell, whom Burgoyne had sent to Clinton on 23 September, returned at last.[9] His news merely confirmed the hopelessness of Burgoyne's position. The long-expected reinforcements had arrived late in New York and had turned out to be a mere seventeen hundred fit for duty. Nevertheless, Clinton had, by a brilliant stratagem, stormed the Highland forts on the night of 6 October. Since, however, he had made no move for several days after that, and then only with a small fleet, any physical threat to dislodge Gates was out of the question. Campbell delivered Clinton's reply to Burgoyne's letter of 21 September in which he had requested orders whether to advance, retreat, or stay where he was. The tone of the reply was singularly cold and unhelpful, indeed reproachful. The gist was that he had offered to make a try at the Highlands, and this he had done. As Burgoyne had said that even the menace of an attack would be of use, he hoped this success would be serviceable; but "General Burgoyne could not suppose that Sir Henry had an Idea of penetrating to Albany with the small Force he mentioned in his last Letter." As for orders, he had this to say:

> Not having received any Instructions from the Commander in Chief [i.e., Howe] relative to the Northern Army and ignorant even of his Intentions concerning the Operations of that Army, excepting his wishes that it should get to Albany, Sir Henry Clinton cannot presume to give any Orders to General Burgoyne.[10]

At eleven o'clock the next morning, the American army marched into the British camp playing an old tune long popular among British soldiers because it mocked the uncouth dress of rustic New Englanders. From that moment "Yankee Doodle" became the unofficial national anthem of the United States of America. Some of the British veterans smashed their muskets in despair, swearing that they ought never to have surrendered and that they would "do Burgoyne's business for him when they returned to England." Some commanders hid their regimental colors. The army then marched down to a meadow where the Fish Kill emptied into the Hudson, the site of the ruined Fort Hardy. With a gesture perhaps unique in the history of war, Gates had ordered that no Americans except Wilkinson were to be present when the British laid down their arms. Burgoyne and Wilkinson, their backs to the scene, rode to the bank of the Hudson. Burgoyne asked if the river was fordable.

"Certainly, Sir," Wilkinson said, "but do you observe the people on the opposite shore?"

"Yes," Burgoyne replied, "I have seen them too long." He then asked to be introduced to General Gates.

Followed by his retinue of officers and the entire army, Burgoyne, in his full-dress uniform with heavy gold epaulets and a hat with long plumes, rode to the American camp. Gates had drawn up the entire American army on both sides of the way to show Burgoyne that his numbers had not been exaggerated. As Burgoyne passed, some drunken American soldiers shouted that it was a good thing he had surrendered, for they intended to massacre the British to the last man. Others then chipped in, saying they merely wanted to tar and feather him, stand him on one of his barrels of gunpowder, and make him read aloud his "Proclamation." By the time he reached General Gates, who was wearing a plain blue coat, quiet and dignity had been restored. When the two reined up within a sword's length of each other, Burgoyne raised his hat in a courtly gesture and declared, "The fortune of war, General Gates, has made me your prisoner."

"I shall always be ready to bear testimony," replied Gates, "that it has not been through any fault of your Excellency." Phillips then approached and, after a salute, he and General Gates shook hands. They had known each other when Gates was in the British army. After that, Baron von Riedesel and the other officers were introduced in order of rank. An American historian of the last century, observing that eyewitness accounts stressed the impeccable spotlessness of the uniforms of the British officers, wondered how this had been managed under such conditions, and came to the conclusion that the stories of hardship must have been British exaggerations to make their surrender appear more justifiable.[11] He does not seem to have understood that dress uniforms were the last things regular officers of European armies would have allowed to become spoiled.

Gates invited his "guests" into his tent. Then, as the British army dressed its ranks for the march to Albany, Gates and Burgoyne emerged from the marquee.

> Not a word was said by either, and for some minutes, to the best of my recollection, they stood silently gazing on the scene before them. . . . Burgoyne was a large and stoutly formed man, his countenance was rough and hard, and somewhat marked with scars, if I am not mistaken, but he had a handsome figure and a noble air. Gates was much the smaller man with much less of manner, and destitute of that air which distinguished Burgoyne.[12]

Burgoyne then stepped back, drew his sword and presented it to Gates, who received it with an inclination of the head, and immediately returned it. They then both stepped into the marquee, while the army, prior to its march, went to eat its first proper meal for several weeks.*

Gates entertained Burgoyne and the senior officers at a luncheon served upon two planks laid across two empty barrels. There were only four plates in the entire company. The meal consisted of a ham, a goose, some beef, and some boiled mutton; the drink was rum and water without sugar. There were only two glasses, which were used by Gates and Burgoyne. The other officers drank from bowls. "Men that can live thus, may be brought to beat half the world," said one of them.[13] A modern reader, however, might find such a meal gargantuan rather than austere. After a few moments, someone announced that the Baroness von Riedesel was outside with her three girls and that they had nowhere to go. General Schuyler, who was present despite threats from New Englanders that if he showed his face they would put a bullet through it, rose and said he would take them to his tent.

In common with the other women of the army, the baroness' greatest terror over the past few days had been that the army might decamp and make for Canada, leaving the women to the Americans, whom she imagined to be like the half-savage "Cowboys" serving with Captain Fraser. She had been surprised, passing through the American camp, that no one had insulted her. On the contrary, she had been treated most chivalrously. Now this "handsome man" appeared, lifted the children out of the cart, kissed them, and, with tears in his eyes, helped her down, telling her to "fear nothing." He took her to the marquee, where she was shocked to see Gates, Burgoyne, and Phillips laughing together. To cover her embarrassment, Schuyler took the baroness and her daughters to his tent, where his staff gave them a meal.

Throughout the luncheon, Burgoyne was affable and pleasant. He flattered Gates but rather undid the effect by going on to praise Arnold highly, especially for the part he had played in the battle of 19 September! Shortly after, Gates was discomforted yet further by the arrival of Daniel Morgan. The previous evening, Gates had tried to enroll

* General Gates ordered the Indians still with Burgoyne's army to be put in an enclosure and surrounded by a strong armed guard, for he had heard that the militia intended to kill them all, including the women and children, in reprisal for the outrages committed by their people during the advance. Who these Indians were, or how many, is not recorded, for they were not included in any list of the "Convention Troops." Their loyalty in remaining to the end was never acknowledged, let alone repaid, by the British, who, on the contrary, disavowed them. Burgoyne's campaign was the first on which Indians were employed in substantial numbers, and it set the direction which relations between Americans and Indians were to take for the next century: uninterrupted and increasingly merciless killing by both sides that continued until the massacre at Wounded Knee. The British were as much to blame as anyone for this tragic history. During the final treaties between Great Britain and the United States at the end of the war, the Indians and their rights were not so much as mentioned, an oversight which the king, who had repeatedly assured the Indians of his protection, did not see fit to remedy. The remains of the Iroquois fled to Canada, where they have lived in decline and increasing poverty ever since.

Morgan in his plan to oust General Washington, and when Morgan had indignantly refused Gates had retaliated by pointedly not inviting him to meet the British officers. Some army business had compelled Morgan to consult Gates regardless, and, when he left, the British asked who he was. As soon as they learned his identity, they rose, overtook him on the road, and gathered around him. Burgoyne shook his hand, saying, "Sir, you command the finest regiment in the world!"[14] The other officers introduced themselves, confessing that they had "felt" him severely on the field. It was a strange scene: a group of regular officers of the British army, dressed in their resplendent uniforms and comfortable in their assurance of belonging to the most privileged class in society, telling this uncouth, provincial character, dressed in fringed hunting jacket, trousers, and moccasins, that his was the best regiment in the world. The fact was that Burgoyne had completely changed his mind about the Americans. Three days later he wrote to Lord George Germain:

> I should now hold myself unjustifiable if I did not confide to your Lordship, my opinion, upon a near inspection, of the rebel troops. The standing corps which I have seen are disciplined. I do not hazard the term, but apply it to the great fundamental points of military institution, sobriety, subordination, regularity and courage. The militia are inferior in method and movement, but not a jot less serviceable in the woods. My conjectures were very different after the affair of Ticonderago, but I am convinced they were delusive; and it is a duty to the state to confess it.
>
> The panic of the rebel troops is confined, and of short duration; the enthusiasm is extensive and permanent.[15]

At the end of the luncheon, Gates asked Burgoyne to propose a toast. Normally, the first toast at a military banquet should be to the king, but this would hardly have been tactful. After a moment's hesitation, Burgoyne stood up and announced, "George Washington!," to which Gates had no choice but to reply, "His Majesty King George III!" Thus, with his usual aplomb in social matters, Burgoyne enabled his officers to toast the king after all.

In Albany, Schuyler invited Burgoyne and his family of officers, as well as the Baron and Baroness von Riedesel and their family, to stay at his house in the town. Schuyler did his best to put Burgoyne at ease, forbidding any mention of Saratoga in the presence of the British. At the same time he assured Burgoyne that he bore no ill will over the burning of his house, for under a similar military necessity, he said, he would have done the same. Nevertheless, there were embarrassing moments. Schuyler's youngest son once locked Burgoyne and his staff in their bedroom (where they slept on mattresses), shouting, "You're all my prisoners!"; and on another occasion one of the von Riedesel children cried in a loud voice, "Mama, is this the palace Papa was to have when we came to America?"

Tiny incidents like these reminded Burgoyne of the grim reality of his situation. He, a most civilized man, had invaded the Hudson valley with what had been intended as a conquering army. A loyalist from this army, fleeing to Canada, described the trail the British left behind them:

> The whole way from Stillwater was marked with destruction, devastation, and of the many pleasant habitations formerly within that distance, some were burnt, others torn to pieces . . . and but the meanest occupied. The inhabitants in general having been forced to flee their once peaceful dwelling to escape the rage of war. This once agreeable and delightful part of the country now displayed a most shocking picture of havock and wild desolation. The inevitable distress of the fugitive inhabitants, their want not only of the comforts but even of the common necessities of life, occurring to my musing thoughts made me impress curses upon the heads of those
>
> Whose last is murder, and whose horrid joy
> Is to tear their Country, and their Kind destroy.[16]

It is not surprising, therefore, that Burgoyne was bewildered by the kindness he received. Sometimes he was deeply moved by it and actually shed tears; sometimes he suspected it was all a political maneuver to trick his officers into changing sides: "The treatment of the officers and troops in general is of so extraordinary a nature in point of generosity that I must suppose it proceeds from some other motive than mere kindness of disposition."[17]

Nevertheless, his stay at Schuyler's gave Burgoyne his first opportunity not only to meet Americans at close quarters but also to collect his thoughts about his own future. He was convinced that the ministers in London would have no scruples in offering him as a scapegoat for their own sins, and he started to look for means to defend himself. Accordingly, he sent off a number of long letters to Lord George Germain, General Howe, General Carleton, and General Clinton.

CHAPTER XVI

"THE UTMOST THAT MALEVOLENCE CAN SAY"

WHEN Howe had sailed off to the Chesapeake, he had given Clinton permission to make a move in favor of Burgoyne if he wished but had left him no men with which to do it. By early September it had become clear that Burgoyne was in difficulties. On the eleventh, Clinton wrote to him, offering to make a try at Fort Montgomery when reinforcements arrived. The reinforcements did not arrive until 24 September. They had taken three months to cross the Atlantic in old Dutch cargo ships, and out of the total of three thousand men only seventeen hundred were fit for duty. Five days later, Burgoyne's answer arrived, saying "do it, my dear Friend, directly."

Since Howe had not bothered to write to him for several weeks, Clinton knew nothing of the whereabouts of Washington's army. He was afraid, therefore, that if he moved north Washington might reappear and capture New York. On the other hand, an attack on the Highlands might well tip the scales in Burgoyne's favor. He had spent weeks planning how the supposedly impregnable forts might be taken, and when information reached him that Putnam had sent some detachments to reinforce Washington and Gates, he saw that he had a heaven-sent opportunity which it would be criminal to waste. On 3 and 4 October, he led three thousand men, with a fleet under Commodore Hotham, up toward the Highlands, having first, by a feint, deceived the Americans into thinking he was making for Long Island Sound. The forts stood perched on cliffs 150 and 200 feet high commanding the west shore of the Hudson. Clinton landed on the east shore. Putnam hurriedly brought more men from the forts to oppose him. Clinton crossed to the west shore and sent two regiments around behind the mountains to attack the forts from their unprotected land side. Putnam frantically tried to cross back again, but it was too late. By dawn (7 October) the forts were stormed and the Americans flying in confusion. During this excitement, Captain Campbell arrived with his really alarming news from Burgoyne and a request for orders, or at least advice. Clinton was intensely annoyed, for he assumed Burgoyne was looking for ways to shift the blame for any disasters onto him, before they happened. How, in any case, did Burgoyne suppose Clinton able to force his way to Albany with a mere three thousand men? He sent a Sergeant Taylor, with the following message, back to Burgoyne:

> Nous y voici, & nothing now between us but Gates. I sincerely hope this little Success may facilitate your Operations. In answer to your letter of 28 Septr. by C.C. I shall only say I cannot presume to order or even advise, for Reasons obvious. I heartily wish you Success.[1]

Unfortunately, Sergeant Taylor rode into an American camp and, hearing soldiers refer to General Clinton, supposed Sir Henry had caught up with him. When he was taken before the American General James Clinton,* he swallowed the silver bullet in which the message had been rolled up. He had been made to vomit and the bullet was about to be opened when the dauntless sergeant grabbed it and swallowed it again. Another emetic was forced into him, and the message was discovered. Sergeant Taylor was hanged on a tree near Hurley churchyard, and the message was sent on to Gates, where at least it influenced the American general to accept Burgoyne's terms of surrender.

On 9 October, while Clinton was wondering what to do next, Captain Scott arrived with his news confirming everything Campbell had said. Clinton sent Campbell and Scott back to Burgoyne next day, with the frigid and reproachful message quoted in the previous chapter. Angry as he was, Clinton was determined to do what he could to save Burgoyne. Further delay was caused, however, by an administrative crisis which called him back to New York until the thirteenth. Meanwhile, the navy was having trouble with a strong *cheveux de frise*, or spiked chain, which the Americans had stretched across the river. Clinton ordered the fleet, with two thousand men under Brigadier-General Vaughan, to cross the chain regardless of danger and make every effort to reach Albany. They carried enough supplies for five thousand men for six months, in case Vaughan succeeded in establishing contact

* The sergeant's confusion is understandable. When Sir Henry Clinton attacked Fort Clinton, it was commanded by General James Clinton and his brother, Governor George Clinton of New York.

with Burgoyne. With great difficulty, the ships scraped over the chain at high tide and disappeared northward.

By the seventeenth, Clinton was feeling more hopeful. Whatever happened, Burgoyne was surely saved, for at least he could now retreat to Canada. Meanwhile, he himself, to his own astonishment, was master of the Highlands, which he had always regarded as the key success in America. Thus, the defeat of Burgoyne and Howe's useless meandering through Pennsylvania could be seen as well worthwhile if the Highlands could be held, for they were the one place that really mattered. The only risk was that until Howe, convinced at last by this *fait accompli*, relented and sent some reinforcements, New York itself would be dangerously undergarrisoned. On that day, however, a letter arrived from Howe, the first since August. As usual, it contained a minimum of information, and, instead of congratulating Clinton on his brilliant success, it merely demanded that three regiments, together with *all* the reinforcements lately arrived from England, be sent to Philadelphia without delay. Clinton could scarcely believe his eyes. Howe had already received copies of Burgoyne's messages and read accounts of Bennington in the local newspapers (which would also have told him that Burgoyne would soon have an army of ten to twelve thousand opposing him from front and rear).[2] He knew perfectly well that in demanding these troops he was removing Burgoyne's only hope of salvation, forcing Clinton to abandon the Highlands and exposing him to the danger that Gates' entire army could now come south and, in combination with Washington, overwhelm New York. Almost numb with anger and disappointment, Clinton wrote to Vaughan to return immediately.

Vaughan, in fact, had reached Livingston's Manor, from where a flood tide could take him to Albany in five hours. Nevertheless, he was in a "desperate" position. He had wasted the whole of 16 October burning the town of Esopus. Along the banks of the river, thousands of American militia were keeping pace with the fleet, and his pilots were refusing to take him further. It was with relief, therefore, that he received Clinton's order to return.

When Clinton first heard of Burgoyne's surrender, he would not believe it, for he had persuaded himself that Burgoyne had never given him reason to suspect matters were so serious. He remained in a state of despair for weeks. His capture of the Highlands had been "one of those extraordinary events which may happen once in a century."[3] It was, indeed, scarcely less brilliant than Wolfe's capture of Quebec. If they had been held, Britain must have won the war. Now his success was totally wasted, and he would never be offered such a chance again. Worse, because his brilliant feat had gone for nothing, it would never receive the fame it deserved. Although Clinton's real hatred was reserved for Howe, who, he believed, had contrived to lose the war single-handed by one blunder after another, each of which defied common sense, he never in his heart forgave Burgoyne either. He wrote a long letter to him in December, saying that he would "not look amiss at anything that passed when you had so much to perplex and distress you." Nevertheless, he wrote to a friend, "Recollect my . . . handsome offer to B---, my fulfilling it and much more, and the return he made of endeavouring in his distress to catch at a poor miserable weak twig as I am, to rend me only to break his fall!"[4] It never occurred to him that when Burgoyne wrote he did not know that Clinton had begun his attack and so did not know he had anything to be grateful for. In asking for orders, Burgoyne was within his rights, for once in America he was technically under the command of Sir William Howe; he was not to know that Howe had left no orders for him. Moreover, despite Clinton's reference to two thousand men, Burgoyne still supposed that the reinforcement would be five thousand, not seventeen hundred fit for duty and arriving two months late. Nor did Clinton remember that while he was sneering at Burgoyne for pitiably craving orders or advice, he himself was just as pitiably craving orders and advice from Sir William Howe.

If Burgoyne and Clinton each thought his own campaign the only important one, Howe, with more reason since he was commander-in-chief, in his turn regarded them as mere sideshows to his capture of Philadelphia. When news of Burgoyne's surrender reached him, he likewise refused to believe it. When he was forced to believe it, he wrote to Germain expressing his surprise that Burgoyne had ever expected cooperation from him, since he had positively told Burgoyne in his letter of 5 April that no such cooperation would be forthcoming. He ended by resigning his command "on account of the little attention, my Lord, given to my recommendations since the commencement of my command."[5]

In Quebec, General Carleton was similarly washing his hands of Burgoyne. Indeed, he seems to have watched Burgoyne's defeat with a certain "I told you so" satisfaction.

On 20, 22, and 23 May he had written three letters to Germain. He repeated his accusations that Germain had deliberately undermined his authority and forced his resignation, for as soon as Germain had been appointed Secretary of State, it had been rumored that "Your Lordship's Intentions were to remove me from the Command the first Opportunity, in the mean time that you would render it as irksome to me as possible, by every kind of Slight, Disregard and Censure. . . ." By placing creatures such as Christie in Canada, the Secretary had encouraged strife and faction in a province already in peril from invaders. Germain had ruined the previous year's campaign by canceling the order for batteaux, and he was now blaming Carleton for slowness in pursuing the Americans and suggesting that had it not been for Carleton's withdrawal from Crown Point Howe would not have been defeated at Trenton. It was true, he went on sarcastically, that being in Canada he had never thought of covering Howe's winter quarters in New Jersey; but then he had not supposed that the minister, knowing that Howe's troops had already gone into winter quarters, would have expected Carleton's army, so much further north, still to be continuing their operations. But then again, such decisions were usually left to the commander on the spot, rather than to "a great General at three thousand miles distance." In the last war, Carleton went on, Amherst had taken a year to cross Lake Champlain and had been praised and rewarded, although he had the full support of the local people. In contrast, Carleton had had to drive out the Americans, who had removed vast quantities of stores and provisions and left the government of the province in chaos and the people in a turmoil. Nevertheless, in two months he had built from scratch and with a much smaller army the largest fleet ever put on the lake and destroyed the fleet the Americans had built to oppose him. For all this he had been censured and had had the command of the troops taken from him and given to General Burgoyne. Germain's policy of paying agents to spread calumny against him had resulted in a public evil and a general contempt for the king's government; if it continued, the troops could well mutiny and the province be lost forever. Next, he complained that Burgoyne had been allotted too many men; for although on paper three thousand men were to be left in Canada, in reality they did not amount to more than 1,534 for the defense of a territory scores of thousands of miles square. Finally, after berating Germain for interfering in the appointment of judges, Carleton ended by handing in his resignation.[6]

Burgoyne, of course, had always been careful to praise Carleton in his letters to Germain for the zeal with which he had assisted in preparing the campaign, despite his obvious disappointment at not being allowed to lead it. However, as I have suggested, there were tensions beneath the surface, especially over the matter of the horses and carts. Then Burgoyne assumed, or was led to assume, that Ticonderoga would be garrisoned by troops from Canada. This, after all, was common sense, for his army was obviously too small to spare a garrison for so large a fortress. Nevertheless, when he wrote to Carleton from Skenesborough to send troops to Ticonderoga, he thought it necessary to remind him of Germain's orders to render Burgoyne's army every assistance he could afford. Carleton wrote back to say that since Ticonderoga was no longer within his command and since he had been told in such insulting detail which units to keep in Canada, this was one assistance he could *not* afford. This was a hint that Carleton knew that it was Burgoyne who had supplied Germain with the facts and figures on which those insulting orders had been based, but he probably forgot that it was he who had asked Burgoyne to supply them in the first place. With a show of commiseration, he added, "I am very ready to acknowledge that I think the whole of our Minister's measures, civil and military, very strange; indeed, to me they appear incomprehensible unless they turn upon private enmity and resentment."[7] Burgoyne wrote again to Carleton just before crossing the Hudson and was again positively refused.[8]

In October Carleton received letter after letter from Brigadier-General Powel in Ticonderoga, reporting that Burgoyne was surrounded and probably capitulating. An army of nine thousand Americans was advancing toward the fortress, which had only just managed to repulse Lincoln's attack two weeks previously. What was he to do? He begged Carleton for orders or at least advice. Carleton was still standing on his dignity and in the midst of another spate of angry letters to Germain. He did not bother to answer until 20 October and then only to say that he could not possibly give orders or even advice. However, he went on (as though Powel did not know it already), the brigadier should either retreat while there was still time or prepare for a long siege, but he should remember that retreat would be "a very pernicious measure" if there was still hope for Burgoyne. Powel hung on until 30 October, when, having withdrawn the post on Diamond Island, he blew up Ticonderoga in a series of tremendous explosions and sailed for Canada.

In his new letters to Germain, Carleton repeated all his accusations once more and congratulated Germain on the success of his plan to force his resignation: "Your Lordship effected with Ease what all the King's Enemies could not have brought about."[9] As for Burgoyne's defeat, he had only this to say, in a letter to Burgoyne himself on 12 November:

> This unfortunate event, it is to be hoped, will in future prevent ministers from pretending to direct operations of war, in a country at three thousand miles distance, of which they have so little knowledge as not to be able to distinguish between good, bad, or interested advices, or to give positive orders in matters, which from their nature, are ever upon the change: so that the expedience or propriety of a measure at one moment, may be totally inexpedient or improper in the next.[10]

There seems to be a veiled hint here that among the interested advisers whom Lord George Germain should have ignored Carleton numbered General Burgoyne. However, Burgoyne was too distraught at this time to take hints of that nature. Instead, he welcomed Carleton's letter because it confirmed his own view that his orders had been "positive." This, indeed, was the basis of the defenses he was now preparing; and in letters to Howe, Clinton, and others, written from Schuyler's house in Albany, he appealed to them to wait until they had read his orders before judging him. They would then see that his orders had been so precise and peremptory that he had been given no choice but to force his way to Albany. If government had deliberately "devoted" (sacrificed) his army as part of some grand design, "it was no more a general's duty to decline proceeding . . . than it would be justifiable in a sergeant who leads a forlorn hope at the storm of a breach to recede because his destruction was probable."[11]

The easy ascendancy of British arms over superior numbers had, until Freeman's Farm on 19 September, given him every expectation of success; and there had been no cause to anticipate the enormous numbers that finally gathered to oppose him. "The contempt of my own army, the condemnation of Government and the world, would have been the consequence of inaction; . . . The utmost that malevolence can say will be that I have been too bold." The Germans had been disappointing. They had encumbered themselves with baggage, allowed themselves to be wiped out in Bennington, run away on 7 October, and deserted in large numbers in Saratoga, and the survivors had intended to surrender after firing one shot if the Americans had attacked. Even the British troops, in the end, had promised to fight only if attacked. "In short, my army would not fight and could not subsist; and under those circumstances I have made a treaty that saves them to the state for the next campaign . . . , for they could be returned to garrison duty in Britain and the garrisons released to fight in America. In a letter to his nieces he wrote,

> I have been surrounded with enemies, ill-treated by pretended friends, abandoned by a considerable part of my own army, totally unassisted by Sir William Howe. I have been obliged to deliberate upon the most nice negotiations, and political arrangements that required the most undisturbed reflection, under perpetual fire, and exhausted with laborious days, and sixteen almost sleepless nights, without change of clothes, or other covering than the sky.

It is not certain who were these pretended friends who had ill-treated him: von Riedesel perhaps, or Phillips less probaby. More likely he meant Clinton, Carleton, and Saint-Luc, who had deserted and was now reviling Burgoyne's name to Carleton in order to conceal his own guilt. Nevertheless, Burgoyne was familiar enough with London society and the ways of ministers and their secretaries to know what to expect when he returned to England. If he had been sacrificed by Germain, he wrote to Clinton, to assist great purposes, he was satisfied;

"but if the minister lays blame upon me for such exertion I have used upon the principle, the spirit, & the letter of his orders, I shall hold myself justified in laying those orders before the world." Indeed, he confided to his nieces, there was really no doubt about this, "for I imagine I am reserved to stand a war with Ministers who will always lay the blame upon the employed who miscarries." Therefore he had already taken the precaution of sending Lord Derby a duplicate of his latest dispatch to Germain, in case the ministers were unscrupulous enough to publish it cut or mangled in such a way as to make him appear more culpable than he was.[12]

Burgoyne left Schuyler's house on 27 October and began his journey to Boston. The army was divided up and sent off by different routes. Some parties were well-treated, others were refused food or shelter, and a few Germans even froze to death. Occasionally they came across a village whose inhabitants were entirely loyalist, who gave the soldiers food and clothing. The British sometimes behaved with their customary arrogance, a few of the officers and soldiers cursing the staring country folk as "damned rebels," a breach of manners that made Burgoyne extremely angry. Burgoyne himself became ill and spent several days as the guest of Colonel Elijah Dwight at Great Barrington. At Hadleigh he was so kindly treated by Colonel Porter, the high sheriff, that he presented him with the dress sword he had surrendered to Gates—and received back again—at Saratoga. Burgoyne's old bodyguard were allowed to camp in the deer yard, where Colonel Porter's six children gazed in fascination at the scarlet and white uniforms until they were shocked into flight by the casual swearing of the British soldiers. At Kinderhoek, Burgoyne was put up at the house of Mr. David Van Schaak, whose daughter caused some embarrassment, when asked for a toast, by proposing in her confusion, "the King and Queen and all the Royal Family."[13]

The Convention Army, as it was now called, arrived in Cambridge in the middle of a violent storm on 7 November. Mrs. Winthrop, in a letter to Mercy Warren, described the muddy, unkempt British soldiers, still surly and tough, followed by their starving horses and a guard of "American, brawny, victorious yeomanry." Then came the Germans.

> I never had the least idea that the creation produced such a sordid set of creatures in human figure—poor, dirty, emaciated men. Great numbers of women, who seemed to be beasts of burden, having heavy baskets on their backs, by which they were bent double. The contents seemed to be pots and kettles, various sorts of furniture, children peeping through gridirons and other utensils. Some very young infants, who were born on the road: the women barefooted, clothed in dirty rags. Such effluvia filled the air while they were passing, that, had they not been smoking all the time, I should have been apprehensive of being contaminated.[14]

Burgoyne, Phillips, von Riedesel, and the American General Glover, who had escorted them from Albany, were given a luncheon in Boston by the commandant, the benevolent General William Heath. Before the meal, Phillips suggested that Heath delegate to Burgoyne the responsibility of seeing his orders were obeyed, but Heath preferred to exercise his own command directly. Burgoyne smiled and Phillips said, "I only meant it for your easement, Sir."[15] After luncheon, Burgoyne returned to Cambridge via Charlestown. The streets of Boston were crowded, and every rooftop and window packed with people trying to catch a glimpse of the famous British general. When Burgoyne said, "There's the former residence of the Governor," someone called out, "And on the other side is the riding school!" referring to Burgoyne's conversion of the Old South Meeting House in 1775. Burgoyne, who must have heard it, merely said to Heath, "Sir, I am astonished at the civility of your people; for were you walking the streets of London in my situation, you would not escape insult." "Insult" was his euphemism for the dead dogs and cats and refuse from the dung hills that the terrible London mob habitually threw at unpopular figures. Bostonian civility, however, was at an end.

After a day's confusion, in which some troops were quartered in Harvard University and others in private homes, to the fury of the citizens (Mrs. Winthrop spoke of residents driven from their homes into the woods by this "inundation of undesirable objects," which was nonsense), the British were sent to Prospect Hill and the Germans to Winter Hill. Here they were given the remains of the old camp of the American army during the siege of 1775. The huts had no windows, "just holes," and often no doors. Wind, rain, and snow were blown through, and there was no wood with which to do repairs. Into these the prisoners were now crowded, between thirty and forty men, women, and children to each hut. In the bitterly cold nights, there was never room for more than half to lie down at a time. Firewood cost $13 a cord, and soon the price rose to $26. Two hundred and fifty cords were needed per camp each week. Burgoyne and his officers were unable to find quarters anywhere, for the citizens of Cambridge were unwilling to continue the hospitality that had been shown in Albany and the other towns on the road. After two nights in the open—and it was now snowing—Burgoyne procured a room at the Blue Anchor Inn for himself and his "family" of officers. He himself was so ill that he could not walk (his disease may have been gout). In vain, General Heath remonstrated with the gentry of Cambridge. Every appeal was met by a refusal and a raising of prices by the tradesmen. The situation was aggravated by a shortage of food and fuel of all kinds and by an unusually severe winter. Burgoyne attempted a gesture of friendliness by giving a ball in a vacant mansion. It was a dismal failure. The local committee forbade any ladies to attend, and the only two who dared were Schuyler's daughters, who happened to be in town.

During this time, Congress had been seeking ways to break the "Convention" of Saratoga. They argued that if the British were returned to England, more troops would be freed to come to America the next year, and, on the advice of Washington, they put forward one pretext after another to delay embarkation. Lafayette also insisted that to keep the treaty would be folly, for should France, as a result of Saratoga, recognize the United States and declare war on England, there was nothing to stop these troops from fighting the French in Europe.

Congress insisted that a roll be made giving physical descriptions of all the officers and men, so that if they broke their parole they could be identified. Burgoyne meanwhile was objecting to signing the parole at all, until proper quarters had been found for the officers. On 14 November he wrote to Gates to protest and stated that in the failure to find quarters "the public faith was broke." Congress seized on this phrase as proof that Burgoyne was intending to break the treaty himself and was clearing the way by accusing the Americans of breaking it first. To support this, they pointed out that the quantity of weapons, powder, and other supplies captured in Saratoga had been disappointingly small. In order to justify the lenient terms he had granted, Gates had told Congress that Burgoyne's army had still had twelve days' supplies on hand when it surrendered. In fact, there had been none. Nearly all the muskets had been found to be old and useless; bayonets, swords, scabbards, cartouche boxes, and belts were few; the military chest and the regimental colors had vanished.

Gates explained that the muskets had been stolen or changed by the American militia immediately after the laying down of arms, and the bayonets, etc., had doubtless been pilfered at the same time. The cartouche boxes and accouterments he had forgotten to specify in the treaty, and most of these had been sold by the troops along the road. Burgoyne had sworn to him that the regimental colors had been left in Canada, while the military chest would obviously have been so easy to dispose of that Gates had not bothered to look for it. He had been so busy moving the army south to cover Albany that he had had no time to attend to such formalities. We now know that at least two of the regimental colors, those of the 9th and von Riedesel's regiments, had been hidden among the personal belongings of the commanding officers; Baroness von Riedesel sewed her husband's flag into a mattress.

Nevertheless, only the colors of the 9th ever returned to England. The *New York Gazette and Weekly Mercury* reported that the military chest had been taken back to Canada by Captain Mackay.[16] The more reliable Digby tells us that the money chest was distributed among the army on the morning of 16 October.[17]

Next, trouble arose over the port of embarkation. The Convention had stipulated that the transports would be allowed to enter Boston in order to take off the troops. However, winter weather and the fact that facilities in Boston were already occupied in unloading a recent consignment of arms from France meant that the troops would not be able to embark before the spring. When Burgoyne applied for the port to be changed to Rhode Island or New York, he was refused. Congress suspected that the British had some scheme of not sending the troops back to Europe, though they never discovered proof. When the Clinton Papers at the William Clement Library, Ann Arbor, were opened to the public in the 1920s, there came to light a letter from Howe to Burgoyne, dated 16 November, in which he advised Burgoyne to instruct the commander of the naval ships escorting the transports to sail not to England but to New York, "my design being to exchange the Officers for those of the Rebels I sent in last Winter, in full Confidence of receiving an equal Number in Return, which, notwithstanding my repeated Applications has been pointedly refused under the most frivolous Pretences."[18] The German troops could go back to Europe. He cautioned Burgoyne to keep this absolutely secret, "as on the least suspicion the Troops wd. infallibly be stopt." Since its discovery, this letter has been offered as proof of the "perfidy" of Sir William Howe. At the same time, American suspicions that the British intended to break the treaty all along are now held to be justified; for the behavior of Congress turned out to be no more shabby than the behavior of the British. The facts are somewhat different.

It was customary in those days to exchange prisoners, on parole or otherwise. Sometimes a direct swap was arranged, so many British for so many Americans, and each side could reenroll its troops in its army. "On parole" meant that the soldier, or officer, could return home but not engage in any warlike activity, his oath being accepted as guarantee. Howe did not propose to smuggle the British Convention troops into New York and put them straight back into the army. He had signed an agreement with the Americans to release a certain number of troops in exchange for an equal number of British. He had released his prisoners, but the Americans had not kept their side of the agreement. By having the Convention troops physically in his possession, he hoped to force Congress to honor its obligations just for once; for not only had the prisoners of his own army not been released, but also the Americans still held the four hundred British soldiers promised in exchange for the four hundred Americans freed after the Cedars affair. In short, he wanted something with which to twist the arm of Congress. He was legally entitled to do this, for Article III of the

Convention of Saratoga said that should any "cartel" (agreement to exchange prisoners) take place, then Article II, by which Convention troops promised not to fight in North America again "during the present Contest," would be void. Howe enjoined secrecy because he knew very well that the Americans did not want to release any prisoners in their hands, knowing as they did that Britain's gravest problem was manpower, and would grasp at any excuse to avoid doing so. Where Howe's "perfidy" comes into this is hard to see.

In any case, Congress was perfectly capable of breaking the Convention without proof of a British conspiracy, and it did so. Washington pointed out that he had refused to release British prisoners because the condition of the American prisoners freed by the British had been so bad that they could not be reemployed as soldiers. To send back an equal number of healthy, well-trained British soldiers would by no means be a fair exchange. Howe conceded this, but pointed out that while the treatment of British troops may not have been especially harsh, the treatment of American Tories, who were the king's loyal subjects no less than British soldiers, had been—and still was—atrocious. It was reported, for instance, that when Clinton stormed the Highland forts, the Americans had burned their ships to prevent their falling into enemy hands. One of these had contained 150 loyalist prisoners. The crew had set fire to the ship and then made good their own escape, but they had not released the prisoners, all of whom had died in the hold. A similar incident, perpetrated perhaps by the same jailer, had occurred during the burning of Esopus. Thus, the dispute over the Convention Army became involved in the greater dispute over the treatment of prisoners in general. As the Americans well knew, arguments of that nature could be carried on for the rest of the war, for every atrocity story on one side could be matched by one on the other.[19]

Having accused Burgoyne of bad faith, demanded a descriptive list of every man in the Convention Army (a measure not required in the Convention), insisted on Boston's remaining the only port of embarkation, and made sure that Boston could never become available for such a purpose, Congress now raised an objection over money. Since the United States paper money was what we now call "inflated," Congress insisted that all expenses incurred by Burgoyne's army should be paid for in coin, preferably gold, although one dollar in coin was worth three in bills and rapidly increasing in value (by April it was worth four, and by the end of the year seven). All money for Burgoyne's army was supplied from the British money chests in Rhode Island or New York, which meant that the citizens of Cambridge, despite their protests at the presence of these "sons of slavery," could not only charge an exorbitant price for everything, but also for each sale get in hard coin three times the value of that exorbitant price. Some idea of what this meant can be seen from two bills covering the period 6 November to 1 January 1778.[20] The first was for food and came to £49,771 10s 10½d. The second, for wood, axes, straw, and hay, came to £12,277 4s 9d. This total of £62,048 represented a value of about $91,000 in specie (hard coin), but in paper money it represented $273,000. This was the sum the Americans demanded in specie for these two bills alone. It was a kind of blackmail, and, knowing how difficult it would be for Burgoyne to find so much coinage, Congress was satisfied that it had presented him with an insoluble problem—for not a single soldier would be allowed to sail until all bills had been paid in full. That done, on 8 January 1778 Congress declared that it had no intention of violating the treaty, but, since the Convention had not been strictly complied with in the matter of cartouche boxes, etc., since Burgoyne refused to give descriptive lists of all the officers and men, and since Burgoyne had accused Congress of breaking its faith and thereby implied that he was about to do the same, the embarkation of the troops would have to be suspended until Congress received an explicit ratification of the Convention notified by the government of Great Britain. Congress knew that if the government did that, it would have to recognize Congress, which it could not do without changing the basic premises of the war. At the same time Congress took care not to inform Burgoyne or his army of these resolutions for several months.

Thus the Convention troops continued under the delusion that they would soon be sailing for home. The inexplicble delays, the rising prices, the growing shortages of everything, and the hardships of the soldiers living in a climate to which they were not accustomed and for which they had neither proper clothing (they had left their winter uniforms in Canada) nor shelter, inevitably caused trouble; and the repeated outbreaks of disorder were aggravated by the appointment of Colonel Henley as the American commandant on Prospect Hill. He bullied and harassed his prisoners without mercy, threatened to "pour shot" into the huts if he heard a sound after dark and "make the flames of Hell jump out of ye, and turn your barracks inside out!" He ordered his guards to arrest anyone who looked at them "insolently" and to shoot on sight anyone, man or woman, who strayed beyond their boundaries, put random groups of men into close confinement, and wounded two or three with his bayonet. In Albany, it is worth noting, Stark, the hero of Bennington, was dealing out similar treatment to the wounded who had been left behind at Freeman's Farm under the care of Doctor Hayes. At the hospital, of which he was temporary commandant, he ordered that any man, or officer even, who went more than ten rods (fifty-five yards) away from his quarters would be given two hundred lashes on his naked back.[21]

At Prospect Hill on 7 January, the day before Congress resolved to break the Convention, Colonel Henley again provoked a brawl and injured a British sergeant, besides sending eighteen men to a guard ship for no apparent reason. Burgoyne brought Henley to a court-martial. In his speeches for the prosecution, Burgoyne, having presented the evidence, which was incontrovertible, and cross-examined the witnesses, appealed to the Americans as a new nation, founded on their proclaimed principles of liberty and self-determination, to distinguish between the honor due to their country and the honor due to Colonel Henley as its delegate in this prison. The greatest danger to liberty came not from outside enemies but from men in authority who made themselves arbiters of the law. If Henley and his like had had their way, and a general massacre of the prisoners had resulted, the victims would have become martyrs;

> but for America the transactions would have remained a foul and indelible blot on the first page of her New History, nor would any series of disavowal and penitence, nor ages of rectitude in government, purity in manners, inflexible faith, or the whole catalogue of public virtues, have redeemed her in the opinion of mankind.[22]

"Here," reported an eyewitness, "the Court was struck with much awe and seemed to be impressed with a resolve to act impartially." The mood soon passed. The judge advocate was not impressed by the pomp of Burgoyne's "Attic language." He admitted that Colonel Henley ("a more generous, honorable or humane man does not live in America") was his old and close friend but assured the court that this would in no way influence his decision in the present case. At the same time, he reminded his hearers of the "palpable dishonour done to my country, by General Burgoyne, in this Court" and of the notorious "pride, contempt and outrage" with which the British troops treated their captors. Burgoyne, he said, had made great play with the law of accomplices and with the doctrine that officers in command were responsible for the actions of their inferiors; but by that logic, one might as well say that Burgoyne was a party to the murder of Miss McCrae. The judge advocate was also critical of the fact that Burgoyne, and not he, had conducted the prosecution. Colonel Henley was acquitted. However, he was soon replaced by Colonel William Lee, who ran the camp sensibly and humanely.

By now it was March, and Burgoyne was endeavoring to obtain permission to return to London. In a letter to Henry Laurens, president of Congress and the man above all others responsible for the breaking of the Convention, he pleaded ill health (not that that would have cut much ice) and the need to deal with financial problems occasioned by money paid by the Treasury against his personal account to help toward the support of his troops. His death before this money was repaid to the Treasury would cause "much embarrassment and great injury to my relatives and friends." His chief motive, however, was to answer the insinuations and accusations which the ministry was now making against himself and his army in his absence. Congress felt by now that Burgoyne would be worth more to them making trouble for the ministry in London than as a prisoner in Cambridge and gave their consent. On 11 March Washington wrote a cordial letter, in which he assured Burgoyne that he was ever ready

> to do justice to the merit of the Gent^{n} & soldier—and to esteem, where esteem is due, however the idea of a public enemy may interpose. You will not think it the language of unmeaning ceremony if I add that sentiments of personal respect, in the present instance, are reciprocal. . . . I can sincerely sympathize with your feelings as a Soldier, the unavoidable difficulties of whose situation forbid his success, and as a man whose lot combines the calamity of ill health, the anxiety of captivity, and the painful sensibility for a reputation, exposed where he most values it, to the assaults of malice and detraction.[23]

There were still some last-minute difficulties and embarrassments. Late in March a British fleet anchored at Holmes's Hole under the impression that it was to take off the entire Convention Army. Trouble arose in the ensuing correspondence when General Heath insisted, regretfully, on opening all the letters sent by Burgoyne and others to officers with the fleet; but after making his token protest, Burgoyne had to acknowledge that Heath was within his rights. Then President Laurens wrote to Heath to say that Burgoyne could not depart until all financial accounts were settled. When Burgoyne asked how they were to be settled, Heath replied, "Strictly conformable to the resolves of Congress." Burgoyne then asked if Congress "could be serious in their resolution, requiring in specie the same sum they had expended in paper money." Heath supposed "that honourable body were serious in all their resolutions." Burgoyne replied that this was unjust, "for the odds was double [in fact by now they were quadruple] and appealed to our General [Heath's way of referring to himself] to say whether he thought it just himself? Our General answered that as an executive officer, it was not for him to judge or determine, whether the orders of his superiors were just or not. General Burgoyne replied, that was true."[24]

Eventually, Burgoyne was allowed to replace in kind what could not be paid for in specie, and the two generals made a pledge of honor, by which Burgoyne promised to arrange the shipment of money and provisions sufficient to clear outstanding accounts and to leave a box of gold as a pledge for any deficiencies in the provisions. It is interesting to note that as soon as these matters were settled, Burgoyne sent a letter to the British captain of the fleet, accompanied with the gift of a large turkey, paid for out of his now slender resources.

Whatever his faults, Burgoyne was unobtrusively generous and, in money matters, more than honest. There is a story that when he was in Albany he was approached by an American woman who had nursed Sir Francis Kerr Clerke before he died and to whom Sir Francis had left a small sum of money in gratitude. Burgoyne referred her to his deputy quartermaster-general, Captain Money. Money, however, paid her in Continental paper bills. When Burgoyne learned of this, he sent for her, politely asked her to keep the bills, and then coldly ordered Captain Money to pay her the same sum again in hard guineas of British coinage.[25] The point here is that Burgoyne paid expenses of this kind, together with presents to wives who had lost their husbands in battle, prizes for valor, and the cost of "entertainment and refreshment of officers coming to headquarters," out of his own pocket, and never claimed them back, although his officers said he was entitled to charge them to the public account.[26] Thus, although most generals of that time regarded war as an occasion for private enrichment (Clinton bought himself five farms), Burgoyne, reputedly a gambler and a man of pleasure, returned to England the poorer by over £20,000 pounds, none of which he ever bothered to reclaim from the Treasury. It should be added that his only source of income in America was his salary as a lieutenant-general.

The last condition required of him was to sign a parole that he was to return to America and surrender himself again to Congress should it request him to do so.

On 2 April, Burgoyne dined in Boston with General Heath. The two men, so utterly different in background, temperament, and outlook, had come to regard each other during these difficult months with a certain respect, perhaps even affection. On leaving, Burgoyne offered to send "any foreign necessaries you may want or wish." "Our General thanked him for his politeness, but was careful not to mention any, choosing rather to suffer with his fellow countrymen the necessities of the times, than to avail himself of so exclusive a favour."[27] Burgoyne sailed for Rhode Island on the fifth. The command now devolved on Phillips, whose arrogance and temper soon led to friction; and Heath came to regret that he no longer had the "good sense" and moderation of General Burgoyne to deal with. In considering the root of this trouble, he touched upon a matter which was to become a major theme in American literature:

> The same feeling which had great weight in the beginning of the war, continued for some time, namely, that Great Britain was one of the greatest and most powerful nations in the world, in arts and in arms;

while the Americans were yet . . . young, weak, and but barely civilized, ignorant of the world, and especially so of arts and of arms. . . . There was frequently, as in the atmosphere, placid intervals; but whenever any cross wind happened to blow (and there is no season without them) then instantly appeared those ideas of self-superiority, and contempt for the Americans, which was the true cause of many uncomfortable hours. Mankind have the same passions, the difference lies in some riding with a double curb, while others give the reins.[28]

CHAPTER XVII

THE ADMINISTRATION CLOSES RANKS

BURGOYNE'S fear that the administration would build up a strong case against him in his absence was well-founded. There are signs that Lord George Germain had begun to prepare his defenses as early as the end of August 1777, when letters and dispatches arrived simultaneously from Burgoyne and Howe. The dispatches were intended to be published in the newspapers, and, therefore, like modern official communiqués, contained little that was true and nothing that was interesting. The private letters were intended for the eyes of Germain and the king only and, therefore, contained a slightly more truthful account of events, as well as plans for the future.

Howe's private letter was the one written on 16 July, shortly before he sailed from New York, in which he declared that if Washington marched to defend Philadelphia Burgoyne should meet little opposition in the north; but if Washington marched toward Albany, Burgoyne was strong enough to keep him busy until Howe came up behind him and caught him between the two armies. Meanwhile, Howe intended going to the Delaware, having given up his plan of approaching Philadelphia from the south, via Chesapeake.

When he sent Howe's correspondence to the king, Germain wrote in his covering letter, "The Private letter confirms the opinion Lord George has always had of the General's pursuing his intended operations to the Southward."[1] What did this mean? Inasmuch as the trapping of Washington's army "between two Fires" had always been an important part of the Hudson plan, this part of Howe's letter, taken out of context, could be said to "confirm" Lord George's opinion; but the letter as a whole showed that Howe had not the least expectation that Washington would march north toward Albany. However, as I mentioned earlier, this private letter was "inadvertently" omitted from the correspondence sent to the king. One historian has suggested that the omission was deliberate because the letter showed how completely Germain had permitted Howe to wash his hands of Burgoyne.[2]

I wish the matter were as simple as that. However, the affair is complicated by Germain's behavior the next day, when he sent Burgoyne's correspondence to the king. This time he wrote, "Lord George has a private Letter from Genl. Burgoyne which he will not now trouble your Majesty to read."[3]

This letter was written from Skenesborough on 11 July. In the version which Burgoyne read out in his defense before Parliament and published later in his book *A State of the Expedition from Canada*, there are two paragraphs as follows:

> Your Lordship will pardon me if I a little lament that my orders do not give me a latitude I ventured to propose in my original project of the campaign, to make a real effort instead of a feint upon New England. As things have turned out, were I at liberty to march in force immediately by my left, instead of my right, I should have little doubt of subduing before winter the provinces where the rebellion originated.
>
> If my late letters reach Mr. Howe, I still hope this plan may be adopted from Albany; in the mean while my utmost exertions shall continue, according to my instructions, to force a junction.[4]

Clearly, if the king had read this and Howe's letter at the same time, he could not but have noticed the startling discrepancy. Moreover, here was proof, if any were needed, that Burgoyne had expected to meet Howe all along. In that case, Germain would have had every reason for not "bothering" the king with this letter and "inadvertently" omitting to send Howe's letter as well. However, in the original of this letter, which is in the Public Record Office in London, these paragraphs are nowhere to be found. Regarding his diversion toward New England, Burgoyne merely says that, since the Americans were fortifying on the Hudson, he would keep his Indians with the main army until reaching Albany, and then perhaps "renew the alarm towards Connecticut."[5] The rest of the letter concerns administrative matters, such as the question of his brigadiers' rank and the organization of the loyalist volunteers, all of which he hoped to resolve when he learned "Mr. Howe's sentiments" on them. Meanwhile, he would disregard the geographical limits of Canada so that his brigadiers could continue to draw the higher pay of their local rank until his army "is the army of Sir William Howe" (that is, until the armies were physically joined). The letter ends with a request for leave to return to England at the end of the campaign, as he had done the two previous years.

When I first discovered this, I wondered if Burgoyne had sent two versions of this letter by different messengers, to guarantee delivery. This was hardly likely, though, for communication to Canada from Skenesborough was perfectly safe after the capture of Ticonderoga. Germain acknowledged receiving only *one* private letter (though that is no proof that he *received* only one), and I have been unable to find a written copy of the printed version anywhere. Where, then, did Burgoyne get this version? It is just possible that he faked it, while preparing his defense, in order to make his case appear stronger. Alternatively, it is possible that he did send two versions, that the printed version arrived on 22 August, and that Germain, having been careful not to show such an incriminating document to the king, quietly destroyed it later. The evidence against both Burgoyne and Germain is so confusing that the matter must be left open.[6] After all, there may be perfectly innocent explanations to all these incidents.

Nevertheless, if one considers the chain of events from the beginning, it is clear that Germain had got himself into an awkward predicament. The root cause of all his troubles had been when, on 3 March, he had too hastily approved Howe's first change of plan and proposal to attack Philadelphia. I have suggested that the next crisis came when Howe's second letter (20 January) arrived after Burgoyne's departure for Canada and not before, as is generally believed. This faced him with three choices: to write to Burgoyne and cancel the campaign; to write to Howe and go back on his previous approval (which would require awkward explanations to the king and probably provoke Howe's resignation); or, finally, to trust that Burgoyne could reach Albany alone and let things take their course in the hope that they would turn out well in the end. If, as I suspect, he kept that letter to himself, then it is only natural that he would have had to keep these later letters to himself as well. This would explain why, when he answered Howe's correspondence on 3 September (but was careful *not* to acknowledge the receipt of Howe's private letter dated 16 July), he expressed the hope that a junction of the two armies would occur earlier than Howe had previously expected. Otherwise, we have to believe that Germain was so muddleheaded as to be almost insane. Since we know that he was not, the only explanation of this affair that is consistent with his behavior is that he was keeping the truth from the king and his fellow ministers in the hope that if Burgoyne and Howe were both successful, and all turned out well in the end, nobody need ever know how close the campaign had come to disaster.

In that case, however, why did he not "bother" the king with Burgoyne's letter? Although the original is less explicit in referring to a junction than the printed version, the whole of the letter was written on the assumption that a junction with Howe would take place sooner or later. That was probably enough to alarm Germain into keeping it from the king. This, of course, does not clear Burgoyne of the suspicion of having faked the printed version, to which I shall return in due course.

When in the late autumn news arrived of Howe's "unaccountable" voyage to Chesapeake, followed by rumors of Bennington and other misfortunes, the general disquiet was so great that even Germain was unable to keep up his outward show of cheerful optimism. Early in October he owned to Lord Hertford "that General Howe had defeated all his views by going to Maryland instead of waiting to join Burgoyne."[7] Nevertheless, while Germain was still uncertain whether to cast the blame for the impending disaster on Burgoyne or Howe, Burgoyne played into his hands. His letter of 20 August, in which he declared his intention of crossing the Hudson and forcing his way to Albany, arrived at the end of the month. Germain confided to his deputy-secretary, William Knox:

> I am sorry to find that Burgoyne's campaign is so totally ruined; the best wish I can form is that he may have returned to Ticonderoga without much loss . . . but what alarms me most is that he thinks his orders to go to Albany to force a junction with Sir William Howe are so positive that he must attempt at all events the obeying of them, tho' at the same time he acquaints me that Sir William Howe has sent him word that he has gone to Philadelphia, and indeed nothing that Sir William says could give him reason to hope any effort would be made in his favour.[8]

By the end of November all London was talking about the stories of Burgoyne's defeat that were arriving with every ship from America. These reports were so obviously true that the subject forced itself into the debates of Parliament before any official confirmation had yet arrived. At first Lord George temporized and kept back those parts of Burgoyne's letters that had criticized the absence of latitude given by his orders. The central issue, however, could not be avoided; and when on 18 November Fox demanded to know why Burgoyne had been ordered to join Howe in New York while Howe had "gone to another country," ignorant that he was supposed to cooperate with Burgoyne, Germain answered that

> the honourable gentleman was under a mistake when he imagined that General Burgoyne had orders to fight his way to New York, there to join Sir William Howe: that his orders were to clear the country of rebels as far as Albany, which town was prescribed to him as the boundary of his expedition, unless circumstances might make it necessary to co-operate with General Howe, in which case he was to assist him to the uttermost of his power.[9]

Thus, if Burgoyne was guilty of twisting his orders in one direction, Germain was just as willing to twist them in the opposite direction. The orders had said nothing about cooperating with Howe *only if "circumstances might make it necessary."*

With the arrival, on 2 December, of Burgoyne's official account of his surrender, the opposition released a tremendous onslaught on the administration. Germain, pilloried as an "ill-omened, inauspicious character," was the prime target, but he maintained for the most part a cool silence. The opposition clamored for copies of all instructions and papers relative to Burgoyne's campaign to be "laid on the table" for inspection. There was one ludicrous moment in the House of Lords. The aged William Pitt, Earl of Chatham, was thunderously denouncing the employment of Indians when someone pointed out that he himself had ordered the employment of Indians in the last war. He refused to believe it, swearing that he would never have put his name to such an order; and when Lord Amherst reluctantly admitted that he himself would never have used Indians unless specifically ordered by Pitt, and that he could produce the very order, Chatham had to sit down, covered with embarrassment and confusion.

The ministry saved itself by adjourning Parliament for the Christmas holiday earlier than usual and keeping it adjourned for six weeks. During that time, Germain was able to persuade the king that a public inquiry into Saratoga would be most unwise, for it would enable the opposition to attack the ministry, make speeches against the war, and spread their republican and prorebel views throughout the land. The king maintained that Burgoyne should be given a fair hearing when he returned. Germain agreed but at the same time pointed out that Burgoyne's insistence that his orders had been positive was unjustified. At this moment, too, he suddenly remembered that letter from Howe, dated 16 July, which he had "inadvertently" left out of the papers submitted to the king the previous August. "It plainly shows," he wrote to the king, "that Sir William Howe thought Lt. General Burgoyne's army in safety even if it had been attacked by all Washington's forces."[10] This remark is so dishonest and the manner in which the letter was produced so pat that it is very hard not to suspect Germain of deliberate duplicity in the matter of all these missing letters.

The king "inclined" to the belief that Burgoyne's orders *were* positive, but agreed, after an indecisive cabinet meeting, that any inquiry ought to be conducted by a board of military officers *in camera*. He also agreed, perhaps hesitantly, to Germain's insistence that so long as Burgoyne was subject to an inquiry into his conduct it would be against court etiquette for him to be admitted into the king's presence. Yet, while he was proferring the inquiry as the reason why Burgoyne should not be allowed to see the king, so that Burgoyne would be prevented from telling the king things Germain did not want His Majesty to hear, Germain was seeking ways of ensuring that the inquiry would never be held, or would at least be abortive. In this he was helped by Burgoyne's own indiscretions.

It will be remembered that Burgoyne had sent Lord Derby copies of his dispatches to Germain, which he had written after Saratoga, in case the ministry published them in a "mangled" version. On the very day the king received the originals, Lord Derby was reading the copies aloud to his friends at Almack's gaming rooms. Such provocative behavior antagonized many people, lost Burgoyne a great deal of public sympathy, and gave Germain grounds for claiming that Burgoyne was determined to incriminate him, regardless of the truth. No one, however, was especially concerned with the truth any more.

The ministry decided to employ Attorney-General Thurlow, the best legal mind they had, to go over the papers and prepare a case for their defense. While Thurlow was searching for papers in the American Office, Knox showed him the précis of plans and operations which he had written, largely at Germain's dictation, and from which I have quoted on several occasions.

"Why," Thurlow said, "this is the very thing I wanted, and you have done it already; pray, do the Ministers know of this?"

"Yes, Sir, they have all had copies of it."

"Then, by God, they have never read it, for there is not one of them knows a Tittle of the matter."

After glancing at Burgoyne's dispatches, he asked Knox why Germans had been sent to Bennington. Knox explained that the Germans had been on the left of the line of march and, because Bennington lay to the left of the army, military etiquette demanded that they be sent. Howe's Hessians had been at Trenton for the same reason.

"So," says Thurlow, "because one damned Blockhead did a foolish thing, the other blockhead must follow his example."

Knox regretted that Thurlow had no chance to display his military talents, for he was sure "they would have appeared superior to any of our Commanders."[11] Thurlow spent an entire night reading the papers and made his report the next morning. Government, he said, would have been right to withhold the papers had not Burgoyne made a public issue out of his misfortunes. "After what he has thought fit to lay to the charge of others, he has no right to complain if ministers do not expose themselves in his behalf even to a temporary censure." An inquiry, by officers, would clear the air, but it would have to be complete, and the ministers would be wise to wait until the opposition demanded it. Among his other remarks, Thurlow claimed that Burgoyne was left sufficient discretion by his orders, that his orders were not peremptory, and, that, to judge by Burgoyne's "Thoughts," "a co-operation of Howe's army was not expected."[12] How he came to the last conclusion is impossible to conceive. Nevertheless he did—and for this service he was later made Lord Chancellor.

Thus reassured, Germain left a few selected papers at his office for perusal by interested persons. In February, France signed a treaty of alliance with the United States, so that France was now, to all intents and purposes, at war with Britain. When Parliament reconvened, the opposition renewed its attack on the ministry with greater fury than ever. When government supporters blamed the generals, and especially Burgoyne, for the present state of affairs, Germain begged them not to throw out wild accusations until Burgoyne had had a chance to defend himself. At the height of this crisis, Germain's wife, whom even Walpole described as a "sensible, good woman," died of measles in tragic, indeed horrific, circumstances. She was prematurely buried and, reviving, broke open her coffin. Germain was distracted by the fear that opposition newspapers would get hold of this story and turn it into a subject of ridicule. With so much going on, it is not surprising that one small incident passed almost unnoticed. Christian D'Oyley, Germain's deputy-secretary who had promised to write that letter to Howe, resigned. He explained that he had taken his employment as a friend of Howe, in order to help him; now that the commander-in-chief was out of favor, he could see no further need to stay in the American Office. Perhaps the real reason was that the enormity of his blunder in not sending a clear instruction to Howe to cooperate with Burgoyne (owing, I have suggested, to the hurry to wind up affairs before Easter) had at last dawned upon him and that he had decided to remove himself unobtrusively before the storm broke over his head. Perhaps here, too, we have a clue to the origin of the story of the famous "forgotten" or "missing" dispatch. It may be remembered that when Germain returned to London on 7 April after his Easter holiday, I suggest that he decided, as a result of receiving Howe's letter of 20 January, not to write to Howe after all. It is probable that he asked one of the clerks what D'Oyley had written, and, on being told that it had been merely a covering note and that no copy had been made, he dismissed the subject from his mind with relief. D'Oyley, hearing no more about it, probably forgot the letter Germain had intended to write until the crisis broke in December. Then, since Germain had never mentioned it to him, he assumed Germain had forgotten it as well. Hence, it is likely that it was D'Oyley and not Knox, as is generally assumed, who told Lord Shelburne the story of the "forgotten dispatch." The story that the dispatch was found, docketed and awaiting signature, after the war, was probably an invention of Burgoyne's biographer, Edward de Fonblanque.

Burgoyne arrived in London in May. Germain received him

> with much apparent kindness; explanations passed, but they were friendly; I was heard attentively . . . and I was led by degrees, and without suspicion of insidiousness, to the most confidential communication, on my part, of facts, observations, and opinions, respecting very important objects. . . . It was not until after the matter of my communication was exhausted, that the Secretary of State drew from his pocket an order that I should prepare myself for an enquiry: at which I expressed my fullest satisfaction, till he followed the order with the information, of the *etiquette* I before mentioned, that I was not to appear at Court.[13]

Burgoyne was then told that the inquiry was not to be a regularly constituted court-martial; it was, rather, to be held *in camera* and was to confine itself strictly to the actual operations of the campaign, rigidly excluding all questions of the strategic plan and of orders to other generals. Since Burgoyne's defense rested on those orders, or the lack of them, to other generals, he was understandably indignant. He demanded a court-martial, a parliamentary inquiry, and an interview with the king. Germain replied that since Burgoyne was not charged with any improper conduct there were no charges for a court-martial to consider; that a parliamentary inquiry was unnecessary because a military inquiry had already been arranged; and that until the military inquiry had made its report, Burgoyne could not see the king.

Yet Burgoyne was cheated even of his military inquiry. The Board was set up. It consisted of five generals, including Gage, Amherst, and Lord Loudon. They did not interview him, but first wrote asking him to explain the exact terms of his parole. Burgoyne answered that he was not a prisoner of war but a free man bound only not to serve in America during the war; but that should the embarkation of the Convention troops be delayed "beyond the time apprehended," he was to return to America and surrender himself to Congress. The next day, the Board advised the king that since Congress had a lien on Burgoyne's person, any proceeding by the Board "which may in any wise tend however remotely to restrain or affect his Person, until such Parôle is satisfied, might operate to the prejudice of Your Majesty's Service and possibly have very serious Consequences respecting the Troops included in the Convention at Saratoga."[14] By adjourning the Board, instead of dissolving it, the ministry was able to postpone Burgoyne's interview with the king indefinitely. Thus, although Germain was declaring in Parliament that he did not wish members to condemn Burgoyne unheard, he was doing all he could to ensure that Burgoyne never would be heard.

The members, however, had little chance of condemning Burgoyne unheard, for the general was nothing if not voluble. The very day after Burgoyne learned that he was not to appear before the Board of Enquiry, he sat in the House of Commons, and when Mr. Vyner (an opposition member) proposed that the House turn itself into a committee to inquire into the state of the Convention Army and the reason for Burgoyne's presence in England, he declared himself ready to answer questions by Mr. Fox, which, he hoped, would open matters he wanted discussed. The House was crowded with members, which enabled the ministry to propose that all strangers be cleared out to make room. Despite Burgoyne's protests, this was done, so that no report of the debate was kept. Burgoyne, however, answered this maneuver by keeping his own report and publishing it himself.

A large part of his speech consisted of his defense regarding the use of Indians, which I have already dealt with. In the course of this, he mentioned that Saint-Luc, who had deserted after Bennington, was now in London and had often been "closeted by a noble lord in my eye" (Germain). Thus, many stories unfavorable to Burgoyne were now being spread about from the American Office—to the effect that if he had not restricted his Indians they would have done great service and that Burgoyne finally discharged them without cause. Germain stood up and answered that Saint-Luc had said Burgoyne was a great officer with the regulars but did not seem to like the savages or know how to retain their goodwill. "He was a brave officer, but as heavy as a German!" For the rest, Burgoyne concerned himself with answering charges about his superfluity of baggage and artillery and with justifying his crossing of the Hudson.

At the end of the debate, an extraordinary scene took place. Temple Luttrell delivered a long attack on Lord George, in which he contrasted Burgoyne's bravery with Lord George's cowardice at Minden. Burgoyne's only crime was that

> he had been too zealous, too brave, too enterprising, too anxious for the good of his country, had strictly obeyed his orders and done all that British valor was capable of, to carry the Minister's plan into execution. Had he, instead of that, receded from his colours, disobeyed the commands of his superiors, and hid himself from danger, he might have had pretensions to one noble lord's patronage [Lord North's] and to the other's [Lord George Germain's] dignities and emoluments!

Lord George started up in a most violent rage, protested that he was never personal in the House, and swore that "old as he was, he would meet that fighting gentleman, and be revenged!"[15] There were cries of "Order!" and general uproar. Luttrell refused to retreat and even alluded to Germain's "private vices or virtues" (his alleged homosexuality, perhaps). Germain apologized; Luttrell said he would rather go to prison than accept this apology, but, on being threatened with prison, he accepted it.

During the next months, the ministry tried various means of silencing or getting rid of Burgoyne. His old enemy, Solicitor-General Wedderburn, tried to argue that since the Convention of Saratoga had been broken Burgoyne's status had reverted to that of a prisoner of war. Therefore he had no right to his seat in Parliament. Parliament, however, had learned painfully from the Wilkes affair what could happen when it tried to expel members duly elected and dropped that line of reasoning hastily. In June Congress formally renounced its obligation to return the Convention prisoners since the Court of St. James had failed to ratify the treaty. The king, offended by Burgoyne's espousal of the opposition, lent his authority to Germain's move to force Burgoyne to return to America, where his presence among his troops, it was claimed, was necessary. Since Congress had not asked for him, this was absurd, and Burgoyne was able to disobey the royal command without incurring serious royal displeasure. There was, after all, a great deal of public sympathy for him still, succinctly expressed by Lord Pembroke, who said: "Burgoyne in my mind always carried more sail than ballast, but he is gallant and honest; and such ought not to be sacrificed to a Minden Buggering Hero."[16]

The more critical said Burgoyne should never have joined the opposition but should have retired into dignified silence. It is true that Burgoyne irritated and bored the House by continually standing up and drawing attention to the injustices he was suffering, regardless of the subject under debate; at the same time people remembered that before leaving for America he had been a supporter of the administration and its policies. On the other hand, the injustices were real, and the shifts to which the ministers in general, and Lord George Germain in particular, were put to deny him a fair hearing, smear his reputation, and cover up the whole affair, were transparently obvious and contemptible. The situation of the Convention troops was especially unfortunate. The ministry made no serious effort to negotiate their return, and Germain pointedly ignored the few officers who had returned, "whilst runaways and fugitives, with Saint Luc at their head, were questioned and caressed; nay, while a menial servant of my own [said Burgoyne] who had been turned out of my family, was heard with attention."[17]

The truth was that the ministry did not want the troops back, for so long as they were prisoners they were unable to cause embarrassment and provided an excuse for ordering Burgoyne to return to America. As for the Germans, the Duke of Brunswick positively refused to have them, for he was afraid they would spread disillusionment about the war and make the future hiring of men to Britain impossible. Then, when Congress finally went back on its promise to release the Convention troops, Clinton declared that they would have to be treated as ordinary prisoners of war henceforth and refused to send them any more money or supplies. Thus Burgoyne was the only man left willing to speak out for them.

Although most of Burgoyne's speeches were as long-winded and pompous as ever, there were moments when he spoke with eloquence. He pointed out, for instance, that every commander in America, as well as Admiral Keppel in England (who was accused of cowardice and incompetence by his subordinate, Sir Hugh Palliser, a ministry supporter), was now in bitter conflict with the administration, which was trying to blame them all in turn for its own blunders. The ministers not only left commanders unprotected but

> laid snares in their way to effect their ruin: in these days, it is said, the principle of disgrace is implanted the very moment of their appointment, like that of mortality which is supposed in the animal kingdom to be coeval with existence. . . . [U]pon the first ill success in the field, or the first defection in this House . . . they are delivered over to those worse than butchers, the tale-bearers and whisperers, and carriers of detraction, who dissect and mangle them at will, and hold them out a spectacle, *in terrorem*, to teach others more servility.[18]

In March 1779 the House of Commons formed itself into a committee to inquire into the conduct of the war in America. There was a great deal of talk over the competence of members to understand military matters, for the general feeling was that if there was to be any criticism, it should be restricted to "measures, not men." In other words, personalities should be kept out of it. This intention, which is professed by all committees, is always a vain one. Measures are devised by men, and when we come to ask why certain measures turn out to be disastrously wrong, we find that we invariably come back to personalities and the conflicts between them. The Burgoyne and Howe affair, and the consequent loss of the American colonies, was a perfect example.

When Howe came to explain why he had not cooperated with Burgoyne, he said that an attack on the Highland forts would undoubtedly have cost him many men, and the only result would have been that Washington would have put himself either between Howe and New York or between Howe and Burgoyne: "in either case . . . our efforts upon Hudson's-river, could not, from the many difficulties in penetrating through so strong a country, have been accomplished in time to have taken possession of Philadelphia that campaign." On the other hand, he would have gained nothing, even by capturing Albany, that he could not have gained more cheaply by drawing Washington away from Burgoyne's army. Then he went on:

> . . . had I adopted the plan of going up Hudson's-river, it would have been alleged, that I had wasted the campaign with a considerable army

> under my command, merely to ensure the progress of the northern army, which could have taken care of itself, provided I made a diversion in its favour, by drawing off to the southward the main army under Washington. Would not my enemies have gone farther, and insinuated that, alarmed by the rapid success which the hon. general [Burgoyne] had a right to expect when Ticonderoga fell, I had enviously grasped a share of that merit which would otherwise have been all his own? And let me add, would not ministers have told you, as they truly might, that I had acted without any orders or instructions from them; that general Burgoyne was directed to force his own way to Albany, and that they had put under his command troops sufficient to effect the march? Would they not have referred you to the original and settled plan of that expedition . . . to prove to you that no assistance from me was suggested?[19]

If, he concluded, the ministers had had any doubts about the success of the plan, or intended that the safety of Burgoyne's army should depend upon Howe's cooperation, surely they would have informed him and sent him instructions?

This is all very strange. Howe said that he did not wish to be accused of envy; therefore, instead of cooperating with Burgoyne he had gone in the opposite direction. He said that there had been a danger that Washington might put himself between the two armies; yet in letter after letter he had expressed the hope that this was exactly what Washington would do, for therein lay the best chance of bringing the Americans to a pitched battle. Did Howe really expect anyone to believe that, with Washington's army destroyed or dispersed, the British in control from Canada to the borders of Pennsylvania, and all Britain rejoicing at such splendid victories, the ministers (his enemies) would have accused him of jealousy, disobedience, and wasting the campaign? He spoke of the Hudson plan as if it were some wild idea he had never heard of before, although he had been a principal proponent of it for over a year. He complained that the country was "strong" (rugged), although he would have possessed the Hudson River itself, with a large fleet upon it, to keep open his lifeline to New York; yet he expected Burgoyne, as I have said before, to have an easy progress with a smaller army over a greater extent of even "stronger" country. The entire speech suggests that it was not the fear of being accused of envy, but envy itself, that prompted General Howe to turn his back on General Burgoyne.

When Burgoyne came to speak in May, he, too, made a mess of his defense. Instead of sticking to the point, which was that if Howe had cooperated as planned there would have been no Saratoga and France would not now be in the war, he tried to blind his listeners with science by going into details of his supply problems, his proportion of artillery (in this case, as I have said, altering the figures slightly), his choice of route, the conduct of his allies and auxiliaries, and his decision to cross the Hudson. A great deal of this was double Dutch to members who did not know where Skenesborough, Fort Anne, and Lake George were. To those who did, it seemed that Burgoyne could be challenged on every point. Thus instead of lulling suspicion he aroused it. Among his witnesses only Carleton was senior enough to have a knowledge of the general picture, and he was so unhelpful, replying to almost every question "I really don't know," as to be positively hostile. This was unfortunate, for it made Burgoyne's efforts to refute the charge that he had schemed against Carleton appear unconvincing. yet Burgoyne, who needed Carleton as an ally, and had praised him to the skies in his opening speech ("Had that officer been acting for himself, or for his brother, he could not have shewn more indefatigable zeal than he did . . ."), could not now reveal that it was Carleton who had compromised him unscrupulously in the quarrel with Germain.

Why, when Burgoyne had such a strong case, did he put up such a weak one? There is a story, told first by Governor Hutchinson, which says that when Burgoyne arrived in England in May 1778 he was met at Hounslow by Charles James Fox, who asked him what his plan was. "To charge Howe with leaving me to be sacrificed," he said.

Fox replied, "If that's your plan we must forsake you, for we are determined to support Howe."[20]

This tale has been dismissed as a fabrication of the ministers to discredit Burgoyne, yet there is probably some truth in it. Burgoyne does not seem to have turned to the opposition until he was informed that there would be no military inquiry, and he did so then only in desperation at finding every other way to justice blocked and his soldiers abandoned to their fate. For their part, the opposition wanted to discredit and unseat the ministry. This they could never have done by taking up the cause of a single general only, no matter how unjustly he had been treated. But if they could have presented *all* the generals as victims of ministerial incompetence and treachery, then they would have had a case. Probably the price of their help to Burgoyne was his restraint toward Howe. This would explain why he never pressed Howe for those two letters written from Plymouth and Quebec, which, if produced (and Burgoyne did actually read out what he claimed to be the content of one of them),[21] would have damaged Howe's defense severely; for even if Howe could reply that he had received no orders from London and had supposed his letter to Carleton would have removed any doubts about his own intentions, surely the receipt of these letters should have prompted him to write again, and at once, to find out what was going on.

Indeed, throughout the debate Burgoyne gives the impression of defending himself, as it were, with one hand tied behind his back, harping on matters of secondary importance and putting up arguments which even he must have seen were flimsy. The flimsiest and silliest of all was his reply to Germain's remark that the plan was Burgoyne's and that, therefore, Burgoyne had no right to say he was carrying out a plan he did not agree with. Burgoyne's answer was that in the final orders two clauses had been removed from the original plan: first, his discretion to change direction from the Hudson to New England; second, his discretion to take the entire army to New York by sea, should he decide a land expedition to Albany was not feasible. Since these clauses had been removed, Burgoyne argued, the plan was altered; since it was altered, no one could say it was his. Shorn of these two important clauses, his orders left him no choice but to force his way to Albany. Thus the entire discussion was sidetracked into the question of whether or not Burgoyne's orders were positive, and there defenders of Germain have kept it ever since.

It did not take unfriendly critics long to find the weak spots in Burgoyne's defense. Stedman summed up:

> In the whole of his vindication, it was observed, his method was to state a *necessity* for every one of his measures taken singly, and not as one chain or system of action, taking care to pass over one material circumstance, that that *necessity* invariably originated, on his part, from some previous omission or blunder.[22]

This overlooks the fact that the omissions or blunders that really decided the fate of Burgoyne's expedition were not his at all. Nowadays, almost every conceivable cause is assigned to Burgoyne's defeat except the obvious one—Howe's failure, or refusal, to cooperate with him. For even if Burgoyne had made no mistakes and had forced his way to Albany against all the odds, it may be wondered how long he could have maintained himself there without strong support from the south. The probability is that there would have been a surrender in Albany in January 1778 instead of the Convention in Saratoga in October 1777. But this failure or refusal on Howe's part was itself due to conflicts of personality. Let us take but one example. Nearly all Burgoyne's troubles on the expedition arose from a shortage of horses and carts. These should have been provided by Carleton during the winter. Instead, Carleton not only forgot about them but also did nothing for two weeks even after Burgoyne remonstrated with him on arriving at Montreal. In the end, Burgoyne had to contract for them himself, at the last minute, although he had no experience of such negotiations in Canada. As a result no more than a third of the horses paid for were ever sent. Carleton's dilatoriness was all a part of his quarrel with Germain (itself originating in the depths of Carleton's personality). This quarrel, among the numerous mischiefs it caused, affected Germain's relations with Howe and prompted him to approve, on 3 March, Howe's first change of plan too hastily. This approval committed Germain to a course of action from which he found it increasingly difficult to pull back. Thus, when Howe's second change of plan arrived after (as I have suggested) Burgoyne's departure for Canada, Germain was caught in a dilemma: either to cancel Burgoyne's expedition or to go back on his approval to Howe. Because of the risks either course entailed, he decided to do neither. He hoped instead that if he let things take their course they might turn out well in the end. But doing nothing meant concealing the truth from the king and from the other ministers, which again led to more and more deception. As things turned out, his hopes were disappointed, first because Howe, resentful at Germain and perhaps at Burgoyne too, stubbornly went his own way and closed his mind to everything but his own concerns; and second because Burgoyne, with an army too small and lacking transportation, was unable to get to Albany by himself. Nevertheless, Burgoyne's failure was contingent upon Howe's. I do not see how this fundamental fact can be argued away.

Nowadays, too, it is customary to assume that Burgoyne had no idea of forcing a junction with Howe until things began to go wrong in August and he began to look around for excuses for his own lack of progress. I suspect that the case was the opposite: That is, he did not think of reaching Albany alone, and then only in the sense of getting there first, until *after* he received Howe's letter on 5 August. If not, how are we to explain the items of evidence which are listed in Chapter XV, all showing that a meeting with the New York army was basic to the plan of the expedition? This brings us once more to the question of that letter dated 11 July from Skenesborough. It will be remembered that in one version, which he read out during his defense (and later printed in his book), he spoke of the precision of his orders to force a junction with Howe but that in the original he said no such thing, merely referring to a junction with Howe in vague terms. I have suggested that Burgoyne might have forged this version while preparing his defense. Such things are not unknown. Clinton forged an order from Germain at the time of Yorktown in order to make his own conduct appear more justifiable. If one day it could be proved that Burgoyne did forge this letter,[23] surely, then, would not his entire defense fall to the ground? I think not. First, the other correspondence I have mentioned above would still have to be explained. Second, there is his motive. When he came to prepare his defense, he might have realized, with something like horror, that he had no document proving beyond a shadow of a doubt that the two armies were to meet in Albany. The items I have listed were either unknown or unavailable to him. The letters he sent across enemy territory to New York clearly could not have been specific on this point, lest they had been intercepted. He might have been in the position of a man who knows he is telling the truth but cannot prove it and is only too aware that people will be more than inclined to disbelieve him. Therefore, he might have taken the desperate step of actually inventing this letter, justifying his deed with the assurance that on this essential point of a junction, he was right and everybody else was wrong.

There remains one more detail to consider. In those two paragraphs, as in his letters to Howe from Plymouth and Quebec (which he might have rewritten in London as well), he harped on his desire to make a diversion, if not a "real effort," toward New England or Connecticut, even going so far as to claim that he had no doubt of subduing those provinces where the rebellion had begun. How, historians have asked, could he possibly have imagined himself capable of such a march? The country was even more difficult than the Hudson valley, there was no waterway to keep open his communication with Canada, and he would have had the entire population, the most inveterate and rebellious in America, rising against him on all sides. In addition, his rear would have been exposed to Schuyler's, or Gates', army at Stillwater. There are two possible explanations. If he wrote this in London in 1778 or 1779, then he probably introduced this idea as part of his argument that the ministry had so altered his original plan, which had included a march into Connecticut as an alternative to a junction with Howe, as to leave him no discretionary powers. In short, this talk of a real effort toward New England was a red herring. If, on the other hand, he wrote this at Skenesborough on 11 July, then it should be remembered that this was just after the capture of Ticonderoga, when it seemed that American resistance in the north was collapsing entirely. Indeed, every time he had seen the Americans in battle so far, even at Bunker Hill, they had ended by running away, and there was no reason to believe they would not continue to do so. He still imagined that the loyalists were numerous and confident enough to make his progress easy. Six hundred of them, after all, joined his army that very week. In any case, he did not insist on the idea very seriously. He was a talkative man, and he probably wanted to reassure Germain that he was energetically exploring every possibility. In this context, it has often been said that Burgoyne's greatest mistake was in underestimating his enemy. If he did so, it was not out of British arrogance and conceit, for his paper, "Reflexions on the War in America," shows that even in the winter of 1775–1776 he realized that Americans as guerrilla fighters were formidable. This, however, was a civil war, and in a civil war it is almost impossible to estimate the enemy in the same way that one can estimate a foreign enemy. One cannot foretell when, or why, or how hard, people will fight for their ideals, because one does not share the ideals for which they are fighting. Thus, Burgoyne's opinions of the Americans were based, as he himself was the first to admit soon afterward, on misinformation.

This brings us to the final question: If the plan had been carried out as intended, and Howe and Burgoyne had met in Albany and established their line of posts from Montreal to New York, would this have ended the war? Here again, we cannot say, because we do not know if the Americans would have gone on fighting. If they had, they would almost certainly have found ways of penetrating the line and keeping the spirit of rebellion alive in New England. Then the war might have dragged on for years, leaving wounds, in the form of memories of bloodshed and cruelty, and a desire for revenge, that would not have healed to this day. If they had not, then the history of the world since would have been so different as to be beyond all conjecture.

When Burgoyne concluded his defense in Parliament, Germain rose and, needless to say, blamed the disaster entirely on Bennington. Until then, no one had dreamed of failure; but Burgoyne's mishandling of that unfortunate venture had changed the entire picture. Thereafter, his delays in "bringing up immense trains of artillery, and a great suite of provision waggons," had enabled the Americans to build up their strength and finally surround him.[24]

Although Burgoyne had explained in great detail that, far from having a "great suite" of provision wagons, he had not had enough even to carry the bare necessities of his army, nobody challenged Lord George on this point. Nevertheless, the ministers were far from happy about the way the inquiry was going. If the public did not exactly veer around to support Burgoyne and Howe, they saw that Germain had a great deal to hide and that at times he gave the appearance of downright dishonesty. On one occasion he had claimed that Howe had first formed his plan to attack Philadelphia on 8 May 1777; when he was corrected (the real date was 20 December 1776) he had airily replied that he could not be expected to carry every date of every letter in his head. A few days after Burgoyne had finished his case, it happened that Sir William Howe was fifteen minutes late arriving at the House of Commons. Seizing on his absence as a pretext, the ministers adjourned the committee. The next day, although there were still witnesses to call, charges to refute, and evidence to be presented, and despite the protests of Howe, Sir William Meredith, and others, the ministers blocked every attempt to form the committee again by simply refusing to answer questions or even to speak. Thus the committee, in the words of the parliamentary historian, "expired . . . without coming to a single Resolution upon any part of the Business."[25] Yet, despite the shabby treatment they had received, neither Howe nor Carleton joined the opposition, and the plan to array the generals in line against the Administration failed dismally. Thus Burgoyne, who had already joined the opposition, now found himself even further isolated from his former colleagues.

At the same time, the ministry renewed its efforts to force Burgoyne to return to America, on 5 June ordering him to depart as soon as he had completed yet another cure at the waters of Bath. Burgoyne ignored this and meanwhile continued to embarrass the government by reminding them of their failure to do anything on behalf of the Convention troops. In September, the smooth and ambitious Charles Jenkinson was appointed Secretary-at-War, and he promptly wrote to Burgoyne: "I am commanded by the King to acquaint you that your not returning to America and joining the troops, prisoners under the Convention of Saratoga, is considered as a neglect of duty, and disobedience of orders. . . ." To this Burgoyne replied that "the time in which I am charged with neglect of duty, has been employed to vindicate my own honour, the honour of the British troops and those of his Majesty's allies, under my late command, from the most base and barbarous aspersions that were ever forged against innocent men, by malignity supported by power." Taking care to separate the king's person from the ministers who shielded themselves behind his authority, Burgoyne demanded to know: if he had been denied a court-martial and an inquiry because, as a prisoner on parole, he had not been considered as under British law, how could they now invoke British law to compel him to return to America, when by the terms of his parole he was to return only when demanded by Congress? Nor could they invoke the Convention of Saratoga when they refused to recognize or ratify it. He ended his reply by resigning all his appointents, except his rank of lieutenant-general; for by keeping his army rank, he would still be entitled to the court-martial which the ministers were denying him.[26]

His governorship of Fort William, his colonelcy of the 16th Light Dragoons, and other appointments altogether came to £3,000 a year, and their loss, in addition to the expenses he had been put to in America, brought him to financial distress. He sold the freehold of "The Oaks" to Lord Derby.* His regiment went to his old friend Colonel Harcourt, and Fort William was given to General Vaughan,

* Perhaps as much to console his uncle, General Burgoyne, as to celebrate his purchase of a house he had always loved, Lord Derby immediately (14 May 1779) founded a new horse race, which he called "The Oaks," at the meetings at Epson nearby. The following year he instituted "The Derby," which has since become both a British national event and perhaps the most famous horserace in the world. Few among the hundreds of thousands who gather there every year know that all this is owing originally, if indirectly, to General Burgoyne.

Burgoyne in 1780. (*From* Political Magazine, *December 1780.*)

who had led the last-minute dash up the Hudson toward Albany.

In January 1780, encouraged by Edmund Burke and other friends, Burgoyne published his defense in a beautifully printed and produced book entitled *A State of the Expedition from Canada*, dedicated to General Phillips and the officers who had served on the campaign. According to Captain Edmonstone, who had been aide-de-camp to General von Riedesel, it did not sell, for it concerned a past affair that was no longer news. "Those interested in the subject are the only readers. The author is a forgotten man, full of misery. He never speaks when he is out walking and is more miserable here than in America."[27] With time, however, sales picked up and a second edition was printed. In the two centuries that have passed since then the book has remained a work of incalculable value, not only to students of the American Revolution, but also as a mine of information, not found elsewhere, on the inner workings of the British army during this fascinating period of its history. If its sales were disappointing to a man in need of money, Burgoyne at least had the gratification of knowing that all the officers whose evidence was recorded in its pages had testified to their confidence in their general from the beginning of the campaign to the end and to their admiration for his bravery, skill, judgment, and generosity. Nor can his "misery" have been of long duration; for while Howe was retired into disgruntled silence and Clinton was occupying his time in the composition of a long, almost interminable, justification of his part in the war, laced with innumerable ill-tempered and ungenerous comments on his one-time colleagues and friends, Burgoyne had turned to the pleasures of literary creation, in the form of musical comedies.

CHAPTER XVIII

GENIUS, POLISHED MANNERS, AND FINE SENTIMENTS

THE ludicrous situation, in which a British government ardently desired to force a British general, on parole but not a prisoner of war, to return as a prisoner of war to an enemy state who did not want him, continued for about a year—whereupon it became, if anything, even more absurd. Washington, believing wrongly that Burgoyne was ill and might die, offered him in exchange for an equivalent number of American junior officers, NCOs, and privates, some at their homes on parole and others still prisoners of the British. But what was a defeated British general worth to the British? Unaware that the ministers longed to be rid of Burgoyne, Washington was puzzled to learn that the British were prepared to exchange him for no less than 1,040 Americans, provided that the Cedars prisoners were included. It will be remembered that four hundred Americans had been released on parole by Carleton in 1776, in accordance with Benedict Arnold's treaty, and that Congress had refused ever since to release the four hundred British agreed for in exchange, except under impossible conditions. The ministers were calculating, therefore, that Congress would continue adamant, that the negotiation would fail, and that Burgoyne might yet be sent back to America. Edmund Burke said that their hatred of Burgoyne was due to the fact that that he had done more than anybody else to discountenance the delusions put out by the administration as reasons for carrying on the war, the gist of them being that those who adhered to the royal cause were numerous and zealous, while those who supported the new American republics were few and wretched.

Now, it happened that Henry Laurens of South Carolina, who as president of Congress had done more than anybody else to persuade Congress to break the Convention of Saratoga and to delay Burgoyne's release, was captured at sea, brought to England, and put in the Tower of London, without so much as pen and paper to relieve his solitude. Congress, forgetting Washington's negotiations, demanded the return of Burgoyne, whom they intended to hold and offer in exchange for Laurens. They did not realize, of course, that if they wanted Laurens offering Burgoyne was the worst thing they could do; for no sooner would the general have been packed on board ship by a British government unable to believe its good luck, than the gates of the Tower would have been doubly locked on the unfortunate Mr. Laurens. Washington urged Congress to forget Laurens and accept the 1,040 troops, the Cedars prisoners included, before Burgoyne died. Meanwhile Edmund Burke wrote to his one-time friend, Benjamin Franklin, who was in France, asking him to intervene on behalf of a gallant officer now being persecuted by *both* sides. Burgoyne, he said, might have been an enemy to the United States, yet he had never aggravated the natural mischiefs of war "by unnecessary rigour; but has behaved on all occasions with that temper which becomes a great military character, which loves nothing so well in the profession, as the means it so frequently furnishes of splendid acts of generosity and humanity."

Franklin must have smiled at such an unusual reason for becoming a professional soldier, but he sent back a good-humored letter which began, "Since the foolish Part of Mankind will make Wars from time to time with each other, not having enough Sense otherwise to settle their Differences, it certainly becomes the wiser Part, who cannot prevent those Wars, to alleviate as much as possible the Calamities attending them."[1] Nevertheless, he had just been authorized to offer Burgoyne in exchange for Laurens and hoped Burke might be able to negotiate the business. Burke started a campaign for the release of Laurens, playing down the Burgoyne exchange and playing up the ill treatment Laurens was said to have received in the Tower. Congress, taking Washington's advice, withdrew its demand for Burgoyne and accepted the 1,040 soldiers instead, but excluded the Cedars prisoners. Burke, unaware of this, finally proposed the exchange of Burgoyne, and Germain was able to turn it down on the grounds that Burgoyne had already been exchanged for 1,040 Americans. This was untrue, and the affair dragged on until the surrender of Cornwallis at Yorktown made the entire dispute academic. Burgoyne was eventually exchanged for the 1,040 soldiers, including the Cedars prisoners, in 1782, a fortnight before Lord George was put out of office. As Burgoyne acidly remarked, every officer of the Convention Army, and even surgeons' mates, had been exchanged long before, save the general.

The common soldiers were not so lucky. They were marched from camp to camp across America, their numbers steadily dwindling through desertions and escapes. Sergeant Lamb managed to reach New York, only to be recaptured at Yorktown. The remaining British Convention troops were returned after the war. Of the Germans, nearly all (more than a thousand) chose to settle in America, where their knowledge of useful trades had already earned them better livings than they had ever dreamed of at home.

One consequence of Saratoga was that the entry first of France, then of Spain, and finally of Holland, dispersed the conflict around the world, to the West Indies (which now became the crucial theater of the war), to Gibraltar and the Mediterranean, to the coasts of Africa, to India, and even to the Far East. With her resources stretched beyond their limits, Britain could do little more than maintain a foothold in America. Philadelphia, whose possession Howe had thought so important, had to be quickly abandoned. Clinton, finding that evacuation by sea was impossible (so much for Germain's hope that Howe would have been able to send a strong force back to the Hudson in time to assist Burgoyne), had to take his entire army and a procession of loyalists on a dangerous march overland to New York. A number of successes, notably Clinton's capture of Charleston and six thousand troops under Lincoln and the unending difficulties Washington encountered in supplying and keeping together his army, maintained the illusion of an imminent, decisive victory, until Yorktown shattered it forever. Some historians have said that the ministry had good reason to believe that Britain could win in the end and that, consequently, to call Saratoga "the turning point" is nonsense. It is true that the number of troops and guns lost there was small, that the British army as a whole did not see in the event any cause to regard the Americans with greater respect, and that in England the reaction to the defeat was a wave of patriotic fervor and recruiting. But whatever the ministers, or the mass of the British people, thought, the Americans thought otherwise. Before the war had ended they spoke of Saratoga as the birthplace of their liberties and have done so ever since.

Throughout these years Burgoyne kept his seat in Parliament. The oposition had supported him, to a certain extent, after Saratoga, and he felt in honor bound to support them in return. Perhaps his close personal friendships with Edmund Burke and Charles James Fox prevented his staying neutral in any case, for he was a gregarious man. Unfortunately, party politics impose obligations, the worst of them being the necessity of talking a great deal of party cant, regardless of private beliefs. Thus on one occasion he said that he "was *ever of opinion* that this country had no right to raise taxes upon America,"[2] as though he had never voted against the repeal of the Stamp Act. On another occasion he wrote to Rockingham, "The prevalence of the term the *King's army* and the *King's fleet* in preference to their being called the forces of the state, was one among the many manifestations of the Tory doctrine of this reign."[3] Finally, he went so far as to say, "The American War is but part of a general design levelled against the constitution of this country and the general rights of man."[4]

It is true that his experiences had changed his opinions about Americans and about the war, and his change of mind was no doubt eased by the persuasive eloquence of Burke, Fox, and Lord Shelburne; but it would have been more seemly to admit that he had come to these unfamiliar republican ideas though a conversion, rather than to pretend he had believed in them all his life. It was with some justice that Walpole said of him, "Such patriots disgraced the cause of liberty, and were little preferable to the ministers."[5] Professional soldiers sometimes may be good diplomats (as Burgoyne would have done), but they rarely make good politicians. Indeed, they often make dangerous ones, and we can only be grateful that eventually they were prohibited from taking their seats in the House of Commons.

Since his return from America Burgoyne had been a celebrity, if at first a slightly disreputable one. Boswell, with his flair for scoops, managed to obtain an interview, at which Burgoyne told him some of the truth behind the Saratoga affair. Thrilled, Boswell sent his verbatim report to William Temple, whose servant, it is suspected, used it to wrap fish in. Thus we have been deprived of what seems to have been the only record of Burgoyne's conversation ever written. Despite Boswell's support, in later years when Burgoyne applied to join "The Club" (the exclusive literary gathering of which Dr. Johnson was the most distinguished member) he was blackballed. It is not known by whom or for what reason.[6] Nevertheless, Burgoyne was soon welcomed back into London society. During the week of the anti-Catholic Gordon Riots in 1780, when mobs burned down entire London streets, he sheltered Edmund Burke and his wife, whose own home had been wrecked (Burke was Irish and "soft" on Catholics), at his house in Hertford Street, doing everything he could to make them feel at ease.[7]

With the collapse of the war came the fall of Lord North's ministry, and Burgoyne suddenly found his friends in power. He was made a Privy Councillor, with the title "Right Honourable" before his name, and given the colonelcy of the 4th, King's Own Regiment of Foot. However, to avoid the embarrassment of meeting the king at Privy Councils, he was sent to Dublin as commander-in-chief of the military forces in Ireland. He had no liking for his post, even if Irish wit and eloquence were a compensation. The Irish, realizing at last that they were a nation and not a mere province of England, were at the beginning of their long and bitter struggle for independence and unity, and this first spasm was to culminate in the violence of Wolfe Tone's rebellion fourteen years later. Burgoyne had no wish to be involved in suppressing another uprising, and when Rockingham's ministry fell, owing first to the death of Rockingham and then to the political maladroitness of Lord Shelburne, Burgoyne thought he had an opportunity to resign. Lord Portland wrote to tell him that to hold an official post, or at least a military one, and yet be in open opposition to the next ministry were not incompatible, and asked him to stay. Portland led a coalition which contained such antagonistic bedfellows as Lord North and Fox, and, not surprisingly, it soon fell to pieces. Burgoyne, pleading ill health, returned to London in 1784. Fox had offered him another colonelcy, this time of the 4th Dragoons; but it turned out that the aged General Severn, the existing colonel, was still alive, and Fox could only promise the regiment as soon as it became vacant. But General Severn did not die until 1787, and the promise was forgotten.[8]

In fact Burgoyne's real interests were changing. Through his friend Sheridan he met stage people and found their company very much to his taste. In 1780 he had tried his hand at writing for the theater again. The result was a comic opera entitled *Lord of the Manor*, to which he wrote a preface setting out his views on what opera, comic or tragic, ought to be. Music and song, he said, should be used only to describe the "passions." The action should always be in speech.[9] The piece itself, derived from Marmontel's *Sylvain* with additions by Burgoyne (such as an elopement), was rather weak on plot but contained some attractive songs:

> The sleepless bird from eve to morn
> Renews her plaintive strain;
> Presses her bosom to the thorn,
> And courts th' inspiring pain.
>
> But ah! how vain the skill of song,
> To wake the vocal air;
> With passion trembling on the tongue,
> And in the heart despair!

There is a scene in which la Nippe, a manservant, persuades another servant, Peggy, to "put your mistress into my master's hands," and, showing her a *rouleau* (fifty guineas wrapped in a cylinder), he adds that he would like "a something as regards ourselves" besides. He then sings:

> The *rouleau* is form'd with a magical twist,
> To conquer caprice or displeasure;
> If your object the offer of one should resist,
> You have only to double the measure.

It finds to all places its way without eyes,
Without tongue it discourses most sweetly;
To beauty or conscience alike it applies.
And settles the business completely.

To which Peggy replies:

Well, who would have thought such wonderful power,
In a compass so small could be hidden;
To sweeten at once the grapes that are sour,
And purchase e'en fruit that's forbidden.

A magic so pleasant must surely be right,
Without scruple I pocket the evil,
I'll show you the proper effect before night,
And leave you to account with the devil.

The music for these airs was written by William Jackson, and the scenery was painted by de Loutherbourg, who had done *The Maid of the Oaks* when it was put on at Drury Lane. In later years he was to have an influence on the painter Turner, an influence the great artist always denied.

There is a passage in which Burgoyne gives a humorous but accurate sketch of a recruiting officer of the period, whom he calls "Captain Trepan" (the perennial confidence man). We meet him erecting his booth at a country fair:

TREPAN. Come, paste up more bills—and the devices—they are not half thick enough—where's the lion rampant, with the grenadier's cap upon his head?

FIRST WORKMAN. Here, Sir, here.

TREPAN. And the marine device?

2ND. WORKMAN. Here it is—done to the life—the prize boarded; the decks running with arrack punch and dammed up with gold dust.

TREPAN. Right, lad, place that next the lion. I don't see the London tailor with his foot upon the neck of the French king.

3RD. WORKMAN. Here he is in all his glory.

TREPAN. Paste him up on the other flank of the lion—so, so, pretty well—what have you left for the corner?

4TH. WORKMAN. The East Indies, Captain, a nabob* in triumph, throwing rough diamonds to the young fifers to play at marbles.

When asked about the secret of his trade, Trepan explains:

* A "nabob" (from the Indian *"nawab,"* a prince or deputy ruler under the Mogul) was a British adventurer who had made a vast fortune in India and returned to England to spend it.

> Suppose new regiments are to be raised—I am applied to. . . . How are skins now?—How many do you want?—Five hundred—Why, your honour, answers I, those that are fit for use, that bear fire, and wear well in all climates, cannot be afforded for less than ten pounds a-piece—we have an inferior sort that we sell by the hundred—I'll take half and half, says my employer! Your place of delivery?—Plymouth!—Agreed!—and they are on shipboard in a month.

When asked if his business is not subject to frauds, he gaily answers, "Yes, there are rogues in all trades—but my word is known. I never ran the same recruit through more than three regiments in my life—and that only when we have been hard pressed for a review." The entire scene was cut from the acted version on the orders of the Lord Chamberlain, who apparently feared it might bring the military establishment into disrepute.

During the production of his play, Burgoyne met Susan Caulfield, an actress and singer in the Drury Lane Company. Her husband was Thomas Caulfield, an actor who specialized in imitations. These he would improvise during a farce, such as *New Hay at the Old Market*, and if they were applauded he would polish them up and play them as an interlude on the following nights. He does not seem to have been very successful, for between 1795 and 1797 several benefits were held at Drury Lane for him and two other destitute actors. He was probably much older than Susan, for when she left his apartment at the Adelphi and went to live in a room Burgoyne rented for her in Queen Street, Soho, he does not seem to have taken offense; indeed they both continued acting together, and in Burgoyne's plays at that, for years after. Susan did not follow Burgoyne to Dublin. A letter has survived in which Burgoyne sends his "dearest Sue" a pheasant and a brace of partridges (she must hang them for a week), adding in a postscript, "Fie! Fie! to get such colds and pains in the stomach by feasting. If you did but take such care as I do!"[10]

Perhaps, however, it was not feasting, for on or about 25 July 1782 she gave birth to a son. Charles James Fox was godfather and the boy was christened John Fox Burgoyne in his honor. In the following years Susan had two daughters, Maria and Caroline, and another son, Edward, by Burgoyne, who was now, it should be remembered, over sixty years old.[11]

In 1785 Burgoyne wrote his best play, *The Heiress*, which was presented on 14 January 1786. It was an immediate success, ran for thirty-one nights (exceptional at a time when shows were changed two or three times a week to satisfy the very small theater-going public), and thereafter became a stock item in the Drury Lane repertoire.[12] The plot was based partly on Diderot's *Le Père de Famille* and partly on a for-

Blackburn New Theatre.

On FRIDAY Evening, May 4, 1787,

Will be preſented a celebrated NEW COMEDY, (never acted here) call'd THE

HEIRESS.

(Written by GENERAL BURGOYNE.)

The chaſte Elegance of this inimitable Piece has perhaps never been equalled on the Engliſh Stage. The ſplendid Talents of the polite Author have been univerſally acknowledged. And the wide range of Obſervation which his rank and high ſituations have furniſhed, has given him ſuch a rich Stock of Materials as poſſibly no Writer before him was ever ſupplied with. Of this Treaſure has he amply availed himſelf in the preſent inſtance. It is furniſhed with every thing that OBSERVATION, GENIUS, POLISHED MANNERS and REFINED SENTIMENTS can beſtow. The ſtruggles of ſuffering VIRTUE; the unrelenting efforts of griping AVARICE; the inſolence of PRIDE; the refinements of FLATTERY, and the exalted Triumph of SENSIBILITY and HONOUR are the rich ingredients of this unrivalled Compoſition.

Sir Clement Flint, Mr CAULFIELD
Clifford, Mr FORESTER
Lord Gayville, Mr GEORGE
Mr Blandiſh, Mr BENTLEY
Mr Rightly, Mr JACKSON
Chignon, Mr MARTIN
Prompt, Mr PARSONS
Porter, Mr STANTON
And Alſcrip, Mr WELCH
Lady Emily, Miſs NAYLOR
(Being her Firſt Appearance Here.)
Miſs Alton, (with a Song) Mrs CAULFIELD
Mrs Blandiſh, Mrs MARTIN
Mrs Sagely, Mrs WELCH
And Miſs Alſcrip, (the Heireſs) Mrs JACKSON

To which will be added, a favorite ENGLISH BURLETTA, call'd

MIDAS

Or, PREJUDICE PUNISHED

Juſtice Midas, Mr WELCH
Jupiter, Mr BENTLEY
Pan, Mr FORESTER
Sileno, Mr GEORGE
Damætas, Mr MARTIN
And Apollo, Mr PARSONS

Daphne, Mrs JACKSON
Myſis, Mrs MARTIN
Juno, Mrs WELCH
And Nyſa, Mrs CAULFIELD

To begin exactly at Seven o'Clock.

Boxes, 2s: 6d.----*Pit*, 2s.----*Gallery*, 1s.

No Admittance behind the Scenes, nor Servants or Children without Paying.
Places for the *BOXES* to be taken at the Theatre every Day from Ten till One.
Tickets to be had of Mr WELCH at the Legs of Man.

Poster for a performance of *The Heiress,* by John Burgoyne, in which his mistress Susan Caulfield, and her husband, both acted. (*Reproduced by kind permission of the Lancashire Record Office; ref. DD. Pr. 28/1.*)

gotten play called *The Sisters*, by Mrs. Lennox. Originality, however, was not so important in the eighteenth century as correctness of form and sound craftsmanship. Moreover, everyone agreed that Burgoyne had vastly improved on his sources. Even the unfriendly Horace Walpole was charmed and read it through twice in one day, liking it better than anything he had read since Sir John Vanbrugh's *The Provoked Husband.* Burgoyne's "delightful play," he thought, would be acted long after his battles were forgotten. The reason for its success was that it was the only play, in the opinion of the public, that gave a true picture of upper-class life and manners, for other writers, such as Sheridan and Foote, were unfamiliar with the habits of behavior and speech of the aristocracy. Thus critics thought of the heroine Lady Emily as "the only approach to a fine lady upon the modern stage." Since the object of the play was to satirize, in a gentlemanly way, the meanness and vulgarity of the new rich, by contrasting them with the unassuming grace, good manners, and natural taste of the "Quality" (albeit impoverished), one suspects this judgment was formed more on wishful thinking than on an exact knowledge of what the upper classes were like. I suspect that the public fell for Lady Emily because Burgoyne, despite or because of the formality of her speech, succeeded in making her *sexually* attractive.[13]

Forty years later (25 September 1823) *The Morning Herald* described *The Heiress* as "the last real comedy produced on the English stage." In fact, *The Heiress* is a perfectly balanced, polished, four-square period comedy, so very much in its period, however, that one cannot be certain how it would be received today. There is only one song, of which the verse is far more tightly controlled than that of his earlier songs:

> For tenderness framed in life's earliest day,
> A parent's soft sorrows to mine led the way;
> The lesson of pity was caught from her eye,
> And ere words were my own, I spoke in a sigh.
>
> The nightingale plunder'd, the mate-widow'd dove,
> The warbled complaint of the suffering grove,
> To youth as it ripen'd gave sentiment new,
> The object still changing, the sympathy true.
>
> Soft embers of passion, yet rest in the glow—
> A warmth of more pain may this breast never know!
> Or if too indulgent the blessing I claim,
> Let reason awake and govern the flame.

we may leave the last word on *The Heiress* to the writer of the poster advertising a performance at the New Theater, Blackburn, Lancashire, in 1787. The general's high rank and situation had furnished him with such a rich stock of materials

> as possibly no Writer before him was ever supplied with. Of this Treasure he has amply availed himself in the present instance. It is furnished with every thing that OBSERVATION, GENIUS, POLISHED MANNERS, AND REFINED SENTIMENTS can bestow. The struggles of suffering VIRTUE; the unrelenting efforts of griping AVARICE; the insolence of PRIDE; the refinements of FLATTERY, and the exalted Triumph of SENSIBILITY and HONOUR are the rich ingrediants of this unrivalled Composition.[14]

Burgoyne also wrote some political satire *(The Westminster Guide)*, the points of which would be apparent only to an expert steeped in the minute details of Westminster elections, and made a translation of Sedain's opera *Richard Coeur de Lion*. Here again he transformed what had been a London flop into a success. It contains a song as elegant as a painted bedroom panel:

> The God of Love a bandeau wears,
> Would you know what it declares,
> And why his eyes are clouded?
> 'Tis to shew us that his pow'r
> Is ne'er so fatal, ne'er so sure,
> As when in darkness shrowded.

Of Burgoyne's last years we know little, except that they appear to have been tranquil and on the whole content. One thing he did was to try with Sheridan to found a Society for the Encouragement of Ancient Games, in an effort to find an alternative to the tormenting and killing of animals as the only universally popular recreation in England.

He was invited to sit on a committee of twenty-three generals, whose purpose was to decide the best means of defending the coasts of Britain. Burgoyne was one of the only two who voted against fortifications, saying that the best means of defense was attack, for which there existed a navy. With the sums proposed for building fortifications, could be built a fleet stronger than all the fleets of all the European powers combined. It was a subject he returned to in Parliament, arguing that fortresses were not only a vast waste of money but also, since they required large garrisons, constituted a threat to liberty, inducing "garrison-mindedness" in the local citizens and becoming nurseries for *coups d'état*.[15]

The East India Company was in trouble once more, and Burgoyne returned to the attack, castigating its officers for their corruption and brutality. He cited the case of one Captain Williams who, under orders, had hanged the Raja Mustapha Cawn. In words that are only too pertinent today, he maintained that an officer's obedience must be limited to *lawful* commands only. The military establishment of a nation stood on certain well-founded laws of humanity, "without which valour is a crime and a curse, without which an army is the heaviest infliction that can fall on a people!"[16]

In his last speech on army affairs (debating the Estimates for 1792) he drily complimented the government on its raising the pay of officers and soldiers, but he regretted that somehow, as usual, they had overlooked the subalterns. These were still expected to live on their scanty pittance, "although every article of subsistence is at least 30 per cent dearer than when their pay was originally settled"; indeed, their pay was the same as when he had been an impoverished young sub-brigadier fifty-four years before.[17]

General Burgoyne was asked to stage-manage the trial of Warren Hastings, who in Burke's view was the arch villain of British misgovernment in India (Burke was wrong, and was tormented by doubts over the Hastings affair for the rest of his life). Fanny Burney tells us in her *Diary* that she went with her brother James (a naval captain who had sailed with Burgoyne to America and was to become an admiral) to Westminster Hall, where the trial was being held. On seeing them, Burgoyne walked over and said, "Captain Burney, I am very glad to see you."

"How do you do, Sir," answered James, "here I am, come to see the fine show!"

Burgoyne "turned short upon his heel and walked abruptly away." In younger days he would have laughed off such a *gaucherie*. Indeed, in his old age he was becoming touchy and peevish, though he was always quick to apologize. Admiring the work of a certain young painter, he made Sir Joshua Reynolds, the first president of the Royal Academy, promise to have a picture by the young artist hung in that year's exhibition (1791). As great men do, Sir Joshua forgot. Burgoyne wrote a furious five-page letter, but then kept it for as many days before sending it with the following postscript:

> DEAR SIR JOSHUA,
>
> After having kept this letter for five days unfinished, I now confess I wrote it in just anger, but upon reflection, I set too high a value on your talents and your virtues not to be placable, and I have the honour to remain,
>
> Your most obedient and humble Servant,
>
> J. BURGOYNE.

During the summer of 1792 he suffered renewed agonies of the gout. On Friday 3 August he spent the evening at the Haymarket Theatre in good spirits, but the next morning he died suddenly, *The Times* tells us, "at Mr. Fox's feet." He had requested a simple funeral, a desire approved of by that august newspaper:

Burgoyne in old age, from James Sayer's *Caricatures*, (1782-1808) p. 2. (*Courtesy of the Trustees of the British Museum.*)

> Yesterday [13 August] at 12 o'clock at noon, General Burgoyne was interred without any military pomp. A hearse of six horses, a few pages on foot, two mourning coaches, and one plain coach, made the whole of the procession. Indeed, after the compliment paid by France to that disgrace to arms (John Paul Jones), funeral honours, until that circumstance is forgotten, rather commemorate the villainy than do credit to the virtues of any man.

The paper described General Burgoyne as "an accomplished gentleman, an able scholar, a benevolent man." The *Gentleman's Magazine*, noting how few people were present "to drop a tear over departed genius," informs us that the occupant of the plain coach was a lady, "whose convulsive agitation showed her to have that within which passeth show."[18]

General Burgoyne had written his will nine years before in Dublin. After affirming his faith in the "Gospel dispensation" and his reliance "upon the oblation of Jesus Christ, as understood by the Church of England, as the only means of salvation," he went on to say:

> During a life too frequently blemished by the indulgence of one predominant passion, it has been a comfort to me to hope that my sensualities have never injured, nor interrupted the peace of, others. Of the greater crimes that originate in the forgetfulness of God, or injustice, or malevolence towards my fellow creatures, my heart is innocent, and upon that ground, though with the deepest consciousness how little my best actions deserve when set against my offences, I commit my soul to the Mercy of its Creator.

He left £4,000 to Susan Caulfield for the education of his eldest son, John Fox Burgoyne, and £2,000 to Nathaniel Day. Day, it will be remembered, had been commissary-general in Canada in 1776–1777, and a friend since the Portuguese campaign. When Burgoyne had resigned his appointments in 1779, Day had sent a gift of £2,000, unsolicited, and Burgoyne had hoped that when he died he would be wealthy enough to surprise Mr. Day with a gift in return. The large diamond ring, presented by the grateful King José of Portugal, he left to Lord Derby.[19]

In the nine years that had passed since the will was written, unfortunately, Burgoyne's financial resources had not improved but worsened. He had even had to borrow another £500 from Mr. Day. Thus, when his debts were paid, there was no money for Susan Caulfield. Her four children were taken from her by Lord Derby, who brought them up in his own household. Whether this was done forcibly on some legal pretext or with her consent there is no record, and still less is known of what her feelings were about the arrangement. Nor is it clear that she ever saw them again. Perhaps her only consolation was that instead of a certain future of poverty and obscurity, her children would grow up to become members of the upper classes. John Fox Burgoyne, for instance, joined the Royal Engineers, became a distinguished field-marshal, and was knighted. There is a statue to him in Waterloo Place, beside the Athenaeum Club, which is an honor that was never granted to his father.[20]

General Burgoyne's end was fitting to his life. It would be hard to think of anyone who was a more complete product of the eighteenth century; his career reads like a novel of the period: the scandal attaching to his birth; his running away from school to join the army and becoming a cavalry officer at that; his charm and good looks; his elopement with an heiress; his wanderings abroad to escape from his creditors; his encounters there with gamblers, adventurers, statesmen, philosophers, and artists; his strange interlude in Portugal; the death of his father in a debtors' prison; his riotous election; his rise as a politician; his fortunes and misfortunes in the momentous drama of the American Revolution, set against an immense and wild landscape complete with Red Indians; his dabbling in poetry, science, and architecture; his mistress; his dying in debt. All the elements—save shipwreck and a capture by pirates—are there. His pomposity and boastfulness remain an enigma, for my suggestion that they may be attributable to some murky secret he knew about his father is merely a guess. But even these were very much in the style of his age; he was not really much more boastful than Boswell or more pompous than "The Vicar of Wakefield." Finally, we have somehow to reconcile the frightful windbag of the public speeches with the civilized, and presumably entertaining, man who was always welcome in the company of Lord Chesterton, Charles James Fox, Burke, Sheridan, Reynolds, and the Duc de Choiseul, none of whom suffered fools gladly.

A Grub Street hack, satirizing the English stage writers of the time, wrote ungrammatically of him:

> Behold a comic Hero formost comes;
> The Muse presenteth him with Fifes and Drums!
> More skillful March ne'er crossed the River Boyne;
> The Marches on the comic Bard Bur . . . e.
> To Arms & Arts in youthful Years been bread
> And Captive Honour to the Field him led:
> But fully eager for the glorious Prize,
> He spurns at Danger, and pail Fears defies;
> He headlong plunges to his utmost Station,
> And risks at all—at e'en Capitulation:
> Oh fickle Fortune! false, inconstant Friend,
> To deign the comic to a tragic end![21]

However, he lived in a comic age, and his mind was not cut out for tragedy. His plays and songs derive their atmosphere from the paintings of those French artists he had known in Italy. An idyllic afternoon light softens the outlines of his characters, the implacable stepfathers and squires, the hard shallow society women, the rich and lecherous merchants, the cheating valets, conniving chambermaids, and blustering recruiting sergeants, and renders their sordid wranglings over lust and money innocent and amusing. Perhaps, therefore, he should not have been a general, for despite his ambition he was not a seeker of power. He was on the side of the young lovers against their elders. He was for freedom, for pleasure, for "every liberal art, that polish'd life or humaniz'd the heart," and successful generals are not usually "for" these things at all. Voltaire once said of Madame de Pompadour that she was "one of us," a phrase Norman Mailer has used about President Kennedy. Burgoyne, too, was "one of us, not one of them." If he could see Lake Saratoga as it is today, covered with sailing boats and people enjoying themselves in the summer sun, he would be the first to concede that it was all for the best that things had worked out as they did.

APPENDIX I

ORDER OF BATTLE FOR THE EXPEDITION FROM CANADA, 1777

Commander-in-Chief: Lieutenant-General John Burgoyne
Adjutant-General: Lieutenant-Colonel Robert Kingston
Deputy Quarter-Master-General: Captain John Money

Other members of Burgoyne's staff, or "Family," included:
Royal Artillery: Captain Thomas Blomefield
Chief Engineer: Lieutenant William Twiss
Commissary: Mr. Rousseau
Wagonmaster: Mr. Robert Hoaksley
Provost: Lieutenant Atherton
Civil Affairs: Colonel Philip Skene
Naval Engineer: Lieutenant John Schank, RN
Captain of Batteaux: Mr. Munro, RN
Pioneers: Captain Wilcox
Paymaster: Mr. David Geddes
Surgeon of Hospitals: ———
Cartographer: Lieutenant of Engineers W. C. Wilkinson, 62nd Regiment

ADVANCE CORPS

Brigadier-General Simon Fraser
Grenadier Battalion: Major John Acland, 20th Regiment
Light Infantry Battalion: Major the Earl of Balcarres, 53rd Regiment
24th Regiment: Major Robert Grant
Marksmen: Captain Alexander Fraser
Canadians: De la Naudière
Loyalists: Colonel John Peters
Indians: Major Campbell, Saint Luc, De Langlade (Captain Alexander Fraser also commanded a group of Indians incorporated with his marksmen)

RIGHT DIVISION

Major-General William Phillips, RA (whom Burgoyne appointed as second-in-command of the expedition).

First Brigade

Brigadier-General James Hamilton
20th Regiment: Lieutenant-Colonel John Lind
21st Regiment: Major George Forster
62nd Regiment: Lieutenant-Colonel John Anstruther

Second Brigade

Brigadier-General Henry Powel
9th Regiment: Lieutenant-Colonel John Hill
47th Regiment: Lieutenant-Colonel Nicholas Sutherland
53rd Regiment: Major William Hughes

It should be remembered that the above six regiments were formed as battalions: That is, they were shorn of their grenadier and light companies, which were detached, together with those of the 24th Regiment, and of the three Regiments remaining in Canada (29th, 31st, and 34th), to make up the Grenadier and Light Battalions of the Advanced Corps. After the capture of Ticonderoga, the 62nd Regiment (together with the Brunswick Regiment Prinz Friederich) was detached to garrison the fort. Later it was replaced by the 53rd and brought up to the front, where it played a vital part in the battle of 19 September. The 9th was echeloned as a reserve during the battle, while the 47th was deployed to protect the camp.

LEFT DIVISION

Major-General Baron Friederich von Riedesel

First Brigade

Brigadier-General Johann Friederich Specht
Regiment von Rhetz (Brunswick): Lieutenant-Colonel Johann Gustav von Ehrenkrook
Regiment von Specht (Brunswick): Major Carl von Ehrenkrook
Regiment von Riedesel (Brunswick): Lieutenant-Colonel Ernst Ludwig von Spaeth

Second Brigade

Brigadier-General W. R. von Gall
Regiment Prinz Friederich (Brunswick): Lieutenant-Colonel Christian Julius Praetorius
Regiment Erb-Prinz (Hesse-Hanau): Colonel W. R. von Gall, Acting Brigadier

Reserve

Lieutenant-Colonel Heinrich Christoph von Breymann
Grenadier Battalion: Lieutenant-Colonel Heinrich von Breymann
Light Battalion: Major Ferdinand Albrecht von Bärner
Jäger Company: Captain von Geyso
Dragoon Regiment von Ludwig (Brunswick): Lieutenant-Colonel Friederich Baum

The German "Reserve" was equivalent to the British Advanced Corps and acted in conjunction with it.

ARTILLERY

Major Griffith Williams
Four companies Royal Artillery
Detachment Royal Irish Artillery
Detachment 33rd Regiment attached to Royal Artillery and intended for their regiment with Sir William Howe's army.
One Company Hesse-Hanau Artillery: Captain Georg Pausch

The battering train of 128 pieces was left behind at Ticonderoga. The Advanced Corps was allotted ten pieces and the other brigades, including the German Reserve, four each.

APPENDIX II

THE ARTICLES OF CONVENTION BETWEEN LIEUTENANT-GENERAL BURGOYNE AND MAJOR GENERAL GATES, SARATOGA, 1777*

1st.

The Troops under Lieut. Genl. Burgoyne to march out of their Camp with the Honours of War, and the Artillery of the Intrenchments, to the Verge of the River, where the Old Fort stood; where the Arms and Artillery are to be left. The Arms are to be piled by Word of Command of their own Officers.

2nd.

A free Passage to be granted to the Army under Lieut. General Burgoyne, to Great Britain, on Condition of not serving again in North America during the present Contest; and the Port of Boston is assigned for the Entry of Transports to receive the Troops whenever General Howe shall so order.

3rd.

Should any Cartel take place by which the Army under General Burgoyne, or any part of it, may be exchanged, the foregoing Article to be void, as far as such exchange shall be made.

4th.

The Army under Lieut. Genl. Burgoyne to march to Massachusetts Bay by the easiest, most expeditious and convenient Routes; and to be quartered in, near, or as convenient as possible, to Boston, that the march of the Troops may not be delayed when Transports arrive to receive them.

* From copies in the Public Record Office, London, at CO 42/37, f. 608 and PRO 30/55, *Carleton Papers*, Vol. 6, No. 705.

5th.

The Troops to be supplied on their March and during being in Quarters, with Provision, by General Gates's Orders, at the same Rate of Rations as the Troops of his own Army; and if possible, the Officers' Horses and Cattle are to be supplied with Forage at the usual rates.

6th.

All Officers to retain their Carriages, Bat Horses, and other Cattle, and no baggage to be molested nor searched, Lieut. General Burgoyne giving his Honour that there are no public Stores secreted therein. Major General Gates will of course take the necessary measures for the due performance of this Article. Should any carriages be wanted during the March for the Transportation of Officers' Baggage, they are if possible to be supplied by the Country at the usual rates.

7th.

Upon the March and during the Time the Army shall remain in Quarters in the Massachusetts Bay, the Officers are not, as far as Circumstances will admit, to be separated from their Men. The Officers are to be quartered according to Rank, and are not to be hindered from assembling their Men for Roll-Callings, and other necessary purposes of Regularity.

8th.

All Corps whatever of General Burgoyne's Army, whether composed of Sailors, Batteau Men, Artificers, Drivers, Independent Companies, and Followers of the Army, of whatever Country, shall be included in the fullest Sense, and utmost Extent of the above Articles, and comprehended in every Respect as British Subjects.

9th

All Canadians and Persons belonging to the Canadian Establishment, consisting of Sailors, Batteau Men, Artificers, Drivers, Independent Companies, and many other Followers of the Army, who come under no particular Description, are to be permitted to return there; they are to be conducted immediately by the shortest Route, to the first British Post on Lake George; are to be supplied with Provisions in the same Manner as the other Troops, and are to be bound by the same condition of not serving during the present Contest in North America.

10th.

Passports to be immediately granted for three Officers not exceeding the Rank of Captain, who shall be appointed by Lieut. General Burgoyne to carry Dispatches to Sir William Howe, Sir Guy Carleton and to Great Britain, by the Way of New York; and Major General Gates engages the publick Faith, that the Dispatches shall not be opened. These Officers are to set out immediately after receiving their Despatches, and are to travel the shortest Route, and in the most expeditious manner.

11th.

During the stay of the Troops in Massachusetts Bay, the Officers are to be admitted on Parole, and are to be permitted to wear their Side Arms.

12th.

Should the Army under Lieutenant General Burgoyne find it necessary to send for their Cloathing and other Baggage to Canada, they are to be permitted to do it in the most convenient Manner, and the necessary Passports granted for that Purpose.

These Articles are to be mutually signed and exchanged tomorrow Morning at 9 o'clock, and the Troops under Lieut. General Burgoyne are to march out of their Intrenchments at three o'clock in the Afternoon.

Camp at Saratoga, 16th Oct. 1777

(Signed),

HORATIO GATES,

Major General

To prevent any Doubts that might arise from Lieutenant General Burgoyne's name not being mentioned in the above Treaty, Major General Gates hereby Declares that it is understood to be comprehended in it as fully as if his name had been specifically mentioned.

(Signed),

HORATIO GATES

NOTES

Abbreviations

BM	British Museum Reading Room or Manuscript Room, London.
HL	House of Lords Records Office.
HMC	Historical Manuscripts Commission publication.
PAC	Public Archives of Canada, Ottawa.
PRO	Public Record Office, London.
State	*A State of the Expedition from Canada* by Lt. Gen. J. Burgoyne (1780).
WCL	William L. Clements Library, University of Michigan, Ann Arbor, Michigan, USA.

FOREWORD

1. *The Devil's Disciple*, which was first presented in 1897 in New York, concerns the goings-on in a small Hudson Valley settlement which happens to be in the path of Burgoyne's invading army. Although its deeper meaning, to which Shaw seems to have attached importance, is far from certain, the play itself remains very enjoyable even today. What is certain is that the play would be much less enjoyable but for the appearance of General Burgoyne himself in the last act. If played by a good actor, he steals the show. Shaw intended to portray the type of aristocratic gentleman who disarms criticism with fine manners, sensitivity, and a skillful use of cool, ironic wit: "martyrdom, Sir, . . . is the only way in which a man can become famous without ability." When learning that his campaign is about to be ruined and his army destroyed by incompetence in Whitehall, he says, "Take it quietly, Major Swindon; your friend the British soldier can stand up to anything, except the British War Office." Shaw was pleased with his creation, which he described in a letter to Mrs. Richard Mansfield (8 January 1897) as "a very clever and effective part" (*Collected Letters 1894–7*, ed. Dan. H. Lawrence, Max Reinhardt, 1965). In the play, Burgoyne is referred to as "Gentlemanly Johnny." In the published version of the play (*Three Plays for Puritans*) one can read Shaw's stage directions, which describe his appearance vividly, and a note on the historical Burgoyne. Now, according to Mr. Lawrence, in his notes to Shaw's *Collected Letters*, Shaw derived all his information about Burgoyne and the American Revolution from one book, de FonBlanque's biography of Burgoyne, in which "Gentlemanly

Johnny" does not appear at all. For this reason, and because I have been unable to find any reference to "Gentlemanly Johnny" earlier than in Shaw's play, I suspect that the nickname was invented by Shaw himself. As for the more frequent "Gentleman Johnny," which is found in nearly every history book nowadays and has been used as the title for two biographies of Burgoyne so far, I can only suggest that this comes from a confusion between Shaw's invention and "Gentleman Jack," a prize fighter of the last century.

CHAPTER I *HINT OF SCANDAL*

1. Rate Books of Absey Ward, Parish of St. Margaret's, Westminster, 1713–58 (Westminster Public Library, Buckingham Palace Road, London). They show that "Mr. Burgin" moved there between 18 June and 26 November 1713 and that John Burgoyne left between July and September 1757. Christening is in *Registers of . . . Westminster Abbey* by J. L. Chester (Harleian Soc., Vol. X, 1876), p. 450. The date is written Old Style (1722/3) which has given rise to the erroneous statement that Burgoyne was born in 1722.
2. Family history from Burke's *Peerage and Baronetage* (1832–1921 editions); *Complete Baronetage* by G. E. Cockayne (1902), Vol. 2, pp. 104–105; *Victoria County History of Bedfordshire,* Vol. 2, pp. 44, 238–248; BM Ad. MSS 24120, f. 170, a letter on Burgoyne family history. Dr. W. Cole's remark is in BM Ad. MSS 5847, f. 378–9.
3. *Political and Military Episodes . . . of the Right Hon. John Burgoyne* by E. B. de Fonblanque (Macmillan, 1876), pp. 5–9.
4. Lord Bingley's will is in Chester, *op. cit.,* pp. 321–322. See also *A Journal Kept in Canada* by James M. Hadden (Munsell, 1884), pp. 387–391.
5. *Record of Old Westminsters* by G. F. R. Barker and A. H. Stennings (1928–1933), Vol. 1, p. 143; *Annals of Westminster School* by John Sargeaunt (1898). The boy's letter is quoted in *Westminster* by J. D. Carleton (Blackie, 1938), p. 28.
6. Burgoyne's *Orderly Book,* ed. E. B. O'Callaghan, p. 99.
7. Burgoyne's first commission is in *The Army List of 1740* reprinted by *The Journl. of the Soc. for Army Hist. Research,* Special No. III, May 1931. Items of clothing, etc., are taken from *The Military Guide for Young Officers* by Thomas Simes (1722), p. 373.

CHAPTER II *OFFICER, GENTLEMAN, DEBTOR*

1. An invaluable work on the British army in the eighteenth century is *The Organization of the British Army in the American Revolution* by Edward E. Curtis. A certain amount of information can be found in *The Universal Military Dictionary* by Capt. George Smith, R.A. (1779). The most useful contemporary work is *The Military Guide for Young Officers* by Thomas Simes (1722). He says that officers' pay had remained unchanged for over a century, while the cost of living had increased many times. The effect of low pay for junior officers is shown by a copy of the *Military Guide* I have before me, which belonged once to a Lt. Watts of the 47th Foot (one of the regiments at Saratoga). Over the list of "constant expenses" he has written

some additional expenses of 11s incurred by his brother, an ensign, which *"will have to come from Mama."* The dates etc. of Burgoyne's promotions are taken from *Record of Old Westminsters* by G. F. R. Barker and A. H. Stennings (1928–1933), Vol. 1, p. 143. E. B. de Fonblanque's statement that Burgoyne succeeded to a troop in the 13th Dragoons in 1744 appears to be erroneous *(Political and Military Episodes . . . of the Right Hon. John Burgoyne).*

2. Burgoyne's verses to Frances Poole are in de Fonblanque, *op. cit.*, p. 389.
3. The date of his marriage is in *Register of Baptisms & Marriages at St. George's Chapel, Mayfair* by George J. Armytage (Harleian Soc. Registers, Vol. XV, 1889). In most biographies, the date of his marriage is given as 1743 and that of his selling out of the army as 1747. Both originate from de Fonblanque and are erroneous. Miss Warburton is quoted in de Fonblanque, *op. cit.*, p. 9.
4. Sources for Choiseul and Chantelop are: *Le Duc et La Duchesse de Choiseul* and *La Disgrace de . . . Choiseul* by Gaston Maugras (1902); *Histoire de l'Architecture Classique en France* by Louis Hautecoeur (Editions A. et J. Picard, 1953), Vol. V, pp. 36–37; there are numerous references to Chanteloup in *Correspondence of Horace Walpole and Mme Deffand* (Yale, 1939), Vol. 3 *passim.*
5. Sources for Burgoyne at Aix, Florence, and Rome are: *Robert Adam and his Circle* by John Fleming (John Murray, 1962), pp. 109–193 and MSS. listed in Bibliography; Maugras' *Le Duc et La Duchesse de Choiseul,* pp. 32 ff. There is a full discussion of Ramsay's portrait in "The Genuine Portrait of General Burgoyne" by Professor Alastair Smart (*Apollo,* September 1971), where the companion portrait of Lady Charlotte Burgoyne is also shown. There is another portrait of Lady Charlotte when young at Knowsley, painted by "Heatley" (Francis Wheatley?). It is listed in *A Descriptive Catalogue of the Collection of Pictures at Knowsley Hall* (No. 423) by George Scharf, FSA (1875).
6. Sources for "The Oaks" are: *A Topographical History of Surrey* by Edward Wedlake Brayley (1850), Vol. 4, p. 49; *Victoria County History—Surrey,* Vol. 4, p. 247; *Portrait of Surrey* by Basil E. Cracknell (Robert Hale, 1970), p. 132; *A Pilgrimage to Surrey* by James Ogilvy (Routledge and Kegan Paul, 1914), Vol. 2, p. 232; *History of the Derby Stakes* by Roger Mortimer (1962). There is a photograph of Burgoyne's dining room in the Penguin *Buildings of England—Surrey* by Niklaus Pevsner *et al.*
7. Burgoyne's letter to Major Warde and his account of St. Cast are in de Fonblanque, *op. cit.*, pp. 11–14. The newspaper letter is quoted in *Gentleman Johnny Burgoyne* by F. J. Hudleston, p. 30. Other details are from Stanhope's (Lord Mahon's) *History of England* (1851), Vol. 5, pp. 204–207. "Breaking windows with guineas" is in a letter from Lord Chesterfield to his son, 27 June 1758.

CHAPTER III *RAISING A REGIMENT OF HORSE*

1. Burgoyne's promotion and captaincy in the Coldstream Guards are in *Army List* 1759, p. 43. *Victoria County History—Surrey,* Vol. 4, p. 247, says

that Burgoyne sold "The Oaks" to Lord Derby. However, there seems to be some confusion, since Wrottesley tells us in his life of Burgoyne's son (*Life . . . of Field Marshall Sir John Fox Burgoyne,* 1873, Vol. 1, p. 4) that Burgoyne did not sell "The Oaks" until 1778, as a result of his financial difficulties after Saratoga. This was to the 12th Earl, Burgoyne's nephew, who instituted the famous Derby and Oaks races at nearby Epsom.

2. Warrant to raise the 16th LD in PRO WO 26/24, f. 18. Burgoyne's advertisement, list of officers, uniforms, etc., are in *History of the 16th, the Queen's Light Dragoons (Lancers) 1759–1912* by Col. Henry Graham (privately printed, 1912).
3. Correspondence on raising the 16th LD is in PRO WO 26/24, ff. 18, 57, 89, 91, 127; WO 4/55, f. 332; WO 4/59, ff. 132–134, 210 (Barrington's first letter of 25 October 1759), 444, 537. Barrington's second letter is quoted in full in *Political Life of William Wildman, 2nd Viscount Barrington* by Shute Barrington (1812), pp. 51–57. It was young Captain Harcourt's elder brother, by the way, who, when he became Lord Harcourt, purchased Lord Bingley's house in Cavendish Square (*Mid-Georgian London* by Hugh Phillips, 1964, p. 302).
4. Letter is in New York Public Library, Emmett Collection, EM 8119.
5. Two standard works on this subject are *The Structure of British Politics at the Accession of George III* by Lewis Namier (Macmillan, 1929, but reprinted many times) and *The History of Parliament—The House of Commons 1754–90* by Lewis Namier and John Brooke (HMSO, 1964). The latter includes biographies of all members (and hence of several of the officers in Burgoyne's regiment) and descriptions of all elections, etc., during those years. Burgoyne's election to Midhurst is in Vol. 1, pp. 395–396.
6. E. B. de Fonblanque, *Political and Military Episodes . . . of the Right Hon. John Burgoyne,* p. 24.
7. Lancashire Record Office, DDX 113/12. The letter is dated 18 November 1761.
8. Numbers sent to Portugal are in PRO WO 1/165, f. 581, and other returns in the same file.
9. The drawing is in *Noticias de Guerra de Hispanha e Francia contra Portugal no Anno 1762,* a book partly printed and partly MS, No. 2,058, in the library of the Academia Militar, Lisbon.

CHAPTER IV *LA GUERRA FANTÁSTICA*

1. PRO SP (Foreign) 89/57, Lippe's letters and dispatches, sheets not numbered. Letter dated 25 July says British arrived 16 July, but this must be a mistake as there are letters by Burgoyne from Portugal dated 26 June (PRO WO 1/165, ff. 693–696).
2. *Political and Military Episodes of . . . the Right Hon. John Burgoyne* by E. B. de Fonblanque, p. 33, quoting as source Varnhagen von Ense's *Denkmaale* (1824); see also "Anecdotes of Count Schaumberg-Lippe" (*European Magazine,* January 1792, pp. 46–48). There are accounts of this campaign in *O Conde Lippe em Portugal* by E. A. Pereira Salas (called Rev. Padre Salas); "La Guerra Fantastica" by Durval Pires de Lima, in *Nacão Poartuguesa* IX, pp. 243–285 (Lisbon 1934); BM George III MSS No. 236, *Memoires de la*

Campaign de Portugal en 1762; and *Noticias da Guerra de Hispanha e Francia contra Portugal no Anno 1762* (Academia Militar, Lisbon, Library, No. 2,058, part printed book, part MS).

3. PRO SP (Foreign) 89/57, sheets dated 4 August 1762.
4. H. Walpole, *Memoirs of George III* (1854 ed.), Vol. 3, p. 8. When Walpole wrote his journal, Pombal was still known as D'Oeyras.
5. De Fonblanque, *op. cit.,* p. 37.
6. PRO SP (Foreign) 89/57, Hay to Egremont, 16 November 1762.
7. De Fonblanque, *op. cit.,* pp. 39–42.
8. PRO SP (Foreign) 89/57, 30 August 1762; de Fonblanque, *op. cit.,* pp. 44–46.
9. PRO WO 1/165, ff. 693–696. Note re court-martial is in Boston Public Library, MS Eng. 79.
10. PRO SP (Foreign) 89/57, 9 October 1762.
11. De Fonblanque, *op. cit.,* pp. 47–49.
12. PRO WO 4/71, f. 141; WO 1/165, ff. 581, 681. Seven hundred and thirteen officers and men of the 16th LD were sent to Portugal, 106 of them from Belle Isle.

CHAPTER V *UPROAR, VIOLENCE, AND A* FÊTE CHAMPÊTRE

1. Extracts quoted in de Fonblanque, *Political and Military Episodes . . . of the Right Hon. John Burgoyne,* pp. 15–22, though the original has disappeared. De Fonblanque says that the "Instructions" were written when the regiment was raised in 1759, but from interior evidence (i.e., Burgoyne refers to the "two late wars," meaning the War of the Austrian Succession and the Seven Years' War) and the general sense, it is more likely to have been written 1763–1764.
2. The regiment was reviewed in 1766, 1767, 1769, and 1770 on Wimbledon Common; 1771 and 1774 on Blackheath. *History of the 16th, The Queen's Light Dragoons (Lancers)* by Henry Graham (privately printed, 1912), pp. 8–9. For a later history of this regiment see *16th/5th Lancers* by James Lunt (1973) (the *Famous Regiments* series).
3. Burgoyne's letter to Grenville (16 February 1764) on general warrants and his part in debates of this period are in *The House of Commons 1754–90* by Lewis Namier and John Brooke, Vol. 2, p. 142.
4. The correspondence with Pitt is in de Fonblanque, *op. cit.,* pp. 56–57.
5. Burgoyne's report on European armies is in de Fonblanque, *op. cit.,* pp. 58–83. Frederick the Great's paper is quoted in full in Appendix I, pp. 469–482. It was first published in the French edition of Frederick's works in 1861. Long extracts in translation, though much edited and changed, can be found in *Frederick the Great on the Art of War,* ed. Jay Luvaas (Freedom Press, New York, 1966), pp. 263–305.
6. Burgoyne's letter on Major Walpole is in de Fonblanque, *op. cit.,* pp. 84–85.
7. The King's Bench Commitment Book (PRO PRIS 4/4, p. 69) has this entry:

   Died 13th July 1768. John Burgoyne Esquire Committed etc. the day of ffebruary 1767 In Execution with the Cause following upon

> a writ of Habeas Corpus directed to the Sheriff of Middlesex and by the return it appears that on the Thirtieth day of January in the Seventh year of the Reign of our Sovreign Lord George the third John Burgoyne Esquire in the said Writ named was taken by the said Sheriff and detained in his Majesty's Gaol under his Custody by virtue of a Writ of Capias ad satisfaciendum returnable before the Lord the King at Westminster on Thursday next after Eight days of the Purification of the Blessed Virgin Mary to satisfye William Shakespear Esquire for Twenty Eight pounds and Ten Shillings for his Damages etc. whereof the said John is convicted And also Eleven pounds for his Damages Costs and Charges in Error of which the said John is also Convicted—Aylett. By R: Aston.

Presumably John Burgoyne spent the ten days between his arrest and committal to jail at a bailiff's "spunging house," or private prison. This was customary so that a debtor might have a last chance to raise the money. He therefore had ample time to inform everybody, including his son, of his predicament. Even if he refrained from doing so, it is impossible, in the small and gossipy London society of that time, that Burgoyne should not have heard of his father's arrest within a day or two. Most newspapers reported John Burgoyne's death in their obituary lists but usually got the date wrong and gave no address. Only the *London Chronicle* (14–16 July 1768) reported: "On Tuesday last, died at his apartments in St. George's Fields, Major John Burgoyne." In fact, he died on the Wednesday. "St. George's Fields" was a euphemism for the King's Bench prison, which would have been understood by readers. Can we be sure this *was* Burgoyne's father? We know from de Fonblanque (*op. cit.*, p. 6) that Burgoyne's father died in the King's Bench at some time or other, the impression being given, perhaps unintentionally, that this occurred when Burgoyne was still a child. The Rate Books (see n. 2 to Ch. I) show John Burgoyne as paying rates until the autumn of 1757. The KB Commitment Books start in 1757, but this is the only entry under "Burgoyne" from then until 1770 (where the author stopped looking). For this *not* to have been Burgoyne's father we should have to assume (a) that he was arrested and died between 1738 (date of Benson law suit) and 1757, and that for some reason Mrs. Burgoyne continued to pay rates in his name; (b) the existence of another "Major John Burgoyne," unconnected with the family and of whom there is no other record whatever, who was arrested for debt and died in just the same manner. Yet if this *was* Burgoyne's father, why was there no mention of the fact in the newspapers when he died? Burgoyne was by then MP for Midhurst, and his exploits in Portugal were still remembered. Moreover, he had been recently in the public eye owing to the Preston election. There are further mysteries. If Burgoyne behaved callously to his father, the Burgoynes of Sutton seem not to have complained. The 6th baronet, Sir Roger, named Burgoyne in the entail of his will in 1770, and the 7th baronet, Sir John, made Burgoyne executor of his will when he died in India in 1785 (de Fonblanque, *op. cit.*, p. 6). Finally, it is odd that Walpole, who heard everything, says no word about this affair, and no one brought it up after Saratoga when every means, fair and foul, were used to blacken Burgoyne's character. To have shown that Burgoyne allowed his poor aged father to die miserably in a debtors' prison would have been marvellous political ammunition. All this argues that Burgoyne did not behave callously.

Suppose he paid for his father's apartments in the jail. It is hard to be sure what the cost would have been, but it would have been high. A private cell in the debtors' wing in Newgate cost £500 down plus £21 a week in the 1720s. A room in the KB would therefore have cost at least £300 down in the 1760s, plus a constant high running expense. To arrive at something like an equivalent in American dollars in 1978, multiply by twenty. It would have been far cheaper, to say nothing of being more humane and less dangerous to his father, for Burgoyne to have paid the debt, rented a room somewhere (if he did not want to install his father at "The Oaks" or wherever), and hired a manservant or two to look after him and keep him out of mischief. Why did he not do this? The move to Chesterfield Street is shown in the Rate Book, St. George's Hanover Square (Westminster Public Library archive). The house, third from Curzon Street on the right, was new, and the first occupant was "Capt. John Burgoyne," before 16 December 1757. By 1760 he was "Coll. John Burgoyne," which proves he was Burgoyne and not the father. After 1760 the rates were paid by "Mrs. Burgoyne" until 1775. There is no record of her death in the parish register. That Burgoyne himself sometimes stayed there is shown by the letter from that address dated 18 November 1761, which was just after he returned from Belle Isle (Lancashire Record Office, DDX113/12). This would suggest that his parents separated in 1757, that Burgoyne took the house in Chesterfield for his mother to live in, and that he continued on good terms with her. Beyond that, there is not enough evidence to support anything more than guesswork. As for the creditor, William Shakespear, I have found no trace of him; though the odd sum suggests he was a tradesman.

8. Details of the Preston election have been taken from "The Preston Election of 1768" by Winifred Proctor, BA; *Parliamentary History of Preston* by William Dobson (1868), pp. 49, 76; *History of Preston* by Henry Fishwick (1900), p. 380; *A History of Preston in Amounderness* by H. W. Clemshea (*Manchester University Press Historical Series No. XIV,* 1912); Burgoyne's own remarks are from his speech at the King's Bench, June 1768, of which a text is in the Lancashire Record Office, DDPr 131/7, together with a bulk of original papers and documents on the subject. See also the *Structure of British Politics* by Lewis Namier (Macmillan, 1929), pp. 105 and 108, and articles under "Preston" and "Burgoyne" in *The House of Commons 1754–90* by Namier and Brooke, *op. cit.* The episode of "Junius" is cited in de Fonblanque, *op. cit.,* pp. 89, 90.
9. Of the king's remark on Fort William, de Fonblanque sarcastically comments, "His Majesty thought it consistent with his duty to withdraw from an officer a reward conferred for distinguished military service, in the event of such officer presuming in his place in Parliament to oppose any political measure introduced by the ministry" (*op. cit.,* p. 93). This is nonsense, for Burgoyne's appointment to Fort William was a purely political reward (see

Grafton's letter to Granby, in Namier and Brooke, *op. cit.*, Vol. II, p. 142), unless the election at Preston be considered as "distinguished military service"!

10. The debates on the East India Company crisis are in *Parliamentary History*, Vols. 17 and 18, *passim*. Burgoyne's committee's report is in *House of Commons Reports*, Vol. III, and occupies two thirds of that enormous book. The anecdote about "Junius" is also in Walpole's *Last Journals* (1910), Vol. 1, p. 203.
11. In a scurrilous note to the same article, the *Town & Country Magazine* claimed that Burgoyne was something of a rake and had many, though no serious, passing affairs. "When this gentleman . . . was met going into the city, if he were asked what business he was going upon to the bank or banker's, his usual reply was (producing an assignation in a female hand) here is my draft upon a very fine woman, Alderman ——— 's wife. . . ." There may be a grain of truth in this, for in his will Burgoyne confessed that his life had been "too frequently blemished by the indulgence of one predominant passion. . . ." Yet it is most unlikely that he would have been so ungentlemanly as to give away the lady's name; nor does it prove that he did not love his wife.
12. The "Dashing White Sergeant" broadsheet is in the BM at 11630, f. 7 (41). Lady Charlotte Burgoyne's letters are in *Intimate Society Letters of the Eighteenth Century*, ed. the Duke of Argyll (Stanley Paul, 1910), Vol. 1, pp. 168–178.
13. The date of Burgoyne's move to Hertford Street is in the Rate Book, St. George's Hanover Square (Westminster Public Library archive).
14. The account of Lord Stanley's wedding is taken from the *Public Advertiser*, 16 June 1774, the *Gentleman's Magazine*, June 1774, pp. 263–265, and the *Public Ledger*, 10 June 1774. The remark by the demolition foreman is in *Portrait of Surrey* by Basil E. Cracknell (Robert Hale, 1970), p. 132. For *Maid of the Oaks* (criticisms, etc.) see *The London Stage* by G. W. Stone, Part 4, Vol. 3, pp. 1846–1847 (Southern Illinois University Press, 1962).

CHAPTER VI *SONS OF LIBERTY*

1. New Hampshire, Massachusetts, Connecticut, Rhode Island, New York, New Jersey, Pennsylvania, Delaware, Maryland, Virginia, North Carolina, South Carolina, and Georgia. Maine was at this time still largely uninhabited except by French Canadians in the northern parts. Vermont belonged to New Hampshire and was called The Hampshire Grants. East Florida and West Florida (which extended to the Mississippi) were, like Canada, still under direct rule from Great Britain. Canada acquired its own government under the Quebec Act of 1774. Each of the thirteen colonies had its own government. That of Massachusetts was the oldest and strongest; that of Georgia was the newest and weakest.
2. See the discussion on this by John Adams, *The Works of John Adams* (1850–1860), Vol. IV, p. 46. The literature on the origins of the American Revolution is immense. The reader seeking a brief, simple, and well-written introduction might start with *The American Heritage Book of the*

Revolution by Bruce Lancaster and J. H. Plumb (1958, now available as a Dell paperback). Those seeking a detailed account are referred to *The British Empire Before the American Revolution* by Laurence Henry Gipson (Knopf, 1939–1965), Vols. IX–XII.

3. *The Writings of John Forbes,* ed. Alfred P. James (Menasha, Wisconsin, 1938), p. 205, quoted in *The War of American Independence* by Don Higginbotham (Macmillan, New York, 1971), p. 21. Wolfe's remark is in HMC *Stopford-Sackville MSS,* Vol. II, p. 266, letter to Lord George Sackville, August 1758. His opinion of the Rangers is quoted in *The War for America* by Piers Mackesy, p. 30.
4. Governor Tryon of New York wrote to Lord Dartmouth (3 November 1773) of pamphlets printed by the radicals at this time "calculated to sow sedition, and make popular the cause of *those who are deepest concerned in the illicit Trade* to Foreign Countries. . . . If the Tea comes *free of every duty* . . . it is then to be considered as . . . a Monopoly of dangerous tendency . . . to American liberties. . . . So that let the Tea appear free or not free of duty, those who carry on illicit Trade will raise objections, if possible, to its being brought on shore or sold." (My italics.) *Documents Relative to . . . New York* by J. R. Brodhead, Vol. 8, pp. 400–401.
5. One has to read loyalist accounts for a picture of what life was like for moderates and "Tories" in those unhappy years; e.g., *History of New York During the Revolutionary War* by Thomas Jones, ed. by Edward de Lancey (N. Y. Historical Society, 1879, 2 vols.), which is very readable because the author is passionately and unfairly biassed against the rebels. For a brief, entertaining summary, see "Those Forgotten Loyalists" by Robert Graves in *The Crane Bag* (Cassell, 1972). Also *The American Tory* by Morton and Penn Borden (Prentice-Hall, 1972, as a Spectrum Book). Radical propaganda is summarized in Gage's letter to Lord Dartmouth, 17 February 1775, *Correspondence of General Gage* (Yale, 1931), Vol. 1, p. 392.
6. *Portrait of a General* by William B. Willcox, (Knopf, 1964), pp. 36–37.
7. *The House of Commons 1754–90* by Lewis Namier and John Brooke, Vol. 2, p. 143, quoting Brickdale's Debates, 19 April 1774. *Parliamentary History* and de Fonblanque, *Political and Military Episodes . . . of the Right Hon. John Burgoyne,* each gives a different version of the speech, but the sense is the same.
8. Burgoyne's own account of his attempts to gain an important post, written with humor and no doubt bias, is in de Fonblanque, *op. cit.,* pp. 120–132.
9. The first speech, 20 February 1774, is in *Parliamentary History,* Vol. 18, pp. 353–357. The second, 27 February, is in *Parliamentary Register,* Vol. 1 (1774), pp. 250–253.
10. Lord North to the king, 14 April 1775, in *Correspondence of George III,* Vol. 3, p. 203.
11. Letter to Sir Horace Mann, 7 May 1775.

CHAPTER VII *A PREPOSTEROUS PARADE OF MILITARY ARRANGEMENT*

1. *The Siege of Boston* by Richard Frothingham (1849), p. 114, says the *Cerberus* heard the news from a cutter bound for Newport. The log of the *Cerberus,*

however, mentions only the sloop *Otter* bound for Yorktown, where Lord Dunmore, the governor, was in trouble; PRO Admiralty Records 51/181.

2. Frothingham, *op. cit.*, pp. 212–213. Also *Life of Joseph Brant-Thayendanagea* by W. L. Stone, Vol. 1, p. 59.
3. Burgoyne to Lord Rochford, 25 June 1775; in E. B. de Fonblanque, *Political and Military Episodes . . . of the Right Hon. John Burgoyne,* p. 143.
4. This was Clinton's reasoning (*Portrait of a General* by William B. Willcox, p. 45). Burgoyne was more critical of the execution of the raid. It was carried out weeks too late; Gage should have arrested Hancock and Adams while they were still in Boston, extended posts along the road, and trained the troops in the kind of fighting they were to expect. However, both Clinton and Burgoyne testified that they were in complete agreement on all these matters; de Fonblanque, *op. cit.*, pp. 137, 140, 143–144; BM Ad. MSS 5847, letter from Burgoyne to Lord Stanley.
5. Burgoyne to General Harvey, 14 June 1775, in de Fonblanque, *op. cit.*, p. 141.
6. Burgoyne to Lord Rochford, 25 June 1775, is in de Fonblanque, *op. cit.*, p. 148; *Correspondence of George III* No. 1663 and No. 1670 are summaries of Burgoyne's letter and Howe's of the same date. The strange spelling is probably the king's.
7. There are two versions of Burgoyne's description of Bunker Hill, both written to Lord Stanley. One is in de Fonblanque, *op. cit.*, p. 156. The other is in BM Ad. MSS 5847, as copied by Dr. William Cole of Cambridge. A slightly different version of this, taken from the British newspapers, is in *New England Historical & General Register,* Vol. XI, April 1857, pp. 125–126.
8. *Narrative of Bunker Hill* by Lt. John Clarke (1775); but see also *The Pictorial Field-Book of the Revolution* by Benson J. Lossing, Vol. 1, p. 548; *Bunker Hill* by Harold Murdoch (Houghton and Mifflin, 1927) discusses controversial points of the famous battle.
9. Burgoyne to Germain, 20 August 1775; in de Fonblanque, *op. cit.*, p. 193.
10. *Ibid.*, p. 152.
11. The text was published in the *London Chronicle*, 18 July 1775.
12. The Burgoyne-Lee letters are in *Lee Papers*, Vol. 1, pp. 180–185, 188–195, 222–225. Two of the letters are in de Fonblanque, *op. cit.*, pp. 161–173.
13. Burgoyne's letter to North is in HMC 10th Report, *Abergavenny MSS*, pp. 8–9; also de Fonblanque, *op. cit.*, pp. 136–139. Also see *Historical Memoirs* by Nathaniel Wraxall (1836), Vol. 2, p. 292, for a verbal sketch of Burgoyne.
14. Lord Rawdon to Lord Huntingdon, 5 October 1775; in HMC *Hastings MSS,* Vol. 3, p. 160.
15. *Dramatic and Poetical Works of . . . J. Burgoyne,* Vol. 2, pp. 238–239.
16. PRO CO 5/92, pp. 199–221, Dartmouth to Gage, 15 April 1775; printed in *Correspondence of General Gage* (Yale, 1931), Vol. 2, p. 194.
17. These figures are taken from a report by Sir William Johnson, Superintendent for Indian Affairs, to Governor Tryon of New York, dated 22 October 1773; printed in *Documents Relative to . . . New York* by J. R. Brodhead, Vol. 8, p. 458.
18. De Fonblanque, *op. cit.*, p. 153; Gage *Corresp.*, Vol. 2, p. 684.
19. Burgoyne's letters on this subject can be seen in de Fonblanque, *op. cit.*, pp.

150 ff, 182, 190, 196; Geo III *Corresp.*, Vol. 3, Nos. 1670, 1693; also Burgoyne's answers to Gage's questionnaire, and a covering letter to Lord Rochford, are at Longleat, *Thynne Papers*, temp. Marquess of Bath (3rd Viscount Weymouth), American Affairs, 1770–1778, War of Independence, items 21 and 22.

20. De Fonblanque, *op. cit.*, pp. 148–149.
21. *Ibid.*, p. 145.
22. Gage *Corresp.*, Vol. 2, p. 203 ff; Germain to Gage, *ibid.*, p. 206. Howe's Orderly Book, p. 300; Geo III *Corresp.*, Vol. 3, No. 1794.
23. Burgoyne to North, 10 October 1775, *Murdock MSS* 6, Houghton Library, Harvard.
24. *History of Canada* by William Kingsford (1893), Vol. 5; *History of the Organization . . . of the Military Forces of Canada* by the Historical Section of the Canadian General Staff (1920), Vol. 2, pp. 1–8; Public Archives of Canada, Series Q, Vol. XI, p. 318.
25. PRO CO 5/235, f. 203, Howe to Germain, 13 December 1775.
26. The statement that Burgoyne was responsible for the stripping of the Old South Meeting House is in Deacon Newell's Diary, quoted by Frothingham, *op. cit.*, pp. 32–38.

CHAPTER VIII *THE GRAND STRATEGY PREPARED*

1. *Life of Lord Shelburne* by Lord Edmond Fitzmaurice (1912), Vol. 2, pp. 75, 248–250, containing a hostile portrait of Germain.
2. PRO CO 5/169, f. 323 ff, recruiting returns.
3. Readers seeking the truth about this strange man, not the grotesque caricature found in "official" histories, should turn to such modern works as *The American Secretary* by Gerald Saxon Brown, *Sackville of Drayton* by Louis Marlow, *Lord George Germain* by Alan Valentine, and *The War for America* by Piers Mackesy.
4. PRO CO 42/34, Carleton to Dartmouth, 20 November 1775; also PAC Series Q, Vol. XI, pp. 263–264.
5. Walpole, *Last Journals* (1910), Vol. 1, p. 527. Brown, *op. cit.*, quotes a long memorandum to Germain, summer 1776, setting out advantages of Hudson plan (pp. 100, 201).
6. CO 5/92, ff. 621–630; also CO 5/235, f. 173, Howe to Germain, 9 October 1775. Printed in Force's *Archives*, 4th Series, Vol. 3, pp. 991–993. In his *Turning Point of the Revolution*, p. 77, Hoffman Nickerson gives the data wrongly as 9 October 1776, thus thoroughly confusing his account of the planning of the Saratoga campaign.
7. Ira Gruber, *The Howe Brothers & the American Revolution*, p. 80.
8. HMC *Hastings MSS*, Vol. 3, p. 166.
9. Extract quoted in E. B. de Fonblanque, *Political and Military Episodes . . . of the Right Hon. John Burgoyne*, pp. 209–210. I have been unable to locate the original of this document.
10. PRO CO 5/253, "Précis of Operations and Plans" dictated by Germain to his deputy secretary, William Knox.

11. All newspapers January-February 1776 *passim*. *London Chronicle*, 28 March 1776.
12. *London Chronicle*, 22 February 1776.
13. In *Last Journals* (1910), Vol. 1, p. 532, February 1776, Walpole wrote:

> If the King in the prosecution of the civil war met with brave and zealous servants, they took care to be well paid for their loyalty. General Burgoyne had left Boston, not much to his credit nor to the satisfaction of the Court, when, by the departure of General Clinton with a detachment for the southern colonies, Boston was left so ill-officered by men of experience, that had General Howe died or been killed, the command must have fallen on the raw Lord Percy. Burgoyne, on his arrival, had been very communicative of complaints, even to Charles Fox and the Opposition, for Burgoyne knew the Ministers, and probably the Opposition too; for had the latter had any activity they would have questioned him in Parliament before the Court had had time to buy off his affected disaffection. But before there was a single question started in the House of Commons, Burgoyne's rank and pay were raised, fifteen men added to each company of his regiment (all to his profit), and four cornetcies given to him to sell; besides an extraordinary promotion for his wife's nephew, Mr. Stanley, which was stopped by the Secretary of War's partiality to Captain Stanhope, Lady Harrington's son, over whose head Stanley would have stepped. After these favours, nobody was more reserved than General Burgoyne on any mention of America in Parliament.

In fact, when Burgoyne left Boston, an expedition southward was only a vague suggestion, to which Howe was strongly opposed. The order for Clinton's departure was not written until 22 October and did not arrive until 30 December, by which time Burgoyne was in London. Besides, he had royal permission and Howe's approval. PRO CO 5/92, f. 539; *Parliamentary Register*, Vol. 11 (1779), pp. 287–290. The 16th Light Dragoons was merely one of twenty-six regiments to be augmented when ordered for American service in August 1775, long before Burgoyne's arrival in London. This was in line with the king's policy of increasing the army by bringing existing regiments up to strength rather than raising new ones. It was cheaper, easier, and more sensible to mix recruits with veterans. Walpole probably got his story from the *London Chronicle*, 5 February 1776, which reported the augmentation of Elliott's and Burgoyne's Light Dragoons (and the Guards), and he wrongly put two and two together. This report, however, referred to something different. Along with his "Reflections on the War" Burgoyne had sent Germain a proposal to increase the effectiveness of the Light Dragoons by having an additional man ride behind each rider and, at the scene of action, dismount and fight as light infantry, much as motorized infantry does today. After some doubts over so unconventional and "unEnglish" an idea, General Harvey finally accepted the proposal on 7 June 1776: PRO 30/55 (*Carleton Papers*, also called *Headquarters Papers*), Vol. 1, No. 27; *Correspondence of Gen. Gage*, Vol. 2, p.

204; *Correspondence of George III,* Vol. 3, Nos. 1702, 1727, 1793, 2125; *Journ. of Soc. of Army Hist. Research,* Vol. 13, p. 241. Burgoyne's appointment to Canada, as we have seen, had nothing to do with the need to buy his silence, but for his qualifications see also PRO SP/37, ff. 30, 42, 81. His promotion was in line with that of Howe, Clinton, and Percy and in any case necessary to his position under Carleton, who was a full general. Captain Stanley's promotion was no favor as it was not granted. Captain Stanhope was Lord Petersham, who commanded the grenadier company of the 29th Foot, sailing in Captain Douglas' advance squadron for Canada (see Ch. IX). Walpole probably picked up the story about Lord Barrington, Secretary of War, and Lady Harrington, from the "Têtes-à-Têtes" (a scurrilous gossip column) in the *Town & Country Magazine,* which had run a story on a love affair between the two in January 1771. As for Burgoyne's complaints, he was no more communicative than Gage, Howe, Clinton, or any of the other officers in Boston. In this example, it is fortunate that proof exists to demolish Walpole's story completely, and it must be wondered how many other of his stories would stand up to a similar checking.

14. Better known perhaps by their later names (modern, post-1958, names in parentheses): 9th = Royal Norfolk Regt. (R. Anglian Regt.); 20th = Lancashire Fusiliers (disbanded); 21st = R. Scots Fusiliers (Princess Margaret's R. Highland Fus.); 24th = South Wales Borderers (R. Regt. of Wales); 29th = Worcestershire Regt. (Worcester and Sherwood Foresters Regt.); 31st = East Surrey Regt. (The Queen's Regt.); 34th = The Border Regt. (King's Own Royal Border Regt.); 47th = Loyal Regt. (Queen's Lancashire Regt.); 53rd = King's Shropshire Light Infantry (The Light Infantry); 62nd = Wiltshire Regt. (Duke of Edinburgh's Royal Regt.).
15. PRO CO 42/35, f. 203; CO 5/254, f. 9; CO 5/162, f. 11; CO 5/93, f. 685, Burgoyne to John Pownall, 19 February 1776.
16. PRO CO 5/162, f. 33; *History of Canada* by William Kingsford, Vol. 6, p. 105.
17. PRO CO 5/162, f. 283, Debbeig to Pownall, 12 March 1776.
18. *The Private Papers of the Earl of Sandwich,* Vol. 1, p. 108.
19. *Morning Post,* 4 December 1776.
20. E. B. de Fonblanque, *op. cit.,* pp. 212–213; HMC *Stopford-Sackville MSS,* Vol. 2, p. 30.
21. PRO CO 5/93, f. 743.
22. PRO CO 5/93, f. 34, Germain to Howe, 1 February 1776.
23. PRO CO 5/93, f. 763.
24. PRO CO 5/93, f. 767.
25. PRO CO 5/93, ff. 783, 803.

CHAPTER IX *PRECIPITATE FLIGHT OF THE REBELS*

1. PRO CO 5/124, f. 246, Douglas to Admiralty, 8 May 1776.
2. *For Want of a Horse,* ed. F. G. Stanley, entry for 6 May 1776.
3. PRO CO 42/35, f. 9.
4. PRO CO 5/125, ff. 60, 66, Douglas to Admiralty, 26 and 27 June 1776.
5. *The British Invasion from the North,* William Digby, p. 98.
6. *Ibid.,* p. 88.

7. HMC *Stopford-Sackville MSS,* Vol. 2, p. 33; F. von Riedesel, *Memoirs,* Vol. 1, p. 277.
8. *Polwarth Papers* L 30/12/17/7, Sir Francis Kerr Clerke (Burgoyne's aide-de-camp) to Lord Polwarth, 13 July 1776.
9. PRO CO 5/125, f. 60.
10. "Some Evidence for Burgoyne's Expedition" by C. T. Atkinson, in *Journ. of the Soc. of Army Hist. Research,* Vol. 26 (1948), p. 133. It is among some papers of Fraser's discovered that year.
11. Digby, *op. cit.,* p. 157.
12. PRO CO 5/125, ff. 68 ff; Major Williams' account of the battle is in his letter to Germain, 23 June 1776, *Correspondence of George III,* Vol. 3, No. 1897. Other accounts in von Riedesel, *op. cit.,* Vol. 1, p. 289; Digby, *op. cit.,* pp. 106–108; *Journal of . . . American War* by Roger Lamb, pp. 107–108. Story about Thompson in *London Chronicle,* 9 August 1776.
13. WCL, *Clinton Papers,* Burgoyne to Clinton, 7 July 1776.
14. PRO CO 5/125, f. 60; also Digby, *op. cit.,* p. 108.
15. *A Journal Kept in Canada* by James M. Hadden, pp. 179, 464.
16. Digby, *op. cit.,* p. 119.
17. WCL, *Clinton Papers,* Burgoyne to Clinton, 7 July 1776.

CHAPTER X *"ALL MY PLANS HAVE BEEN DISAPPOINTED"*

1. Bedfordshire Record Office, *Polwarth Papers,* L 30/12/17/7, Sir Francis Kerr Clerke (Burgoyne's aide-de-camp) to Lord Polwarth, 13 July 1776.
2. WCL *Clinton Papers,* Richard Cox to Clinton, 20 June 1760, quoted in *Portrait of a General* by W. B. Willcox, p. 24.
3. *A Journal Kept in Canada* by James W. Hadden, p. 359.
4. *Ibid.,* pp. 12–15.
5. PRO CO 5/78, f. 23 ff, Claus to William Knox, Deputy Secretary of State, 1 March 1777; printed in *Documents Relative to . . . New York* by J. R. Brodhead, Vol. 8, pp. 700–704.
6. In *London Chronicle,* 20 March 1776, there is a story concerning the king's review of troops on Wimbledon Common, which the two Indians attended in the uniforms of ensigns; however, by this time Brant-Thayendanagea had been promoted to captain, for that was his rank when he met Germain on 14 March. The Mohawks stayed at "The Swan with Two Necks" inn in Southwark. Brant was interviewed by Boswell, who published an article on him in the *London Magazine* in July 1776 and had his portrait painted by Romney. At the review of the troops at Wimbledon, he said "This may do here, but it won't do in America!"
7. *Life of Joseph Brant-Thayendanagea* by W. L. Stone, Vol. 1, p. 104.
8. PRO CO 42/36, f. 76 ff; *London Chronicle,* 3–6 February 1776; *Military Forces of Canada* by E. A. Cruickshank (1920), p. 125; PRO CO 5/77, ff. 39, 67; Brant's speeches to Germain on 14 March and 9 May also printed in Brodhead, *op. cit.,* Vol. 8, pp. 670, 678.
9. PRO CO 5/94, ff. 167–169, Howe to Stuart (Superintendent of Indian Affairs for Southern Colonies), 23 May 1777.

10. *Parliamentary History,* Vol. 19, p. 1179, Burgoyne's speech on Vyner's motion for an inquiry into Saratoga. This speech was published as a separate pamphlet. Burgoyne's Mohawk proposal is in WCL *Clinton Papers,* Burgoyne to Clinton, 7 November 1776.
11. PRO CO 5/253, f. 26. This is a *Précis of Operations & Plans* drawn up by Germain some time afterward. The number of Indians remaining is in *Journ. of Soc. for Army Hist. Research,* Vol. 26 (1948), p. 137, letter from Phillips to Fraser, 10 September 1776. Curiously, the Mohawk expedition was believed in London to be a fact. The *London Chronicle,* 22 August 1776, said that the two expeditions, one up Lake Champlain and the other via the Mohawk, were already under way and were to meet at Albany. The *Remembrancer,* 26 September 1776, added that Howe would join the two armies "about Albany." Finally, Howe was told on 25 September by American deserters that Burgoyne was advancing down the Mohawk toward Albany. HMC *Stopford Sackville MSS,* Vol. 2, p. 41.
12. Congress' letter to Burgoyne is in *American Archives,* 5th Series, Vol. 6, pp. 684–685. For the Cedars affair, see PRO CO 43/35, f. 415; also *The Authentic Narrative of Facts Relating to . . . the Cedars,* rare pamphlet (1777); *History of Canada* by William Kingsford, Vol. 6, pp. 46–64; *History of New York* by Thomas Jones, Vol. 1, pp. 92–94.
13. *For Want of a Horse,* ed. F. C. Stanley, 25 July 1776.
14. PRO CO 5/125, f. 163, Douglas to Admiralty, 21 July 1776; *Travels Through the Interior Parts of America* by Thomas Anburey, Vol. 1, p. 119, an account, however, which should be read with caution. Accounts of the building of the fleets and the naval battle at Valcour Island can be found in *Naval Operations of the American Revolution* by A. T. Mahan (1913), pp. 18–27; *Navies in the Mountains,* by Harrison Bird (1962); various numbers of the *Fort Ticonderoga Museum Bulletin; The Private Papers of the Earl of Sandwich* (Navy Records Society), Vol. 1.
15. Phillips to Fraser, 7 September 1776, in *Journ. of Soc. for Army Hist. Research,* Vol. 26, p. 135.
16. *Ibid.,* p. 136, Christie to Fraser, 12 September 1776. Burgoyne's letter to Clinton, 7 November 1776, in WCL *Clinton Papers,* and Phillips' to Burgoyne, in E. B. de Fonblanque, *Political and Military Episodes . . . of the Right Hon. John Burgoyne,* p. 219, refer to the disappointment of the officers at Carleton's rejection of the plan.
17. PRO CO 5/125, f. 353, Douglas to Admiralty, 21 October 1776.
18. Hadden, *op. cit.,* p. 30.
19. *The British Invasion from the North* by William Digby, pp. 164–165.
20. *Autobiography of John Trumbull,* pp. 28–34.
21. *Ibid.,* p. 34; *Fort Ticonderoga Museum Bulletin,* July 1934, "Return of American Artillery by Major Stevens"; Digby, *op. cit.,* pp. 161, 169.
22. PRO CO 42/36, f. 1; HMC *Stopford-Sackville MSS,* Vol. 2, p. 222; WCL *Germain Papers,* undated paper at end of 1778 volume; WCL *Shelburne Papers* LXVI, f. 149.
23. De Fonblanque, *op. cit.,* p. 219.
24. WCL *Clinton Papers,* Burgoyne to Clinton, 7 November 1776.
25. *Ibid.*

26. WCL *Germain Papers,* Gordon to Germain, 11 September 1777. The *London Packet,* 13 December 1776, reported that Gordon had already resigned.

CHAPTER XI *HIGH COMMAND*

1. *Last Journals* (1910), Vol. 1, p. 522. The entire affair is discussed by A. L. Burt in "The Quarrel Between Carleton and Germain."
2. PRO CO 42/35, f. 219 ff, "Conversation between Lt. Col. Christie and Lt. Genl. Burgoyne 25 June 1776"; E. B. de Fonblanque, *Political and Military Episodes . . . of the Right Hon. John Burgoyne,* p. 219; *Journ. of Soc. for Army Hist. Research,* Vol. 26, pp. 135, 136.
3. PRO CO 43/13, f. 111, Germain to Carleton, 14 May 1776.
4. HMC *Stopford-Sackville MSS,* pp. 33–36.
5. *State,* Appendix II. House of Lords papers, 8 February 1778, No. 2.
6. WCL *Germain Papers,* 23 August 1776; HMC *Stopford-Sackville MSS,* Vol. 2, p. 39.
7. PRO CO 42/35, f. 171, Carleton to Germain, 28 September 1776.
8. 5 December 1776. On 11 December the newspaper proudly referred to this report as proof that its "American Intelligence" was the best in London. Since they published quite a lot of information that would now be "classified," including a summary of the plan of the Hudson campaign, they clearly had a "source" among the clerks of Germain's office.
9. All newspapers 10–14 December, *Morning Post,* 5 December, and its rival *New Morning Post,* 11 December, carried stories of Burgoyne's quarrel with Carleton.
10. *Last Journals,* Vol. 1, p. 592, quoted in *Geo. III Correspondence with Lord North,* ed. W. B. Donne (1867), and thus passed into the realm of historical authenticity.
11. PRO CO 42/35, f. 449, Burgoyne to Germain, 9 December 1776.
12. PRO CO 42/36, ff. 11–27; the document says "submitted to Lord George Germain" and is signed "J. Burgoyne."
13. PRO CO 43/13, f. 138, Carleton to Germain, 22 October 1776. This is a copy in the entry book; the original is not in the file CO 42/35, where it should be. The *London Chronicle* says Carleton's dispatch was presented to Germain at his house in Pall Mall by Lt. Haynes, RN, on the night of Monday, 9 December, in which case Germain had had the whole night to digest the implication of its contents and would have been even angrier by the time he received Burgoyne. The memorandums and dispatch were then sent by Germain to the king, whose agreement that three thousand troops should be kept in Canada (a figure stipulated by Burgoyne but not by Carleton) proves that Burgoyne's "Observations" were written *before* and not after this interview with Germain. They were then returned to Burgoyne, who again left such as required expediting at Germain's office on 1 January (*State,* Appendix 1). Some of them have disappeared, including one concerning Indian presents, which Germain inquired after on 20 January (CO 42/36, ff. 50, 57). I mention this to remove the suspicion, which may well occur to a future researcher, that the memorandums were written by Burgoyne at Germain's request, as part of an intrigue against Carleton.

14. *State,* pp. 2, 94.
15. The second occasion was after Valcour Island. Carleton told General Waterbury, captured on board the *Washington,* that he was not to be blamed for carrying out the orders of his superiors (in this case, Governor Trumbull) and sent the general, with all the captured American crews, to Ticonderoga on parole. Gates was so alarmed that he would not allow them to land. So again, Carleton's action was due partly to humanity and partly to political calculation.
16. The only reference to this conversation is in Germain's own *Précis of Operations & Plans* in CO 5/253, f. 26. This page deals with the advantages of the Mohawk expedition and Carleton's "inexplicable" refusal to employ Indians. In the right-hand margin is written, in different ink and another hand, "Conversation with General Burgoyne after his arrival in England." The point is that it was this volume which Lord Thurlow took away to read when he was looking for evidence against Burgoyne during the inquiry into Saratoga in 1778. The note, therefore, may be his, on Germain's verbal confirmation. Since the entire passage was dictated by Germain long afterward and at a time when he was defending himself against the opposition, Howe, and Burgoyne; and since the information in it could have been gathered from other men, such as Christie, Guy Johnson, Captain Gordon, etc., as well as Burgoyne, it makes only a weak case against Burgoyne.
17. A. L. Burt, *op. cit., passim.* The first to suggest that Carleton held back deliberately seems to have been William Kingsford (*History of Canada,* Vol. 6, p. 74), who may have got the idea from Stedman's discussion of Howe (see following note).
18. *The Command of the Howe Brothers During the American Revolution* by Troyer Steele Anderson, pp. 134–135 and Ch. IX, discusses this in detail. Charles Stedman put forward this suggestion in *History of the American War* (1794), Vol. 1, p. 199. Although he had served in America, Stedman admitted he did not know what Howe's real motives were.
19. PRO CO 43/13, f. 125, Carleton to Germain, 10 August 1776.
20. *Correspondence of George III,* Vol. 3, No. 1936, Germain to king, 11 December 1776.
21. All newspapers reported this interview after the levee. Geo III *Corresp.,* Vol. 3, No. 1938, king to Lord North, 13 December 1776.
22. HMC *Hastings MSS,* Vol. 3, p. 189, Hans Stanley to Lord Huntingdon, 18 December 1776, speaks of the jealousy among army officers of Burgoyne, probably on account of his rapid rise, and of how they all felt he should not have protected Carleton. After Saratoga, no doubt, these same officers complained that Burgoyne *had* criticized Carleton.
23. *London Evening Post,* 17–19 December 1776, also in other papers.
24. HMC *Various Collections,* Vol. 6, WCL *Knox Papers,* p. 128, Germain to Knox, 31 December 1776.
25. Geo III *Corresp.,* Vol. 3, No. 1964, king to North, 24 February 1777. *State,* Appendix I.
26. WCL *Clinton Papers,* Burgoyne to Pownoll, 2 March 1777.
27. PRO CO 42/36, f. 37 ff; copy in WCL *Germain Papers;* printed in *State,*

Appendix III, and in Hoffman Nickerson, *The Turning Point of the Revolution,* pp. 83–89.

28. PRO CO 5/93, ff. 609–615; HMC *Stopford-Sackville MSS,* Vol. 2, pp. 49–50; CO 5/253, p. 299.
29. Geo III *Corresp.,* Vol. 3, Nos. 1996, 1997.
30. BM Ad. MSS 18,738, f. 196, in king's handwriting, no date. An extract is given by E. B. de Fonblanque, *op. cit.,* pp. 486–487.
31. WCL *Clinton Papers,* Letters from Burgoyne to Lord Sandwich and Pownoll, 20, 23, and 24 March 1777.
32. PRO CO 42/36, ff. 25–32, Phillips to Carleton, 9 November 1777, two letters.
33. PRO CO 42/35, ff. 50, 57, Burgoyne to Germain, 21 January 1777.
34. *A Journal Kept in Canada* by James W. Hadden, pp. 169–171; CO 5/163, f. 261, Blomefield to Townshend, 7 March 1777.
35. PRO CO 5/163, ff. 257, 265, 273; CO 5/125, ff. 105–106, with more letters in Vols. 126 and 127. The *London Chronicle* gives report of capture of the *Mellish; State,* p. 9.
36. PRO CO 5/93, ff. 609–615, Howe to Germain, 30 November 1776; printed in HMC *Stopford-Sackville MSS,* Vol. 2, p. 52; referred to in *The Narrative of Sir William Howe* (1780), p. 11. Germain's reply, 14 January 1777, is in CO 5/94, ff. 1–12, and printed in *Stopford-Sackville MSS,* Vol. 2, p. 56.
37. PRO CO 5/94, ff. 41–50, Howe to Germain, 20 December 1776; HMC *Stopford-Sackville MSS,* Vol. 2, p. 52; Howe's *Narrative,* p. 11.
38. *The Howe Brothers & The American Revolution* by Ira Gruber (1972), p. 154.
39. Lee to Rush, 4 June 1778, in *Memoirs of Charles Lee,* W. C. Langworthy (1792), pp. 422–425.
40. PRO CO 5/94, f. 215; HMC *Stopford-Sackville MSS,* Vol. 2, p. 58. Howe's *Narative,* p. 12.
41. In June 1776, Howe had expressed his "utter amazement" at Germain's "decisive and masterly strokes for carrying such extensive plans into immediate execution" (*Parliamentary Register,* Vol. 11 (1779), pp. 328–329). In his *Narrative* (in fact, a speech before Parliament), he described his disillusionment. Piers Mackesy (*War for America,* p. 111) claims Germain was justified in his reasoning, owing to the ambiguous meaning of the term "effective men."
42. PRO CO 42/36, f. 449, Carleton to Burgoyne, 10 June 1777. "These," said Burgoyne, "were the only orders I had to act upon"; *State,* p. 3.
43. PRO CO 42/36, ff. 101–113; other copies in PRO 30/55, *Carleton Papers,* No. 462; BM Ad. MSS 21,697, f. 161 ff; WCL *Germain Papers;* printed in HMC *Stopford-Sackville MSS,* Vol. 2, pp. 60–63; with passages offensive to Carleton omitted in *State,* Appendix IV, from which Nickerson, *op. cit.,* pp. 91–93, took his version.
44. *Gentleman Johnny Burgoyne* by F. J. Hudleston, p. 131.
45. *Daily Advertiser,* 28 and 29 March 1777; *Gazeteer,* 3 April.
46. HMC *Various Collections,* Vol. 6, p. 129; *Daily Advertiser,* 9 April 1777.
47. *Life of Lord Shelburne* by Baron Edmond Fitzmaurice (1912), Vol. 1, pp. 247–248.
48. HMC *Various Collections,* Vol. 6, p. 222.

49. CO 5/94, f. 505, Howe to Germain, 5 July 1777, Howe having delayed a month before acknowledging receipt. Printed in HMC *Stopford-Sackville MSS*, Vol. 2, p. 63; Howe's *Narrative*, p. 15; *Private Papers of the Earl of Sandwich*, Vol. 1, p. 281.
50. Howe's *Narrative*, p. 15.
51. This argument was first made against Burgoyne in two pamphlets: *Remarks on Gen. Burgoyne's State of The Expedition from Canada* (1780) and *A Brief Examination of the . . . Expedition in America* (1779), both of which asked Burgoyne to confess that he had always expected to reach Albany, or even New York, alone. Their reasoning was revived, with little alteration, by Jane Clark, in a well-known and influential article entitled "Responsibility for the Failure of the Burgoyne Campaign." See also her "Command of the Canadian Army in 1776–7." Since then, and following her lead, have appeared the discussions of T. S. Anderson, *Command of the Howe Brothers*, pp. 245–273; G. S. Brown, *The American Secretary*, Chs. 6 and 7; Piers Mackesy, *War for America*, Chs. 5 and 6; and William B. Willcox, "Too Many Cooks," and *Portrait of a General*. All except Willcox believe Burgoyne invented the story of an expected "junction" as an excuse after Saratoga. These, being works of original scholarship, have given rise to a new "orthodoxy" of belief in this matter (e.g., *Saratoga* by Rupert Furneaux or *The War for American Independence* by Don Higginbotham, New York, 1972. The conversation between Clinton and Germain is given by Willcox, *Portrait of a General*, pp. 140–141.
52. Geo III *Corresp.*, Vol. 3, 1966; BM Ad. MSS 18,738, f. 196.
53. PRO CO 5/163, f. 183, Germain to Howe, 19 April 1777. This letter was printed in *Remarks on Gen. Burgoyne's State of the Expedition* (1780).
54. PRO CO 5/94, f. 269, Germain to Howe, 19 April 1777.
55. PRO CO 42/36 and 37, CO 5/94 and CO 167–9.
56. *Journ. of Soc. for Army Hist. Research*, Vol. 26 (1948), p. 139.
57. PRO CO 42/37, f. 335, St. Leger to Burgoyne, 11 August 1777.
58. E.g., by Furneaux, *op. cit.*, p. 26 ff, who says Burgoyne was "in and out of Germain's office . . . at the vital time." Burgoyne's dinner with Clinton is in *Portrait of a General*, by Willcox, p. 135.
59. *State*, p. 11.
60. Howe's *Narrative*, pp. 11–12; original letter is in PRO CO 5/94, f. 201–203. For its importance, see, for instance, G. S. Brown, *op. cit.*, p. 96.
61. Nor is this letter copied into the entry book. For the other letters referred to, see HMC *Stopford-Sackville MSS*, Vol. 2, pp. 52, 53, 58. Some letters from Howe dated 17 January had arrived on 3 March but this letter of 20 January was not among them. However, when Germain's undersecretary Thomas de Grey laid Howe's papers before Parliament during the inquiry in 1779, this letter was included with those arriving 3 March—a mistake which I think gave rise to Howe's mistake. It is printed in *Parliamentary Register*, Vol. 11 (1779), pp. 377–378.
62. Newspapers throughout the week. The *Morning Chronicle*, 29 and 31 March, reported that Germain left for his holiday on Friday afternoon; he was to spend a week at his home.
63. Mackesy, *op. cit.*, p. 136.

64. *Daily Advertiser,* 10 April 1777.

CHAPTER XII *"THIS ARMY MUST NOT RETREAT"*

1. *A Journal Kept in Canada* by James W. Hadden, p. 346, Carleton to Phillips, 8 May 1777 (given as 8 April, which must be a misprint).
2. *Journ. of Soc. for Army Hist. Research,* Vol. 26 (1948), p. 139, Burgoyne to Fraser, 6 May 1777.
3. *State,* Appendix XII, p. xxxi, Burgoyne to General Harvey, 19 May 1777; *Morning Post,* 29 March 1777. The *London Chronicle,* 22 August 1776, and *The Remembrancer,* 26 September 1776, had not only described the plan but had assumed the Mohawk expedition had already been undertaken that year (see Ch. X, n. 11, and Ch. XI, n. 8).
4. PRO CO 42/36, f. 421, Carleton to Burgoyne, 29 May 1777.
5. PRO CO 42/36, ff. 401, 402, 421, 423, correspondence between Carleton and Burgoyne, 20, 26 and 29 May 1777.
6. PRO CO 42/36, f. 417, St. Leger to Burgoyne, 25 May 1777.
7. CO 5/78, ff. 443–461, Claus to Knox, 16 October 1777; another copy, also by Claus, in New York State Library, MSS 1108, dated 11 October 1777. Printed in Brodhead, Vol. 8, pp. 718–723.
8. CO 5/79, f. 139, Guy Johnson to Germain, 11 November 1777, printed in *Documents Relative to . . . New York* by J. R. Brodhead, Vol. 8, p. 726. Johnson had stayed on in New York in expectation of rejoining his Indians when the junction of Howe's and Burgoyne's armies took place. When he began to doubt that Howe intended to move up the Hudson, he asked leave to go to Canada by sea but was refused.
9. HMC *Stopford-Sackville MSS,* Vol. 2, pp. 65–66, Howe to Germain, 5 April 1777. The date of Sir John Johnson's arrival in Canada, and consequently the receipt date of this letter, is in *Invasion du Canada* by l'Abbé Verreau (1873), Vol. 1, p. 143.
10. PRO CO 5/94, ff. 523–527, Howe-Germain, 7 July 1777; HMC *Stopford-Sackville MSS,* Vol. 2, pp. 70–71, same. For Howe's letter to Burgoyne, see *State,* p. 7, and Appendix X, p. xxvi; *Political and Military Episodes . . . of the Right Hon. John Burgoyne* by E. B. de Fonblanque, p. 280.
11. One hundred and fifty more Indians under Saint-Luc joined the expedition at Skenesborough about 20 July. There were eighty-three loyalists at the beginning of the campaign, who were joined by some six hundred more after the fall of Ticonderoga. Of these, many were captured by, or deserted to, the Americans. These figures are taken from *State,* pp. 9, 74, and Appendix XI; Digby's *Invasion from the North,* p. 20; and de Fonblanque, *op. cit.,* pp. 487–488. For an interesting discussion of them, see *Turning Point of the Revolution* by Hoffmann Nickerson, Appendix II.
12. Hadden, *op. cit.,* p. 478.
13. *Ibid.,* p. 51.
14. *State,* Appendix VI; Digby, *op. cit.,* pp. 356–361; *Travels Through the Interior Parts of America* by Thomas Anburey, Vol. 1, pp. 248–257. Most modern accounts assume that Saint-Luc and de Langlade were present at this

meeting, but it is clear from Lord Harrington's evidence (*State*, p. 48) that they did not join the army until the middle of July.

15. *Memoir of His Own Life* by Roger Lamb, p. 172.
16. Bedfordshire Record Office, *Polwarth Papers,* L30/12/17/11, Clerke to Lord Polwarth, 19 May 1777.
17. Hadden, *op. cit.*, pp. 59–62; Digby, *op. cit.*, pp. 189–192.
18. Burgoyne's *Orderly Book*, p. 3.
19. Hadden, *op. cit.*, p. 81; Digby, *op. cit.*, p. 200; Anburey, *op. cit.*, Vol. 1, p. 273.
20. PRO CO 42/36, f. 213 ff, "Intelligence Reports . . ." A to E, plus two reports by Captain Mackay, who led a reconnaissance in March as far south as Sabbath Day Point on Lake George. It is curious that Mackay's Indians refused to go to Skenesborough. Could it be that they had heard rumors about the corpse of Philip Skene's mother (kept, it will be remembered, on a table) and were afraid of encountering her restless ghost?
21. *Revolutionary Journal* of Col. Jeduthan Baldwin, p. 60.
22. *Military Journal of the American Revolution* by James Thacher, p. 84.
23. *Journal of . . . American War* by Roger Lamb, p. 143.
24. Digby, *op. cit.*, p. 210.
25. De Fonblanque, *op. cit.*, p. 247.
26. Digby, *op. cit.*, pp. 229–232.
27. PRO CO 42/36, ff. 719–728, printed with important changes in *State*, Appendix VIII.
28. *New Hampshire State Papers,* Vol. 8, p. 640; Hadden, *op. cit.*, p. 487.

CHAPTER XIII *"A GLORIOUS SPIRIT IN OUR GENERAL"*

1. *Schuyler Papers,* Box 41, and Letter Book, letters 1250, 1254, 1258, 1261, 1266.
2. *Ibid.*, letter 1275.
3. PRO CO 42/36, f. 731, Williams to Germain, 12 July 1777; ff. 737–751 contain his journal. Hadden (*A Journal Kept in Canada,* pp. 101–102) criticizes Williams for his "Brutality" to the American prisoners. Two hundred of them were kept in a single barn, were forced to work on repairing roads, etc., or beating hemp (as in a London workhouse), and to attend the *feu de joie* celebrating the capture of Ticonderoga. They should, Hadden felt, have been treated either as prisoners of war or as rebels. Nevertheless, at the *feu de joie*, some of the Americans "threw up their Caps & Huzza'd with the Troops, in spite of many pushes from their Comrades."
4. *Ibid.*, p. 96.
5. Hoffman Nickerson (*Turning Point of the Revolution,* Appendix IX) notes that there may have been a road from Ticonderoga to Fort George down the west shore of Lake George. Such a road is shown on some maps (e.g., Holland-Pownall map of 1776 in the so-called "Holster Atlas") but not on others (e.g., Burgoyne's own in *State of the Expedition*). Local tradition maintains that the road had been cut during the last years of the Seven Years' War, and that in 1777 Burgoyne's draft horses and cattle went south by it. Nickerson believes that Burgoyne made no mention of this road afterward because it would have weakened his case for using the Skenes-

borough-Fort Anne route. It should be mentioned that whereas Nickerson's maps show this road passing through Fort George, the very detailed map of New York by Sauthier, engraved for Governor Tryon in 1779, shows the road bypassing Fort George by some miles and leading to Fort Edward via Queensbury and Kingsbury.

6. PRO CO 42/36, f. 633, de Peyster to Carleton, 13 June 1777.
7. *The British Invasion from the North* by William Digby, pp. 235–237.
8. "Influence of the Death of Jane McCrae on the Burgoyne Campaign" by James Austin Holden prints Standish's application for a pension and gives an exhaustive bibliography up to that date.
9. Houghton Library, Harvard University Library *Sparks MSS* 141g. (10 f. 2), "Journal—Traveling notes for historical research 1829–31, pp. 206–211. In his notes to Digby *(op. cit.)*, however, J. P. Baxter pointed out (pp. 236–237) that both Fraser and, later, the American General Morgan Lewis dug up and examined the corpse, Lewis finding three distinct gunshot wounds. Fraser and Lewis, therefore, both believed she had been shot by Americans. If this is to be reconciled with Standish's story, a possible explanation is that the Indian had filled his musket with loose shot, such as stones. The local geography does not support the story that she was shot by Americans from the fort, for the distance is too great and the angles are wrong. Mrs. McNeill only adopted this story many years later. She was Fraser's cousin; so perhaps she first got the idea from him and revived it because she became more intolerantly anti-American as she grew older and would say anything that might put blame on the Yankees. Burgoyne himself never doubted that the Indians had killed her in the manner described.
10. *Journ. of Soc. of Army Hist. Research,* Vol. 26 (1948), p. 142, Burgoyne to Fraser, from Fort Anne, 8 p.m., 26 July 1777.
11. *State,* p. 36, question 5.
12. B. F. Stevens, *Facsimiles,* Vol. XVI, No. 157.
13. PRO CO 5/163, f. 195, Townshend to Germain, 22 March 1777. Lord Harrington (Lord Petersham during the campaign) told Parliament that "cannon always creates a delay that armies have been content to put up with"; *State,* p. 58, question 113.
14. *State,* pp. 9–10. Having given his total of forty-two pieces, but not having added them up, he then gave a breakdown of their distribution: twenty-six pieces, instead of the customary twenty-eight, to fourteen battalions, plus ten more pieces of Park artillery, making only thirty-six all told. Somewhere during his patter, he "lost" two howitzers and six mortars. No one noticed at the time, nor does anyone seem to have noticed since. Nevertheless, Nickerson (*op. cit.,* pp. 164–168) has used other arguments to show that Burgoyne had too many guns.
15. Digby, *op. cit.,* pp. 227–228; Hadden, *op. cit.,* pp. 94–95.
16. F. von Riedesel, *Memoirs,* Vol. 1, pp. 121–122.
17. *Sexagenary* by J. P. Becker (1866), pp. 73–74.
18. PRO CO 42/36, f. 771, Burgoyne to Germain, 30 July 1777.
19. HMC *Stopford-Sackville MSS,* Vol. 2, p. 72; this letter was forwarded by Howe to Germain on 15 July and received in London on 22 August.

20. PRO CO 42/36, ff. 771–775, Burgoyne to Germain, 30 July 1777, private letter. There is another copy in CO 42/37, ff. 163–169. Burgoyne did not print this letter in his *State of the Expedition.* In fact, however, one letter dated 16 July did reach New York on the 25th and was forwarded by Clinton to Howe, who had just sailed. It said nothing "material" beyond recounting the capture of Ticonderoga and the actions at Hubbardton and Fort Anne. A copy is in the *Clinton Papers,* WCL. Burgoyne wrote another, more or less the same, dated 20 July, of which Clinton sent a précis to Howe on 6 August (CO 5/94, f. 711). Some of these ten messages, therefore, were probably no more than statements of success, not reminders of the need for a junction.
21. WCL *Clinton Papers;* printed in *State,* Appendix X.
22. That is, Howe's letter to Germain of 20 December 1776, and Germain's reply of 3 March 1777, if my supposition is right that the 20 January letter did not reach Germain until after Burgoyne's departure (see Ch. XI).
23. Not an unreasonable assumption for Burgoyne to make, although in his speech before Parliament he wrongly dated the letter 17 *June.* It has already been mentioned that orders sometimes took six months or more to reach commanders. Nevertheless, the *Somerset,* bearing a copy of Germain's orders to Carleton under a covering letter from D'Oyley, did reach New York on 3 June. Howe read them immediately, as is shown by his observing, in a letter to Germain of 5 June (WCL *Germain Papers*), that Fraser was serving in the northern army. On 5 July he sent Germain a formal acknowledgment, but without comment (also in *Germain Papers* and printed in HMC *Stopford-Sackville MSS,* Vol. 2, p. 70).
24. This was an attempt by Peter Livius, chief justice of Quebec, to buy over General John Sullivan, who had been captured in New York and was now back on parole at his home. His treason was to be secret, and he was to arrange troop movements, etc., in such a way as to benefit the advance. The letter was discovered at Fort George, and Schuyler forged a reply, purporting to be from Sullivan, accepting the offer. Charles Stedman, *History of the American War* (1794), Vol. 1, p. 336, says Burgoyne received this letter as intended and was completely duped and puzzled by it for several days, not knowing whether to advance or retreat. This is unlikely, for why should Burgoyne not have known whether to advance or retreat because of a doubtful letter merely accepting the proposal? For further confusion, see *Visits to Saratoga Battlegrounds* by W. L. Stone, Appendix I, "Schuyler's Faithful Spy," where this letter turns up again amid some complete fiction, parading as truth, concerning one Moses Harris, who is supposed to have forged many letters between Burgoyne and Clinton, thus causing the failure of the campaign. For a factual account of this affair, see *Secret History of the Revolution* by Carl Van Doren, a marvellous book, pp. 43–49. Burgoyne's letter of 6 August 1777 is in PRO CO 5/94 ff. 707–712.
25. *State,* pp. 41, 71, 75.
26. *Parliamentary History,* Vol. 19, p. 1191.
27. See, for instance, Hoffman Nickerson, *op. cit.,* p. 376, where it is offered as a proof of Burgoyne's weak character, and Furneaux, *Saratoga,* p. 35.
28. Hadden, *op. cit.,* p. 315.

29. Bedfordshire Record Office, *Polwarth Papers,* L 30/12/17/4, Clerke to Lord Polwarth, 10 September 1777, near Saratoga.
30. *Baroness von Riedesel and the American Revolution,* p. 56. *Town & Country Magazine,* February 1777, "The Devoted General and the Fair Virginian" (one of the "Tête-à-Têtes" series of scurrilous gossip).
31. *State,* pp. 49, 99, 100; *History of New York* by Thomas Jones (1871), Vol. 1, pp. 883–885.
32. B. J. Lossing, *Pictorial Field-Book of the Revolution,* Vol. 1, p. 45. Other accounts of Bennington can be found in Nickerson, *Turning Point of the Revolution;* Appendix V, Vol. 1, of von Riedesel's *Memoirs; The History of Pittsfield* by J. E. A. Smith (Boston, 1869), pp. 499–501 (Parson Allen's account); *Reminiscences* by Levi Beardsey (1852); and *A History of the Battle of Bennington* by F. W. Coburn (1912). Burgoyne's orders to Baum and Skene are in *State,* Appendix XII, pp. xxiii–xi.
33. PRO CO 42/37, f. 335, St. Leger to Burgoyne, 11 August 1777.
34. HL 9 February 1779, p. 32.
35. *State,* Appendix IX, p. xxv.
36. *Parliamentary History,* Vol. 19, Burgoyne's speech on 26 May 1778.
37. PRO CO 42/36, f. 453 ff.
38. St. Leger's account of his campaign is in *State,* Appendix XIII. Claus's account is printed in *Documents Relative to . . . New York* by J. R. Brodhead, Vol. 8, pp. 723–726. Claus's original is in PRO CO 5/78, ff. 443–461; another copy is in New York State Library at Albany, MSS 1108 ff. See also *Life of Joseph Brant-Thayendanagea* by W. L. Stone (the elder), Vol. 1; and *The Campaigns of Burgoyne* by W. L. Stone (the younger), which is a condensation of his father's narrative.
39. Digby, *op. cit.,* pp. 260–266.
40. *Advance & Retreat to Saratoga* by Clarence E. Bennett (Schenectady, 1927), Vol. 2, p. 41, quoting a Philadelphia newspaper of about 1 September 1777, which reported that the Indians had been scalping Burgoyne's own men, including a red-haired lieutenant.
41. Digby, *op. cit.,* p. 259.

CHAPTER XIV *"OH FATAL AMBITION!"*

1. *Last Journals,* Vol. 2, p. 41.
2. PRO CO 5/94, f. 288 (also CO 5/253, f. 146 and WCL *Germain Papers*), Howe to Germain, 2 April 1777; printed in HMC *Stopford-Sackville MSS,* Vol. 2, p. 63.
3. PRO CO 5/94, f. 339 (also WCL *Germain Papers*), Germain to Howe, 18 May 1777; printed in HMC *Stopford-Sackville MSS,* Vol. 2, pp. 66–67. Received by Howe on 16 August while sailing up Chesapeake Bay.
4. PRO CO 5/94, p. 619, Germain to Howe, 3 September 1777; Howe's letter of 16 July is printed in HMC *Stopford-Sackville MSS,* Vol. 2, pp. 72–73; Burgoyne's of 11 July from Skenesborough is printed in *State,* Appendix VIII, p. xxi. There is an original in PRO CO 42/36, ff. 719–728. There are important differences, however, between the original and the printed versions. The question of whether Burgoyne may have faked the printed

version after his return to England in 1778 is discussed in Ch. XVII, pp. 258 and 270, and in the notes to that chapter, n. 4, 5, 6, and 23, pp. 327–328 and 329.

5. There is a full account of this affair in *Portrait of a General* by William B. Willcox, Chs. IV and V.
6. WCL *Clinton Papers,* copy in Lord Rawdon's hand, with cypher; printed in *The American Rebellion* (Clinton's *Narrative*) by William B. Willcox (1954), p. 70.
7. WCL *Clinton Papers, Germain Papers;* printed in HMC *Stopford-Sackville MSS,* Vol. 2, p. 74.
8. PRO CO 5/94, f. 583; printed in HMC *Stopford-Sackville MSS,* Vol. 2, p. 73.
9. Burgoyne's *Orderly Book,* p. 113.
10. *The British Invasion from the North* by William Digby, p. 269.
11. *Polwarth Papers,* L 30/12/17/14, Clerke to Lord Polwarth, 10 September 1777.
12. *History of the British Army* by Sir John Fortescue (Macmillan, 1899–1920), Vol. 3, p. 231. For American view, see Nickerson, *Turning Point of the Revolution,* pp. 303–305.
13. Burgoyne may not in fact have been so ignorant of the American positions as is sometimes believed. On 17 September, Fraser paid £5 13s 4d to "men who brought in an exact account of the rebel army, cannon & dispositions." (PRO Treasury Papers, T.1/572, Bundle 3, "Brig. Fraser's Accounts of Contingencies." The bundle is of separate sheets and a notebook, not in any order.)
14. *Battle of Saratoga* by Ellen Hardin Walworth (1891).
15. The paper is quoted by E. B. de Fonblanque, *Political and Military Episodes . . . of the Right Hon. John Burgoyne,* p. 469 ff, who says the copy was in Burgoyne's hand. The relevant passage is between lines 8 and 16, p. 474. There is a translation of this essay, considerably rearranged and differing from Burgoyne's transcript in many ways, in *Frederick the Great on the Art of War* by Jay Luvaas (The Free Press, N. Y., 1966); the relevant passage is on pp. 268–269.
16. This is according to information given to me by a ranger at Saratoga Battlefield National Historial Park. W. L. Stone, Jr. (*Visits to Saratoga Battlefields,* p. 67) says that the farm was owned at this time by a Quaker farmer called Isaac Leggett, who was also a loyalist, and whose daughter was cross-examined by Arnold and Gates.
17. Digby, *op. cit.,* p. 273.
18. American fire would seem to have been more accurate than British. Neilson told Jared Sparks that balls found in the trees showed that whereas British shot was rarely found lower than five feet high and sometimes forty feet high, American shot was rarely higher than six feet. He once cut fifty-nine bullets from one tree alone (*Sparks MSS* 141g, *Journal*). British sergeants, by the way, still carried halberds, many of which were found on the battlefield in the years after the war.
19. *Memoirs of My Own Times* by James Wilkinson, Vol. 1, p. 251 ff, who was told this by Phillips after Saratoga. Digby (*op. cit.,* p. 275) says that it was Phillips and Fraser who wished to attack and Burgoyne who refused. This version is

always given by those who wish to argue that Burgoyne was incompetent. They support it by reasoning that since the Advanced Corps had not been heavily engaged, Fraser would not have claimed it was exhausted. It could be argued, therefore, that Wilkinson's memory deceived him and that he wrote the story backward. Yet if that were so, it is curious that von Riedesel *(Memoirs)*, who missed no chance of criticizing Burgoyne for being hesitant, has nothing to say about the matter. Therefore, I suspect Wilkinson was right and Digby, who admitted he was only repeating a rumor, wrong.

20. WCL *Clinton Papers.*
21. WCL *Clinton Papers.*
22. WCL *Clinton Papers,* original and many copies.
23. WCL *Clinton Papers,* memorandum in Clinton's hand filed under 6 October 1777. Also Clinton's *Narrative* (*The American Rebellion* by W. B. Willcox), p. 72.
24. *Emmett Collection* EM 4336, Burgoyne to Powel, 21 September 1777, original. The other letter, EM 8119, is the one printed in James Wilkinson's *Memoirs of My Own Times* and is a copy.
25. *Sparks MSS,* 1419, *Journal,* p. 169 ff.
26. PRO CO 5/94, f. 713, Burgoyne to Clinton, 23 September 1777; also WCL *Clinton Papers.*
27. F. von Riedesel, *Memoirs,* Vol. 1, p. 156.
28. WCL *Clinton Papers;* also PRO CO 5/94, f. 717.
29. PRO CO 42/37, f. 567 ff, Burgoyne to Germain, 20 October 1777; printed in *State,* Appendix XIV, p. xlix.
30. Here I have followed the argument of Charles E. Shedd, Jr., late Park Historian at Saratoga National Historical Park, in his paper "Burgoyne's Objective in the Second Battle of Saratoga, October 7, 1777," written 15 December 1952. My thanks are due to Michael Phillips, the present Park Historian, for kindly letting me see this essay, which has not been published.
31. Digby, *op. cit.,* p. 283. Neilson's assertion that Arnold was not on the battlefield on 19 September is in *Sparks MSS, Journal.* Sparks's guide, "Major" Bud, said he saw General Poor and two or three other officers "quite in the rear and taking no part" and that the fighting was led by Morgan, Scammell, and Cilley.
32. *Baroness von Riedesel & the American Revolution.* "Poor Mrs. Fraser!" was no mere exclamation. During the campaigns of 1776–1777, Fraser had spent £675 14s 10d out of his own pocket in sundry expenses (e.g., payment for intelligence, for cattle, to army widows, etc.) and had incurred heavy debts. In April 1778 she petitioned the Treasury for this money to relieve her distress. By May 1782, she still had not been paid but had remarried to a Mr. George Hepburn; PRO T 1/572, Bundle 3, "Brig. Fraser's Accounts of Contingencies." Some of the items are of considerable interest: on 31 July 1776, Fraser paid £8 17s to some Ottawa Indians "for bringing in their prisoners humanely, according to General Carleton's instructions." On 8 September 1776, he paid £2 to an Indian chief for "a Silver laced Hat . . . having lost his own in a Skirmish with the Enemy." On 20 June 1777, he

paid £11 13s 4d for two bullocks furnished to the Indians at the conference with General Burgoyne.

33. Von Riedesel, *op. cit.*, Vol. 1, p. 169.

CHAPTER XV *HAVOC AND DESOLATION*

1. Quoted in *The Price of Independence* by Broadus Mitchell (Oxford University Press, New York, 1974), p. 234.
2. *Baroness von Riedesel and the American Revolution,* p. 54. Her husband's own account and comments are in his *Memoirs,* Vol. 1, pp. 169 ff.
3. *Rebels & Redcoats* by George F. Scheer and Hugh F. Rankin (World Publishing Co., 1957; reprinted as a Mentor Book), p. 324.
4. *State,* p. 59, Lord Harrington's evidence.
5. *The British Invasion from the North* by William Digby, pp. 297–298.
6. *State,* p. 129.
7. *A Journal Kept in Canada* by James M. Hadden, p. liv.
8. *Journal of . . . American War* by Roger Lamb, p. 181.
9. *History of the Rise, Progress & Establishment of the Independence of the United States of America* by William Gordon (1788), Vol. 2, p. 573. Although Campbell's return is not mentioned in other early accounts, the name of "Capt. Alexander Campbell" among the officers included in the Convention shows that he must have returned. Von Riedesel *(op. cit.)* mentions only a loyalist who came in on the night of the fifteenth, adding that since he was known to nobody in the army his information was treated with caution. This must be the informant referred to in the "Minutes of the Last Council of War," given in *State,* p. lx. Hence, I have assumed that Campbell returned *after* the signing of the Convention and not before as is said in some accounts. The most detailed first-hand account of the negotiations of surrender is given by Wilkinson *(Memoirs of My Own Times),* though he was not the most reliable of witnesses. The various proposals and emendations of the Convention are to be found in Charles Stedman (*History of the American War* [1794]), the only contemporary to give them.
10. WCL *Clinton Papers,* several copies; PRO CO 5/94, ff. 718–719.
11. *Visits to the Saratoga Battlefields* by W. L. Stone, Jr.
12. *Sexagenary* by J. P. Becker, p. 119. The eyewitness appears to have been Simeon De Witt, a friend of Schuyler's. Neilson, in his more famous account *(An Original . . . account of Burgoyne's Campaign)* uses almost identical words, except to say that Burgoyne's face was "harsh," not "hard." One of these authors was, therefore, copying from the other.
13. W. L. Stone, *op. cit.*
14. *Ibid.*
15. *State,* Second Appendix No. XIV, p. liv.
16. My thanks are due to Mr. Richard S. Allen, of the New York State Bicentenary Commission, for showing me a typescript copy of this letter. Source not given.
17. HMC *American MSS in Royal Institution,* Vol. 1, p. 141, Burgoyne to Howe, 20 October 1777.

CHAPTER XVI *THE UTMOST THAT MALEVOLENCE CAN SAY*

1. WCL *Clinton Papers;* PRO CO 5/94, f. 721.
2. PRO CO 5/94, f. 630, copy of *Maryland Journal*, 26 August 1777.
3. *The American Revolution* (Clinton's *Narrative) by William B. Willcox, p.* 83.
4. *Portrait of a General* by William B. Willcox, p. 183, quoting letter to a friend filed at end of 1777 volume.
5. HMC *Stopford-Sackville MSS,* Vol. 2, pp. 79–80, Howe to Germain, 21 October 1777.
6. PRO CO 42/36, ff. 271–279; CO 43/14, pp. 12–19; the 20 May letter is printed in *Canadian Archives* (1885 volume). For a discussion of these extraordinary letters, see *The American Secretary* by G. S. Brown, pp. 118–120, and "The Quarrel between Germain and Carleton" by A. L. Burt. In an article in the *New England Quarterly,* Vol. 3, No. 4, 1930 (reprinted as a pamphlet by Southworth Press), entitled "Burgoyne's Great Mistake," George B. Upham argued that Carleton should have arranged to harass the upper Connecticut River valley in the region of Haverhill and Newbury. This would have drawn Stark north and held him there. It would also have encouraged the large number of local Tories in the area, who had been cowed by the trial and execution of some Tories in Claremont, New Hampshire, in December 1775. However, if Carleton's figures were correct, and they presumably were, then it is hard to see where he could have found the troops for such raids. Moreover, Germain's orders specifically forbade him to cross the Canadian frontier. Burgoyne's "Great Mistake," according to Upham, was sending Baum to Bennington.
7. PRO CO 42/37, f. 43, Carleton to Burgoyne, 19 July 1777.
8. *History of the American War* by Charles Stedman (1794), Vol. 1, p. 154. Curiously, it was at this very time that Germain, whom Carleton blamed for not allowing Ticonderoga to be garrisoned from Canada, first heard that Burgoyne intended to garrison it from Canada. He immediately sent off his warm approval "of this wise measure," adding, "I shall be sorry if any occurrence has obliged you to alter your design." PRO CO 42/37, f. 165.
9. PRO CO 42/37, ff. 413–511, cover the correspondence between Carleton and Powel and Carleton and Germain, October 1777.
10. *State,* Appendix X, p. xxvii.
11. *The Private Papers of the Earl of Sandwich,* Vol. 1, pp. 306–310; also E. B. de Fonblanque, *Political and Military Episodes . . . of the Right Hon. John Burgoyne,* pp. 313–316.
12. *Ibid.;* also HMC *American MSS in Royal Institution* (1901), Vol. 1, pp. 140–142; WCL *Clinton Papers,* Burgoyne to Clinton, 25 October 1777.
13. F. J. Hudleston, *Gentleman Johnny Burgoyne,* pp. 246–247, quoting *A History of the Town of Great Barrington* by C. J. Taylor (Gt. Barrington, 1882); *Historic Hadley* by Alice R. Walker (New York, 1906); and *A History of Old Kinderhoek* by E. A. Collier (New York, 1914).
14. B. J. Lossing, *Pictorial Field-Book of the Revolution,* Vol. 1, pp. 82, 593.
15. *Memoirs of the American War* by William Heath, p. 146.
16. Hudleston, *op. cit.*, p. 207.

17. *The British Invasion from the North* by William Digby, p. 312.
18. "The Convention Troops and the Perfidy of Sir William Howe" by Jane Clark (*American Hist. Review,* Vol. 37, July 1932, pp. 721–723); the original letter is in WCL *Clinton Papers.*
19. For the American viewpoint, see, for instance, Lossing, *op. cit.,* in the index under "Prisoners"; or *The Price of Independence* by Broadus Mitchell (Oxford University Press, 1974), pp. 167–184. For the other side, see, for instance, *History of New York* by Thomas Jones (1879), in the index under "Prisoners" and Vol. 1, p. 220.
20. PRO PRO 30/55 *Carleton Papers,* Vol. 8, Nos. 868, 910.
21. De Fonblanque, *op. cit.,* pp. 321–323, Dr. Mcnamara Hayes to Burgoyne, 4 September 1778.
22. *Proceedings of a Court Martial . . . of Colonel D. Henley* (1778); much of this is quoted by Thomas Anburey, *Travels Through the Interior Parts of America,* Vol. 2, pp. 92–175.
23. De Fonblanque, *op. cit.,* pp. 329–330.
24. Heath, *op. cit.,* p. 172.
25. Hudleston, *op. cit.,* p. 201.
26. *State,* p. *86,* evidence of Major Kingston.
27. Heath, *op. cit.,* p. 173.
28. *Ibid.,* p. 195.

CHAPTER XVII *THE ADMINISTRATION CLOSES RANKS*

1. *Correspondence of George III,* Vol. 3, No. 2048, Germain to king, 22 August 1777.
2. *Lord George Germain* by Alan Valentine, p. 237. Mr. Valentine's point is that without a knowledge of that letter, the king would regard Howe's move by sea as indefensible, should the campaign end in disaster; but with a knowledge of that letter, which showed that Howe was acting with the approval of Germain, especially if there was a reply from Germain approving the letter too, then it would be Lord George's position that would be indefensible. I am inclined to agree with Mr. Valentine for two reasons: Germain's reply to Howe's correspondence of that month was written on 3 September 1777 and is in PRO CO 5/94, f. 619 ff. The letters acknowledged in that are Howe's of 8 June, and 5, 7, 8, 9, 15, and 17 July 1777, that is, every letter *except* the private letter, which was dated 16 July. I have not been able to find any acknowledgment of this letter at all, not even in the *Germain Papers* in the WCL. It looks as if Germain, as he had been with Howe's letter of 20 January, was being careful not to acknowledge receipt of the letter. It should be remembered that his reply of 3 September would be read by the king before being sent. My second reason is explained in the text—that the next day Germain kept back Burgoyne's letter as well.
3. Geo III *Corresp.,* Vol. 3, No. 2052, Germain to king, 23 August 1777.
4. *State,* Appendix VIII, p. xxi, Burgoyne to Germain, 11 July, from Skenesborough. I have been unable to find an original of this version of the letter anywhere: It is not among the papers relating to the Burgoyne inquiry in the House of Lords papers, nor listed in the *House of Lords Journal* (9

February 1779—the letter given under No. 26 is his *public* dispatch of the same date), nor among the *Germain* or *Clinton Papers* in the WCL. That this is the version that Burgoyne read out in Parliament is proved by the fact that this is the text quoted in the *Parliamentary Register* ed. J. Almon, Vol. 11(1779), pp. 473–475. De Fonblanque *(Political and Military Episodes . . . of the Right Hon. John Burgoyne)* tells us that Burgoyne often copied his letters into his letter books from memory after they had been sent off. This may be true, although the letter books have disappeared; but we are concerned not with what Burgoyne thought he wrote, but with what he did write, and with what Germain read at the time.

5. PRO CO 42/36, ff. 719–728, Burgoyne to Germain, 11 July 1777, from Skenesborough. This letter and the printed version (see n. 4 above) are more or less the same, but with slight differences of phrasing, until par. 3; after that they are completely different. I have found no other copy of this letter.
6. The evidence in fact points both ways. For instance, in the middle of the original letter (see n. 5 above), Burgoyne accidentally left two blank pages, for which he apologized in a postscript. He could perhaps have added the paragraphs concerning a junction with Howe on a separate sheet and slipped it in between the blank pages; in that case, Germain could have surreptitiously removed it. Against Germain it could be asked why, when Burgoyne read the printed version out in Parliament, as evidence that he had always understood he was to force a junction with Howe, did Germain not protest, if he knew that Burgoyne had written no such thing in the original letter? There is no answer to this question. One can only say that this circumstance, together with the suspicion that Germain was not above holding back some of Howe's letters and the complete disappearance of any original to the printed version of Burgoyne's letter, suggests, but does not prove, that Germain once possessed this original but, because of the awkward nature of its contents, held it back and afterward either lost or destroyed it. On the other hand, in Germain's favor, it should be mentioned that in his reply to Burgoyne's letters of 11 and 30 July (private and public), he acknowledged the receipt of only one copy of each (PRO CO 42/37 f. 163 ff, Germain to Burgoyne, 15 September 1777). The possibility that Burgoyne himself rewrote his own letter, adding the incriminating paragraphs and deleting other ones to suit his defense, and his possible reasons for doing so, are discussed on pp. 258, 270, and 271, and below, n. 21 and n. 23.
7. Walpole, *Last Journals* (1910), Vol. 2, p. 9.
8. HMC *Various*, Vol. 6, WCL *Knox Papers*, p. 170, Germain to Knox, 31 October 1777.
9. *Parliamentary History*, Vol. 19, p. 434.
10. Geo III *Corresp.*, Vol. 3, No. 2098, Germain to king, 9 December 1777.
11. HMC *Various*, Vol. 6, *Knox Papers*, p. 270; the précis itself is in PRO CO 5/253.
12. HMC *Stopford-Sackville MSS*, Vol. 2, pp. 88–89; original is in WCL *Germain Papers*.
13. Burgoyne's *Letter . . . to his Constituents*, p. 5.

14. PRO CO 1/616, f. 85. The Board was proposed on 15 May and adjourned on 25 May.
15. *Parliamentary History,* Vol. XIX, pp. 1200–1202.
16. *Henry, Elizabeth & George, 1734–1780; Letters & Diaries of Henry, Tenth Earl of Pembroke and his Circle,* ed. Lord Herbert (Cape, 1939).
17. *Parliamentary History,* Vol. 19, p. 1278. Germain denied this, but his denial appears as an evasion; for he referred only to an officer who claimed to have been badly treated by Burgoyne, and this officer he had refused to see. I suspect this officer to have been Major Paulus Aemilius Irving of the 47th Regiment, who was complaining at this time that Lord Balcarres had jumped over him in obtaining the Lieutenant-Colonelcy of the regiment. He accused Burgoyne of favoritism, saying that all a commander had to do nowadays to assist a friend was to put him into the Advanced Corps, where promotion was swift and sure. The correspondence is in PRO WO 1/1004, ff. 361–363.
18. *Parliamentary History,* Vol. 20, p. 713.
19. *Parliamentary History,* Vol. 20, p. 693, 22 April 1779.
20. *Diaries of Thomas Hutchinson* (1886), Vol. 2, p. 210, 22 June 1778.
21. E. B. de Fonblanque, *op. cit.,* p. 233, quotes Burgoyne's letter from Quebec as follows:

    > I wish that a latitude had been left me for a diversion towards Connecticut, but such an idea being out of the question by my orders being precise to force the junction, it is only mentioned to introduce the idea still resting upon my mind, viz., to give the change to the enemy if I could, and by every feint in my power to establish a suspicion that I still pointed towards Connecticut.
    >
    > But under the present precision of my orders, I shall really have no view but that of joining you, nor think myself justified by any temptation to delay the most expeditious means I can find to effect that purpose.

    However, it is clear that de Fonblanque is quoting not from an original letter, but from Burgoyne's own speech in Parliament, as printed in *State,* p. 7. As I suggest in n. 23 below, Burgoyne may in fact have written this not in Quebec in 1777 but in London in 1778–1779, when he was preparing his defense. For this reason, and because the original is missing, I have not included this letter among the items of evidence to show that Burgoyne expected a junction with Howe from the beginning. Nevertheless, he did write to Howe twice in April and May 1777, and the text was probably similar, for he could hardly have dared invent such a letter with Howe sitting a few seats away and able, for all Burgoyne knew, to produce the original. As I have said before, Howe probably read this letter but did not take in its implications because he was no longer interested in what Burgoyne did.
22. *History of the American War* by Charles Stedman (1794), Vol. 1, p. 356.
23. The questionable paragraphs in the printed version of Burgoyne's letter are quoted above, page 257. The similarity of phrasing between this and the letter to Howe quoted above in n. 21 suggests to me that the two letters

may have been faked, if they were faked, at the same time. Burgoyne did not start to use expressions such as "the precision of my orders" until the end of August 1777. On the other hand, on 19 May 1777 he did discuss in his letter to Germain his desire to make a strong feint toward Connecticut (*State,* Second Appendix V, p. xi; original in PRO CO 42/36, ff. 299–302). On the whole, I think it unlikely that Burgoyne would have dared to doctor this letter, for the reason, as with Howe, that he could so easily have been found out. Germain never took up this matter, either in Parliament or in any of the pamphlets which ministerial journalists wrote against Burgoyne afterward, although they went through his book with a toothcomb. Yet the discrepancy between the two versions of this letter remains puzzling, unless it was Germain who lost or destroyed the original of the printed version.

24. *Parliamentary History,* Vol. 20, p. 805.
25. *Ibid.,* p. 818.
26. The letters between Burgoyne and Jenkinson (afterward Lord Liverpool) are in the BM, *Liverpool Papers,* Ad. MSS 38210, 38212, ff. 144–147, 38383. See also *Lord George Germain* by Alan Valentine, pp. 290–304.
27. Morristown National Historical Park, *von Riedesel Papers,* Capt. A. Edmonstone to von Riedesel, 21 January, 6 March, and 15 April 1780.

CHAPTER XVIII *GENIUS, POLISHED MANNERS AND FINE SENTIMENTS*

1. *Correspondence of Edmund Burke,* ed. John A. Woods (Cambridge University Press, Chicago, 1963), Vol. IV, p. 378, Franklin to Burke, 15 October 1781. There is an account of this affair in James M. Hadden, *A Journal Kept in Canada,* pp. 406–425.
2. *Parliamentary Register,* Vol. 3 (1781), p. 551.
3. *House of Commons 1754–92* by Lewis Namier and John Brooke, Vol. 2, p. 145.
4. Parliamentary Register, Vol. 5 (1781–1782), pp. 138–139.
5. *Last Journals* (1910), Vol. 2, p. 768, 2 June 1780.
6. *Boswell in Extremes* (Journal 1777–1779), ed. Frederick Pottle (Heineman, 1971), pp. xiv, xv, xxi, xxii.
7. Burke *Corresp.,* Vol. IV, p. 245.
8. E. B. de Fonblanque, *Political and Military Episodes . . . of the Right Hon. John Burgoyne,* pp. 424–429.
9. *The Dramatic & Poetical Works of the late Lieut. Gen. J. Burgoyne* (1808). His plays were published separately, some running into many editions, but all quotations hereafter are from the 1808 edition.
10. Quoted by F. J. Hudleston, *Gentleman Johnny Burgoyne,* p. 300, no source given.
11. After the birth of John Fox, Susan went to Dublin, where she stayed with Burgoyne for the months remaining before he returned to London. She lived in Park Street. J. L. Chester's *Registers of Westminster Abbey* (Harleian Soc., Vol. X, 1876), p. 450.
12. *The London Stage 1660–1800,* ed. Charles Beecher Hogan (Southern Illinois University Press, 1968), Part V, Vols. 1, 2, and 3 (see index for Part V

under "Burgoyne"). The reviews praised the acting: "We never saw a play more admirably performed in all its parts" (*Gazeteer,* 16 January 1786).

13. Lady Emily was played by Elizabeth Farren. She became the second most famous actress in England (after Mrs. Siddons) and married Lord Derby, who met her through Burgoyne, in 1797, three weeks after his wife died. (It will be remembered that she had run away twenty years previously with the young Duke of Dorset, Germain's nephew.)
14. The poster is in the Lancashire Record Office, DDPr 28/1, dated 4 May 1787. Thomas Caulfield played Sir Clement Flint, while Susan played Miss Alton, the romantic lead (who sings the song). This fact further suggests the difference between their ages.
15. *Parliamentary History,* Vol. 27, p. 1320. Hudleston, *op. cit.,* p. 303, tells us that Lord Cornwallis, who was on the board, thought Burgoyne was the biggest blockhead and sycophant he had ever seen. What Cornwallis actually said was: "Of all the blockheads and sycophants in the world, I believe ——— is the greatest." As there were twenty-three members of the board, this could have meant anybody. (*Correspondence of Charles, 1st Marquis of Cornwallis,* ed. by Charles Ross [1859], Vol. 1, p. 190, Cornwallis to Lt.-Col. Ross, 8 May 1785.)
16. *Parliamentary History,* Vol. 28, p. 535.
17. *Ibid.,* Vol. 29, pp. 811–812.
18. *The Times,* 7, 10, and 14 August 1792; *Gentleman's Magazine,* August 1792. Burgoyne was buried beside Lady Charlotte in the north cloister of Westminster Abbey. Having no inscription, the site of the graves was forgotten, and was not rediscovered until a few years ago. The grave is now inscribed, though the birth date is wrong.
19. Chester, *op. cit.,* p. 450; de Fonblanque, *op. cit.,* pp. 463–465.
20. His son, Captain Hugh Burgoyne, RN, won the Victoria Cross for an act of extraordinary gallantry during the Crimean War. He was drowned when his ship, HMS *Captain,* foundered during trials in the Bay of Biscay, in 1877, the centenary of his grandfather's defeat.
21. "The Poetical Review of the British Stage," among a miscellany of pamphlets and broadsheets in the BM at 644. k. 18(12).

BIBLIOGRAPHY

MANUSCRIPTS

The biographer of General Burgoyne works under one great disadvantage: Nearly all Burgoyne's private papers, letters, and (if he kept any) diaries seem to have disappeared. De Fonblanque, author of the first full-length biography in 1876, quoted from letter books, etc., but gave no hint as to where they could be found, and my efforts to trace them through his descendants have achieved nothing. The papers of the Burgoyne family in Bedfordshire were lost in a fire in the last century, but none of these may have belonged to the general, who had little contact with them and lived in London or Lancashire. Inquiries at county record offices have proved equally fruitless. This is the more regrettable when we are told, in a biography of his son, that General Burgoyne's private letters were not only entertaining and amusing, but quite free of the windy rhetoric that makes so many of his public and official writings extremely tiresome.

The most valuable manuscript collections relating to Burgoyne's American adventure are in the Public Record Office in London and in the William L. Clements Library, University of Michigan, Ann Arbor, USA.

Public Record Office

I COLONIAL OFFICE (CO) PAPERS

These are the correspondence between the Secretary of State for America (Lord Dartmouth until 10 November 1775 and after that Lord George Germain), the commanders-in-chief in America, and the various government departments. Files of original correspondence contain enclosures from officers commanding armies and corps (and so contain Burgoyne's original dispatches, letters, and memorandums), together with reports, etc., from Indian Superintendents, spies, and a host of other officials. The entry books contain copies of letters in the "original correspondence" files, in chronological order but without enclosures. They are essential as a check, for there are entered copies of some letters of which no originals exist.

(1) *Original Correspondence*

CO 5/76–79	Indian affairs, 1775–1778.
CO 5/92–95	Commanders-in-chief, with enclosures.

CO 5/125–126	Admiralty 1776–1777.
CO 5/136	Post Office 1777–1782 (contains lists of packet boats, etc.).
CO 5/139–140	Other Secretaries of State (contains correspondence on recruiting of Hessians).
CO 5/162–163	Board of Ordnance, 1776–1777 (extremely useful for information on supplies and artillery of Burgoyne's army).
CO 5/167–169	War Office, 1772–1777.
CO 5/170	Convention troops.
CO 5/179	Burgoyne-Heath correspondence at Cambridge, Massachusetts.
CO 42/35–37	Commander-in-Chief, Canada (contains Burgoyne's dispatches and letters to Germain).

(2) *Entry Books*

CO 5/250	In-letters, Ordnance.
CO 5/253	*Précis of Operations & Plans, 1774–1777.*
CO 5/254	Out-letters, Admiralty.
CO 5/256	In-letters, War Office
CO 5/258	In-letters, Treasury.
CO 5/259	In-letters, Admiralty.
CO 5/261	Out-letters, War Office.
CO 43/13	In-letters, Canada.
CO 43/14	Out-letters, Canada.

II OTHER CATEGORIES

(1) *War Office*

WO 1/2, ff. 459–461	Burgoyne-War Office.
WO 1/11	Carleton-War Office.
WO 1/165	Portuguese campaign (administrative).
WO 1/616, ff. 65–86	Board of Inquiry into Saratoga.
WO 1/682, f. 149	Burgoyne letter.
WO 1/683, f. 305	Burgoyne letter.
WO 1/948, f. 207	Burgoyne letter.
WO 1/1001 and 1004	Burgoyne letter.
WO 4/55, 59, 61, 71	16th Light Dragoons.
WO 4/274	Saratoga Convention.
WO 5/60	Marching Orders, 1776–1778.
WO 26/24	16th Light Dragoons.
WO 26/29, f. 470	Convention of Saratoga.

(2) *Treasury*

T 1/387	Clothing, 16th Light Dragoons.
T 1/537, ff. 48–52	Intelligence letter re Burgoyne.
T 1/572, Bundle 3	Brigadier Fraser's expenses on campaign.
T 64/102–103	Nathanial Day, commissary-general, Canada.

(3) *Audit Office*

AO 199/637	Jacob Jordan's contract for Burgoyne's horses.
AO 219/737	Colonel St. Leger's expenses on Mohawk expedition.
AO 325/1289	Loyalist expenses on Burgoyne's campaign.

(4) *State Papers*

SP 37/18 and 19	Miscellaneous items relating to Howe and Burgoyne.
SP 87/31	Cherbourg raid.
SP 89/57	Portuguese campaign (dispatches, etc.).

(5) *Headquarters (or Carleton) Papers*

PRO 30/55, Vols. 1–10	*passim.*

(6) *King's Bench*

PRIS 4/4, f. 69	Commitment to prison, and death, of Burgoyne's father.

Williams L. Clements Library, Ann Arbor, Michigan, USA

This is the second most important collection of papers relating to Burgoyne. Items are to be found among the *Germain, Clinton, Knox, Shelburne,* and *Howe Papers.* Of these, the *Germain* and *Clinton Papers* are by far the most useful. Since the papers, unlike those in the PRO, London, are very well indexed and cataloged and are arranged according to date, there is no need to say more than a few words here.

I GERMAIN PAPERS

When Germain left office, he took with him a large quantity of documents. These have found a permanent home in Ann Arbor. Most of them are duplicated in the PRO, London, or vice versa; but there are some important items not in London, just as there are some important items not in Ann Arbor. The printed catalog of the *Germain Papers* published in 1910 by the Historical Manuscripts Commission (entitled *Stopford-Sackville MSS*) before they left England is very unreliable, most letters being abridged without indication where and some being omitted altogether.

II CLINTON PAPERS

These are essential for reconstructing the sequence of messages between Burgoyne and Clinton in the autumn of 1777. They also contain one or two letters from Burgoyne not found elsewhere. Those wishing to find their way about the *Clinton Papers* would be wise to consult *The American Rebellion* (Clinton's *Narrative*) and *Portrait of a General* both by William B. Willcox, and *The American Secretary* by Gerald Saxon Brown.

British Museum

Ad. MSS contain a number of letters from, to, or concerning Burgoyne, but they are mostly of secondary importance: 5847, f. 378; 18,738 f. 196 (the king's "Observations" on Burgoyne's "Thoughts for Conducting the War from the Side of Canada"); 21,697, f. 158; 21,698, f. 25; 24,120, f. 170; 29,475; 32,413 (Digby's MS); 32,913, f. 257; 34,413, f. 202, 207; 34,414; 34,415, ff. 3–7; 35,614; 36,046, f. 162; 36,570, f. 13; 38,200, f. 278; 38,204; 38,209, ff. 224, 265; 38,210, ff. 63, 64, 67, 68; 38,212, ff. 144, 175, 184; 38,306, f. 47; 38,343, ff. 130, 131, 206, and 136–205 (Heath correspondence); 47,579, f. 69.

House of Lords Record Office

These are copies of all the papers submitted for the inquiry into Burgoyne's campaign, including some not in the PRO files. Printed lists are in *House of Lords Journal,* Vol. 35, pp. 290, 297–299, 315–316.

Other Collections

I GREAT BRITAIN

There are papers relating to Burgoyne in: Bedfordshire County Record Office *(Polwarth Papers, Burgoyne family muniments); Longleat, Wiltshire (Thynne Papers, American Affairs);* Lancashire Record Office, Preston (concerning Burgoyne's election of 1768); Sheffield Central Library *(Rockingham Papers);* Royal Artillery Institution, Woolwich (a few MSS, including an artillery officer's orderly book during the campaign of 1777). Frank Sabin has a diary of the campaign written by Lord Napier. There may be additional references in the great collection of letters in the *Newcastle Papers,* Nottingham University Library.

II USA

The quantity of MSS relating to Burgoyne's campaign from the American side is vast, and it is beyond the scope of this book to list them here. Those of immediate use to understanding the campaigns from Burgoyne's point of view are the *Schuyler Papers* and *Emmett Collection,* etc., in New York City Public Library; *Sparks MSS* in Houghton Library, Harvard; a letter by Burgoyne in Boston Public Library. The Henry E. Huntingdon Library, San Marino, California, has sundry items including *Richard Pope's Book,* the diary of a British officer of the 47th during the campaign, a photostat copy of which is in the New York City

Public Library. The New York State Library at Albany has photostat copies and some original MSS of documents of the campaign, including Colonel Klaus's account of the Mohawk expedition. MSS in Library of Congress, relating to Burgoyne, are copies of papers in PRO London, William Clements Library, etc.

III CANADA

Public Archives of Canada, Ottawa. Series Q, Vols. 12, 13, 14, are Carleton's duplicate copies of letters, etc., in PRO CO 42/35–37. I have not been able to examine these, and there may be copies of papers whose originals in London are now missing. There are also related papers in the *Haldimand Papers*, though these concern the period after Carleton's resignation in 1778.

Published Manuscript Collections

American Archives by Peter Force (1857–1863), IVth Series, Vols. 4 and 6; Vth Series, Vols. 1 and 2.

History of the Organization, Development & Services of the Military Forces of Canada, ed. Ernest A. Cruickshank, (Historical Section of the General Staff, 1919–1920), Vol. 2.

Canadian Archives, 1885 volume.

Letters of Members of the Continental Congress, ed. E. C. Burnett (Carnegie Institution, 1921–1936), Vols. 2 and 3.

Facsimiles of MSS in European Archives relating to the American Revolution by Benjamin Franklin Stevens (1889–1898, 25 vols.).

Heath Papers (Massachusetts Historical Society, 1904), 7th Series, Vol. 4.

Correspondence of George III, ed. Sir John Fortescue (Macmillan, 1927–1928), Vol. 3.

Historical Manuscripts Commission: *Abergavenny; American MSS in Royal Institution; Carlisle; Dartmouth American papers; Dropmore; Fortescue,* Vol. 1; *Hastings,* Vol. 3; *Kenyon; Lothian; Round; Stopford-Sackville; Various Collections,* Vol. 6, *Knox Papers.*

Lee Papers (New York Historical Society Collections, 1871).

Documents relating to the History of New York by J. R. Brodhead (1857), Vol. 8.

St. Clair Papers, ed. W. H. Smith (1882).

Private Papers of the Earl of Sandwich (Navy Records Society, 1932).

Writings of George Washington, ed. J. C. Fitzpatrick (U. S. Government Printing Office, 1933).

BOOKS AND PERIODICALS

Biographies of Burgoyne

(1) De Fonblanque, Edward Barrington, *Political and Military Episodes in the Later Half of the Eighteenth Century, Derived from the Life and Correspondence of The*

Right Hon. John Burgoyne, General, Statesman, Dramatist (Macmillan, 1876). Although a brief sketch of Burgoyne's life was supplied as a foreword to the 1808 edition of his poetical and dramatic writings, and a similar one written by Mrs. Inchbald for her introduction to *The Heiress* (*The British Theatre,* Vol. 20), no full biography appeared until this book by Edward de Fonblanque. As a work of literature, it is still the best, the most readable (Burgoyne's own interminable letters apart), and the most moving. This is to some extent explained by the fact that de Fonblanque deliberately set out to make a hero of his subject. If the facts did not fit, he ignored them or changed them to make them fit. While this gives his book artistic unity, it makes it very unreliable, and sometimes downright misleading, to someone in search of the truth. Nevertheless, it is essential to anyone studying Burgoyne, for de Fonblanque quotes from papers and letters not found elsewhere.

(2) HUDLESTON, F. J., *Gentleman Johnny Burgoyne* (Cape, 1928) is again rather unreliable, although hidden among the hearty jokes is a lot of good history. His interpretation of the Burgoyne-Germain-Howe-Clinton tangle is quite wrong.

(3) HARGROVE, Richard John, *General John Burgoyne* (Archive Ph.D. Thesis, 4 October 1970; xeroxed by University of Michigan and distributed to some libraries in America). Although this is not a published book, I mention it in order to acknowledge my debt to it. I found it most useful, even if I disagree with many of the author's interpretations and conclusions.

(4) LEWIS, Paul (pseud. Noel Bertram Gerson), *The Man Who Lost America* (Dial, 1973). This is published as a biography and was reviewed as such. It contains some surprising statements not found elsewhere. Not only does the author name Burgoyne's mistress in Canada and quote letters to her hitherto unknown, but also he tells us, for instance, why Burgoyne was chosen to command in Canada. The king, it seems, was getting fat. "Gentleman Johnny" pointed this out to His Majesty and suggested riding as a cure. During the rides, the king was so enchanted by Burgoyne's wit and conversation that he gave him the Canadian command as a mark of his esteem and confidence. Since Mr. Gerson does not tell us where he found out all this, he has only himself to blame if his authenticity is doubted.

(5) PAINE, Lauren, *Gentleman Johnny* (Robert Hale, 1973).

(6) LUNT, James, *John Burgoyne of Saratoga* (Macdonald & Janes, 1976; Harcourt Brace, 1976); and

(7) GLOVER, Michael, *General Burgoyne in Canada and America* (Gordon & Cremonesi, 1976). Both these books, published almost simultaneously, are serious works of military history. However, they have not been based on research among the original documents, where their respective authors would have found answers to many of the questions they have consequently been compelled to leave open.

(8) General Burgoyne has appeared in several works of drama and fiction: *Tales of Military Life* by George Robert Gleig (2nd Series, 1833); *The Devil's Disciple* by G. B. Shaw (1897); *Sergeant Lamb of the 9th* by Robert Graves (1941);

Rangers by D. P. Thompson (1851); *The Guns of Burgoyne by Bruce Lancaster* (1939); *Gentleman Johnny* by S. Styles (1967); *For Want of A Nail—If Burgoyne had Won at Saratoga* by Robert Sobel (1973).

II Burgoyne's Writings

(9) *Maid of the Oaks* (1774).
(10) *Substance of General Burgoyne's Speech on Mr. Vyner's Motion on 26 May & Mr. Hartley's Motion on 28 May, 1778* (J. Almon, 1778).
(11) *A Letter from Lt. Gen. Burgoyne to his Constituents* (J. Almon, 1778).
(12) *A State of the Expedition from Canada, As Laid Before the House of Commons, by Lieutenant-General Burgoyne* (J. Almon, 1780).
(13) *A Supplement to the State of the Expedition from Canada* (J. Robson, 1780). A selection of Burgoyne's orders on the campaign.
(14) *Lord of the Manor* (1780).
(15) *The Heiress* (1786).
(16) *Richard Coeur de Lion* (1786).
(17) *The Dramatic and Poetical Works of the late Lieut. Gen. J. Burgoyne* (1808, 2 vols.).
(18) *Orderly Book of Lieut. Gen. John Burgoyne,* ed. E. B. O'Callaghan, M.D. (Munsell, 1859).

III Career, Politics, and Campaigns Outside America

(19) *Gentleman's Magazine,* 1762.
(20) *London Political Magazine,* December 1780, an article on Burgoyne.
(21) NAMIER, Sir Lewis, and John Brooke, *The History of Parliament: The House of Commons 1754–92* (HMSO, 1962).
(22) SALES, Rev. Padre E. A. Pereira, *O Conde Lippe em Portugal* (Vila Nova de Famalicae—Publicacões da Comissão de Historia Militar II, 1936).
(23) "Substance of Col. John Burgoyne's Speech before the King's Bench, relative to his Election in Preston" (1769), a contemporary pamphlet in Lancashire Record Office.
(24) *Town & Country Magazine:* "History of the Têtes à Têtes Annex'd." 1 March 1779, p. 65.
(25) "The Preston Election of 1768" by Winifred Proctor (*Trans. of the Hist. Soc. of Lancashire and Cheshire,* 1959). With bibliography.

The above list contains merely the principal items; others will be found in the notes to the text.

IV Journals, Orderly Books, etc., of the Campaigns of 1776–1777

BRITISH AND LOYALIST

(26) ANBUREY, Captain Thomas, *Travels Through the Interior Parts of America* (1789, 2 vols.; also Arno reprint). This is a book to be read with caution, for it is possible that the author was neither with Burgoyne's army nor even in Canada or America. He certainly makes some suspicious errors. For instance, in a letter purporting to have been written from Quebec in December 1776, he describes the spectacle of Bur-

goyne's departure for England aboard the *Apollo*. Burgoyne in fact sailed on the *Isis* and returned on the *Apollo* six months later. Since the *Isis* was the most famous ship in Canada, every man in the army would have known this fact. For such reasons, although Anburey is liberally quoted in accounts of Burgoyne's campaigns, I have forborn to do so except in one or two instances where he is obviously telling the truth. For a discussion of this book, see "Thomas Anburey's Travels Through America: A Note on Eighteenth-Century Plagiarism" by Whitfield J. Bell, Jr. (*Papers of the Bibliographical Soc. of America*, XXXVII, 1943, pp. 23–36).

(27) DIGBY, Lieutenant William, 53rd Regiment, *The British Invasion from the North*, ed. James Phinney Baxter (Munsell, 1887). Taken from an MS in the British Museum.

(28) HADDEN, Lieutenant James M., Royal Artillery, *A Journal Kept in Canada Upon Burgoyne's Campaign in 1776 and 1777*, ed. Col. Horatio Rogers (Munsell, 1884).

(29) LAMB, Sergeant Roger, *An Original & Authentic Journal of Occurrences During the late American War*. (Dublin, 1811).

(30) LAMB, Sergeant Roger, *A Memoir of His Own Life* (Dublin, 1811).

(31) MACALPINE, John, *Genuine Narrative etc.* (1788). This was a Canadian who, with Mackay, was ordered to build the bridge at Fort Edward but deserted to Canada and left the army to its fate.

(32) M'GAURAN, Major Edward, *Memoirs* (1786).

(33) PELL, Joshua, "Diary of an Officer of the British Army in America" (*Magazine of American History*, January–February 1878). Pell was a loyalist whose descendants own Fort Ticonderoga.

(34) STANLEY, Lieutenant-Colonel F. G. (ed.), *For Want of a Horse; Journal of an Officer who Served with Carleton & Burgoyne* (Tribune Press, Sackville, New Brunswick, 1961). Journal and orderly book of an unnamed officer of the 47th Regiment, in Fraser's Advanced Corps in both campaigns, from an MS in the library of the US Military Academy, West Point.

GERMANS

(35) DU ROI, Major August Wilhelm, the Elder, *Journal*, trans. and ed. Charlotte S. J. Epping.

(36) EELKING, Max von, *German Allied Troops in the North American War of Independence*, trans. and ed. J. G. Rosengarten (Munsell, 1893).

(37) PAUSCH, Captain Georg, Chief of Hanau Artillery, *Journal*, trans. and ed. W. L. Stone (Munsell, 1886; also Arno reprint).

(38) PETTENGILL, R. W. (ed.), *Letters from America 1776–9* (Houghton Mifflin, 1924).

(39) RIEDESEL, Major-General Friedrich von, *Memoirs, Letters & Journals*, ed. Max von Eelking, trans. W. L. Stone (Munsell, 1868; also Arno reprint).

(40) RIEDESEL, Mrs. General von, *Letters and Journals Relating to the American Revolution*, ed. Max von Eelking, trans. W. L. Stone (Munsell, 1867; also Arno reprint).

(41) RIEDESEL, Baroness von, *Baroness Von Riedesel & the American Revolution*, trans. and ed. Marvin L. Brown, Jr. (Chapel Hill, 1965).

(42) STONE, W. L. (ed.), *Letters of Brunswick & Hessian Officers during the American Revolution* (Munsell, 1891).

AMERICANS

(43) BALDWIN, Colonel Jeduthan, *Revolutionary Journal* (1906; also Arno reprint).

(44) BOARDMAN, Oliver, *Journal* (*Connecticut Historical Society Collections*, VII, Hartford, 1899).

(45) COLMAN, Colonel Dudley, "An Eyewitness Account of Burgoyne's Surrender" (*Magazine of American History*, March 1893).

(46) CROSS, Ralph. "Journal" (*Historical Magazine*, New York, January 1870).

(47) GORDON, William, *History of the Rise . . . of the United States* (1788–1789), Vol. 2.

(48) HEATH, General William, *Memoirs of the American War*, ed. R. R. Wilson (1798; reprinted by Wessels, 1904).

(49) HUGHES, J. M., aide-de-camp to General Gates, "Notes Relative to the Campaign Against Burgoyne" (*Massachusetts Hist. Soc. Proc.*, Vol. 3, February 1858).

(50) KIDDER, Frederick, *History of the First New Hampshire Regiment* (Albany, 1888). Includes journal of Lieutenant Thomas Blake.

(51) *Orderly Book of the Northern Army at Ticonderoga* (Munsell, 1859). Most of this has been republished in the *Fort Ticonderoga Museum Bulletin, passim.*

(52) SMITH, Reverend Hezekiah, *Journals, Letters & Addresses*, ed. R. A. Guild (American Baptist Publication, 1885).

(53) SMITH, J. E. A., *History of Pittsfield* (Boston, 1869), includes Reverend T. Allen's account of Bennington.

(54) THACHER, James, *Military Journal of the American Revolution* (1823).

(55) TRUMBULL, John, *Autobiography* (1841; reissued, ed. T. Sizer, Yale University Press, 1953, but with some letters at end of Vol. 2 not included).

(56) WILKINSON, General James, *Memoirs of My Own Times* (1816).

(57) WILLETT, Colonel Marinus, *Narrative* (Arno Reprint). Only first-hand account of siege of Fort Stanwix from American point of view.

V Burgoyne's American Campaigns, Later Accounts, Histories, Etc.

A complete list of these would run to many hundreds of books and articles. For the planning of the campaign and the reasons for its failure, the following have been the most useful:

(58) *A Brief Examination of the Plan and Conduct of the Northern Expedition in America, in 1777* (T. Hookham, 1779). This is typical of the scathing personal attacks published on behalf of the ministers after Burgoyne's return to England.

(59) ADAMS, Charles Francis, *Studies Military & Diplomatic* (1911); also an essay on 1777 in *Mass. Hist. Soc. Proceedings*, 1883.

(60) ANDERSON, Troyer Steele, *The Command of the Howe Brothers during the American Revolution* (Oxford, 1936).

(61) BROWN, Gerald Saxon, *The American Secretary* (Ann Arbor, 1963).
(62) BURT, Alfred L., "The Quarrel Between Germain and Carleton, an Inverted Story" (*Canadian Hist. Review,* Vol. XI, No. 3, September 1930).
(63) CLARK, Jane, "The Command of the Canadian Army in 1777" (*Canadian Hist. Review,* June 1929).
(64) CLARK, Jane, "Responsibility for the Failure of the Burgoyne Campaign" (*American Hist. Review,* Vol. 35, No. 3, April 1930, pp. 542–549). Jane Clark was secretary and archivist of the William L. Clements Library during the 1920s and 1930s and the first to use the *Clinton* and *Germain Papers* in the collection. Until her article appeared, opinion among historians was generally sympathetic to Burgoyne. She reversed the trend, as it were, and her work has been used as a starting point by the "anti-Burgoyne school" ever since. Yet her article says little that was not said in 1780 by the author of (72) below; a fact she herself did not acknowledge.
(65) EGERTON, H. E., "Sir William Howe and General Burgoyne" (*English Hist. Review,* October 1910).
(66) *Essay on Modern Martyrs* (1780), supposedly written by a "Mr. Dallas"; another attack. Also *A Reply to . . . Burgoyne's Letter* . . . (1780).
(67) GEE, Olive, "The British War Office in the later Part of the American War of Independence" (*Journ. of Modern History,* June 1954).
(68) GRUBER, Ira D., *The Howe Brothers & the American Revolution* (Atheneum, 1972).
(69) GUTTRIDGE, G. H., "Lord George Germain in Office" (*American Hist. Review,* Vol. 37, p. 30).
(70) MACKESY, Piers, *The War for America* (Longmans, 1964).
(71) POLWHELE, Richard, *The Spirit of Fraser to Gen. Burgoyne* (Bath, 1778).
(72) *Remarks on General Burgoyne's State of the Expedition from Canada* (G. Wilkie, 1780). Perhaps written by Israel Mauduit, this summarizes the anti-Burgoyne case with such thoroughness that very little has been added since, despite the opening of the *Clinton Papers* in the 1920s.
(73) TOWER, Charlemagne, *Essays Political & Historical* (1914).
(74) VALENTINE, Alan, *Lord George Germain* (Oxford, 1962).
(75) WILLCOX, William B. (ed.), *The American Rebellion* (Yale, 1954). A modern publication, with notes and edited texts, of Sir Henry Clinton's *Narrative,* written in retirement after the war.
(76) WILLCOX, William B., "Too Many Cooks: British Planning Before Saratoga" (*Journ. of British Studies,* November 1962).
(77) WILLCOX, William B., *Portrait of a General; Sir Henry Clinton in the War of Independence* (Knopf, 1964).

For the campaigns themselves, I have found the following useful:

(78) ADAMS, James Truslow, "The Burgoyne Expedition" (*North American Review,* September 1927).
(79) ANDERSON, George B. (comp.), *Our Country and its People; a descriptive & biographical record of Saratoga County* (Boston, 1899).
(80) ARNOLD, Isaac N., *Benedict Arnold at Saratoga* (1880).

(81) BECKER, J. P., *Sexagenary* (Munsell, 1866). Authorship also attributed to Simeon DeWitt Bloodgood.

(82) BENNETT, Clarence E., *Advance & Retreat to Saratoga* (Schenectady, Robson and Adee, 1927, 2 vols.) A very rare book with items of local information not found elsewhere.

(83) BIRD, Harrison, *Navies in the Mountains* (Oxford, 1962).

(84) BIRD, Harrison, *March to Saratoga* (Oxford, 1962).

(85) BRANDOW, John H., *The Story of Old Saratoga* (Albany, 1919). Partly reprinted as guide to Saratoga battlefield, from an original article in *NY State Hist. Assoc. Proc.*, 1913.

(86) BROOKS, N. C., "The Fields of Stillwater & Saratoga" (*Graham's Magazine*, April 1847).

(87) COBURN, F. W., *A History of the Battle of Bennington* (1912).

(88) CULLUM, George Washington, "The Struggle for the Hudson (Narrative & Critical History of America" by Justin Winsor, Vol. 6, 1888).

(89) DE PEYSTER, Brevet General J. W., *Maj-Gen. Philip Schuyler and the Burgoyne Campaign* (1877).

(90) DRAKE, Samuel Adams, *Burgoyne's Invasion of 1777* (Boston and New York, 1889).

(91) FURNEAUX, Rupert, *Saratoga: The Decisive Battle* (Allen and Unwin, 1971).

(92) GORSSLINE, R. M., "Medical Notes on Burgoyne's Campaign 1776–7" (*Canadian Defence Quarterly*, April 1929).

(93) HOLDEN, J. A., *The Burgoyne Campaign* (1913).

(94) JONES, J. H., *History of the Campaign for the Conquest of Canada* (1882).

(95) LEES, Major A. W. H., "The True Account of Saratoga" (*Journ. of the Royal United Services Institution*, 1913).

(96) MAINE, H. C., *The Burgoyne Campaign* (Troy, 1877). Contains some very interesting illustrations.

(97) MILLS, Borden S., "Troop Units at the Battle of Saratoga (*NY State Hist. Assoc. Proc.*, 1916).

(98) NEILSON, Charles, *An Original . . . account of Burgoyne's Campaign* (Munsell, 1844).

(99) *New York State Historical Association Proceedings*, Vol. XII, 1913, Sixteen Essays on Saratoga Subjects. The most valuable of these is "The Influence of the Death of Jane McCrae on the Burgoyne Campaign" by James Austen Holden, pp. 249–310, with exhaustive bibliography up to that date.

(100) NICKERSON, Hoffman, *The Turning Point of the Revolution: Burgoyne in America*. (Houghton Mifflin, 1928). The most detailed account of the campaign to date, from the American side, but lacking references. In some important respects, such as the Burgoyne-Howe-Germain affair and Burgoyne's tactics at the two Battles of Freeman's Farm, he is seriously wrong.

(101) NICOLAY, John G., *The Battles of Saratoga* (Chautauqua, 1892).

(102) O'BRIEN, Michael, "Morgan's Riflemen at the Battle of Saratoga" (*Journ. of the American Irish Hist. Soc.*, 1927).

(103) OSTRANDER, William S., *Old Saratoga and the Burgoyne Campaign* (Schuylerville, 1897).

(104) REID, Arthur, *Reminiscences of the Revolution, or, Le Loup's Bloody Trail from Salem to Fort Edward* (Utica, 1859). Fanciful and novelettish but contains some authentic local information. For further details of Fort Edward and Jane McCrae, see *Old Fort Edward* by William H. Hill (Fort Edward, 1929) and 2 vols. of *Addenda* by the same author (1957).

(105) SHEDD, Charles E., *Burgoyne's Objective in the Second Battle of Saratoga, October 7, 1777.* (Unpublished typescript, File No. 834, Saratoga National Historical Park, 15 December 1952). Written while Mr. Shedd was Park Historian, this is the best analysis of the battle so far made.

(106) SNELL, Charles W., *Saratoga National Historical Park* (National Park Service Historical Handbook, Series No. 4, 1950).

(107) STONE, William L., Sr., *The Life of Joseph Brant-Thayendanagea* (1838; also Kraus reprint).

(108) STONE, William L., Jr., *The Campaigns of Burgoyne and St. Leger* (Munsell, 1877).

(109) STONE, William L., Jr., *Ballads and Poems relating to the Burgoyne Campaign* (Munsell, 1893).

(110) STONE, William L., Jr., *Visits to the Saratoga Battlegrounds* (Munsell, 1895; Kennekat reprint, 1970).

(111) SWEETMAN, John, *Saratoga* (*Knight's Battles for Wargames* series, Charles Knight, 1971).

(112) UPHAM, George B., "Burgoyne's Great Mistake" (*New England Quarterly*, October 1930).

(113) WALWORTH, Mrs. Ellen Hardin, *Battles of Saratoga, 1777* (Munsell, 1891).

VI Convention and Convention Troops

(114) BACHTELDER, Samuel F., "Burgoyne & His Officers in Cambridge" (Cambridge Hist. Soc. Publications XIII, *Proceedings 1918*, pub. 1925). Republished as a separate pamphlet in 1926.

(115) DABNEY, William M., *After Saratoga; The Story of the Convention Army* (University of New Mexico Press, Albuquerque, 1954).

(116) DEANE, C., *Lieut. Gen. Burgoyne & the Convention of Saratoga* (1877).

(117) *Proceedings of a Court Martial . . . of Col. David Henley, for ill-treatment of a British Soldier* (1778).

(118) WALL, Alexander J., *The Story of the Convention Army, 1777–83* (New York Hist. Soc., 1927).

VI Miscellaneous

In addition to the general works cited in the notes or above, the following have been drawn upon:

(119) ALDEN, J. R., *The American Revolution* (1954).

(120) BEATSON, Robert, *Naval & Military Memoirs* (1804), Vol. 4.

(121) CARRINGTON, Henry B., *Battles of the American Revolution* (1876).

(122) CHAPELLE, Howard L., *The History of the American Sailing Navy* (W. W. Norton, New York, 1949).
(123) CUMBERLAND, Richard, *Memoirs* (1807).
(124) CURTIS, Edward E., *The Organization of the British Army during the American Revolution* (Humphry Milford, Oxford University Press, 1926; reprinted by EP Publishing, 1972).
(125) DAWSON, Henry B., *Battles of the United States* (1857).
(126) DONKIN, R., *Military Collections & Remarks* (1777).
(127) DUNCAN, Captain Francis, *History of the Royal Artillery* (1872), Vol. 1.
(128) FULLER, J. F. C., *British Light Infantry in the Eighteenth Century* (1925).
(129) HALE, Horatio, *Iroquois Book of Rites* (1880).
(130) HUGHES, Major-General B. P., *British Smooth Bore Artillery* (Arms & Armour Press, 1969).
(131) HUME, Ivor Noel, *1775, Another Part of the Field* (Eyre and Spottiswood, 1966).
(132) KATCHER, Philip R. N., *King George's Army, 1775–1783* (Osprey, London; Stackpole Co., Pennsylvania, 1973).
(133) KINGSFORD, William, *History of Canada* (1893), Vols. 5 and 6.
(134) LOSSING, Benson J., *Pictorial Field Book of the Revolution* (1851; republished by Charles Tuttle, Rutland, Vermont, 1972). Although this book has been cited several times in the notes, it deserves a special mention here. It is not only invaluable as a mine of quickly accessible information (which, despite the early date, is remarkably accurate), but it is also a delight to browse through or to read from beginning to end. Fortunately it has been rescued from oblivion by an excellent modern reprint. This should be especially welcome in Britain, where the original is virtually unobtainable (even the British Museum copy has most of the first volume missing).
(135) MULLER, John, *Treatise of Artillery* (1768).
(136) POUND, Arthur, and Richard E. Day, *Johnson of the Mohawks* (Macmillan, 1930).
(137) Regimental histories: most of the regiments of Burgoyne's campaign are by now included in the *Famous Regiments* series published by Leo Cooper, under the general editorship of Sir Brian Horrocks. The volume for the 16th/5th Lancers (Burgoyne's 16th Light Dragoons) is by Major-General James Lunt. Cannon's *Historical Records* series published by HMSO in the last century provide dry chronologies. Colonel Graham's history of the 16th Light Dragoons has already been cited, and many other notable regiments, such as the 20th, have been the subjects of books by themselves.
(138) SCHEER, George F., and Hugh F. Rankin, *Rebels & Redcoats* (World Publ. Co., 1957; also a Mentor Book paperback). Useful source book of first-hand accounts from letters and diaries, etc.
(139) SMITH, John Jay, *American Historical & Literary Curiosities* (New York, 1860).
(140) STUART WORTLEY, Mrs. E., *A Prime Minister and his Son* (1925).
(141) TREVELYAN, George Otto, *The American Revoluion* (New York, 1905–1912).

(142) VAN DOREN, Carl, *The Secret History of the American Revolution* (1941; Popular Library, 1969).

(143) VAN TYNE, Claude H., *The Loyalists in the American Revolution* (1902).

(144) VAN TYNE, Charles H., *The War of Independence, The American Phase* (1929).

(145) WHITTON, Lieutenant-Colonel F. E., *The American War of Independence* (1931).

INDEX

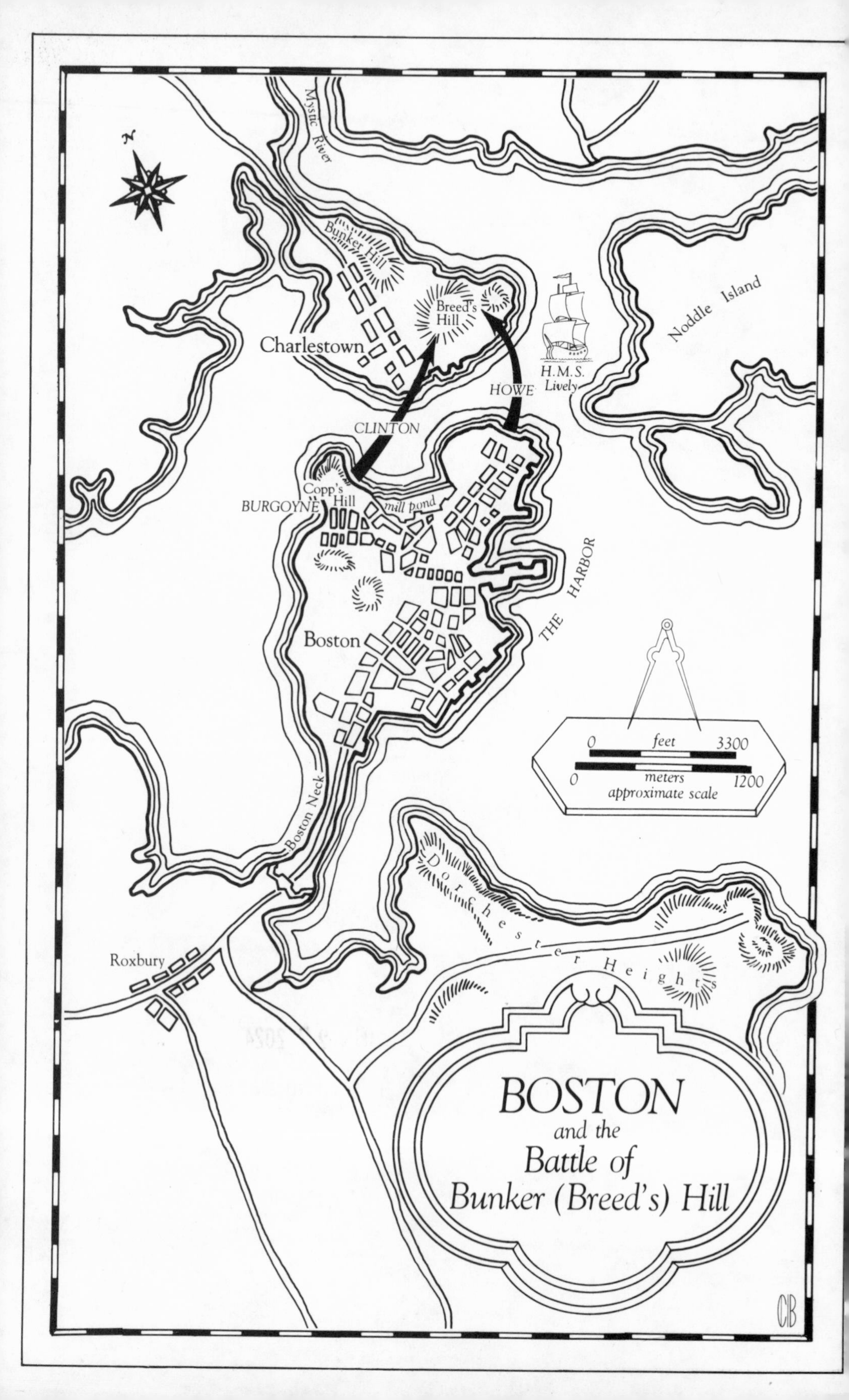
N
Mystic River
Bunker Hill
Breed's Hill
Charlestown
H.M.S. Lively
HOWE
CLINTON
Noddle Island
Copp's Hill
BURGOYNE
mill pond
THE HARBOR
Boston
0 feet 3300
0 meters 1200
approximate scale
Boston Neck
Dorchester Heights
Roxbury
BOSTON
and the
Battle of
Bunker (Breed's) Hill
CIB